Led Zeppelin

1968-1980

Led Zeppelin
The story of a band and their music
1968-1980

Keith Shadwick

Led Zeppelin
The story of a band and their music, 1968-1980
Keith Shadwick

A Backbeat Book
First edition 2005
Published by Backbeat Books
600 Harrison Street
San Francisco
CA 94107, US
www.backbeatbooks.com

An imprint of The Music Player Network, United
Entertainment Media Inc.

Devised and published for Backbeat Books by
Outline Press Ltd, 2A Union Court, 20-22
Union Road, London SW4 6JP, England
www.backbeatuk.com

ISBN-10 0-87930-871-0
ISBN 13: 978-0-87930-871-1

EDITOR: **Tony Bacon**
BOOK DESIGN: **Balley Design Associates**
JACKET DESIGN: **Paul Cooper Design**

Origination and print by Colorprint (Hong Kong)

05 06 07 08 09 5 4 3 2 1

CONTENTS

" I think our music is an excitement thing: it has to be impromptu. You know, it just drops out of your mind – it falls out of your head and onto the floor and you pick it up as it bounces. That's how we work. But what else would you expect? We hire this recording truck and trudge off to some cruddy old house in the country. The last thing you'd expect is the music to fall right into place. But it does. We even spent one night sitting around drinking ourselves under the table telling each other how good we were. "

Robert Plant, 1974

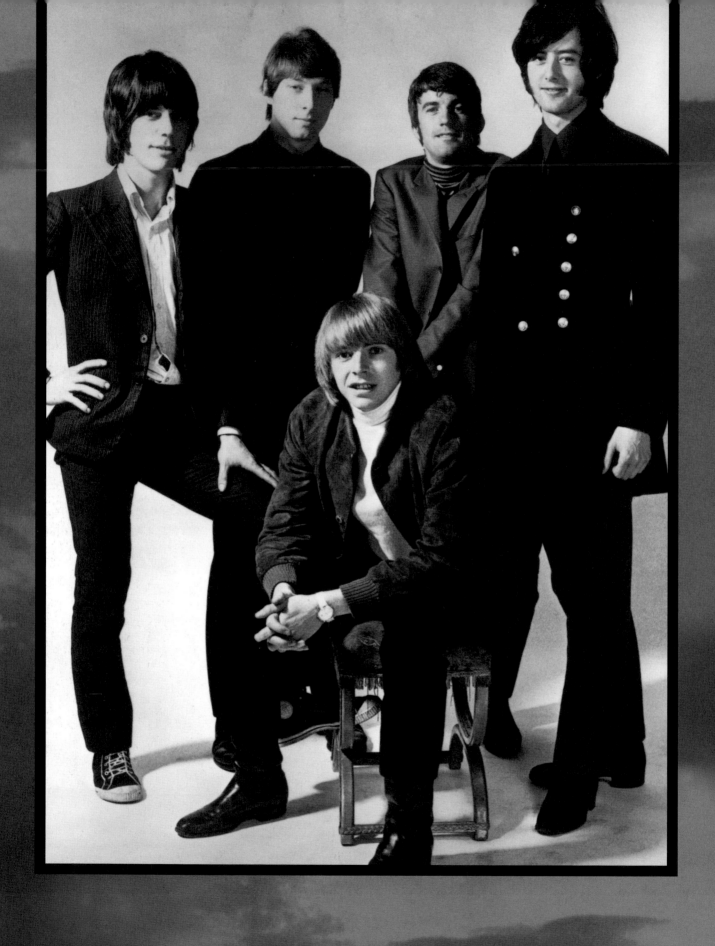

GOODNIGHT, JOSEPHINE

It is a simple fact about Led Zeppelin that is easily overlooked: they were not part of the first or even the second wave of 1960s blues and R&B-based British groups. For that reason alone, the way they came together and the music they made was likely from the start to be different from what had gone before.

The band's early identity was inextricably bound up with the evaporating fortunes of The Yardbirds, a once-popular beat group from London that suffered from a permanently unstable personnel, a variable home-grown ability to come up with winning songs, and a singer whose looks were generally more persuasive than his vocal talents.

The first great wave of beat groups in Britain had mainly been formed in distinct localities and stayed on their own local territory, with occasional stints on the road for the more successful and adventurous. The Beatles came together this way and, as we all know, became a battle-hardened and efficient live act long before they auditioned for George Martin. So did The Rolling Stones before they signed to Decca. The Animals and The Yardbirds, from different ends of the country, were two more bands who followed a similar path.

A second wave of bands – Fleetwood Mac, Cream, The Spencer Davis Group – emerged from the wreckage of mostly unsuccessful local groups and suddenly clicked with record companies, with managers and with the public in a previously undreamed-of way.

The third generation in the 1960s followed the Cream model more than any other. Traffic, for example, were drawn from the elite of other bands around at the time. Led Zeppelin were typical of this third wave in that its members were drawn from disparate parts of the country, all were experienced and thoroughly professional even though they were still very young, and they had more than a passing knowledge of how the industry worked before they even signed their first deal as a unit. They were part of a London-based scene that had developed a pool of professional rock talent capable of playing on any sessions around, and could swap from working band to working band in search of that elusive perfect combination.

When The Beatles had first hit back in 1962-3, such a pool of professional rock talent simply hadn't existed, in London or in Liverpool or anywhere else in Britain. The work – and the opportunities that work would offer – did not exist. Professional musicians playing in groups were almost certain to be jazzmen moonlighting with hit-parade fodder and 'variety' entertainment acts. The climate was very different in the late 1960s, and that is one of the reasons that Led Zeppelin took off so quickly once assembled.

All the industry machinery for putting exciting new acts out into the market now existed, and with the high levels of musicianship and the collective charisma the band possessed, it was going to reach its audience very quickly – and not just locally.

Earlier in the decade, The Yardbirds had enjoyed their two or three years of major chart success in a pop industry as prone to swift changes of musical fashion as it is today. But as their rabid type of 'rave up' music had become passé, they had sunk into rapid and irreversible decline. Not even maverick producer Mickie Most had been able to re-float the good ship Yardbirds with a sequence of increasingly inconsequential singles through 1967 and into 1968.

With all that, plus increasing disaffection in the ranks and continual personnel changes, a band can go one of two ways. Like The Pretty Things, The Rolling Stones, The Kinks and (much later) Fleetwood Mac, it could retain an original core personnel and preserve the name while waiting for a return to the good times. Some indeed succeeded; others waited but the good times never came back. The other option was to break up. The various members could then look for a new set of people to play with, as well as a new repertoire and a new group name.

This would seem a pretty simple – if stark – choice. Yet, oddly, The Yardbirds would eventually follow neither course. To show why, we need to wind the story back to its proper beginnings, when everyone was younger, more innocent, and still looking for that first big step into fame – and, of course, the fortune that all musicians expected but so few achieved.

The Yardbirds more than most personified the opportunities and the dilemmas faced by ambitious young British musicians fired up by the raw and exciting blues and R&B that seemed to have been exported almost as an afterthought from the USA. In May 1963 the group consisted of Keith Relf, Anthony Topham, Chris Dreja, Paul Samwell-Smith, and Jim McCarty, but by mid October Eric Clapton had replaced Topham. They took over the residency of the Crawdaddy club in Richmond, south London, from the upwardly mobile Rolling Stones, benefiting from a burgeoning audience and its attendant press.

A rejection by the UK Decca label in February 1964 virtually guaranteed them success. Their first single was released on Columbia in May 1964, and by spring of the following year The Yardbirds registered a worldwide Top 10 hit in 'For Your Love'. This was not without cost, for Clapton quit the group in protest at their willingness to deviate from R&B and blues orthodoxy. In a comment that could equally apply to Led Zeppelin or any of the scores of British R&B-based bands that grew to fame in the 1960s, rhythm guitarist Chris Dreja later summed up the period. "For all of us," he said, "the initial inspiration was hearing American blues music – that's where the passion came from. But I mean we were white guys in post-war England. We were never gonna play it the same way, so we played it our way, and any sort of natural progression and experimentation in the music was [done] our way."[1]

Ironically, considering subsequent Yardbirds history, manager Giorgio Gomelsky first approached Jimmy Page to be Clapton's replacement. But Page was busy playing pop sessions on the London studio scene and instead recommended Jeff Beck for the job. By March 1965 Beck was the group's lead guitarist. For the next 14 months they enjoyed a stable personnel and their most sustained period of commercial success. Their willingness to experiment with songs, arrangements and sound, and their thirst for rave-up jamming and full-on live performances, put them at the forefront of British rock.

The Yardbirds became widely influential, not only in their individual choice of repertoire – R&B classics, dressed-up blues, bespoke outsourced originals, and, later, material written by group members – but in their treatment of that material. The group had an innate sense of drama, could play the blues with genuine drive (Keith Relf was a fine blues-harp man), and could invest rather odd songs with a real sense of unvarnished honesty.

As 1965 turned into 1966 they went into an American studio to record 'Shapes Of Things', their first self-penned hit single. It benefited greatly from a carefully developed arrangement with a simple and economical form that allowed its message to unfold naturally, inviting the type of sound enhancement at which Beck and bassist Paul Samwell-Smith were quickly becoming expert. The Yardbirds specialised in a 'big' studio sound, which suited this single only too well. It also suited Beck's taste for shaping and sculpting guitar sounds through the control and manipulation of sustain and, on occasion, feedback.

Beck was a very unusual guitarist for the time. He was both a virtuoso and a player interested in moving beyond simple imitation of American blues models. He was as interested in 'other' sounds, including those from the East, as any guitarist around at the time, including George Harrison – as can be heard from the 'oriental' line he contributes to the previous single, 'Heart Full Of Soul'. He was arguably the first British guitar virtuoso of the 1960s, primarily because he was so flexible and so imaginative – and all at the drop of a hat. Chris Dreja said: "We'd even got an Indian session player in to try that out but it sounded so 'tagged on' it was ridiculous. That was done at Advision and Jeff came in with his guitar, played the riff and it fitted perfectly. … At that time, Jeff's sound was fuzzbox and feedback. Really, he wanted that raunch. … He wanted to 'sit on top' of everything."[2]

Beck's liquid sound and easy technique gave a sinuous quality to the group's sound and was unique, even within more traditional blues numbers. When it came to the sounds he created on 'Shapes Of Things', the record became something of a manifesto for change – and a manifesto that Jimi Hendrix, for one, studied assiduously. For close on a year, The Yardbirds were putting out singles that carried the imagination and urgency of The Beatles, and prompted a popular worldwide reaction. They were at the cutting edge.

The group had landed major international success on the back of songs written by outsiders such as Graham Gouldman, and while this was hardly unusual at the time – check out the songwriting credits for The Animals or Manfred Mann, for example – it didn't augur well for long-term security. 'Shapes Of Things' and 'Over Under Sideways Down' were the sum total of their self-penned 45rpm hits and they were two of their most influential sides, along with some set-piece album tracks such as 'The Nazz Are Blue'.

Drummer Jim McCarty said the session for the classic 'Over Under Sideways Down' was typical of how the group worked with Beck aboard. "When we made records we would record all together, then Jeff would come in and do his bit. We'd never know what he was going to do! On something like 'Over Under' we just worked on the basic boogie, and Jeff came up with that riff which, the first time I heard it, I didn't think fitted at all. But the more you heard it the more it became spot on."[3]

After Samwell-Smith's swansong with the group, The Yardbirds LP, recorded in early June 1966 (also known as Roger The Engineer), they again approached Jimmy Page to join the group, initially as their bass player. Page was known not only to the original members but also in particular to Beck: their friendship pre-dated the group.

Beck and Page had been working on a project just prior to Page joining The Yardbirds. Encouraged in May 1966 by Simon Napier-Bell and Mickie Most to try something on his own in the studio, Beck collaborated with Page on a rock re-arrangement of Ravel's 'Bolero', retitled 'Beck's Bolero'. Beck asked Page along, to play electric 12-string guitar, while sessionman Nicky Hopkins played piano, Mickie Most regular John Paul Jones was on bass (a late inclusion when John Entwistle pulled out), and The Who's Keith Moon played drums.

Beck and Page have both said since that more than one song was recorded at this hastily convened session; Page recalled that 'Louie Louie' was one of the others. But 'Beck's Bolero' is the only one to have appeared on an official release. The two guitarists have suggested that the group was at least initially considered as one that might last. "I didn't really like The Who then," Beck admitted later. "They were annoying me because they had my drummer! … The session started at 10 and we were done by 12. I wanted to see that band come out of there cemented with that one record. But Keith obviously couldn't [carry on with it] because of The Who, although he led us to believe he was leaving them – probably just to make The Who jealous. And John Paul Jones was a fabulous bass player. It was the obvious solution, going with that band. But it never happened."[4]

What happened was that 'Beck's Bolero' waited in the

can for close on a year before it was released as the B-side to 'Hi Ho Silver Lining' – and so the first putative 1960s supergroup never got off the ground. Led Zeppelin, indeed. Many years later Jimmy Page agreed that this dry run was a first attempt to put something together that was seriously heavyweight. But it was never a realistic option: after all, they never got as far as recruiting a lead singer. Page said it was "not Led Zeppelin as a name: the name came afterwards. But it was said afterwards that that's what it could have been called. Because Moony wanted to get out of The Who, and so did John Entwistle, but when it came down to getting hold of a singer … the group was dropped because of [Steve] Marriott's other commitment, to Small Faces. But I think it would have been the first of all those bands, sort of like Cream and everything. Instead, it didn't happen – apart from the 'Bolero'. That's the closest it got."5

Beck may well have decided that if he couldn't get his supergroup going, then he'd do the next best thing and inveigle his mate Page into The Yardbirds. There is third-party evidence that it was Beck's idea to get Page to swap to guitar and Dreja to bass: Yardbirds manager Simon Napier-Bell recalled that he told Beck it was madness to bring in someone as good as himself "but Beck absolutely insisted".6 Page remembered that Beck "often used to say 'I wish you could join and we could play together' and I agreed that it would be good". Page said that after he took over on bass "the idea was that Chris Dreja, who was the rhythm guitarist, should learn bass, and when he became proficient enough we'd switch".7 This gave The Yardbirds a line-up with two lead guitarists.

The division between what they wanted to play onstage at this time and what they were pushed into recording was revealed when film-maker Michelangelo Antonioni recruited The Yardbirds for his movie *Blow Up*. Originally he intended to use a different group from the London scene but changed his mind after attending a concert at the Royal Albert Hall in late September 1966, headlined by The Rolling Stones with The Yardbirds as one of the support acts.

John Kerr, reporting for *Music Maker*, observed that "the hall was filled to capacity by girls aged between 12 and 16 and a smaller percentage of boys around the same age. At sight of the Stones the audience went wild and rushed the stage. … [They] repeatedly rushed the stage and kept up such a barrage of sound that any assessment of the musical abilities of the group was quite impossible. The fact emerges that 1966 pop fans – certainly in the case of The Beatles and The Rolling Stones – are interested in stage presentation as a means of actually seeing their idols. When they want to listen to them, they play records." After defining Jagger as the Nureyev of pop, Kerr turned to The Yardbirds. He said they "do not rely on their frontman, Keith Relf, for their audience appeal. He does cavort, strain over a harmonica and sing

with a thin smoky voice, but he's not in the same pop ballet élite as Jagger. It's the music that is so attractive about The Yardbirds. In particular, the fast, bluesy playing of Jeff Beck."8

The whole event also impressed a director looking for a way to summarise the contradictions of a society attempting to reconstruct itself from the roots up – while having as much fun as possible. So he slotted The Yardbirds into his shooting schedule. With the Stones a non-starter for a cameo in the film, he decided that the support band had the musical edge to serve his purposes. They were his fourth choice for the slot.

At Antonioni's request the group performed a thinly-disguised version of 'The Train Kept A-Rollin'', by far the wildest and most anarchic tune in their repertoire. The version they made is brutal, menacing, and teetering on all-out violence, with Keith Relf's blues vocals struggling to be heard amid the overdriven guitars. This is what Antonioni heard at the Albert Hall, and is what made The Yardbirds such an exciting live act with their own dedicated following. 'Train Kept A-Rollin'' would remain a firm favourite of Jimmy Page, too. But nothing The Yardbirds would record in the studio in the next year came close to this level of adrenalin rush.

Chris Dreja felt that the heady coupling of Beck and Page on twin lead guitars was only a limited success at best. Jim McCarty recalled that it started with the best of intentions. "Jeff was quite happy with that at the time – and then ego sort of took over. It became a bit competitive. They started trying to outdo each other with solos and things, although I always thought that Jeff had a natural showmanship anyway. He'd put the guitar on the top of his head. Eric did as well, in fact, but Jeff was just a natural, really. I don't think he really cared so much about doing a show, he just did what came into his head. When we were touring with the Stones, I was playing away, looked up, and Jeff was playing his guitar behind his head! So you never really knew with Jeff what he was going to do."9

Some have speculated that Beck and Page didn't exactly work hard to fit in together, but that not only runs counter to Page's perfectionist instincts, it is also contradicted by Page's memories of the work that both guitarists put in at the beginning. "We rehearsed hard on all sorts of riffs to things like 'Over Under Sideways Down' which we were doing in harmonies," Page said, "and we had sections worked out where we'd play rehearsed phrases together. It was the sort of thing that people like Wishbone Ash and Quiver [later] perfected, that dual-lead-guitar idea. Of course, that was all very well in theory and at rehearsal, but onstage Beck would often go off into something else."10

The ever-mercurial Beck was temperamentally incapable of sticking to routines night after night and was also perhaps in the early stages of burn-out after so much touring and the effort of carrying forward the group's inventive edge. So the initial excitement didn't sustain itself. Page recalled a few years later that both men respected each other too much to enter into mere carving contests onstage. "It was never a case of trying to blow each other off," he said, "because I was trying to get it working, so you had this stereo effect on the guitars. There was no point in doing battle: that would have just led to a useless sound."[11] An eyewitness of the Beck-Page guitar combination onstage in late September 1966 reported that "every note that Jeff Beck played was played in unison by Jimmy Page. It was interesting, but very strange. It seemed … that Beck was showing Page the set by learning his licks".[12]

Beck was probably feeling the pressure of his position rather too keenly and was hoping to move some of the burden onto Page's capable shoulders. It is also possible that Beck was – perhaps subconsciously – planning his exit. The events of the next US tour would confirm the wisdom of this foresight – however instinctual it may have been. Everyone involved has acknowledged that there was already tension in the group with no obvious outlet.

Before that, however, the Beck-Page group managed one studio single, 'Happenings Ten Years Time Ago', recorded in September 1966 around the time of the Albert Hall appearance with The Rolling Stones. It was the last single of which everyone in the group remained proud, and with good reason, and it is the last time that The Yardbirds showed themselves to be ahead of what was going on around them. The single was a testimony both to Beck's quicksilver brilliance and to the way Page could double that effect.

But whatever potential the twin-guitar approach may have had, by late October 1966 Beck was no longer in the group. The parting of the ways came at the tail end of a gruelling, ill-judged US package tour. They were co-billed with Sam The Sham, Gary Lewis & The Playboys, and Bryan Hyland. Chris Dreja said: "I suppose today [Beck] would have had time off and therapy and everything else." But no one did that sort of thing then. You just plugged on. Everyone was feeling the strain and, when someone blew up, the others looked to manager Simon Napier-Bell to clean up the mess. There was no tradition in the group for reading the warning signs, especially from a junior member.

Dreja recalled: "Jeff had a kind of major emotional blow-up and decided he'd had enough. … He walked off the tour and left us with it. Obviously, Jimmy was a lot fresher and had done a lot of sessions in his time, so he had a pretty professional approach, and we realised we could make it work as a four-piece."[13] That said, this was a tour Page would refer to repeatedly in later interviews as an all-time on-the-road low.

Recently, Beck said that he was "thrown out of The Yardbirds" probably as a direct result of the group being "unable to cope with my moodiness at the time. I wasn't easy to be around then."[14] This suggests that the group decided this was one walk-out too many and they didn't want Beck back. They'd soldier on alone.

Beck was clear about what had hurt him and the group the most. "The management was the real reason the group broke up," he said. "We could have been enormous. We were limited by bad management, and the gigs were wrongly chosen. … I would have liked to see them develop a bit more, that's the regret I had, but physically I couldn't wait to get out of the band."[15] Jim McCarty had similar feelings. There was no overall strategy – or if there was, it was never explained to the group. "I don't know what [manager Napier-Bell] was up to, because we never really saw him very much. He never sat down with the band and said, 'Well, this is where I think we can get to and this is how we're going to get there.' We had meetings, but we never talked about overall strategy and so on. Nobody did that, apart from [previous manager Gomelsky] in the early days. It was a shame really that it never happened."[16]

Page, ever the professional (indeed he was known by the rest of the group as Mister Cool), took over Beck's duties in addition to his own, and the group completed the disastrous tour. That it took place against a rapidly changing and fraught political and social backdrop in the country passed them by at the time. Dreja only later realised just how deeply this affected them all. "There was all of this hidden stress that we didn't really pick up on. We just carried on doing our thing. … We didn't sort of analyse it too much, I don't think. We just got on the next plane and lived through the next bit. But it was all going off. … We were all so new to the Americans – and they had a lot of problems of their own. Also, don't forget the British invasion had killed off their homegrown music. It's amazing, really, that they welcomed us with such open arms."[17] The tour was completed, and with Page on guitar and Dreja on bass the group now functioned efficiently as a quartet. But the exposure to an uncomprehending teen audience in the Southern States did the group no good at all.

Page did not fail to notice and learn as standards slipped around him. He was keenly observant and would put all these lessons to good use later. For the moment he stayed with the group in order to calm The Yardbirds for the next phase of their life. Page was habitually loyal and conservative in his actions. He'd taken years to get out of studio work and would now be equally reluctant to abandon his first major group. He would give The Yardbirds everything in a bid to return the group to its glory days. But the odds were turning against such a result.

By the end of 1966, Paul Samwell-Smith had overseen his last Yardbirds recording session, on December 22nd, walking out on an abortive attempt to record Graham

Gouldman's song 'You Stole My Love' after a row with Page.

Napier-Bell's interest was flagging too, and by January 1967 he had signed over his management rights in the group to Peter Grant, an ambitious man on the lookout for an act with whom he could make an impact. Prior to leaving, Napier-Bell also made over his recording and production interests in The Yardbirds to Mickie Most's RAK Productions. Most and Grant had separately set up the RAK Music Management company together in 1966 and shared an office in London's Oxford Street. They had known each other since the 1950s and, after going their separate ways in the business for some years, decided to join forces in this area, although Most's production and record dealings were kept separate.

Napier-Bell had told Grant that the worldly Page was a "troublemaker" who showed an unhealthy interest in the group's finances. Grant recounted to a *Melody Maker* scribe years later: "So then I met [The Yardbirds] and I said to Jimmy, 'I hear I have to give you the bullet because you're a troublemaker.' 'Troublemaker?' he said. 'You're dead right! We did *Blow Up*, four weeks in America, and a Rolling Stones UK tour, and we got just £118 each.' I took them on."[18] Page, used to the relatively straightforward and lucrative financial arrangements of studio work, had been shocked by the standard of financial practice in the world of rock groups.

Not long after, Napier-Bell sold his interest in the new Jeff Beck Group to Grant too. Beck said later this was a key move for him, calling Grant "a great manager, the best of his day".[19] Grant plotted a new course for them, concentrating on the USA and successfully appealing to the newly emerged 'underground' there. It was a formula Grant would soon repeat for another band under his charge and with even more impressive results.

Meanwhile, in the first weeks of 1967, Page accompanied Keith Relf to a *Melody Maker* interview. Relf said gloomily: "The Yardbirds are stale to British fans – like The Animals and the other groups we came up with." Page was more inclined to look on the bright side, saying: "We are still going down very well in America. It's still fresh to them. ... I've been on three American tours – on the first two there was nothing happening there at all. I was shocked by the groups we played with. Now you find good guitarists and good ideas everywhere – especially on the West Coast. They aren't just reproducing Beatles and Stones any more."[20]

The Yardbirds now had a choice to make. They could follow the implications of their live act into the burgeoning 'album-band' market, soon to be exploited brilliantly by Cream and The Jimi Hendrix Experience in Britain and by The Grateful Dead, Jefferson Airplane, Spirit, Iron Butterfly and others in America. All were allowed to reproduce often sprawling but hard-hitting onstage performances on their studio albums. The other option for The Yardbirds was to side with the 'hippy-power' tendencies of the psychedelic folk-rockers and acoustic-electric artists, such as Donovan, Fairport Convention, and The Pretty Things. The Yardbirds and their new management/production team opted to do both, after a fashion.

Nothing was clear-cut about the decision. Keith Relf, for example, felt that 'Happenings Ten Years Time Ago' was "much too clever. ... It may have been all right for the States but it was never a single for Britain".[21] Page saw it from a different angle. "The trouble is we're not allowed to record in the States," he told that same *Melody Maker* interviewer, "and that means we must do everything in a terrible rush when we are here [in Britain]."[22]

That rush would not ease up during 1967. In fact, the group found studio time increasingly difficult to prise out of their new production team. Relf spelt out their underlying lack of confidence about their place in the home-country scene. "Who knows how we will go down here? The whole scene seems to be one of artistic confusion with nobody knowing which way to turn."[23] If the group members themselves didn't know what they wanted, nobody else was in a position to help. Chris Dreja saw it clearly in hindsight. "The best manager we ever had was Peter Grant. ... Unfortunately for us, by the time [he] came on the scene we were going downhill and we were knackered."[24]

Musicians who find themselves in struggling bands deal with the experience in different ways, although most opt to do nothing much and complain a lot. Some stick immovably to the formula that has given them success but is now helping to bury the group's future, while others adopt wholly new (and sometimes appropriate) musical personas. With time, patience, judgement and luck, this last scheme can revive the fortunes of a struggling band and give it a completely new image and audience. It can also create a new set of problems.

With The Yardbirds in early 1967 there was a sense of renewal through the new management and production team run by Grant and Most. But there was little time to take stock. Almost as soon as Grant took over the reins in January, the group were off on an extensive package tour of Australasia with The Walker Brothers and Roy Orbison, plus different local bands in each city. They arrived at the peak of a hot Australian summer and took advantage of the fact that, with the long summer holidays still in full swing, their performances were well attended by school and college kids. These audiences were the first to see Page take a bow to his guitar onstage.

Dreja relished his new role as bassist and found the new quartet a more 'emotional' vehicle. The Yardbirds had enjoyed steady chart success in Australia since 'For

The final Yardbirds line-up in late 1967: Chris Dreja, Jim McCarty, Jimmy Page, Keith Relf.

Your Love' and had even managed a minor chart placing with 'I Wish You Would' in 1964, followed by a strong cult following for the influential LP *Five Live Yardbirds*. Unfortunately, in Melbourne one fan became a little too enthusiastic at the successful concert at the Festival Hall: after the gig, Page's black Gibson Les Paul Custom (which the Australian press reported had been "loaned to Jimmy by Keith Richards") was stolen, along with a Fender guitar owned by the guitarist from local support band The Mixtures. In an uncanny premonition of what would happen again to Page in 1970, neither guitar was recovered.

Despite the group's popular success in Australia, they were away from Britain at a time when the scene was going through another of its lightning shifts that before long would result in a schism between 'pop' – in 1966 still a perfectly respectable word – and 'rock', which was attempting to convey something of the artist's sensibility along with continuing commercial success. Rock was associated with the emerging 'underground' culture, with young fans looking for their own heroes and philosophies through word of mouth rather than adopting those found in advertising and other media channels. During 1967 this division would widen to become an unbridgeable chasm. Commerciality was being redefined with the rise of Cream and The Jimi Hendrix Experience. The Yardbirds were in danger of being left behind by this new wave.

Page, keenly aware of any shift on the London scene, tried to keep on top of events. In February 1967, The Yardbirds' Far East tour ended in New Zealand after dates in Hong Kong and Japan were scrapped. The rest of the group headed back via San Francisco to the sobering prospect of a spattering of small gigs in England and Scotland and their first single under Mickie Most.

Page, in no hurry to return to London and that bleak scenario, returned via Bombay, India, making the first of his regular sorties to the East to pick up on the music there. Years later he said: "I remember arriving at three o'clock in the morning, getting off the plane with just a small bag and my guitar. I had no hotel organised or anything; I really busked my way through the trip."[25] On this occasion he brought back a few instruments, including a tambura (a sort of four-string sitar, used in Indian music usually for a drone behind other instruments or singing).

In February 1967 the group reassembled in a London studio to make their first single under Mickie Most's direction, 'Little Games' and 'Puzzles'. Or at least that was the plan; the reality turned out to be rather different. Most, used to being the boss on his own sessions and to using freelancers on a hire 'em-fire 'em basis, promptly decided that The Yardbirds' bassist and drummer, Dreja and McCarty, the driving heart of the group, were not to his liking. He thought that as unschooled musicians they would be too much like hard work in the studio. This

decision taken, he drafted in two replacements – bassist John Paul Jones, a trusted Most freelancer, and drummer Dougie Wright – and promptly knocked the stuffing out of the group before they'd recorded a note.

"I think Peter Grant had ultimate faith in Mickie Most," McCarty said later. "Mickie would suggest a single or something and we'd say, 'Let's go along with it: he's Mickie Most.'

"Also, we knew Peter had faith in Mickie's judgement. It's a shame, really, the choices that were made. We weren't really strong enough or confident enough in our own abilities to steer where we wanted to go."[26]

Page had joined The Yardbirds in a bid to escape the debilitating facelessness and lack of group identity during his years in the freelance recording scene. On this first session since Jeff Beck left the group, he was in effect functioning again in his old role as a sessionman. This disappointment, and the frustrations of the album sessions spread between February and the start of May, would make it clear to Page that he needed to exert control over all aspects of his music as soon as he had the opportunity.

The fate of 'Little Games', released as a single in April, was a salutary lesson, underlined by its successors and the album it decorated. 'Little Games' was a poor song given a half-baked treatment to toughen it up for a group like The Yardbirds. This did no one any favours, and it would have been better cast in triple time, sung with a smile by the likes of Sandie Shaw. It was at best foolhardy to ask a beat group to iron out the natural waltz-like melody into a driving beat and a singer with the narrow stylistic range of Keith Relf to lift the song through Tom Jones-like chutzpah.

Relf was good at a young man's soul-searching angst and could make a passable stab at the breezy self confidence of blues lyrics like 'Good Morning Little School Girl', but he had little vocal technique. He was certainly not alone in this among pop-group singers of the day, but his small voice and limited vocal range were at their best when he used his natural baritone to good effect. This song asked him to do nothing that suited him.

All these mismatches resulted in a single that didn't even chart in the UK and Australasia and reached a high of 43 in the USA. Thus began the era when fans would buy a Yardbirds single not for the A-side, which was invariably unmitigated chart fodder (and not very good), but for the B-side, where you could still find the group's musical values and energies intact. Intact, that is, outside Britain; 'Little Games' was their last British single.

The B-side of 'Little Games' was 'Puzzles', a stronger group composition recorded the same day. It features an attractive rhythm guitar pattern on acoustic and electric guitars – a Page trademark – that betrays close listening to Jefferson Airplane and The Byrds. The simple arrangement at least furnishes the song with an appropriate setting for the melody and lyrics.

Unfortunately, the words and their delivery are a poor match for the rhythm patterns of the melody. There are stresses in the wrong places adding syllables to words that didn't have them, hampering Relf's efforts. Considering he was the lyricist, he really didn't help himself.

The most exciting part of the track is the closing guitar solo. Page is back in England and very much aware of what Hendrix, Beck and Clapton are doing in the studio. He quickly asserts his mastery of the guitar licks, a Hendrix-inspired combination of legato Indian-music melodies and furious, descending, sitar-like runs. Page also seems at ease exploiting the immediacy of the studio sound and the excitement offered by guitar effects (here an octave-divider). The tempo change just prior to it provides a welcome shift of pace – an arranging touch that Page would develop greatly in the coming years – and the solo ends the track in compelling style, even with the then-fashionable fade.

The Yardbirds appeared on the BBC's *Saturday Club* radio show in April, serving up three numbers – a Dylan cover, a version of the new single, and 'Drinking Muddy Water', a thinly disguised version of Muddy's own 'Rollin' And Tumblin''. The purity of its blues lineage reached back to the earliest days of The Yardbirds when Eric Clapton played on 'I Wish You Would' and 'Smokestack Lightning'.

The Dylan cover was 'Most Likely You Go Your Way (And I'll Go Mine)' and is hardly revelatory. Relf closely approximates Dylan's own delivery of the song, injecting little of his own interpretation. The group plays it competently but quite straight, with Page very busy in his accompanist's role, while Dreja and McCarty stick to simple things correctly done. 'Little Games' here benefits from the extra space of a live performance that allows Page to cut loose a little in his solo and his closing obligato phrases, giving the song some of the bite its studio production had removed. 'Muddy Water' suffers from the inadequacy of the way the BBC recorded rock bands live: no distortion allowed, and the bass and drums sound puny compared to the studio version of a month later. But Page plays uninhibitedly and with as much blues authenticity as Peter Green or Eric Clapton.

The new album was issued in the US in July 1967 as *Little Games*; EMI turned it down for the UK. Only Cream at this time could compare to The Yardbirds for the breadth of their endeavours and the general originality of material on their parallel LP, *Fresh Cream*. If that had been Cream's last (as was the case with The Yardbirds) rather than their first, then a case could be made that Page's group were the more assured creative stylists at this point.

Yet the making of *Little Games* had not been a happy experience for any of the musicians. Jim McCarty saw it as the point at which the group lost its momentum. "I don't think Mickie Most was even there. He was just interested in singles. He would just say, 'Oh well, you've got a good engineer; get on with it yourselves.' Maybe he'd come in from time to time, but albums were not a priority." They were also missing the departed members who had contributed so much. "We seemed to run out of ideas creatively when Jeff [Beck] and Paul [Samwell-Smith] left,"[27] McCarty said.

'Smile On Me' and 'Drinking Muddy Water' come direct from the predictable Chicago-blues sources of Howlin' Wolf and Muddy Waters, and 'Smile On Me' shows just how much Page had absorbed from his short time alongside Jeff Beck. His first solo offers a staccato attack with a bitingly distorted tone; the second has the crazily bent long tones so beloved of Beck but preserving Page's long-term homage to B.B. King's phrasing and pauses. Both solos are exciting, offset satisfyingly by an octave-picked theme with wah-wah added as the track fades. This is hard-hitting contemporary blues, with Relf toughening up appropriately for the occasion.

'Drinking Muddy Water' benefits from Page's double-tracking and the addition of a rather eccentric piano accompaniment from Stones keys man Ian Stewart. Relf's harmonica playing is slashing and idiomatic, adding to the excitement, and Dreja adds powerful locked-in bass. Page plays some beautiful slide guitar as well as a stiletto-point solo wail using more standard techniques. He would mostly keep this type of playing under wraps in the early Led Zeppelin years as he concentrated on building their songwriting credentials, but it would be in full evidence by the time of Zep's third album.

The final blues, 'Stealing Stealing', reaches further back to jug bands and minstrel outfits of the 1920s and 30s, from Cannon's Jug Stompers to The Memphis Jug Band, whose original it is based on. Obviously included for light relief and a radical contrast to the more progressive and serious-minded material on the album, it works on its own terms without being memorable.

The Yardbirds passed off these derivative blues numbers as their own, raising the vexed question of song ownership. The Yardbirds – and later Led Zeppelin – were not the only bands at the time accused of taking from their lesser-known and less fortunate elders. Furthermore, everybody in the blues had always borrowed from everyone else. It was the way the genre worked, although some borrowings were closer to the bone than others. McCarty felt that this went back to the group's earliest performing days, individually and collectively. "I suppose we'd always been a cover band, originally. And then we'd done our own versions of various things, and they'd got changed quite radically. I guess we felt that those changes justified the songwriting credits."[28]

With 'No Excess Baggage' the group could have been forgiven for a creeping feeling that they were being pushed towards becoming a low-rent substitute for

Manfred Mann – a band itself going through an identity and popularity crisis after the defection of singer Paul Jones. This song fits the Manfreds mould with its simple melody, sunny lyrics and strutting chorus. Only the band's arrangement makes it serviceable: Page's rocking guitar lines and imaginatively varied effects bring it alive between the poppy verses. The only other feature of the track worth dwelling on is the outstanding bass playing by one John Paul Jones, ghosted in for this recording at Mickie Most's insistence.

As with many of Page's later creations, his solo-guitar cameo on *Little Games*, 'White Summer', shows the confluence of traditional Eastern and Western music in its instrumental techniques, musical theory and style. Page listened widely and was never averse to combining influences. Many years later, he talked about his fascination with alternative guitar tunings and specifically the DADGAD tuning he adopted for 'White Summer'. Regular guitar tuning pitches the strings at EADGBE; the DADGAD variation lowers the first, fifth and sixth strings by a tone. "I used to call DADGAD my C.I.A. tuning – Celtic-Indian-Arabic – because that's what it was," said Page. "DADGAD was something going around the folk scene during the 1960s, and it was when I first started playing that that I became really interested in Arabic and Indian music."[29]

'White Summer' presents Page as an acoustic guitarist and studio technician of considerable sophistication. He uses guitar techniques derived from pioneer East-Wester Davy Graham and the remarkable Bert Jansch, rubbing shoulders with tuning, fingering, and melodic conceptions inspired by Indian and Arabic music. The folk melody of the piece is specifically derived from 'She Moved Through The Fair' in the 1963 version by Graham, which he in turn credited to Padraic Colum.

Page freely admitted on more than one occasion that he was not in the same league as the top acoustic guitarists, and so it proves. But as he correctly surmised, he doesn't have to be; his strengths lie elsewhere. From the start of his version, Page is thinking less as a guitarist and more as an arranger. He gives the performance a more certain and symmetrical form than Graham's mostly improvised version (Graham recorded it live, too, in February 1967). Rather than relying on technical virtuosity like most guitar specialists, Page is unafraid to add other instruments to develop the piece's character and bring new colours. An oboe on the melody line helps tease out its folkish roots, while in the middle section the Indian mood is underlined by the addition of a tabla drum player – shades of Most's work with Donovan. This is one of the pieces that would be brought over from The Yardbirds when Led Zeppelin began regular live playing.

'Tinker Tailor Soldier Spy' is a Page-McCarty attempt to revisit the puzzled optimism of 'Shapes Of Things', posing that song's "come tomorrow" question in a rather more detailed way. It is not a memorable composition, nor was it a successful single, but it has two claims to fame. Its chime-like opening chord sequence is at least in part a direct anticipation of Led Zeppelin's 'The Song Remains The Same', and Page takes his first guitar solo on record using a violin bow.

'Black Rose' is Relf's attempt to re-invoke the monkish atmosphere of 'Still I'm Sad', this time with just Page's acoustic guitar and the lightest of (backwards) drum touches from McCarty as accompaniment, pointing the way to Relf's future with his band Renaissance as well as Page's interest in production techniques. Relf sings poorly on this track and really should have been given more time to record his vocals to a higher standard. Page, of course, plays his part impeccably, the complete studio professional. 'Little Soldier Boy' is another message song from Relf and the gang – military beat and all – and seems more like a second-string Kinks album song than a searing Yardbirds original.

'Glimpses' is not a gripping piece of collective writing by the group, but they do show themselves well capable of using the studio and instrumental effects available at De Lane Lea studio in May 1967. Page's great washes of phased guitar sound, his use of an electric sitar, and the presence of voices as background chanting and scrambled monologue make for stimulating listening as Dreja and McCarty drive the track along on a strong 6/8 beat and insistent riffs. It is little more than the sum of its effects, but it shows a very different approach to song-making, stressing open-ended forms and unresolved patterns that became central to progressive pop in the following year. Many groups would try this type of thing but The Yardbirds were one of the few to pull it off successfully, largely because of Page's inventiveness with the effects.

The Yardbirds were in Stockholm in early April attempting to support their new recording efforts with live and radio appearances, one of which would be preserved and appear on the 1997 set *Yardbirds … Where The Action Is!*. In a routine run-through of hits – 'Shapes Of Things', 'Heart Full Of Soul', 'Better Man Than I', 'Over Under Sideways Down' – the group's tightness is impressive, as is Page's committed guitar work. Each solo he takes – and of course he is the only soloist in the group now – is impassioned, with a keening electrified sound and a concentration on legato melodic shapes made red-hot by his urgent, overdriven sound. On the climactic 'I'm A Man' Page follows the time-honoured course of the rave-up, his solo peaking as he strums on the other side of the guitar's bridge, but he introduces his own variations by adding an atmospheric bowed-guitar passage over which Relf can improvise some words. It's a strong premonition of what Led Zeppelin would later develop into a cornerstone of their onstage performances.

The Yardbirds spent the late spring and early summer of '67 playing a motley selection of gigs around Britain and Europe, their live act still delivering while their records failed to chart. They made another attempt at a hit single in July with the gobsmackingly awful 'Ha Ha Said The Clown', yet another attempt to become Manfred Mann clones – an ironic quest given that Manfred Mann also thought the song feeble. It is hardly a surprise that expert opinion today suggests the only Yardbird present on the recording is Keith Relf. The rest is supplied by New York session musicians. Perhaps the single's failure in the USA was a blessing in disguise (it wasn't even released in the UK). Imagine where a hit might have led a group with a good record in the pursuit of follow-up success.

The September 1967 issue of *Music Maker* carried a reader's letter from Australia, published in the Sound Sense pages, asking Jimmy Page "what type of guitar, strings, amplifier and tuning" he employed. His detailed answer is revealing. "I have a … Gibson Les Paul Custom guitar with three pickups, but for stage and recording work I play a 1956 Fender Telecaster given to me two years ago by Jeff Beck. I have a 100-watt Vox amplifier and two Vox [AC-30] amplifiers, all linked to distribute the sound.

"I use Ernie Ball Rock'n'Roll strings, but these are not obtainable outside the USA, as far as I am aware. However, a close equivalent are Fender Rock'n'Roll. I use the sixth, fifth and fourth strings straight from the set and the second for the third, the first for the second, and a banjo octave for first. This is a very light-gauge stringing. For 75 percent of the time I use standard tuning, but the rest of the time I retune the instrument to chord shapes, [for example] when the guitar is tuned to a G chord, the first string is let down to D, the second stays at B, the third at G and the fourth at D, but the fifth is let down to G and the sixth is to D. This system has been employed for a long time by acoustic country-blues and folk artists and it gives opportunities for interesting experiments on the electric guitar."[30]

In the Led Zeppelin years, Page became reluctant to talk in detail about his technical arrangements, and especially about the tuning and stringing of his guitars, so it is useful to have his thoughts so early in his career when he had less reason to be guarded about such things. The choice of strings not only gave him a great degree of pliability when phrasing and bending, it also added to the unusually edgy sound he achieved, no matter which pickup or tone settings he was using.

Page's approach differs quite radically from Eric Clapton at this time. Clapton, asked similar questions a couple of months earlier, replied: "I favour standard light-gauge strings, rather than doctoring the strings to make them lighter. Messing around with strings and altering their position makes them even lighter and I never agree with it. … I like Fender Rock'n'Roll strings, which used to be obtainable only in the States but are now marketed in Britain as Fender No.150."[31] Asked a few months earlier about how he achieved his sound, Clapton said: "My sound results from finger vibrato, applying a lot of bass and volume on the guitar, and turning everything right up on the amplifier, which is a Marshall 50-watt. I don't use a fuzz-box."[32]

Clapton was looking for very different sounds and practical uses for those sounds than Page, and it is fascinating to read in these contrasting responses how they realised those aims. Clapton's inspiration lay almost completely within the traditional blues at this time, while Page's enquiring mind led him to explore many other styles and techniques, happily borrowing from a range of different genres and traditions and looking for expressive flexibility in every musical situation.

This was not the only appearance of Jimmy Page's name as a writer in the British music press of autumn 1967. Page was either feeling homesick or unusually communicative at this time, for in the September 9th issue of *Melody Maker* he wrote an open letter describing what is was like to be on the road in the US of A that summer. Although this was something the British press had encouraged band members to do since The Beatles had conquered America in 1964 – often ghosting the pieces for them when time got tight – it was a dying art by 1967 as journalists began touring with bands and filing intercontinental stories under their own bylines.

Page wrote: "There's never been a tour like this! Not because of the enthusiasm of the fans or the music, or even the size of the crowds that turned out to see us. No, this is a tour we will always remember because of the violence. To call this an explosive tour would be an understatement. We've encountered problems everywhere – the bulk of them racial in origin. And from what we've seen it would seem that there is a large scale revolt against American society.

"Take our three days at the Fillmore Auditorium. [The Yardbirds appeared there in late July supported by The James Cotton Band and Richie Havens.] It started out nice enough, with people like Julie Christie and the Jefferson Airplane coming along to hear us. We also heard that Bob Dylan was in the audience, but we never met him.

"That first night was a ball, both for us and the Jimmy Cotton Blues Band, who were also on the show. Then, on the second day, a coloured guy was shot in a supermarket and before we know it there was a race riot in full swing. Molotov cocktails were thrown, road blockades were put up, and the militia were called out to control the crowds. It was a pretty ugly scene all round and didn't make for a happy stay."[33]

Page goes on to detail another riot at Griffith Park in Los Angeles right in the middle of a Love-In. The letter concludes with a platitude so flat it reads like a sub-editor's attempt to add a neat and polite ending, in contrast to the contemporary critique of the rest. Page is describing the famous 'Summer of Love', centred on San Francisco – and he is describing riots. It is commonly accepted today that the following year, 1968, saw the peak of such civil unrest in the USA, but perhaps it was more the year when the media could no longer ignore what was going on.

Another event on this late-summer Yardbirds tour – notable only in hindsight – was their August 27th appearance at the Village Theater in New York City where they shared the bill with The Youngbloods and folk singer Jake Holmes. Holmes had recently written and recorded an album's worth of material for the small Tower label. On it, he performed a version of his own song, 'Dazed And Confused'. It was also issued as a single by the same company.

The original included all the compositional elements that Led Zeppelin would reveal on their treatment of the song on their own debut album: the descending walking bass line, the eerie, harrowing atmosphere, the paranoid lyrics (although Holmes's were about a bad acid trip). Drummer Jim McCarty heard Holmes's set at the New York date and was sufficiently impressed by the song to go out and buy a copy of the album. Quickly, the rest of the group came to agree with him. According to McCarty, Page also bought a copy of the album at the time.

The Yardbirds began to work a version of 'Dazed And Confused' into their live set, gradually altering the arrangement and – as so often happened with the group – re-casting the lyrics to suit their own style. As the group continued to tour during the next nine months, the song became a staple of their live act. Although they never laid down a commercially recorded version, they did tape it for the BBC in March 1968. That take shows a strong affinity with the version that would soon become a centrepiece of the Led Zeppelin live show.

A Harry Nilsson song, 'Ten Little Indians', was released as The Yardbirds' new single in October. It was another effort coaxed from a weary group by Mickie Most in his frustrating and ultimately doomed attempt to make the group commercial. At least Page gained some long-term benefit.

In a desperate attempt to salvage what he called "an extremely silly song" with "a truly awful brass arrangement", he had the idea to add 'pre-echo' to the brass. "The result was very interesting," said Page later. "It made the track sound like it was going backwards. Later, when we recorded 'You Shook Me' [on the first Zeppelin LP], I told the engineer Glyn Johns that I wanted to use backwards echo on the end. He said, 'Jimmy, it can't be done.' I said, 'Yes it can. I've already done it.'

"Then he began arguing, so I said, 'Look, I'm the producer. I'm going to tell you what to do, and just do it.' So he grudgingly did everything I told him to, and lo and behold, the effect worked perfectly. When Glyn heard the result, he looked bloody ill! The funny thing is, Glyn did the next Stones album and what was on it? Backwards echo! And I'm sure he took full credit for the effect."[34]

The 'Ten Little Indians' single deservedly disappeared without trace. By then The Yardbirds had completed their sixth US tour to ever-diminishing returns and were pining for home. Page felt that the Most-produced A-side was "the sort of thing that led to a lack of confidence within the group and its eventual split".[35]

A new US tour in October and November '67 was a disaster from the start, with McCarty missing due to various complications at the start, gigs regularly cancelled, and the group reduced to supporting Ramsey Lewis at The Cheetah club in Chicago. The highlight was another night at the Village Theater in Greenwich Village, this time with Vanilla Fudge and Tiny Tim – a bizarre line-up even for the late 1960s. The members of Vanilla Fudge would soon welcome Page's next band onto another American tour, easing Led Zeppelin's entry into the rock rat-race.

Everyone in The Yardbirds knew this was not the way to run a tour. Page determined that when he went out with his next group, nothing like this would be repeated. In fact, when McCarty attempted to address the question of where The Yardbirds should be going, Page proved a willing listener.

"He did keep himself to himself," said McCarty, "but when I used to talk to him about the problems in the band and that maybe we should take another direction, develop the quieter side of things, he used to say, 'Well, I'm willing to change. I'll go along with you.'"[36] But time was running out for the group, and there were no studio opportunities to develop another direction. Life on the road was the only financially viable option, especially in the States.

Back in Britain they faced virtually no work at all, and no mention in any of the end-of-year pop awards and ceremonies. During 1967 The Beatles had of course released *Sgt Pepper*, the Stones had delivered the bizarre but newsworthy *Their Satanic Majesties Request*, Jimi Hendrix had hoovered up acclaim with *Are You Experienced*, and Cream had created a small masterpiece in *Disraeli Gears*. Even The Pretty Things, a band drifting commercially for some time, had at least got their overlooked masterpiece *S.F. Sorrow* released in Britain. The Yardbirds, once at the cutting edge of pop, hadn't even managed to get their album out in the UK.

The group's final single, 'Goodnight Sweet Josephine', appeared in April 1968, another US-only release. The commercial radar that had detected so many hits until 1967 had apparently gone blank. How did they choose this banal song, with lyrics laddishly celebrating a whore, as their next shot at chart fame? Their ex-guitarist, Jeff Beck, had scored hits with such chart fodder as 'Hi

Ho Silver Lining', 'Talleyman', and 'Love Is Blue' – all produced by Mickie Most, who still shared an office with Peter Grant, the manager of both Beck and The Yardbirds. Beck had found time to put together his Group with Rod Stewart and Ronnie Wood to make the *Truth* album and headline in the States. Surely something was terminally wrong when the best anyone could conjure for The Yardbirds was a single like 'Josephine'?

The only redeeming feature of the whole exercise was the B-side, 'Think About It', a brooding, medium-fast minor blues that takes the listener back to The Yardbirds' origins and their very first single, 'I Wish You Would'. Relf delivers one of his best vocals, while Page's arrangement is simple, imaginative and exciting, starting with a guitar rendition of the verse melody and then settling into a stark, menacing blues riff. The tension is built well to the point where Page bursts in with what for a single must be considered a long guitar solo.

True to his arranging instincts, Page doesn't merely play blistering blues runs and patterns (although he does that too) but introduces the solo through a recapitulation of the melody, providing a proper framework. His frantic solo is not his best by a long shot, burdened by familiar guitar-hero patterns and a lack of continuity, but it does have a good feel and a fair dose of beautiful melody. He double-tracks a brutal, compelling chordal accompaniment on two guitars, one of which sounds almost like a cello, suggesting it may be bowed. 'Think About It' ends with a repeat of the first vocal verse, followed by a throbbing guitar and backwards hi-hat beat reminiscent of Hendrix's 'Are You Experienced' as well as earlier Yardbirds efforts.

With Fleetwood Mac's 'Black Magic Woman' a minor hit around the same time as this single's release, it seems almost perverse to have played to the group's weaknesses rather than its strengths and not to have made 'Think About It' the A-side. At least it would have been an honourable exit for a group that had lost its way and its own self-belief.

Certainly the single's producer had no idea what to do with it. Simon Napier-Bell, who from the start did not consider the teaming with producer Mickie Most a good idea, felt that Jimmy Page as well as Peter Grant learned something important from the string of failed singles. "The funny thing was, with Mickie Most, chart success with singles was all-important. Yet Peter thought that if you put a single out you were competing to get in the chart and if you didn't get in the chart you are then a failure. If you don't put a single out – you can't be a failure!

"Maybe working with Mickie made him think about this, because charts ruled Mickie's life – or perhaps Jimmy Page had given him the idea."[37] Grant, who regularly went out on the road with his group and knew their real capabilities, would have been quick to detect the gap between what they were doing live and what came out of the recording sessions.

Against this miserable background, in spring 1968 The Yardbirds prepared for their final US tour, already flagged as their last due to Relf and McCarty's decision to leave at its conclusion and form a new group together. Bizarrely, this period of preparation included another session at the BBC where they performed not only the hard-hitting 'Think About It' and the classic 'My Baby', made famous by Garnett Mimms, but also 'Goodnight Sweet Josephine'.

At least this time 'Josephine' was given a rousing performance, full of high spirits and a complete lack of respect. This is what it deserved, lifting it from an embarrassment to a bit of silly fun. 'My Baby' exhibits similar levels of enthusiasm and also preserves one of Keith Relf's best-ever vocals, where he gives his all at the top of his range and sounds completely convincing as a soul balladeer.

'Think About It', stripped of much of its production, preserves the same arrangement and the same haunted feel, while the superior recording of McCarty's drums gives the track a better bottom-end than the studio version. Page's solo flows better 'live' here than in the studio as he links his phrases more logically, showing that he could deliver a powerful solo on the spot and also maintain exact control of the guitar's tone and dynamics to maximise impact. But now he and the group had their last tour to play.

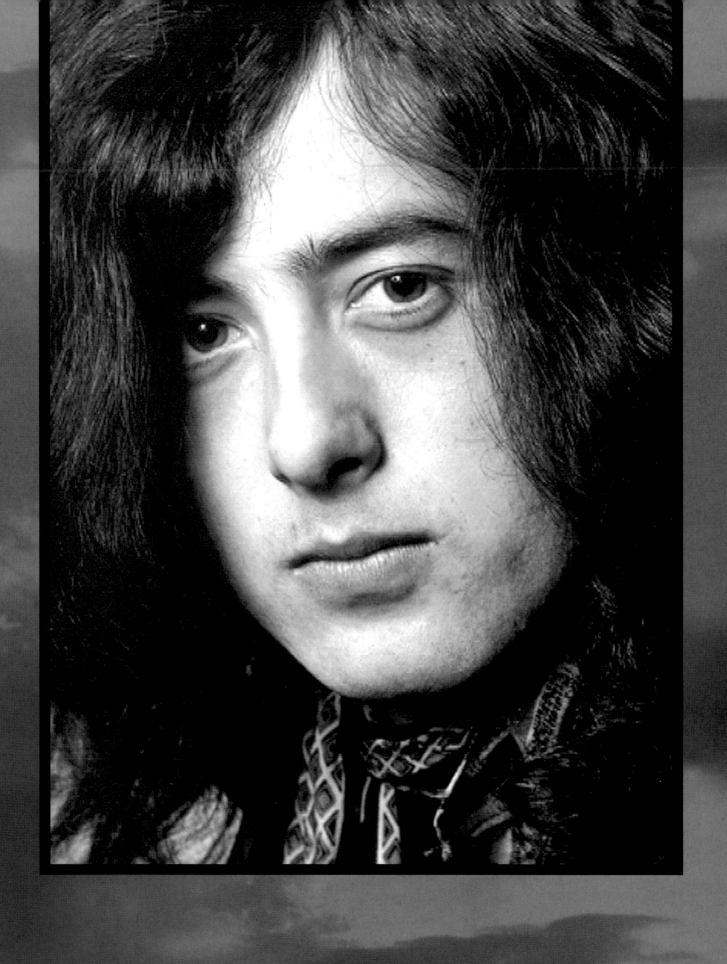

AN IRON BUTTERFLY BY ANY OTHER NAME

- YARDBIRDS FINAL AMERICAN TOUR
- YARDBIRDS SPLIT
- LED ZEPPELIN FORMED
- 1ST EUROPEAN TOUR
- SESSIONS FOR 1ST ALBUM

The Yardbirds' final US tour, which stretched from March to June 1968, was at least conducted in a relaxed atmosphere between the four group members, because they had already taken their decisions and knew that this was the parting of the ways. Relf recalled later that he and McCarty were by then looking for different things in their music than The Yardbirds allowed. He was especially aware of the gap between their live and recorded work, and was irked by their lack of freedom in the studio. "Towards the end … we were more into the psychedelics. That was the thing that was happening for us. Whatever happened in the studios was the producer's idea of what the band should be. What we were actually doing was getting off on sound and feedback – just letting it go."[1]

Page was well aware of the group's diverging musical interests. He recalled that Relf and McCarty "were into very light things like Simon & Garfunkel, The Turtles, and people like that, and they wrote some songs in that vein, which they wanted to go off and record. I was in favour of us keeping the group together and tried to persuade them to stay and record their songs as The Yardbirds because I knew we had the potential to pull it off, but they just wouldn't have any of it. Keith was the instigator, I think, really."[2]

Before the group's departure for America, Page had a brief talk with Peter Grant. "I can remember distinctly … driving Jimmy around Shaftesbury Avenue near the Saville [Theatre, central London] after the split," said Grant. "We were in a traffic jam and I said to Jimmy, 'What are you going to do? Do you want to go back to sessions, or what?' And he said, 'Well, I've got some ideas.' He didn't mention anybody. I said, 'What about a producer?' and he said, 'I'd like to do that too, if you can get a deal.' So I thought, 'Great, let's do it.'"[3]

With that settled, the group flew out to the USA. Chris Dreja remembered: "It was a good tour. I think the playing was more fun, actually, because we knew we didn't have to do this for much longer. It was a sort of release. … I preferred playing then and Jimmy got into his stride at that point. We were doing arrangements of things that, when I hear some of them now, I can't believe that's what we were doing. … All sort of medleys and riff links … exciting stuff, and you could tell the audiences were turned on. If we'd taken six months off, who knows what would have happened?"[4] This description of Page's last phase with The Yardbirds is an uncanny anticipation of Led Zeppelin's working methods.

But the group did not take six months off and did not survive. They even went into a studio in New York City in early April to record four numbers, possibly in order to honour contractual commitments, but these were never commercially issued. One of the tracks was 'Knowing That I'm Losing You', a Relf-Page song that Page later

reworked into 'Tangerine' for the third Led Zeppelin album. The marriage of the hard-driving group with Easy Listening-producer Manny Kellem – his big hit had been Paul Muriat's 'Love Is Blue' – was close to perverse. Maybe no one else was in town at the time. Much of the material recorded in the three days was below par, but the two songs from the last day, the rip-roaring 'Avron Knows' and a further version of 'My Baby', prove that The Yardbirds remained a potent and powerhouse group when in the mood.

None of these recordings was cleared for release by producer Kellem, so they were filed and forgotten, rendering Epic's attempt to stockpile tracks before the group split something of a non-starter. In a sense, Epic did attempt a cash-in, but it would be with an abortive live album three years later – *Live Yardbirds! Featuring Jimmy Page* – when Page was a guitar god running another band. The cash-in was shortlived, with Page's lawyers successfully demanding the record's recall.

In May 1968 The Yardbirds played their last nights at San Francisco's Fillmore Ballroom, on a bizarre bill that included the uncompromising jazz pianist Cecil Taylor and electric-violin-led rock band It's A Beautiful Day. The dope-heads in the audience must have been even more confused than usual on those three nights. But it was all played in the knowledge that, whatever happened to The Yardbirds, this line-up would not be carrying the name forward. The tour wound its way across the country before ending with two nights on June 4th and 5th at a racetrack in Montgomery, Alabama. That same night of the 5th, in a hotel in California, Senator Robert F. Kennedy was assassinated, once again bringing to the surface the violence in American society that Page had noted in his letter to *Melody Maker* a year earlier. It certainly put the group's problems into perspective.

News of the impending split had been leaked in the music press in the UK. *Melody Maker* carried a brief note. "Break-up of The Yardbirds is expected on their return from America. … Lead guitarist Jimmy Page is to re-form the group with a new lead singer and drummer, to replace Keith Relf and Jim McCarty." In an equally short second and concluding paragraph the item summed up the group's history, ending with the observation that "they have spent much of their time in America in recent years",[5] almost as if British readers needed to be reminded who they were.

A year later, Page himself would have a clear perspective on this period, telling *Oz* magazine's Felix Dennis: "It was a shame The Yardbirds eventually folded out. Towards the end, Keith and Jim McCarty just didn't have their heart in the music. They were almost ashamed of the name Yardbirds in the finish, though I don't know why; on the last tour we were getting better reaction than we'd ever had. They were a great band; I was never ashamed of playing in The Yardbirds."[6]

Relf and McCarty flew back to London on June 6th, ready to start work on their own joint ideas. The following week's music press carried stories of the group's two-way split – and rave reviews of The Jeff Beck Group's US concert debut. Beck's band, newly signed exclusively to Peter Grant's management, was booked by Grant into the Fillmore East in New York City for two nights, June 14th and 15th. The Group's heavy, wild, blues-based sound was an instant hit with the underground audience there – an uncanny anticipation of the impact that another Peter Grant band would soon have at the venue.

The New York Times claimed that the Beck Group "upstaged, for one listener at least, the featured performers, The Grateful Dead".[7] Page and Peter Grant were both on hand to witness this triumph and read the press raves. Grant forwarded the *Times* review to Clive Davis at Epic Records, and Davis released The Jeff Beck Group's first album, *Truth*, later that year. It peaked at Number 15 that August – a triumph for an unknown band that had concluded its first US tour with six nights at the Fillmore West earlier that month, supporting headliners such as Sly & The Family Stone and Albert King.

Early in the summer of 1968, back in the disintegrating Yardbirds camp, it was now Page and Dreja's job to find new personnel. After agreeing a basic strategy with Page, Dreja returned to London. Page stayed back a few more days, seeing music-business friends and meeting up with Peter Grant. Before Page left New York he gave interviews announcing that he and Dreja would be continuing the group. He told *Go* magazine: "The others were in The Yardbirds for four or five years. They had lost all of their enthusiasm. Keith Relf, the singer, was fed up for a long time and he was always threatening to leave the group." Page went on to say that they were keeping the Yardbirds name because "people have associated a type of sound with the name. It's a heavy beat sound and I want to keep that".[8] The beat would remain; the name would not.

It is understandable that the demise of The Yardbirds has been overshadowed in most fans' minds by the creation of Led Zeppelin, with Zep's mythology towering over the earlier group. But in such transitions dissolution comes before creation. The Yardbirds had to unravel before Led Zeppelin could take flight.

Page had already committed to working with Yardbirds manager Peter Grant and knew that, in terms of band management, Grant would be ideal. Grant was as ambitious as Page himself, but his ambition expressed itself in an unusual way for pop managers of the late 1960s. Grant wanted ultimately to focus upon one band and make that band phenomenally successful. To that effect he wanted a small stable of acts, all of whom he felt personally close to, and who had the ability to make that breakthrough.

So far in the short time that Grant had been running his own show he'd had chart success with The New Vaudeville Band and, subsequently, attracted some talented performing artists to work with him. But he had not fixed on the act he thought would do it.

Yardbirds drummer Jim McCarty saw the developments at first hand. "When Peter Grant came in he was just an extension of a tour manager, really. He was never one to sit down and talk about strategy and that with us as a group. I guess he might have developed it as he went along – maybe he built up a relationship with Jimmy and they developed a strategy. They certainly had a very good strategy when Led Zeppelin formed."[9] McCarty remembered Grant as someone who was very loyal to his acts and diligent in his efforts to get them paid properly – and promptly – for live work. This was a trait that would become increasingly dominant as Led Zeppelin rose to new heights over subsequent years.

Grant and Page were quick to recognise fellow spirits. Grant's informal chats with Page and the subsequent follow-through quickly changed Grant's angle on The Yardbirds and what might follow them. As Page's plans developed that summer and Led Zeppelin was created, Grant kept in close contact with his thinking, although he already had a major success on his hands that summer with The Jeff Beck Group.

But the Beck success was in close tandem with Mickie Most, who still inhabited the role of record producer. Although his relationship with Most remained close, Grant was soon to discover that there were other ways to achieve his aims. When he realised how well his and Page's ideas dovetailed and how brilliant Page was at the overall strategy of making a band successful both live and in the studio, he gradually relaxed his grip on the other artists with whom he was involved. In particular, The Jeff Beck Group – with Rod Stewart as tyro vocalist – was increasingly left to Mickie Most to steer, though Grant continued to book the band and plan their US tours. This would ultimately hasten the Beck Group's demise.

McCarty felt that Page and Chris Dreja only decided to continue with The Yardbirds after the last US tour had concluded. "[Relf and I] were the ones who were going," said McCarty. "So we said, 'If we're leaving, you can have the name.' Chris and Jimmy had the rights to carry on with it." McCarty and Relf waved goodbye to Grant at the same time. "We weren't involved with Peter," McCarty added. "We went with different management. We went our separate ways."[10]

The two ex-Yardbirds, Relf and McCarty, were first off the mark with their new post-Yardbirds venture. Teaming up with producer and ex-Yardbird Paul Samwell-Smith, they recorded some sessions in July at Abbey Road under the name Together. On these tracks the two defined the musical directions they wanted to pursue – heard in embryo on certain Yardbirds tracks of the past few years, especially brooding singles such as

'Still I'm Sad' or 'Heart Full of Soul'. Unfortunately for the two, these recording ventures met commercially with the same absolute indifference that had sunk the previous few Yardbirds releases. A single from these sessions was eventually released in November 1968 and disappeared without trace.

With half the band gone and no immediate replacements to hand, the two remaining Yardbirds, Page and Dreja, wanted to keep the name going and bring in new recruits on drums and vocals. Page flew back to London on June 15th, hooking up again with Dreja to think through their needs and who might be drafted in. Peter Grant began making forward bookings for what would become Led Zeppelin – still billed for now as The Yardbirds – including an autumn tour of Scandinavia and a projected brief US college tour in October.

Page spent the rest of June 1968 pondering his next moves and catching up on old business connections. After all, the old line-up still had one gig to play before permanent disbandment. That was on July 7th, at Luton College of Technology, about 30 miles north-west of London. It would be the last gig by the quartet featuring Relf and McCarty.

One early decision had been that the new band would not need an outside producer any more. Page himself, by then an experienced hand in the studio and with definite ideas of his own, would take over the producer's role. It was also clear that a clean break was needed with current record company arrangements. After all, Epic had not exactly landed the group any recent Stateside hit singles, and the *Little Games* album had been largely ignored; in Britain, Columbia had not even released the LP or the last couple of singles.

The new band would not be looking to outside songwriting teams for material. There were a number of reasons for this, some artistic and some financial. Relying on material from third parties meant little real control over the direction and development of musical style and character. It also meant that, in terms of wielding power, a band that could not produce and arrange its own material was in a weak position, individually and as a band. And the real money from records was in the publishing rights, so it was important for a band to generate its own compositions and arrangements.

Page told *Go* magazine he was chasing "a couple of singers and drummers"[11] but that the band would not fundamentally change its sound. At the outset Page intended to go for a big-name vocalist in the hope of giving the band a fresh image and direction as quickly as possible. He was taking his examples from John Mayall's Bluesbreakers, Small Faces/Faces, and Traffic, all of which experienced periodic personnel upheavals but retained their name and, largely, their identities.

If this could work, then the new band could prove continuity with The Yardbirds' past and be off to a flying start with their remaining fans. Page had once before approached ex Small Faces frontman Steve Marriott. As noted earlier, back in 1966, Page, Jeff Beck, Keith Moon and John Entwistle briefly considered pooling their resources to form a new band, but had been warned off Marriott in no uncertain terms by the singer's manager, Don Arden. He could see that finding an outstanding vocalist not already in a binding deal was going to be something of a problem.

Drummers were not seen as such a problem by a guitarist who had played with so many good professionals on the studio scene for years. All that Page and Dreja had to do was to make a list. Then Dreja and Peter Grant's office would make contact with them and see who was available and up for a change. In early July several drummers were approached to see if they were interested in reviving the fortunes of The Yardbirds. They included Clem Cattini, who had played as a sessionman on a late Yardbirds single, Jimmy Page's preferred choice B.J. Wilson, of Procol Harum, session drummer Paul Francis, and Aynsley Dunbar, who'd missed playing with The Jimi Hendrix Experience by the toss of a coin. For various reasons none was immediately available or willing to take a chance with an untested band. After all, The Yardbirds were showing every sign of terminal decline. They would have to look further afield – possibly as far as the ranks of the unknowns in working bands outside London.

For the vocal slot, Page approached Terry Reid, a singer managed by Peter Grant and with Midlands roots. (The 'Midlands' indicates a region of central England, centred on Birmingham, whose industrial areas are often called the Black Country.) Reid had come to Page's attention while a member of Peter Jay & The Jaywalkers but had recently gone solo, signing with Most and Grant's RAK organisation. This move, plus Reid's determination for a solo shot at fame, meant he had no desire to join.

According to Grant and Page, it was Reid who suggested they check out a singer he knew from the Midlands, Robert Plant. Others (including Plant himself) claimed that Page and Grant were directed Plant's way by two others: musical matchmaker Alexis Korner, who had seen Plant in London in 1967 and played with him later in the Midlands; and Tony Secunda, then managing Procol Harum and The Move. Secunda had long been an admirer of The Yardbirds but felt they were poorly served by Keith Relf's vocals and onstage persona. He'd known of Plant's abilities for some time and stayed alert to possible new openings for him.

Meanwhile, on July 19th Page received a speculative phone call from John Paul Jones, a session musician he knew well from his days in the studios. Jones had worked

John Paul Jones joined Led Zeppelin as bassist and keyboard player. He knew Jimmy Page from their London studio-session days.

together with Page on many Mickie Most sessions and had participated in the 'Beck's Bolero' session in '66. Jones, who also knew Peter Grant well from visits to the RAK office, was offering himself primarily as a bassist but also had a combination of talents and accomplishments rare on the rock scene of the day.

Jones came from a musical family, the son of Joe Baldwin, a professional pianist who played in jazz and dance bands, including Ambrose's orchestra. He could play a wide range of instruments, including keyboards, and was also a fine arranger. In magazine interviews at the time, Page claimed he was after a singer who could also play keyboards so that they could experiment with the Mellotron (a tape-replay keyboard something like a mechanical sampler).

Given this, Jones knew that there was at least a chance the new band might need someone with his versatility. His wife had seen an interview with Page in *Disc & Music Echo* around this time and suggested he make contact with his old studio mate. According to Grant, Jones initially checked out the gig through Grant's office, then made the call. Page made no immediate commitments on the phone, but kept Jones in mind. Within a few days he would have reason to call Jones and make him an offer that the musician, jaded by years of studio work, would be only too keen to accept.

The day after Jones's call, Page, Dreja and Grant drove to Birmingham to check out Terry Reid's recommendation. Robert Plant had spent most of his time in and around Birmingham and nearby Midlands cities fronting a series of groups. But so far he had failed to progress further than a couple of singles for CBS that did nothing, some highly enjoyable and occasional gigs with Alexis Korner, and a long stint leading local Birmingham outfit The Band of Joy. At the time of Terry Reid's recommendation, Plant was fronting another group, Hobbstweedle, which he admitted later "wasn't very good. The band overplayed and there was a lot of hubbub and flash but no real content."[12]

Contacted by Grant to undergo a working audition, Plant arranged for the Yardbirds contingent to see him in action onstage. On the evening of July 20th 1968, standing in the hall of Birmingham Teacher Training College, all three men agreed that Plant had something worth developing, even if the rest of his band didn't. Plant had a very strong voice, good pitch, a wide range, natural rhythmic feel, and good stage presence. His harmonica playing was authentic and enthusiastic. He was not a singer hung up on the current Northern Soul obsessions of many of the mighty-voiced UK vocalists of the time.

Jim McCarty remembered Chris Dreja telling a different story about that evening in Birmingham. Dreja was markedly less impressed with Plant than Page or Grant had been, but after a quick discussion between the three men they decided they would try him out –

although Plant knew he was by no means hired. Dreja's lack of enthusiasm for Plant's singing may well have been a factor in his subsequent removal from the reshaped band.

Page asked Plant to spend a few days at his boathouse down at the River Thames at Pangbourne (about 40 miles west of London) to see if the combination would work. Plant was pencilled in for the lead-vocal role, pending developments. Once ensconced at Page's boathouse, Plant discovered that he and the guitarist had a near-instant communication on common musical ground. He said later: "I looked through his records one day when he was out and I pulled out a pile to play, and somehow or other they happened to be the same ones that he was going to play when he got back … to see whether I liked them!"[13]

Plant's own musical inclinations led him to two differing sources for his singing style: British folk music and earthy American blues, both acoustic and electric. This was an unusual combination, even for a period when individuality was highly valued. Although completely unschooled, Plant had good instincts and an arranger's ear. The two found they could work together quite naturally.

"Jimmy wasn't dominating or anything as I might have expected," Plant remembered years later. "I could suggest things, and the two of us re-arranged 'Babe I'm Gonna Leave You' – although it doesn't say that [on the LP] because I was under contract to somebody else. … It was good to be able to hit it off like that."[14] (The original vinyl album credit for 'Babe' was "Traditional/arranged by Jimmy Page", but that would be changed later.) The Page/Plant collaboration would be crucial on several levels to the way the band was to develop. Plant said: "[Jimmy's] ability to absorb things and the way he carried himself was far more cerebral than anything I'd come across before, and so I was very impressed."[15]

It was proving a little more tricky to find a drummer. Over the same few days in late July, Dreja had phoned Paul Francis, only to discover that he was about to leave the country on a short tour. Dreja and Francis agreed to resume talks when he returned. Dreja was sufficiently sure of Francis to include him when he was interviewed around this time and gave the line-up of the new version of The Yardbirds as himself, Jimmy Page, Robert Plant, and Paul Francis.

Some have since questioned Dreja's readiness to go back on the road, but there was no sign of such reluctance in the interview. "Now we're starting to get things together with the new group, we're very keen to get on the road," Dreja said. "Our first set of new shows will be starting in September – ironically enough in Scandinavia, where we have a ten-day tour arranged. After this it'll be down to work in England. We've done a fair amount of rehearsing, with some new songs and also plenty of the old Yardbirds hits."[16]

Dreja was being a little economical with the truth: Francis had never hooked up with the band and there had been no rehearsals. Dreja's hint that recording had taken place was wishful thinking too, although there is no reason to doubt that he felt it would only be a matter of a week or two before it would. But much would happen in a very short space of time to completely alter the landscape as far as The Yardbirds were concerned.

Page later had no memory of Paul Francis being offered a position in the band, commenting: "He must have been someone who Chris had in mind."[17] According to McCarty, Page may have been thinking of adding a rhythm guitarist. "Jimmy sent [original Yardbirds guitarist] Top Topham a telegram as well. Asked him to join Led Zeppelin. Maybe Jimmy wanted a rhythm-guitar player to help out."[18] Such things often happen in the formation of bands, with plans changing almost daily.

New arrival Plant proved his worth by dipping into another pool of talent largely unknown outside the local scene: Birmingham. The city would later become notorious as a breeding ground for stylish rock drummers in particular. Cozy Powell and Carl Palmer both eventually made it out of local bands, but at the time Birmingham and environs were largely ignored as a talent centre. Plant himself had for years been going down to London in repeated attempts to find success. As he later commented: "Everyone in Birmingham was desperate to get out and join a successful band. Everyone wanted to move to London."[19] On the brink of such a move, Plant decided that recommending Birmingham drummer John Bonham, who was playing with folkie Tim Rose, might quickly get his new band out of a hole.

By the end of July 1968, Rose and band were back in London from a tour and, on the last day of the month, Page, Dreja and Grant went to watch them, with Bonham on drums, at the Country Club in Hampstead, north-west London. Page in particular was impressed by Bonham (even then known as Bonzo to his mates). Later he said: "When I saw what a thrasher Bonzo was, I knew he'd be incredible. He was into exactly the same sort of stuff as I was."[20] Bonham was asked to come down to Page's Pangbourne boathouse and meet the others. But what constituted 'the others' quickly changed too. Some time between Page's invitation to Bonham and the meeting itself, Dreja was eased out of the band and John Paul Jones installed in his place. The changeover took place on the first weekend in August.

Page knew Plant was his new singer and that Plant was not going to be playing an instrument onstage. This meant that Page needed an all-rounder who would major on bass but who could, when required, move quickly to other roles, onstage and in the studio. Dreja, as a bassist and guitarist, would have filled the role adequately, but he was not a keyboard player. He was also a holdover from the first band and, in theory at least, the senior partner.

The way things were developing, Page was no longer sure he wanted to put together a new band with such

potential for conflict arising from the previous arrangement. Reflecting on this, he saw a role for his old session colleague John Paul Jones. Page already knew the man, so a rehearsal would not be so much a testing of his abilities as a simple matter of seeing whether he fitted in. Dreja's involvement in developments was allowed to wither. Dreja turned to another passion, photography, quickly kick-starting a professional career. He would take the photograph of Led Zeppelin that appeared on the back jacket of their first LP.

With the events of the weekend of August 2nd-3rd confirmed, Page told Peter Grant, now in New York, that Robert Plant and John Paul Jones were two of the three newcomers who would make up the new band. Grant issued a press statement on August 5th in New York confirming this move. That week, John Bonham followed up the invitation of July 31st to come down to Page's boathouse at Pangbourne, on the Thames just west of Reading, for a meeting and an informal jam. Bonham said: "It was quite strange meeting John Paul Jones and Jimmy, me coming from the Midlands and having only played with local groups. ... I was pretty shy and I thought the best thing was not to say much but suss it all out. We had a play, and it went quite well."[21]

After the success of the second Pangbourne meeting Page was sure he wanted Bonham to be the fourth member. He quickly told Grant and the London office to contact the drummer with a firm offer. Although Bonham had completed his commitments with Tim Rose, he proved elusive for a few days, having picked up some work on a Chris Farlowe tour. Lying low and weighing his options, the drummer finally responded to one of a number of telegrams addressed to his local pub.

Bonham later explained this short pause as time taken to get a grip on the situation. He was a jobbing drummer from Birmingham with a history of short-term commitments to bands in return for average wages. Page's band was – potentially at least – a very different proposition. "That's why I had this thing about the telegrams. ... It seemed like a gift from heaven."[22] Bonham needed to know it would not all evaporate with a change of mind. He also needed some reassurance about income. Plant recalled later that there were "all sorts of negotiations about retainers and so on, and Bonzo was very keen to get an extra £25 a week [about $60 at the time] to drive the Transit van."[23]

However, time was short if the band were going to rehearse a set to fulfil their concert commitments in Scandinavia in September. Around a week after the Pangbourne meeting, with Plant's encouragement, Bonham agreed to give it a chance. A London rehearsal was quickly set up with the other three members of what was becoming an entirely new band. Page knew already which numbers he wanted to play, but with Dreja's exclusion he was now the only one person who knew how

to play them. He and Plant had also agreed on a fresh bunch of songs that they felt equally enthusiastic about from their exploratory meeting at Pangbourne in July, and these too would have to be routined.

The combination of ordinary luck and Page's astute choices for the personnel of his new venture is all too easy to take for granted. It is thrown into relief when compared with the tribulations of The Jeff Beck Group, already a success that summer and seemingly headed for glory. Beck was never happy with the choice of drummer and kept swapping around, while his relationship with singer Rod Stewart was so tenuous as to find them not speaking for much of the time. The strain was exacerbated by Mickie Most's refusal to allow Stewart a headlining role in the band. Most considered Beck the star and insisted it stay that way. Later, Epic Records executives would in all innocence greet Rod Stewart backstage after a concert as "Jeff". All this was compounded by the fact that Beck, by his own later admission, was going through something of an ego trip at the time.

In contrast, Jimmy Page was building his new band from the ground up, carefully and thoroughly, making sure that things gelled properly on every level and that the support machinery was both efficient and equitable. His quiet insistence that he alone would produce their records removed all the conflict that had embroiled The Yardbirds – and was still hindering Jeff Beck – and allowed the band to find their own sound and repertoire. It was no accident that the personnel of Page's new band would remain stable for 12 years.

All four musicians have said that the first official rehearsal was an unqualified success. It took place in a basement rehearsal space in Gerrard Street, Soho, central London. According to John Paul Jones: "We set the amps up and Jimmy said, 'Do you know 'Train Kept A-Rollin''? By The Yardbirds?' I said no, so he said, 'Well, it's a 12 bar with a riff on G.' That was the first thing we ever played."[24]

That simple, crunchingly raw blues – the same tune that had captivated film-maker Antonioni two years earlier – was a good place to start. It allowed everyone to release any nerves or tension in sheer speed and adrenalin. Everyone knew the blues, there was no arrangement to worry about, and the song's nature gave everyone license to cut loose. That is, of course, if it really was the first tune they played. According to Robert Plant, it was "a Garnett Mimms thing, 'As Long As I Have You', which we used to do in The Band Of Joy – that was the first number Zeppelin ever rehearsed".[25] It's possible that Plant is remembering the Pangbourne get-togethers, because Jones recalled "an early rehearsal at Jimmy's place [where] there was a Hohner organ and we did a couple of

things with that. One of them was 'A Tribute To Bert Burns' and I recall we also rehearsed 'Chest Fever' by the Band."[26] All three numbers – the Mimms song, 'Burns', and 'Chest Fever' – required organ, an instrument not present in the tiny Gerrard Street rehearsal space.

Whatever came first, it worked. The confidence of the new members grew apace. Crucially, Jones and Bonham realised within minutes that they made an ideal team. As Jones explained later, he'd had plenty of experience playing sessions with drummers and knew very quickly which he clicked with and which he didn't. "As soon as I heard John Bonham play I knew this was going to be great – somebody who knows what they're doing and swings like a bastard. We locked together as a team immediately. … He was a strong drummer, and we were playing rock'n'roll – you don't want somebody tapping about. He was loud from the bottom up, if you know what I mean. Which is how I like it, being a bass player."[27]

Jones was not just a bass player, but a very particular one. At a time when many bassists at the more progressive end of rock were experimenting with fast, high, complex patterns, Jones thought his key quality was solidity. "I don't like bass players that go 'boppity boppity bop' all over the neck," he said later. "You should stay around the bottom and provide that end of the group. I work very closely with the drummer; it's very important."[28] A trained musician and virtuoso, Jones was a team player – a vital ingredient as far as Page was concerned.

With the bottom end meshing from the start, Page knew he had the right musicians. In Plant, already an accomplished blues shouter and someone he privately knew to be interested in and capable of a great deal more than that, Page was also aware that he had the perfect front-of-stage focal point. The band already had more potential than he could reckon with; the only questions now were ones of timing and gathering together a repertoire that was both fresh and provided a continuity with The Yardbirds' recent past.

This was important because, remarkably, the guitarist wanted to continue the new group under the old name, even though the final original member had now departed. In a measure of his conservatism and caution, Page was attempting to minimise risk, retain the old fans, and provide continuity while announcing the new era with his idea to re-christen the band The Yardbirds Featuring Jimmy Page. The new foursome had legitimate reasons for going to Scandinavia under the original name – they tour had been booked for The Yardbirds in the first place. Page saw no reason why they should not continue with the name afterwards. Others, though, would feel differently.

Meanwhile, the new band had an opportunity for something of a dry run at recording when Jones arranged for them all to help him fulfil his existing session commitments by playing as backing musicians for an album for singer P.J. Proby to be cut at the end of August.

> **Robert Plant was a singer on the Midlands scene before he joined Led Zeppelin. The band, still billed as The Yardbirds, played their first dates in September 1968 in Scandinavia.**

Jones said: "I was committed to doing all the arrangements for the album. As we were talking about rehearsing at the time, I thought it would be a handy source of income. I had to book a band anyway, so I thought I'd book everyone I knew. We had Robert on tambourine."[29]

After another week of rehearsals, mostly at Page's boathouse, the band had learned a live repertoire not too far from that played on the last Yardbirds US tour. They were ready for the brief Scandinavian jaunt. Peter Grant accompanied them, eager to see and hear his new charges.

The band's public debut during the afternoon of September 7th 1968 at the Gladsaxe Teen Club in northern Copenhagen, Denmark was followed by a late-evening gig at the Pop Club in Copenhagen's southern seaside suburb of Brondby. These were typical of the sort of gig The Yardbirds had dealt with latterly, trifling affairs compared to their earlier reputation as hitmakers. For the new band, however, it was a perfect low-key introduction both for themselves and a live audience. Pictures from the evening show have the band on a small, low stage in front of a moderate-sized crowd in a room about the size of a small gymnasium. They all look very young.

Again following the recent Yardbirds model, this tour consisted of 14 performances across two weeks with a couple of short breaks woven into the fabric, probably due to a lack of other bookings rather than a planned rest on such a short tour. They worked in three countries – Denmark, Sweden and Norway – all closely linked by road and rail, so it was by no means a punishing schedule.

Peter Grant was back from New York where he had shaken hands on a deal with Atlantic Records. The company would get first offer on Jimmy Page's new band. Grant got his first glimpse of the new Yardbirds on this tour and quickly came to the view that Page had chosen his new musical partners astutely. This band had all the power, enthusiasm and life that had slowly drained away from the old line-up between 1966 and 1968.

At times, in fact, Page felt that the new drummer was showing a little too much enthusiasm and was overplaying, getting in the way of his guitar and Plant's vocals. Such minor adjustments were being made constantly in bands at the time. Jimi Hendrix would knock Experience drummer Mitch Mitchell's cymbals with his guitar if he felt Mitchell was overplaying and disturbing the mood that Jimi was trying to set onstage. Page, more discreet in such matters, told Bonham offstage: "You're going to have to keep it a bit more simple than that."[30] When Bonham got back onstage, only to cut loose again, Page asked manager Peter Grant to intervene. Not one to mess around, Grant simply told Bonham that if he wanted to keep his place in the band, he would do what Page told him to do. "Behave yourself, Bonham, or you'll disappear."[31] The lesson was learned – musically, at least.

Grant was convinced that this new line-up had what it

takes. With a record company firmly interested in the results, the manager was happy to book time at Olympic studio in Barnes, west London, for the band to record their first album. Page paid for this, a total outlay of £1,782 (then about $4,300). Page said later that he managed this from money he'd saved from his earnings as a session musician, because he'd made virtually nothing with The Yardbirds. It was a risk but gave him complete artistic freedom, while owning their product gave Grant great latitude in dealing with record companies.

Page elaborated later: "I wanted artistic control in a vise grip, because I knew exactly what I wanted to do with these fellows. In fact, I financed and completely recorded the first album before going to Atlantic. It wasn't your typical story where you get an advance to make an album: we arrived at Atlantic with tapes in hand. The other advantage to having such a clear vision of what I wanted the band to be was that it kept recording costs to a minimum. We recorded the whole first album in a matter of 30 hours. That's the truth. I know because I paid the bill."[32]

Logs from the recording sessions show that the band was booked by Grant as 'The Yardbirds'. By the standards of the day, they were not given freedom to record when they wanted, but neither were they set unrealistic deadlines that would have compromised their performance. Glyn Johns, a man adept at creating fine albums and a good atmosphere in the studio, was brought in to oversee proceedings, but the arrangements and treatments had been prepared in advance by Page and the band at their Pangbourne rehearsals. Page had clear ideas of what he wanted to do with the production. This would be a very different experience from the *Little Games* sessions. No one was desperately seeking hit singles: this was an album project. The first day of recording was September 27th 1968 and the sessions lasted around nine days, into early October.

Jones said the album was "pretty much a recording of the first show, which was why it had so many covers on it. That's all we had ready to play at that time."[33] He remembered the band making a virtue of necessity. "Robert did some guide vocals in the studio and we couldn't get rid of them, so we turned them into an effect. That sort of thing happened all the time. I remember there was a Hammond organ in the studio which I used, and I wrote the riff to 'Good Times Bad Times'."[34] Page recalled Plant "singing the vocals live … which helped him because he'd make up lyrics as he went along."[35]

Like any sensible co-producer and bandleader, Page had prepared more material than would fit onto a single LP, so that there would be a choice. Live and studio are two very different things, with songs that don't really work onstage suddenly blossoming on tape, and vice versa. With a surplus, what worked best would be used, rather than including everything that was made because there was nothing else. Tracks worked on during these sessions were: 'Good Times Bad Times', 'Babe I'm Gonna Leave You', 'You Shook Me', 'Dazed And Confused', 'Your Time Is Gonna Come', 'Black Mountain Side', 'Communication Breakdown', 'I Can't Quit You', 'How Many More Times', 'Tribute To Bert Burns' ('Baby Come On Home'), 'As Long As I Have You', Spirit's 'Fresh Garbage', and 'Flames' by Elmer Gantry.

Of the tracks attempted at Olympic that were unissued at the time, only 'Tribute To Bert Burns' has since surfaced on an official release, turning up on the second *Led Zeppelin* boxed set (1993) and the ten-CD *Complete Studio Recordings* set (same year) under the title 'Baby Come On Home'. As its original title suggests – the correct spelling is Bert Berns – this is a tilt of the hat to the famous songwriter and producer who died in 1967. He had worked with The Drifters, Ben E. King, and The Isley Brothers before scoring success with British acts such as Lulu and Them, helping set the tone and style for a whole generation of rock and soul acts. Zeppelin recorded a close and affectionate imitation of the mid-1960s slow pleading ballad, as favoured by many black American soul singers of the day such as Garnett Mimms and complete with arpeggio'd piano accompaniment. While it is superbly played, it would not have sat comfortably with the rest of the music on the first LP.

Peter Grant kept well clear of all these musical decisions: his policy was that music matters were solely the band's concern. As Jones put it: "He dealt with the record companies and trusted us implicitly with the music. That was one of his great strengths, I always thought. There was no pressure to change anything and his only comment was, 'That sounds great.'"[36]

How did this first effort fit into what others were doing that year? LPs released in the UK during the summer and autumn of 1968 included: Cream's *Wheels Of Fire*, released mid August as the new Zeppelin line-up was coalescing; Dylan's *John Wesley Harding*; The Beatles' *Yellow Submarine* soundtrack; The Jimi Hendrix Experience's *Smash Hits* collection; Jeff Beck's *Truth*; Small Faces' *Ogden's Nut Gone Flake*; Big Brother & The Holding Company's *Cheap Thrills*; The Band's *Music From Big Pink*; Fleetwood Mac's *Fleetwood Mac*; The Kinks' *Village Green Preservation Society*; Simon & Garfunkel's *Bookends* and *Parsley, Sage, Rosemary & Thyme*; Vanilla Fudge's *Renaissance*; Donovan's *A Gift From A Flower to A Garden*; Pink Floyd's *Saucerful Of Secrets*; The Doors' *Waiting For The Sun*; and Iron Butterfly's *In-A-Gadda-Da-Vida*. Traffic released *Mr Fantasy* in late October, while Hendrix's *Electric Ladyland*, released in the US in September, appeared in the UK in November. The Beatles' *White Album* showed up around the same time, as did The Rolling Stones' *Beggars' Banquet*.

Perhaps the most comparable LP issue of that time was Beck's *Truth*. This had hit the US stores in August but had to wait until early October to find a British release.

Along with *Wheels Of Fire* and *In-A-Gadda-Da-Vida*, it was arguably the prototype heavy metal album that many later claimed for Led Zeppelin.

All this worthy endeavour on 12-inch vinyl is put into another perspective when we glimpse the type of material hitting the top of the British singles charts at the time: Esther & Abi Ofarim with 'Cinderella Rockafella'; Cliff Richard with 'Congratulations'; The Equals with 'Baby Come Back'; Des O'Connor with 'I Pretend', 'Young Girl' from Gary Puckett & The Union Gap; Louis Armstrong with 'What A Wonderful World', and 'Those Were The Days' by Mary Hopkin, leavened by more memorable moments such as Manfred Mann's 'The Mighty Quinn'; The Beatles with 'Lady Madonna' and, later in the year, 'Hey Jude'; Arthur Brown with 'Fire!'; and 'Jumpin' Jack Flash' from The Rolling Stones.

With the album recorded, mixed and edited, Grant booked the band into a series of clubs and university venues, still calling them The Yardbirds. With a US deal already in the making, he had phoned some British record companies about a possible UK deal even before the music was recorded. None was interested in a revamped Yardbirds. It was a similar story on the gig circuit, where he simply couldn't get agencies to come and see the band.

The first London booking Grant managed to land for the new line-up was at London's famous Marquee club in Wardour Street, on Friday October 18th. That, and the gig at Liverpool University the following night, were the band's last as The Yardbirds. Some weeks earlier, Page had given an interview to *Melody Maker* to announce the formation of "a New Yardbirds" as the article put it. It appeared just a few days before these gigs. He said: "The new chaps are only about 19 and full of enthusiasm. It was getting a bit of a trial in the old group."

The article's author, Chris Welch, then listed the band's new members, mentioning in passing that Page was "not sure whether to call them Yardbirds or not". Page felt the style of the band was "blues basically, but not Fleetwood Mac-style. I hate that phrase progressive blues. It sounds like a hype, but it's more or less what The Yardbirds were playing at the end, but nobody knew about it because they never saw us. We're starting work on an LP and we're going to the States in early November".[37]

Whether Grant and Page intended to continue to use the Yardbirds name is arguable, although there are indications that they meant to. What has emerged in recent years is that it would have been in contravention of a legal arrangement made in 1965, as well as the agreement reached by all four of the line-up that had called it a day in late June. In 1965, Yardbirds Ltd had been established in such a way that every musician who was or would become a group member retained a share in

Overleaf: Birmingham drummer John Bonham was headhunted for Led Zeppelin from folkie Tim Rose's group.

the group's name. In 1968, Relf and McCarty had given formal permission for Dreja and Page to continue using the name, at least until all prior commitments had been met and possibly beyond that. But with Dreja's departure from the set-up, that agreement was no longer appropriate. Grant and Page's extension of the use of the name past the tour of Denmark and Sweden alarmed Dreja, in particular, when he saw gig ads in the music press in late September, and he acted. As he later told Greg Russo: "I have a letter from my solicitor to Peter Grant saying, 'My client is concerned over the use of ['The Yardbirds']. Please desist.' ... I never, ever signed any documents that gave Peter Grant and Jimmy Page rights to the name The Yardbirds, and quite the opposite, in fact."[38]

This exchange occurred in the days immediately preceding the Marquee appearance, leaving Grant and Page with a problem to solve in a hurry, for they wanted not only to effect a change of name but also to catch the music press deadlines that would allow that change to be publicised in the weeklies appearing on the same day as the Marquee show itself, October 18th. Page has occasionally talked subsequently to journalists about this, with perhaps the most accurate summation of his and Grant's thinking coming in a 1970 interview. "We dropped that name," said Page of 'The Yardbirds', "because we felt it was working under false pretences."[39] No matter that it was Dreja who pointed this out to them.

In retrospect, Robert Plant thought it a good thing that the name had to change. As he told Chris Welch in 1970: "They'd always put The New Yardbirds on the posters, and they'd drag along the audience who'd come four years before to hear The Yardbirds, and of course there we were doing stuff like 'Communication Breakdown'."[40] Whatever new name they might choose, Page wanted it to accurately reflect the key qualities he felt the music should have: a paradoxical combination of heaviness and lightness, finesse and bombast. It should also have a touch of wit. As it transpired, the new name had all those things and more.

No name – especially a band name – comes out of a vacuum, and the one quickly agreed upon, Led Zeppelin, is no exception. There is a long tradition of anecdote that ascribes the name to two members of The Who, John Entwistle and Keith Moon. As we've seen, back in 1966 The Who's rhythm team grew tired of the stresses and strains inside their band and seriously contemplated leaving to form a new supergroup with Jeff Beck and Jimmy Page. In 1968-69, supergroups were a new and very fashionable phenomenon in rock, and though this earlier prototype never got off the ground, in conversation one night Entwistle and Moon had joked that such a line-up, had it ever become a reality, would have gone down like a lead balloon ('lead' as in metal, not as in 'lead guitar') – an old English expression for

something that is a complete disaster. Elaborating on the joke, the image became altered to a lead zeppelin – an even more spectacularly amusing image of self-immolation. Page liked not only the idea but also the image conjured – the perfect combination of heavy and light, combustibility and grace. Filed away for future reference, two years later he decided it fitted his needs.

This could well be the real origin of the name, but there are, of course, alternatives. A friend of Page's from the mid 1960s has related that during 1968 Page, like many stars of the day, often sported badges, trinkets, and other accessories on his clothes. One of these was a small replica zeppelin made of – you guessed it – lead. Perhaps contemplating the clever heavy-and-light contradictions contained in Iron Butterfly's name, Page found what he was looking for pinned to his own shirt. Perhaps it was a combination of circumstances – a timely coincidence.

During the week preceding the Wardour Street Marquee gig, the name was quickly agreed upon by Page and Grant – with Grant adapting Lead to Led so as not to confuse the Americans, and also as another little flash of witty wordplay – and released the news to the music press. The band's first appearance billed as Led Zeppelin came at Bristol Boxing Club on Saturday October 26th and then two weeks later on November 9th at The Roundhouse in London.

In a *Melody Maker* interview published in mid October, Page had talked about the band members, his immediate plans, and his wonderment at the potential of his current position. "I'm hoping the Marquee will be a good scene. Robert can get up and sing against anybody. He gets up and sings against Terry Reid! Those two are like brothers together. I thought I'd never get a band together. I've always shied of leadership in the past because of all that ego thing. I know old Eric [Clapton] wanted to get a thing together with Stevie [Winwood] but neither of them like leading. ... It's refreshing to know that today you can go out and form a group to play the music you like and people will listen. It's what musicians have been waiting for [for] 20 years."[41]

A new company, Superhype Music Inc, was registered in Page and Grant's names on October 22nd and the band name Led Zeppelin officially adopted. Grant flew out to New York at the end of October to conclude the Atlantic Records deal for Led Zeppelin, not The Yardbirds as he'd previously assumed. In the November week that saw Richard Nixon elected to the White House over the disconsolate Democrat Vice President Hubert Humphrey (after a bitterly divisive campaign and a wholesale lurch to the right among US voters), Grant was locked in record-company negotiations. As with Nixon and Humphrey, there would be winners and losers.

Jimmy Page: leader, main songwriter, producer and guitarist of Led Zeppelin.

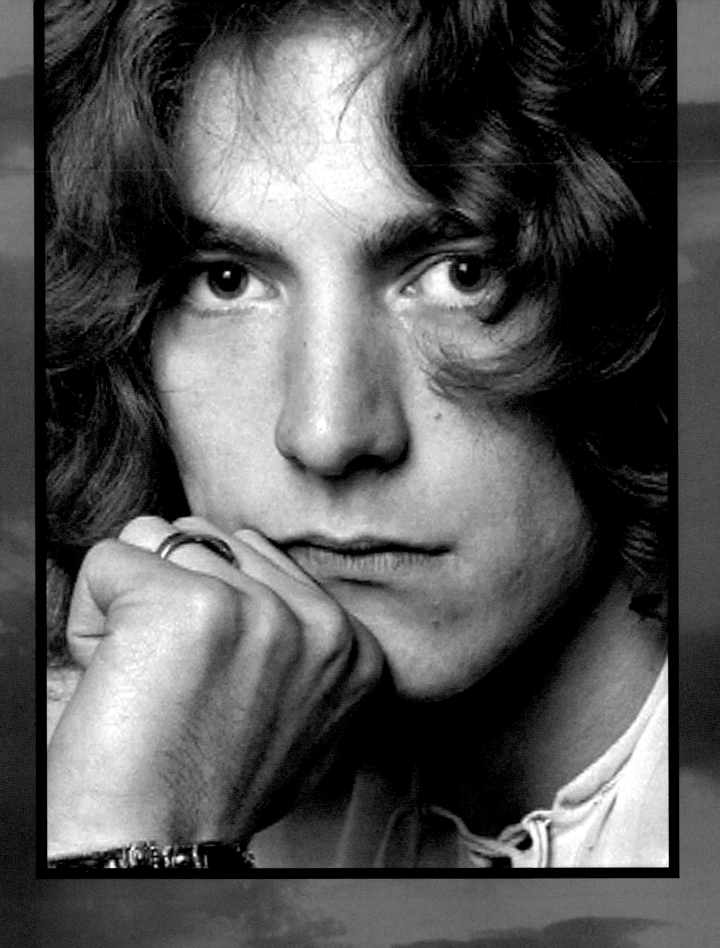

HAPPY CHRISTMAS, MR NIXON

- ◼ LED ZEPPELIN SIGN TO ATLANTIC
- ◼ 1ST AMERICAN TOUR
- ◼ 1ST ALBUM RELEASED

When Peter Grant flew to New York City at the end of October 1968 to conclude a record deal for Led Zeppelin, he took with him tapes of the finished first album. It was an extension of many of the concepts behind The Yardbirds' final LP, *Little Games*, and yet was something quite different. It had to be: Grant could not have got a major deal on the back of an album as obviously scraped together as *Little Games*.

Grant, mindful of his handshake agreement, met first with Ahmet Ertegun and Jerry Wexler at Atlantic Records. Ertegun and Wexler were old hands when it came to sniffing out major talent and two of the few industry big-shots of the day with ears for rock. Ahmet and his brother Neshui had broken Ray Charles internationally in 1954 and, more recently, Atlantic had taken on Cream for North America. In 1968 they were in the process of signing Crosby Stills & Nash for the world as Buffalo Springfield came apart at the seams. Ertegun and Wexler needed only a single listen to Grant's tapes. They knew that Page's new band had that elusive combination of musical quality and sheer raw excitement that would translate to consumer reaction. And they believed that in Grant the band had the management to deliver success.

The Led Zeppelin deal was part of a wider pattern at the time in the way that Atlantic signed UK talent. They had an established process of picking up on North American options for bands already signed to UK companies such as Polydor, Island and others. Dusty Springfield had recently come to them for the US, and during 1968 Ertegun signed Yes, undoubtedly because he saw them as a possible successor to Vanilla Fudge and their elaborate cover arrangements.

The five-year deal was done without a great deal of jockeying. Curiously, the one minor hitch in negotiations was to do with production and mixing. Atlantic had their own internal pecking order that they wanted to protect. Grant later claimed he recalled Atlantic "saying they wanted to remix it, and Jimmy said, 'What are they talking about?' But I said, 'It's just politics.' Tom Dowd [an Atlantic studio regular since the 1950s] was there and Jimmy foxed him with a few technical questions. That was an early battle we won."[1]

Grant obtained a healthy six-figure advance in order to fund the first six months or so of their activities, when the album would be new and the band still establishing an audience. Grant's timing had been perfect: Cream, Atlantic's biggest-selling British act of the day, had completed their Farewell Cream tour of America in the very week he was in New York. Cream played at Madison Square Garden on November 2nd 1968 and completed their commitments in Rhode Island on the 4th. They gave their final farewell concert at the Albert Hall in London on November 26th, just two weeks later. Atlantic, who had been aware of the coming split since the summer, were definitely in the market for a follow-up British heavy-rock act. The other heavyweight ex-Yardbirds guitarist, Jeff Beck, had stayed at Epic and his first LP was doing good business. Atlantic didn't want to miss out on the only other alternative.

The deal Grant won for Led Zeppelin was unusual in its day, although hardly unique. (And they were not the first white British rock act on the Atlantic label; The Shadows got there in 1961.) Atlantic were used to doing deals with production companies, either over a limited licensing period or over much longer periods of time. What was different with the Zeppelin deal was that the production company involved was not a third party, like Mickie Most's RAK, but one set up by Page and Grant to oversee all professional band activities. This meant the two had direct control over the band's output and image. Few bands and their managers at this time would have inspired the trust and commitment of a major label like Atlantic: The Beatles had only that same year managed to re-negotiate their commitments with EMI to incorporate Apple Corps into all future recording agreements, with 'Hey Jude' the first Beatles release on the Apple label. Many other first-rank artists were owned by the production company that licensed their releases to record labels. Those signed direct to record companies had no more room in which to manoeuvre, because the companies themselves made most of the important musical and marketing decisions.

In an echo of the old USA-UK Yardbirds split, Grant had initially retained UK rights separately from the otherwise worldwide Atlantic deal. But none of the British companies Grant approached was prepared to sign them. It was because of such knock-backs that Grant and the band built up their later belief that Led Zeppelin had been rejected by their home country in their early days. While it is true they struggled to be taken seriously by the UK music business, they never experienced problems in drawing a crowd, and the first album, when it came in early 1969, found an eager audience in Britain. Eventually, Grant threw in the UK for Atlantic as part of the deal. Before he left New York, he dropped by Epic Records, with whom he still had business dealings through The Jeff Beck Group, and informed company boss Clive Davis that Led Zeppelin had signed with Atlantic. Another link with The Yardbirds was severed.

Back in Britain, the new band was not exactly rushed off its feet with interest from bookers and agents. Page had time to reply at length to someone who had written a letter to *Melody Maker* asking about technical aspects of his artistry as well as basics about which guitar he used. Page initially dealt with how he produced sustain on his instrument – a topic then much discussed in amateur guitarist circles. Page claimed he did it "with the use of a

Tone Bender [distortion unit]. It is virtually a standard model, but with a few modifications carried out by its inventor, Gary Hurst, which provide more sustain and a harmonic overtone." Page went on to relate that he used a Fender Telecaster with pickups that he has personally rewired. He also discussed his violin bow. "I use an ordinary violin bow on the guitar, given a little more tension on the horsehair than one would employ for violin playing, plus lots more resin. It gives an infinite variety of sounds, ranging from violin to a Boeing 707 taking off."[2]

The seriousness with which Page addressed these questions reflected his earnestness about devising and applying such unusual techniques to his guitar playing. He is not out for cheap effects, but a genuine broadening of the guitar's colouristic and expressive properties. That these were being harnessed for the sake of his band's overall sound and impact is amply displayed on the set of recordings he'd just concluded for Led Zeppelin, though *Melody Maker's* readers were hardly in a position to know that at this juncture. In fact, Page's British fans were not going to get much of an opportunity to see his new band in the near future, for on Grant's return to London the manager lost no time in choosing to prioritise the new band's Stateside career.

The reasons for this were straightforward. Grant had signed them to a record label based in New York. America was by far the largest audience for rock, both live and on record. The US album market had grown at a faster rate than the British one, which was still in transition between relatively simple singles-based careers and the more expensive and arduous variety based on albums.

There was also the problem that every other act faced in Britain: a lack of suitable venues. With the demise of the old package tours – 1968 was the last year these were at all financially or culturally viable – there was a yawning gap between low-grade gigs that paid next to nothing and the theatre circuit that, while hardly lucrative, was at least a paying proposition. Apart from the Albert Hall in London and one or two other larger venues, the infrastructure for larger rock events was still in its infancy in Britain. By the end of 1968 the United States, by contrast, was routinely redeploying baseball fields, grid-iron football stadiums and other larger sites as rock concert venues for an evening. There was also a thriving college circuit that paid well and countless smaller gigs populated by groups still in the netherworld between local popularity and nationwide management or a record deal.

A further factor was Page's popularity in America and his feeling that it was a natural market for the new band. As he said much later: "To tell you the truth, I had a bigger following in the States – The Yardbirds were very popular there. But above and beyond that, I could see the potential there. The audiences were much more aware of what was happening musically, and the USA was so massive that there were naturally more places to play and more opportunities for the band on every level."[3]

Grant did in fact try agents in Britain but got a lukewarm response: The Yardbirds had faded from chart action some 12 months earlier and few seemed interested in trying out a new band led by the group's final guitar hero. The smattering of gigs the new band did actually play in November and December 1968 under their new name created little or no music-business buzz, although audiences were enthusiastic.

A short review in *Melody Maker* by Tony Wilson in late December combined praise and puzzlement. "Led Zeppelin, the re-grouped Yardbirds, … are now very much a heavy music group, with singer Robert Plant leading and ably holding his own against a powerful backing trio. … Amp troubles didn't help them on this particular occasion but there seemed to be a tendency for too much volume, which inevitably defeats musical definition. … Drummer Bonham is forceful, perhaps too much so, and generally there seems to be a need for Led Zeppelin to cut down on volume."[4] Faced with such bemusement, Grant didn't hesitate: he would have the band over to America as soon as possible and get them touring. The album would be released over there early in 1969 and the more people who knew about them by then, the better.

Grant pulled together a short US tour for the band, booked under the new name Led Zeppelin and once again in some instances relying on old Yardbirds connections. They would play support roles for established name bands such as Vanilla Fudge, Country Joe & The Fish, and Iron Butterfly. Reflecting how quickly the rock word was evolving, it was less than 12 months since Vanilla Fudge had debuted as a support act for a US Hendrix tour.

This was Lyndon Johnson's last Christmas as President of the United States and Richard Nixon's first as President-elect. Meanwhile, the Vietnam War raged on, the overwhelming backdrop for the Western world. The music that Led Zeppelin was about to unleash on the world, live and on record, had the slightly crazed violence of the day, mixed with an exuberance that stemmed at least in part from an apprehension that Western culture and values were changing rapidly. Many felt they were changing for the better, despite the riots in Paris and London that summer, the assassinations of Martin Luther King and Robert F Kennedy, and the bloodbath on the streets around the Democratic convention in Chicago that autumn. John Lennon had written 'Revolution' in response, Jagger & Richards 'Street Fighting Man', while Hendrix had recorded 'House Burning Down' after observing the events of spring/summer '68. Led Zeppelin,

Overleaf: The first American tour ran from Christmas 1968 through January and into February 1969, with enough time to dash off this promo shot.

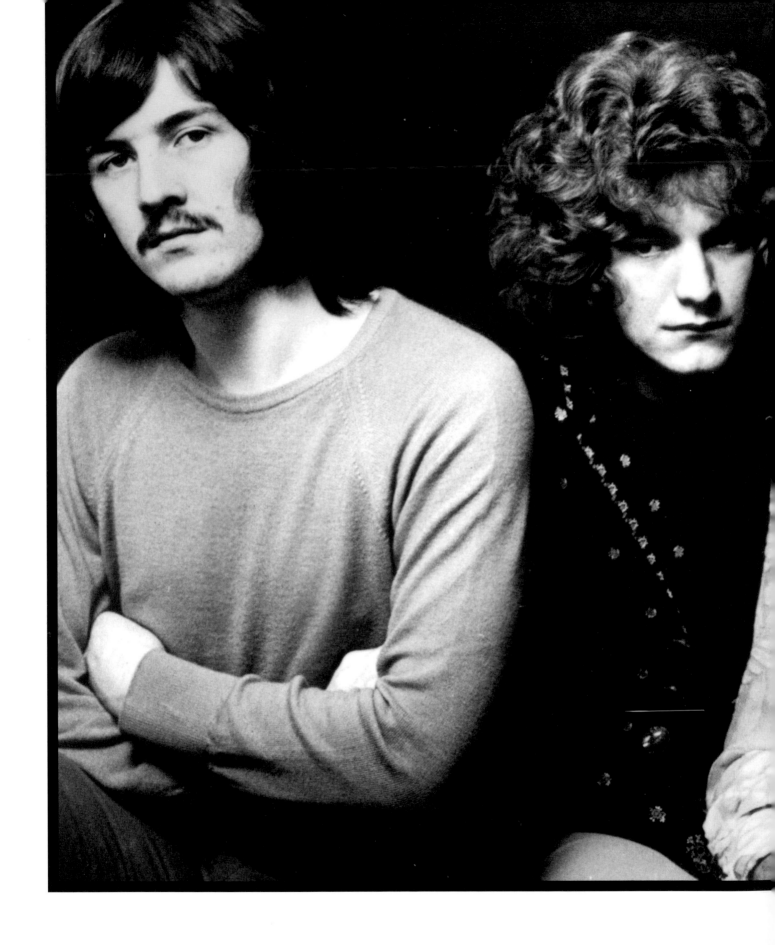

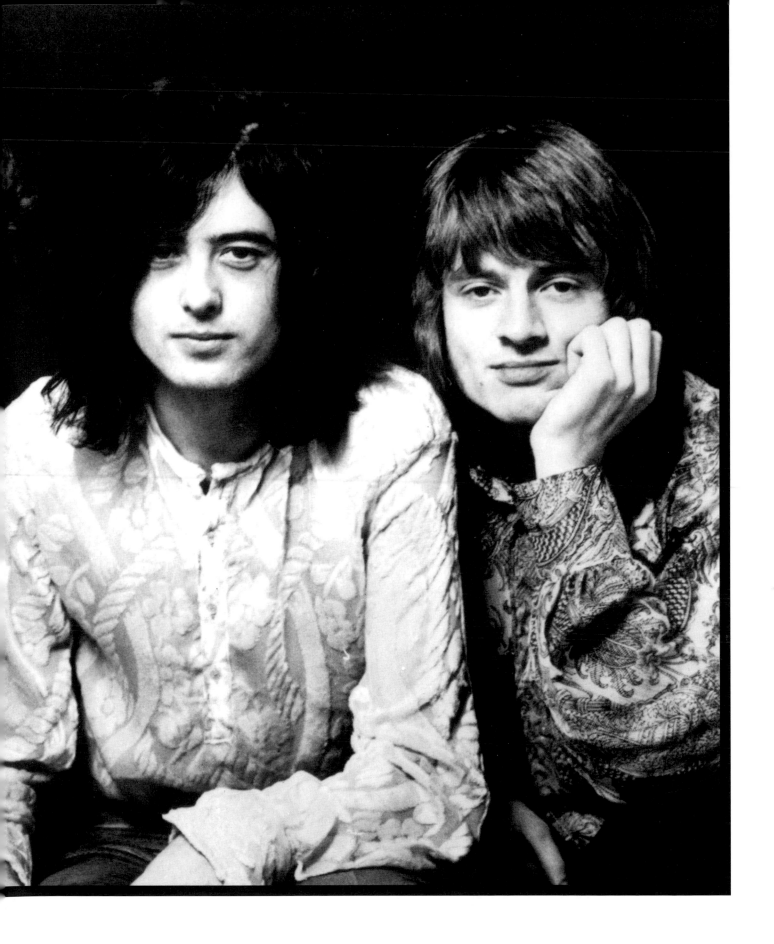

by contrast, would stay with the basics, at least for the time being: love, sex, and the angst of youth. It worked.

Led Zeppelin's first US tour was, like the Scandinavian jaunt before it, a case of fitting into venues and places where The Yardbirds had enjoyed something of a local following. After landing in Los Angeles on December 23rd and spending Christmas Eve and Christmas Day there, they flew to Denver, Colorado, for the opening of the tour, and stayed on the West Coast until mid January, gradually moving southwards.

This gradual southward journey became legendary in Led Zeppelin circles as the time the band came closest to death while on tour, battling through virtually impassable roads amid snowstorms in a rented vehicle, desperate to make the connections for the following night's gig. Life on the road has always been a tough and dangerous business, and most bands and performers have hair-raising stories to relate. There have been enough deaths to deprive the music business of some major talents and to show that the hazards are real enough. The good luck that Zeppelin experienced on this trip, when they were poor, unknown, and bottom of the bill, was precisely the kind of thing every band needs if it is to survive, both physically and as a team. Such experiences, in retrospect, usually knit a group together more tightly. With this new and largely untested band, a musical kinship was quickly deepening into a formidable band spirit that would see it through bigger crises in the future.

Things moved very fast in many ways. As Robert Plant said years later: "When we started the tour on the West Coast, we weren't even listed on the bill. By the time we got across to the East Coast, we were up to second on the bill – it was quite a feeling."[5] From the first show in Denver, where they opened for Vanilla Fudge and Spirit, Zeppelin were provoking a response from their American audiences that made them believe they would be a successful live act. The volume was high, of course – that was mandatory during this period of increasingly ramped-up amplification for the heavy bands, who were finding new sounds and expressive properties in extreme volume. But it was the depth of sound, right the way through the band, that was a particular hallmark – as it was on the yet-to-be-released debut album.

A review in the *Sunday Denver Post* noted: "The concert was kicked off by another British heavy, the Led Zeppelin, making its first US tour. Blues oriented, hyped electric, the full routine in mainstream rock, done powerfully, unifiedly, inventively, and swingingly. Singer Robert Plant a cut above average in style, but no special appeal in sound. Guitarist Jimmy Page of Yardbirds fame exceptionally fine." The reviewer said he found Bonham's drum solo "uninventive, unsubtle, and unclimactic".[6] He didn't like them much, by the sound of it.

From the start, this band not only enjoyed making music together – which is not as common as most fans

might think – they thrived on spontaneity. They were taking their cues from the very elite of contemporary bands – Cream, Grateful Dead, the Hendrix Experience – and from the blues masters of a previous generation – Muddy Waters, Howlin' Wolf, Buddy Guy, Albert King. They would re-fashion a tune from night to night, allowing inspiration to take it where it may. Again, this was something that The Yardbirds had made a proud tradition, from the Eric Clapton days onwards, but with Page in control of the overall shape and sound of this band, and with Plant able to dominate a performance by sheer vocal presence, there was a clearer overall structure and a sure storytelling touch about the band's renditions.

Just as Page had a keen arranging ability with other people's music, his ability to orchestrate the quartet's spontaneous interpretations was a key quality in its onstage success. This was something he shared with Miles Davis, another innovative musician who had more than a touch of genius when it came to creating a definitive shape and sound for a song, in the studio or live.

Zeppelin generally made a good impression on the bands with whom they shared bills. Bonham and Vanilla Fudge's Carmine Appice became good travelling companions and long-term friends. Appice later recalled talking to Bonham about his stunning bass-drum triplets on 'Good Times Bad Times', an innovation that had every heavy rock drummer of the time applauding. He was knocked out when Bonham replied: "I got it from you." Appice couldn't remember ever having played such a thing. Bonham said: "It's on 'Ticket To Ride' on the first Vanilla Fudge album." Appice went back and listened to the Fudge record again. "Yes, I did a triplet between the hand and foot. But he did it all with his foot. That blew me away. We became good friends on that tour."[7] Appice contacted the Ludwig drum company early in 1969 and smoothed the way for Bonham to land an endorsement deal from the manufacturer. It proved a sound business move for both parties.

With 1969 just a few days old, Zeppelin arrived in Los Angeles for the first of four nights at the Whisky A Go Go alongside Alice Cooper. Zeppelin's tour manager, Richard Cole, described the Whisky as "on the cutting edge of the transformation occurring on the Sunset Strip. Old clubs like the Crescendo and Ciro's had closed down, replaced by rock venues that attracted kids as young as pre-teenagers. … The Whisky occupied a building that had once been a branch of the Bank of America. It had been painted green, and the safes and desks had been replaced with a stage, oversized speakers, and glass-enclosed cages bulging with dancing girls who could keep you entranced for hours."[8]

Vying with the caged dancing girls for four nights, Zeppelin made a reasonable impression on the locals. They in turn made an impression on the band, especially the groupies. Los Angeles quickly became a town in which Zeppelin enjoyed hanging out as well as playing. They were in their element musically, socially, and sexually, all but Page discovering for the first time the other side of the L.A. rock'n'roll life. Page had other troubles during the Whiskey dates: he'd come down with flu, and on the first night had a temperature of 104. But he was a trouper, and made it through the engagement. Most of the repertoire was from the still unreleased first album, with a smattering of rock'n'roll numbers when encores were called for, so the crowd at these early American gigs came to the music cold. In an effort to help them overcome unfamiliarity, Grant and his allies at Atlantic in New York got some white-label promo copies of the LP printed up for use by disc jockeys on the burgeoning FM radio album scene. This was a relatively new but vital window onto America's rock-loving public.

A newly-emerging youth movement wanted more from their music than the three-minute thrills of the pop single, whether it was played live or on a record, and there was an inevitable reaction from radio stations to supply that demand. This was not a change of direction by the teenage audience that appreciated The Monkees and similar groups – this was a financially powerful youth sub-culture that wanted to go to concerts and open-air gigs where they could sit around, get stoned, chat, have sex, all accompanied by long raves from their favourite acts. It was never a universal trend – no musical trend ever is – but during 1968-69 it became the latest thing, and a very cool thing to do.

FM radio stations were programming late-evening and overnight shows run by knowledgeable jocks who were happy to play tracks much longer than the average three-minute single. They were also pleased and flattered when artists dropped into the local FM station to promote their albums and upcoming gigs in town. This was the media outlet targeted by Atlantic and Grant, and it was exactly the right place to start a campaign to get the band noticed nationwide. While Zep were not headlining their own shows, many in the crowd would at least have heard of them and in some cases heard them on their radios.

Led Zeppelin went straight from sharing the bill at LA's Whisky A Go Go to a four-night support slot at San Francisco's Fillmore West, a venue The Yardbirds had headlined last time out. Grant made clear to them in advance that this was the key event on the tour. Make a splash here and they could succeed anywhere in the USA. "Peter told us," Plant recalled later, "if we didn't crack San Francisco, we'd have to go back home. That was the place that was considered to be essential, the hotbed of the whole movement. … If we weren't convincing, they would have known right away."[9]

By this time, Page had recovered from his flu bout. "The group was happy to see me better and we really started to play from that point on. The rest of the boys had got more accustomed to the American audiences –

they had never been to America before, and they were able to gauge things a little better … so right there is when it started happening. From then on we could see there was some sort of reaction to us."[10]

Along with Taj Mahal they were a support at the Fillmore to Country Joe & The Fish, a local favourite with a nice line in acerbic political commentary, hippy philosophy, and musical throwbacks to stomp and jug bands of the 1920s and '30s, as well as more contemporary acoustic influences. In the current political climate they were both an insiders' band and an act with a genuine popular standing on the West Coast. The bill was a typical mix-and-match affair of the type Fillmore owner Bill Graham specialised in. Country Joe was a favourite who knew how to speak to this crowd, so no matter who had been on before him, he could quickly establish a mood. Taj Mahal was also by this stage a popular performer in his blues-drenched style, so the audience certainly got their money's worth over those four days.

There is no doubt that the British band did well, making its mark on a town that at that time had about the coolest and most publicised scene in rock. It was fitting that their first album, *Led Zeppelin*, was released in the USA on January 12th, the final day of their Fillmore West run. From now on the crowds on this tour would have a chance to buy the record before hearing them live. Or rush out the next day to confirm their new rock discovery. Zeppelin's accessibility and their no-frills live show steadily won them their own loyal fans as they moved around the country.

After San Francisco and a date in San Diego there was a swing across country, arriving at Boston for another short season, this time at the well-known Tea Party venue where they were the sole act for three nights towards the end of January. Jones felt that the final Boston date defined the course of their career. "As far as I'm concerned, the key Led Zeppelin gig – the one that just put everything into focus – was one that we played on our first American tour at The Boston Tea Party," he told *NME*'s Nick Kent in 1973. "We'd played our usual one-hour set, using all the material from the first album and Page's 'White Summer' guitar piece, and by the end the audience just wouldn't let us off the stage. It was in such a state that we had to start throwing ideas around – just thinking of songs we might all know. … So we'd go back on and play things like 'I Saw Her Standing There' … and the response was quite amazing. There were kids actually bashing their heads against the stage – I've never seen that at a gig before or since – and when we finally left the stage we'd played for four-and-a-half hours. Peter Grant was absolutely ecstatic. He was crying – if you can imagine that – and hugging us all. … I suppose it was then that we realised just what Led Zeppelin was going to become."[11]

Grant had recently established a pattern for US tours with Jeff Beck – who had also made a breakthrough at the

Tea Party – and Zeppelin were primed next to make an all-out push for a breakthrough in New York at Bill Graham's other rock palace, the Fillmore East. They did two days there, closing out January and kicking off February. As Plant recalled, they were second on the bill to Iron Butterfly, with gospel group Porter's Popular Preachers the other act on the first night. An eyewitness reported years later: "The impact of Led Zeppelin that night is forever burned into my temporal lobes – the loudest, sexiest, most exciting thing I have ever seen. Even the people who had seen The Yardbirds the previous year and already heard Zeppelin's first album were unprepared for the full frontal assault of the band live, and the crowd's response was thunderous and immediate.

"They played for 40 minutes before leaving the stage, returning for a loudly-demanded encore and then seemingly leaving for good with many thank-yous and smiles at the audience response. But the crowd wouldn't let them go. As the house lights went up people continued clapping, stomping, and shouting for more, to the point where the light-show screen, now a static shade of bright blue, flashed the phrase 'more??', causing an even louder eruption from the crowd.

"The lights went down and Zeppelin returned to play 'Communication Breakdown', an unprecedented (or at least unusual) second encore for an early-show warm-up act. They finally left the stage, leaving the audience buzzing and still emitting occasional whoops as they filed into the lobby for the break or sat waiting for the now anti-climactic headlining set."[12]

The situation is notorious in rock circles: every up and coming band tries to blow the headliner out of the water, and with two groups that had superficial stylistic similarities and an equal fascination with volume and sheer drive the competition was bound to be intense. Iron Butterfly – ironically also signed to Atlantic – and their management tried to make it as difficult as they could for Zeppelin, while Peter Grant, by making sure the two bands played back-to-back, placed the pressure firmly on the bigger act. The usual ploy is for the headliner to make sure the support has its sound ruined by lack of soundcheck time or by sabotage at the mixing board, but old campaigners like Grant, Cole and Page made sure that this did not occur.

Led Zeppelin made an impression not only on their audience but also on entrepreneur Bill Graham and the Atlantic top brass who attended. Graham had seen them do it on both sides of the country now, while Atlantic were confirmed in their judgement in snapping up the band at such an early stage. The Tea Party, followed by the Fillmore East, and then a big breakthrough in Chicago at the Kinetic Playground, showed the band and its management that Led Zeppelin were going to succeed on both coasts and all areas in between where rock was enjoyed. The only hesitation in this progress came with a

family accident back in Britain that necessitated Bonham's quick return for a few days, obliging the band to pull out of The Scene Club in New York at very short notice. After the Chicago triumph, Zeppelin's tour wound down through the South to end in Miami, Florida, on February 15th. Each gig confirmed that their reputation was building and that they could deliver the goods onstage.

The first Led Zeppelin album was released in America on January 12th 1969 (Britain had to wait until March). The first staccato guitar chords on the opener, 'Good Times Bad Times', punctuated by dynamic drum fills, announce that this is an arrangement meant for an album, not a quickly-made single. There is time to develop ideas, especially that interplay between guitar and drums. The riff that underscores the descending vocal melody is crisp and colourful, a descendent of the riffs that Jeff Beck had so often supplied for Yardbirds recordings.

The stops and breaks that give the song so much of its drama – and which would become an identifying trait of Zeppelin – are not thrown in gratuitously, but serve to set up and delineate each section, be it vocal verse, guitar solo, or drum fill. Only the early fade suggests a band and an arranger not yet sure of their ground and anxious not to let the listener's attention wander at the start of the record: a fully confident working band would have pulled together a natural end rather than a studio fade. This is underlined by Page delivering not one but two short solos, both featuring heavily treated guitar and plenty of frenetic fretboard runs – so much is going on that the listener doesn't get a chance to think about the structure.

Standard for the time, Plant's lead vocal is double-tracked to strengthen his impact. One of the most important parts of 'Good Times' is Page's confidence in his new singer to carry a tune – Plant is left all by himself high up in the song's melody during the verse, with no rhythm guitar 'cushion' to support him, apart from the jabbing riff, seconded by bass and drums.

As a statement of intent, this opening track has forcefulness, impressive depth of sound, and plenty of intense character. It announces a new and different band. It also shows quite clearly where the precedents lay for Led Zeppelin's working methods. One of the most immediate – and least heralded – is the American band Vanilla Fudge. Another more obvious antecedent for placing blues-based material at the heart of a band's personality, and then building on that in new and imaginative ways, is Cream.

Both Vanilla Fudge and Cream were impressive live acts (and both released recordings of their live act) and admirably disciplined in their studio work. Both had

John Paul Jones said a key gig on the first US tour was an ecstatic night in Boston in January 1969. "I suppose it was then that we realised just what Led Zeppelin was going to become."

intense, driving drummers in Ginger Baker and Carmine Appice who emphasised the bottom end of their beat in order to nail down a juggernaut of sound on top. Baker, Appice and Zeppelin's John Bonham also had the technical flexibility and a sufficiently sophisticated concept of time to produce sudden, unexpected and attention-grabbing fills to enliven a song's arrangement: indeed, they could each quite comfortably become an essential part of any song's arrangement. All three supplied a rock-solid basic beat that rarely relied on any complex or advanced ideas about polyrhythms or other notions imported from jazz. Mitch Mitchell and others were doing that kind of thing in music more suited to it, such as that of Mitchell's leader, Jimi Hendrix.

This is pointed up very clearly on the album's following track, Page and Plant's treatment of a folk song made famous by Joan Baez, 'Babe I'm Gonna Leave You'. At the time of its release it was thought an odd choice for a band like Zeppelin, though both Plant and Page have spoken many times since about their affinity for the song as sung by Baez. Maynard Solomon, a musicologist and owner of Vanguard Records, made some interesting points in the liner notes to Baez's famous recording on her 1962 album *Joan Baez In Concert*. He calls it "a white blues, a form which was created early in our century by the meeting of the Southern lyric lament (with its ties to the old ballads) and the Negro blues. The strange quality (and power) of the song is that the narrator inwardly desires exactly the opposite of what he will do, and is torn by the prospect of self-imposed departure".

Solomon also noted that Baez "learned the song at Oberlin College from Janet Smith."[13] The original Vanguard release had no composer credits or publishing details, although the writers of other songs on the album were noted in Solomon's commentary. The original vinyl Zeppelin release credited Page and Plant alone. The Vanguard CD reissue of Baez's *In Concert* lists Anne Bredon alone. So what happened? What seems to have confused everyone is the absence of a composer credit on the original Vanguard release. Solomon's liner notes hardly clarified matters. But eventually the facts came to light in a most unlikely way. Anne Bredon, who had written the song back in the late 1950s, had not ever concerned herself with the problems of owning songs, but her son, who knew Led Zeppelin's music and who chanced upon her authorship, persuaded her to contact a lawyer in the early 1980s. A settlement was duly reached. Recent Zep CDs credit the song to "Anne Bredon / Jimmy Page & Robert Plant".

There is no doubt that Page added a compelling hard-rock arrangement to 'Babe I'm Gonna Leave You' in a way that expanded it beyond its original conception and added new elements, much as Jimi Hendrix had a year before with Dylan's 'All Along The Watchtower'. Whether that justified adding Page and Plant's names to the composer credits is uncertain, although it must also be acknowledged that such practices were hardly unique to Led Zeppelin at the time. This was only one step away from taking a traditional song in the public domain, copywriting whatever minimal arrangement any group may make, and hence claiming all publishing royalties.

At least Page went to the trouble of genuinely reinventing the song. That he created this arrangement was made very clear by Page himself in an interview years later. He was refuting one of the many assertions made by ex-Zeppelin tour manager Richard Cole, whose book about his years with the band had first been published in 1993. "The book," said Page, "claims that Robert picked up my guitar and started playing me the arrangement that eventually appeared on the album. Arghh! Can you believe that? First of all, I had worked out the arrangement long before Robert came to my house, and secondly, Robert didn't even play the flippin' guitar in those days. Thirdly, I didn't ask him if he could imagine playing that song, I told him that I wanted to do it."[14] Point made.

As with the album's first song, the arrangement for 'Babe I'm Gonna Leave You' has stylistic antecedents, none greater than Big Brother & The Holding Company. Their second album, *Cheap Thrills*, was released in summer 1968 and contained a dramatic rendering of George Gershwin's 'Summertime' decked out with Janis Joplin's fever-pitch vocals, interludes of screaming guitars, pounding drums, and contrasting whisper-quiet passages. Big Brother were extending the more studied dramatisations of existing material that Vanilla Fudge had started in 1967 with 'You Keep Me Hanging On'.

Other more tangential influences might include Eric Burdon's manner of elaborating a lyric during his time fronting The New Animals, and Joe Cocker, whose 'A Little Help From My Friends' single was Number 1 in Britain the week Page's new band went into the studios and whose band Robert Plant saw around the time he and Page met for the first time. Page the session man played the fine lead guitar so prominent on Cocker's treatment of Paul McCartney's tune, and the single inaugurated a new fashion for re-dressing earlier rock songs in pomp-rock arrangements – a trend that Hendrix's 'All Along The Watchtower' had deftly avoided the year before.

Page's introduction of two interlocking full-band sections helps develop the song's story. It also doubles the tune's length. Baez managed it in under three minutes; Led Zep do it in over six. Plant's vocal, in particular, suggests close listening to Janis Joplin's approach, if not her style. He is paraphrasing from the first word, stretching the lyrics and altering the line, first in whispers, later in more strident declamation, while the acoustic guitars accompany. The cadential rhythmic pattern of two guitars and timpani at each verse's end nicely anticipate the full-on electric guitar riff tagged on after the second verse, substituting for the acoustic treatment. Following Page's repeat of the acoustic intro and a short overdubbed acoustic solo, Plant is reintroduced front and centre, this time almost hysterically jabbering broken words and phrases in a manner that reduces the performance's unity and continuity of mood.

When the electric-guitar-driven riff re-enters, it seems detached from what Plant is doing. This disjunction is not resolved as the band go through their cycles twice more and Plant mainly ad-libs new lyrics of no great originality or import. The rendition has lost its forward momentum. It is perhaps with performances such as this in mind that Plant later said often that he felt his work on the first album could have been better had there been more time to work his way into the material and the band. 'Babe I'm Gonna Leave You' is a courageous performance – and the arrangement is very imaginative for its day – but it is only partially successful. The concision, consistency and intensity of Baez's original marks it as superior.

Willie Dixon's 'You Shook Me' takes everyone back to the blues, and the resulting ease and good humour is immediately apparent. This track, which gives the impression of a late-night jam in a juke joint, is in fact very tightly arranged, even down to Bonham's strict limitation of his cymbals to a ride splash in each bar and hi-hat beats in unison with his bass-drum pedal. At this ultra-slow shuffle tempo, the space opened up allows the rest of the band to try some spectacular effects, none more so than Page's superb blues guitar solo, starting at 4:01. It also allows Plant room to display some first-rate blues harp playing, chasing his own vocal lines and using slurs and distortion to good effect. In the now famous guitar-vocal duet at the end – a duet that would do as much to establish Plant as a front-rank vocalist in 1969 as anything during 'Dazed And Confused' or elsewhere on the album – Page uses some of his studio wizardry, employing backwards tapes as well as standard playing to create a strange rushing effect around his guitar phrases.

This version of Willie Dixon's modern-day blues classic compares well with the one by Jeff Beck's group on his album *Truth*. Beck's drummer Mick Waller provides a similarly controlled slow shuffle beat in the verses, with tight use of the hi-hat, but cuts loose in order to support Beck's fluid wah-wah blues playing elsewhere. Rod Stewart's vocal is closer to soul than blues, his voice pushed back in the mix, while the piano embellishments from Nicky Hopkins dissipate rather than concentrate the mood. It's a good performance with some stunning Beck guitar, part of the British Blues genre of the time, and its highlights are very enjoyable. But it lacks an overall focus and purpose. Beck's liner-note description is revealing: "Probably the rudest sounds ever recorded, intended for listening whilst angry or stoned. Last note of song is my guitar being sick."[15]

The production values and discipline of Beck's recording are nowhere near those of Page's. The quite proper focus on Plant's voice in the mix is absent on Beck's version. Beck later complained that Page nicked his idea – *Truth* had come out in summer '68 – but the fact is that such material was hardly unique to Beck's band, and Page's treatment is more imaginative. This may be explained – in part or wholly – by Page now being in complete control of all matters in the studio, while Mickie Most was still nominally producing Beck.

There are moments of pomp and splendour on *Truth* that parallel what Led Zeppelin would soon be doing, including the instrumental 'Beck's Bolero', with that 1966 prototype line-up of Beck, Page, John Paul Jones, and Keith Moon. There is some truly sensational guitar playing. There are even a couple of good updates of traditional songs ('Old Man River', 'Greensleeves') that hint at what Page was doing with Led Zep. But there is no overall vision of how the music should be presented.

This is presumably because, as with The Yardbirds, Most simply didn't bother turning up to the album sessions, letting Beck produce in the absence of a producer. Beck was an outstanding guitarist but was not at that time an outstanding producer. Consequently the band's message is inconsistent, Beck and Stewart never really reach a rapport, and the sum is less than the parts. The dubbing of obviously fake applause onto the sprawling and in parts boring 'Blues De Luxe' epitomises the group's approach and applies to the performance as much as the applause: is this a piss-take or do they really mean it?

Such questions certainly don't cross the listener's mind when absorbing the first Led Zeppelin album. Page's production is meticulous and highly imaginative. He has thought through the sounds he wants on each number before the recording starts and concentrates on realising that idea. Thus Bonham, naturally a bottom-heavy drummer with a stupendous beat, is given a depth of sound on the record that simply had not been heard before. The way Page captured Bonham's sound all over his kit was a revelation at the time.

Years later, Page detailed how he arrived at that conception of recording the drums. "One of my suspicions regarding the sound was validated right from the earliest recordings of the band," he told Joe Bosso. "I had been on sessions with other drummers who, while they played pretty well, sounded like they were just hitting a cardboard box. The whole reason for that was they were sitting in the little drum booth, which just sucked the sound out of the drums. So right from the first album I insisted that the drums were gonna breathe, and that we were gonna get a proper tone on them.

"Of course you couldn't get a better drummer than John Bonham, given that set of circumstances. He knew how to tune his drums. See, I always felt that the drums were the backbone of the group. ... You have to base everything around that – the bass and the drums."[16]

Page also gives a true and accurate feel to the other instruments recorded, allowing a full spectrum of tone and timbre to emerge on the bass and various guitars. He had few peers in the studio, even as early as autumn 1968. Jimi Hendrix had an equal breadth of vision for the sounds he wanted translated into an overall studio performance, as evidenced on *Electric Ladyland*, but he didn't have the hands-on expertise of Page, relying on others in the manner of Lennon & McCartney to realise the sounds he heard in his inner ear.

Page was canny enough to know that a hard-driven small amplifier, along with other aids such as wah-wah and boost pedals, could give his guitars all the knock-flat power and tonal edge he would need in a studio. He didn't need wall-to-wall Marshall stacks because he knew how to use microphones. "The first album was done totally with a Supro [amp]. It's got a twelve-inch speaker. ... I spoke about it in interviews and then people bought them up and I could never find one again!"[17]

A simple but effective production technique segues the end of 'You Shook Me' with the walking bassline of 'Dazed And Confused'. It's a brilliant juxtaposition that pulls the listener into the brooding mystery of the descending chord sequence of 'Dazed'. Whatever the real paternity of this particular song – and The Yardbirds played an arrangement of it on the last '68 tour that shares much of its arrangement with this one – it had been reinvented by the time of this recording. Page's extended arrangement effectively evokes a hellish, tortured atmosphere illustrating the anguish that Plant sings about. This mood – and the subject that provokes it – is more suited to Plant's early vocal style than 'Babe I'm Gonna Leave You'.

What Plant does with 'Dazed And Confused' points out specific differences between The Yardbirds and Led Zeppelin. The BBC recording of the song that The Yardbirds made in March '68 finds Keith Relf singing very well and adopting a Donovan-type style that recalls his 'Season Of The Witch' and 'There Is A Mountain'. Relf sings at the top and tail of the song but otherwise stays out of Page's way, leaving the guitarist to take what amounts to an extended solo. This may have been gratifying onstage, allowing Page to develop his bowing technique in front of an audience, but the guitarist was ultimately looking for nothing so conventional. He wanted a more varied and unusual approach to instrumental features. And he got it with Plant's attitude.

Plant becomes an active participant with Page throughout the Zeppelin arrangement. His screams, grunts and cries allow Page to re-think his own involvement and develop a more 'orchestral' approach to the overall arrangement, progressing from one stage to the next in a skilful mixture of instruments and vocals that avoids the stereotypical vocal-solo-vocal routine. This interaction would prove decisive in allowing Page's new band to evolve in a new and distinctive way. Much later, in an interview, Plant would wince at his earliest Zep work. "I think in retrospect I was slightly hysterical. I took it way too far with that open-throated falsetto. I wish I could get an eraser and go round everybody's copy of Led Zep 1 and take out all that 'Mmm, mmm, baby, baby' stuff. ... I was caught up with the power and the excitement of it, but that doesn't stop me thinking now it would have been better just to shut the fuck up a bit more. I was floundering in the middle of a very open, free-form, extended rock'n'roll thing."[18]

Nonetheless, at the time Plant was willing to give it a shot. At this stage of his career he was adept at conjuring a post-adolescent (and pre-coital) angst, but not so versatile as to be able to convey more complex emotional settings. With 'Dazed' this is simply not a problem. The hell-fire agonies of the love-smitten narrator who has bitten off more than he can chew with the woman at the centre of the song – "soul of a woman was created below" – sit perfectly for Plant's wailing, pain-filled style. One oddity of his singing on the first-album recording is that he never phrases the verse within the normal bar structure. He always lags behind, deliberately on the wrong side of the beat. This creates an off-balance effect that emphasises the disorientation that is the song's central message. The ground is shifting in front of the listener before the song has got entirely into it stride.

'Dazed' epitomises many of the central aspects of Zeppelin's early style. Its sheer weight of sound was virtually unprecedented at the time, from the brutal bottom end of Bonham's drums and Jones's bass to the elaborate, slashing, imaginative guitar. Many groups were heading towards this type of breadth and depth in the recording studio in 1968-69, but it's arguable that Zeppelin got there first. It isn't sheer volume, or distortion, or edge: Hendrix had all three in abundance on *Electric Ladyland*, as did Cream on *Wheels Of Fire*. It is the size of the sound, its depth.

In the middle of 'Dazed' there is a sudden introduction (3:29) of a cut-time instrumental passage. It never fails to provoke an adrenalin rush in the listener, no matter how many times one has heard it before. Before the idea of headbanging had even been developed, this passage builds to classic headbangers' music: heads down, air guitar, ecstasy all round. Then there is Page's own mix of bow and unorthodox picking in his solos.

Page can feel justifiably proud of his production job on the entire album, but especially on this track, with his deft manipulation of echo, reverb, and varying guitar mixes and textures, all to serve the interests of the piece.

Hints of great things to come as Led Zeppelin pose together upon the release of their first album, early in 1969.

The versatility alone is astonishing, dealing with different tempos, instrumental combinations and vocal approaches, but sustaining a consistent overall sound canvas. His ear for sound colour is remarkable, not only in the range of patinas he manages on his guitars, but also the brightness and presence he delivers for each musician's efforts. Engineer Glyn Johns deserves credit too for extracting from the board all the required tones and timbres.

'Dazed And Confused' closed side one of the vinyl LP. On today's CD versions it segues into the following track, 'Your Time Is Gonna Come', as it had from 'You Shook Me'. Considering Page's close involvement in all things Zeppelin up to the present day, one can only assume that this unbroken movement of songs is intended. Certainly the César Franck-chorale-like organ intro to 'Your Time' (played by Jones) is in the same key in which 'Dazed' concludes, so it may well have been the original intention, thwarted by the time limitations of vinyl at the time.

When Jones makes the transition into the riff of 'Your Time Is Gonna Come', the tune's roots are laid bare. The verse's structure is very close to 'Hey Joe', as performed by Jimi Hendrix, down to the detail of the cadential guitar tag. Plant's vocal follows a different route to 'Hey Joe', although the lyrics have a similar message about women paid back for alleged wrongdoings to long-suffering lovers. The song, another Page composition, is undistinguished, with a hackneyed chorus that even Page's arranging skills can't mask. He uses pedal-steel guitar for the first time in a studio, but by his own later admission it is out of tune. The song does however give Plant the opportunity to deliver an entire song without having to resort to screeching, and he does well.

'Black Mountain Side', once more introduced through a segue, is a Page acoustic-guitar instrumental that again has roots in Yardbirds days. It is in turn lifted from another performer, this time Bert Jansch, who recorded the piece in 1966 with the addition of a simple folk melody. It was not Jansch's creation: he freely admitted that he had first heard it from singer Anne Briggs.

"Anne Briggs was what was called a revivalist singer, absolutely stunning," Jansch told Colin Harper in 1994. "They were so old, these songs, and they were coming alive through her singing. … I remember learning 'Blackwater Side' from Anne, basically by playing on the guitar exactly what she'd sung and then fitting various riffs to it. I actually used that 'Blackwater Side' kind of backing for quite a few folk tunes."[19] Page said that "Annie Briggs was the first one that I heard do that riff. I was playing it as well, and then there was Bert Jansch's version. He's the one who crystallised all the acoustic playing as far as I'm concerned."[20]

Briggs had quit the folk scene by the early 1970s. Interviewed in 2003, she said she didn't even know who Page was and had only once heard Zeppelin's recording of 'Black Mountain Side', as Page had titled it. She realised immediately where they'd got it. She had originally learned the song, she said, "from Bert Lloyd, who was a splendid collector of folk songs, now dead. The song I learnt from him was unaccompanied. The riff I learnt from a friend called Stan Ellison. It was Stan who designed the musical accompaniment, the one I recorded, which was nothing like Bert Jansch's version." Briggs went on to say that she thought if Led Zeppelin had made a massive amount of money, they should give some to Bert Lloyd's widow, plus perhaps Stan Ellison, and not her. She did not see her role as an originator. Besides, the folk tradition was built upon the principle of patchwork borrowing. "When people sang for pleasure and nobody got any money," she observed, "then it was great, no problem. The problems come into it when money starts flying around."[21]

Page said later: "Bluesmen borrowed from each other constantly, and it's the same with jazz; it's even happened to us. As a musician, I'm only the product of my influences. The fact that I listened to so many various styles of music has a lot to do with the way I play. Which I think set me apart from so many other guitarists of that time: that fact that I was listening to folk, classical, and Indian music in addition to the blues and rock."[22]

As with the Davy Graham's solo outing that Page transformed into 'White Summer' for The Yardbirds, he has changed and augmented much for 'Black Mountain Side', introducing Eastern elements, most obviously through the use of a tabla percussionist, Viram Jasani. Page darkens the harmonies, emphasising the latent minor tonality as Jansch played it and giving the piece the form of the opening two sections of an Indian raga.

Using a 12-string rhythm guitar as the base, he adds some frenetic, sitar-like improvisation in a short but intense middle section. The whole performance is only a little over two minutes – shorter than Jansch's effort by some considerable distance – and, once again, as with the Graham adaptation, Page's take is more coherent and to the point. It is also blessed once more with high production values. The quality of sound on the guitars is a thing of beauty, and an ear to Jansch's original will provide instant appreciation of this often-overlooked part of listening pleasure.

Another segue introduces 'Communication Breakdown', a fast rocker based on the eternal triangle of E-D-A-D chords and with roots in Eddie Cochran's 'Nervous Breakdown'. There is a nice pattern of rhythmic breaks to help structure the verse and give something for Plant to shape his vocals around, although there is little more than a simple pop-song structure to prop up the whole thing. The arrangement builds well, organ and extra guitars lifting the out chorus, and the band maintain an impressive degree of excitement. It is a fine piece of pop confection in the Vanilla Fudge mould.

The final pure blues performance on this debut

album, Willie Dixon's 'I Can't Quit You', comes hard on the heels of 'Breakdown'. Its form and arrangement closely follow the Otis Rush version recorded for Vanguard and released in 1966 on Volume 2 of *Chicago/The Blues/Today!*. The obvious difference comes with the presence of an alto saxophonist on Rush's version – approximated by a Page overdub on the Led Zeppelin recording. Page said later that it was "a pleasure"[23] to borrow from Otis Rush for this song, indicating that on this first album he and Plant were in part paying tribute to their common inspirations.

'I Can't Quit You' follows the procedure of 'You Shook Me', keeping the lid on during the verses and using violent punctuations on the turnarounds. Page's belief in Plant's ability for blues singing is patent, given the amount of space he leaves for the vocalist to float around, and Plant takes full advantage. This slow triple-time blues suits Page's own blues phrasing, and after the neat tip of the hat to Jimi Hendrix's triple-time solo on his 1966 blues classic, 'Red House', Page moves into a flowing and relaxed outing that for the most part is well considered and full of passion.

Page does however make a fist of the last chorus, where he gets on the wrong side of the beat during a series of fast runs and comes out of the blues sequence early, momentarily confusing both Jones and Bonham before the band is back together again. It is a tribute to their honesty that Zeppelin left it in because the feel was so good, rather than patching and editing. Time would not have been too tight to do that, had Page wanted to. 'Quit You' ends up as one of the most successful pieces on the first album, with no flat spots and a perfectly symmetrical form, all within the classic blues tradition.

The record's last piece, 'How Many More Times', is famous now for its sledgehammer walking riff borrowed from Albert King's 'The Hunter' and played in tandem by Page and Jones. King's riff was in effect a generic modern blues riff, found amongst other places in the work of Howlin' Wolf, but there are other qualities that make 'How Many More Times' an unusual and provocative performance that in many ways was quite ahead of its time. The rendition quite likely had a long gestation. Elements of it had been present in The Yardbirds' live performances while Page was in the band: in one section of their late-period live version of Howlin' Wolf's 'Smokestack Lightnin', for example, they used the same bolero rhythm of 'Beck's Bolero' now co-opted into 'Times' (3:11).

The constant movement from section to section in 'Times' is a valid and exciting way of telling the song's story and providing plenty of contrast. Another forward-looking step is the unusual way that Page makes his guitar a prominent feature. There are a number of instrumental passages dominated by the guitar but there are no guitar-hero solos. Page instead uses his featured spots for some

serious sound-painting. At one point (starting at 3:39) he uses the guitar-bowing technique he had first developed while in The Yardbirds, creating an eerie and wholly musical sound full of imagination and yearning.

It is exciting to hear Page doing such things. Of his contemporaries, only Beck and Hendrix were capable of looking beyond blues-based scramblings up and down the fretboard. Here, he shows the breadth of his musical imagination by considering the entire sound of the music and how his guitar could help shape it effectively, rather than simply pouring hundreds of rapid-fire notes over its surface. This in itself gives Page the space to structure the song unusually, pacing it through tempo changes and different dynamic levels and thus helping to retain its impact at each stage. Page creates part of this variety and contrast through discerning use of effects (wah-wah and Tone Bender distortion), amplifiers, speakers, and even the mixing board in the studio.

It wasn't just heavy-rock fans who were listening closely to this heavyweight track. Roxy Music's title track on *For Your Pleasure*, recorded in 1972, features at its conclusion a long and close imitation of the two-chord ostinato punctuated by Bonham's tom-tom drum fills of 'How Many More Times'. Roxy smothered it in Bryan Ferry and Eno's electronic approximations of Page's guitar landscapes, but the resemblance is uncanny.

There were other songs completed during the first-album sessions. Page's discerning ear for selecting the best and most typical performances for the album was confirmed with the arrival of 'Baby Come On Home' on 1993's ten-CD *Complete Studio Recordings* set (as well as the more affordable two-CD 'Boxed Set 2'). It was cut on October 10th 1968, late in the sessions, and is a hybrid homage to Atlantic and Stax soul and the Northern Soul ballad-style that had been in vogue in Britain for much of the 1960s. It is a competent and tasteful homage, with Page doing a Steve Cropper impersonation and Jones contributing Hammond organ licks straight from Muscle Shoals. But it heads in a completely different direction to the rest of the album and its inclusion would have been a mistake. There are echoes of this direction on 'Your Time Is Gonna Come', the album's weakest track, but not enough to dilute the essential thrust of the band's style. A track with an even stronger gospel-soul flavour would have drastically altered the balance.

On the band's return to Britain in mid February following the American tour they learned that the album, after a month on release in the USA, had crept into the charts, making it to Number 90. This was impressive for a band that had arrived in the country as unknowns and who were not even billed on their first handful of concerts, even if it was eclipsed by the Jeff Beck Group's Number 15 the previous autumn. Led Zeppelin's first US tour could be counted as a popular success, and the band were eager to follow up with similar progress back home.

TEA PARTIES IN BOSTON, FESTIVALS IN BATH

- **2ND EUROPEAN TOUR**
- **2ND AMERICAN TOUR**
- **SESSIONS FOR 2ND ALBUM**
- **1ST SINGLE RELEASED**
- **1ST UK TOUR**

Following their first US tour in January and February 1969, Led Zeppelin returned to a rapidly changing British music scene. While they were away, Traffic had announced they were breaking up: Stevie Winwood was to join up with Eric Clapton, Ginger Baker and Ric Grech to form the shortlived but phenomenally successful Blind Faith. The Beatles were struggling to survive the traumatic experience that winter of recording and filming *Get Back* (later retitled *Let It Be*), while Jimi Hendrix was back in London for a filmed and recorded Albert Hall concert in late February that would mark the last UK performance of the original Experience.

Commentators have often suggested that Led Zeppelin couldn't get arrested in Britain at this point in their career, so weak was the demand for them live and in the media. Years later and with the benefit of hindsight, Jimmy Page saw it quite differently. The idea that success in Britain lagged behind the US was, according to Page in 1998, "a myth, it's just not true. When we started playing in England it might have been a little difficult in the beginning because the first album wasn't released [there] yet and people hadn't heard the band. And it's hard to start out that way, even if you're really, really good and knocking people dead in their tracks. But I had a big reputation in The Yardbirds and people were really keen to see what I was doing. And as soon as they saw us, word of mouth started spreading, and we became popular pretty quickly".[1]

The evidence supports Page's view. They were playing regular gigs around London and further afield – Plymouth, Cardiff, Leicester – and from all reports these gigs attracted many local fans, often provoking queues beforehand. It was more that the type of venue so plentiful for profitable live work in the US just didn't exist in Britain outside a handful of major city centres. For an ambitious man like Page, this grated. He wanted to get back to America as soon as possible to further the band's career there and capitalise on that country's vast potential.

Still, the band did land a 'live' spot on BBC Radio on March 3rd, recording three songs for a *Top Gear* broadcast on Radio 1 later that same month. March was when the first LP was released in Britain – on the 28th – so it was apt timing. A month later, Page talked to *Record Mirror* about those performances. "Working in America pulled the group together a lot. ... After we'd recorded [the first LP] we had a 50-minute stage act together. But at the end of our US tour, that had stretched to two-and-a-half hours – and it happened naturally. At places like the Fillmore, where you play encore after encore, you just have to stretch the numbers out. ... The trouble is, of course, that now we're back in Britain the numbers are too long, and that's our main problem at the moment. Radio, especially, is used to short numbers – on *Top Gear*, for example, we had to tailor all our songs to fit them in."[2]

The three performances from that *Top Gear* are the first live Led Zeppelin efforts since given official release (on *BBC Sessions*, 1997). Two are at the blues end of Led Zep's repertoire, ensuring that the majority of BBC listeners did not lose track of what was going on. Both 'You Shook Me' and 'I Can't Quit You Baby' are indeed shorter than their LP counterparts but are given a minor shift in focus thanks to the harder-edged BBC production of the day. Jones's Hammond organ playing is higher in the mix while Page's lead guitar work, given more space by the absence of any rhythm guitar track, is both more subtle and more incisive than on the record.

Page's solo spot on 'You Shook Me' recycles much of his album solo but has no echo or other devices. Instead he relies on the remarkable edge of his tone plus authentic blues phraseology in an effective solo. Bonham's drum patterns follow the original except that he allows himself to be busier and more inventive in his fills; this is, after all, nearly six months and a lot of playing away from the original. Plant is perhaps the most changed. Singing with much less anxiety and much more confidence, he is no longer so unvaryingly at the top of his considerable range, giving himself the options of light and shade to develop his storytelling powers.

This development is also one of the most notable features of 'I Can't Quit You'. Plant becomes a little over-excited in the second verse, almost losing his voice for a moment, but he quickly pulls himself back and delivers a more measured – and effective – message from that point. Page's accompaniment is something of a revelation, for he plays with virtuoso blues skills but doesn't attempt to smother Plant. Instead he opts for the type of classic blues guitar-vocal accompaniment that has been at the heart of amplified blues since T-Bone Walker plugged in his guitar. In the quieter passage after Page's solo, Zep show just how much a listening band they are. They respond to each other's nuances like very few other outfits in rock could manage at the time. These are four musicians who have learned to breathe together musically, especially in a blues structure that allows them plenty of latitude.

All of this was also deployed on the version of 'Dazed And Confused' served up for Radio 1. The studio technology that had helped to make such an impact on the album was of course unavailable in the setting of a 'live' BBC recording, but Page shows that he is capable of whipping up an equal soundscape with his regular onstage gear. The band is not as tight as on other occasions, with Jones and Bonham slipping from the rhythmic precision that is their normal hallmark in an attempt to add more swagger and style. Plant sounds assured, changing his vocal timbre, exploiting its various emotional messages, blending more exactly with Page's guitar and also providing Page with the scope to play when needed, such as in the violin-bow passage. The band cook like crazy in the up-tempo passage, showing its credentials and casting off any sloppiness they may have had at the outset. They wrap things up with poise and impact.

During March and April, manager Peter Grant gave the band as much work around Britain as he could profitably find in order to back up the album's release. As in America, these club and theatre appearances were very well attended as word on the band spread. Tour manager Richard Cole, whose antipathy to small-time rock'n'roll ventures is made very clear in his book about the years he spent with Led Zeppelin, remembered a string of poorly-paying venues that nonetheless had vibrant atmospheres.

"They were cramped little clubs," wrote Cole, "often bursting with audiences of no more than 300 or 400. Some had no dressing rooms. The fees were small, too – £60 [about $145 then] against 60 percent of the gross was typical, although they sometimes went as high as £140 per night [$330]. Amazingly, word of mouth helped sell out nearly every performance. But even with packed houses, no one would make much money."[3]

A brief Scandinavian jaunt preceded a full-fledged UK tour, showing little material progress from the one there six months earlier, except that the band could now carry off the Stockholm Konserthuset (once again in the company of Country Joe & The Fish) rather than just stick to the smaller clubs in the suburbs. They packed into three days of intense appearances the sort of coverage that had taken them almost half of the previous September. They also landed an extended appearance on a Danish television show. A large slice of their performance on March 14th would be issued as a bonus on the 2003 *DVD* collection. It has remarkably good sound for the television technology of the day (but the poor sound generated on other shows this year would quickly convince Page and Grant that TV was generally not for them). The band delivered four songs from the first album with absolute conviction allied to professionalism.

It is clear from the footage that, even after just three months on the road, this band has gelled into a superb live unit. The interdependence between all four players and their ability to listen closely is the key to their impact. Each of the four tunes has moments where someone – usually Page – does something different, departing from the written text, and heads off into the musical unknown. Without fail, the rest of the quartet are with him in a flash. Even in a well-routined piece like 'Communication Breakdown', during the instrumental break Page, playing Fender Telecaster for the entire set, goes this time for a more funky, Hendrix-like rhythm when he pulls the band back from its half-time metre, with Bonham and Jones responding with relish to the idea of a snatch of near-funk. At the end of this opening number the studio audience, all seated on the floor, are completely silent for about five seconds: they are stunned by what they've just heard. Then the applause begins. This was typical of the reactions the band were now generating every night.

Led Zeppelin were already into their own unique image by this time. Page adopts one of his shimmering full-length robes, Plant is buttoned up in a stylish dark velvet jacket, Jones wears a dark turtleneck, Bonham a red singlet. Plant is also showing flexibility and growth in his approach to the band's repertoire. On 'Dazed And Confused' he brings considerable light and shade to his opening verse, and alters the melodic path to introduce variation and different meanings. He seems quite certain of his place onstage. He spends his time when not singing either simply grooving to what the others are doing or following the twists and turns of Page's guitar playing. This is not a lead singer with an onstage attitude or ego problem: he quite simply enjoys what the entire band is generating and gets off on it in a wholly unselfconscious way. This is a finely honed team with a rare natural internal balance, working hard together and for each other, each member playing a role with which he is comfortable and ready to react to whatever the others give out at any moment.

There is little overt showmanship. Plant occasionally talks to the audience and attempts to win them over through charm or humour, and once or twice he puts on a display. There is plenty of sex and attitude being strutted, but it comes out from the nature of the music, so it feels congruous rather than a showbiz afterthought.

One of the most gratifying elements of this TV performance is the fluidity of Page's playing. He has often said over the years that he much preferred live situations to studio when it came to his own guitar work, and this whole set bears that out. He plays each fill, each riff, each featured section with great elegance and ease. His note choice, the cleanness of execution, the rhythmic security are all a revelation for anyone who had no chance to see the band live and only ever heard them on records.

Page for the most part sticks to well-known blues lines and intricate but quite static fretwork, often moving his fret position to generate pattern-variation rather than extending phrases into different areas. But the ease with which he connects it all up puts him in the premier league of rock guitarists of the day. All the potential that was glimpsed fleetingly in Yardbirds days has coalesced into a well-formed and completely expressive technique. Furthermore, that technique is beautifully complemented by bassist Jones and drummer Bonham, their playing perfectly in sync, no matter what the feel.

The tour concentrated local media minds more than the previous visit. Led Zeppelin were catching the attention of the pundits, who were comparing them to Hendrix and Cream as the latest British rock mega-export. Inevitably, this meant that judgements would be made. Stockholm's *Dagens Nyheter* made some worthwhile points. "Led Zeppelin first impressed me," wrote the reviewer, "because they played so hard and loud. Not in that typical thin English way. They had an almost

American heaviness and depth to their music. But the group is just a few months old and haven't found their place yet. The guitarist Jimmy Page is good, a skilful and imaginative soloist. His bassist was good too and the drummer was promising. The singer I didn't like. He mostly screamed and the lyrics he was screaming were banal."[4]

The *Expressen* man was unimpressed, concluding that "they played the same kind of blues most English bands play today. Not much more original and definitely not the new Cream".[5] And the *Svenska Dagbladet* perceptively noticed some key distinguishing traits. "The band plays a very hard and intensive blues. Their music has room for much experimenting and is, to a great extent, built on an exciting dialogue between former Yardbirds guitarist Jimmy Page and singer Robert Plant. This man has a strange voice. He sings more tones than words and lets the tones and intensity stand in for a song's content."[6] It was generally agreed that Zeppelin were a great deal more appealing than the group they were supporting, Country Joe & The Fish.

Back in Britain, on March 25th 1969 Led Zeppelin filmed an appearance in *Supershow*, a multi-artist showcase that, unusually for its time, was shot on colour film rather than video, intended for cinema release. (Unfortunately, distributors were never found.) The other artists featured in this amazing cornucopia of talent were Stephen Stills, Buddy Guy and Roland Kirk. A version of 'Dazed And Confused' from this show was included on the same 2003 *DVD* set.

Compared to the Danish TV performance, this suffers from poorly balanced and distorted sound. The rendition is further fractured by then-trendy zoom camera techniques and even a barrage of dry-ice fog that makes it hard for the band to communicate with each other as they play. Plant's vocal on this occasion begins in a notably subdued mood, allowing him to build the tension slowly and deliberately rather than start at full stretch. He had quickly learned how to take music that was created in a recording studio and adapt it for optimum live performance. Among the visual and audio disappointments of the filming there are compensations, including the revelation that Page's Telecaster had been hand-painted in greens, reds and oranges (in black & white these colour swirls had been almost unnoticeable). The band is unified and its power undeniable, but the conditions are less than ideal.

If manager Peter Grant had got his way, Zeppelin would also have appeared on a BBC TV show just three days later. He invited the production team from *Colour Me Pop* to come down to the Marquee Club and shoot the band's set on the evening of the 28th; Grant saw it as an ideal opportunity to show the band in its natural habitat,

Seen through the eye of an American photographer's lens during the second US tour, May 1969.

onstage and wailing, and also to show just how popular the band had become in Britain. The queues to get into their shows on this short tour ran into the hundreds. But the TV crew didn't show up. In fact, they not only didn't show but, according to Grant, they didn't even bother to contact the manager later to offer an apology or excuse. It signalled a hasty but complete turnaround in Grant's attitude to accommodating TV companies. Until then he was willing to at least consider TV requests on their merits. Now he would reject any such ventures, especially where the BBC was concerned. If there was to be any filming of Zeppelin, the band would endeavour to own and control the use of all footage.

It was apparent that there was a groundswell of live support in America and Britain, and a surprisingly strong showing for the first LP amid Atlantic's all-out campaign in both countries. But this was not reflected by the reception from the music media in some quarters, especially *Rolling Stone* in the USA. On the national scene, record-trade magazine *Billboard* was broadly sympathetic, but *Rolling Stone*, already the US rock industry's bible of choice and alarmingly ready to pontificate when they felt like it, took what proved to be a long-term dislike to the band's blues-laden, high-decibel approach.

The magazine had by then made its antipathy to hugely popular British blues-rock bands clear, its demolition job on Cream's Eric Clapton in May 1968 helping precipitate that band's demise with its shattering effect on the guitarist's self-belief. They championed US rock acts they thought had 'authentic' written all over their music , and any whiff of hype spelled critical doom – unless your name was Grateful Dead, Jefferson Airplane, The Band, or Bob Dylan, or you lived in San Francisco. This attitude would persist towards many new British acts well into the next decade.

The magazine's reviewer John Mendelsohn dismissed Zeppelin's first album – and the band – as formulaic. "The popular formula in this, the aftermath era of such successful bluesmen as Cream and John Mayall, seems to be: add, to an excellent guitarist who, since leaving The Yardbirds and/or Mayall has become a minor musical deity, a competent rhythm section, and a pretty soul belter who can do a spade imitation. The latest of the British groups so conceived offers little that its twin, The Jeff Beck Group, didn't say as well or better three months ago."[7]

Mendelsohn's carefully chosen words – especially those pairing Robert Plant with Rod Stewart in such gratuitously derogatory terms – were designed to inflict maximum pain and impute the most cynical of motives to the band and its management, as if Led Zeppelin were nothing more than a group of clones programmed to play ersatz heavy blues and pocket the rewards. But as the review makes clear, Zeppelin were hardly alone in suffering such condescending cynicism.

Most of the other press notices at this early stage were

a great deal more balanced. Plant was the only member of the band singled out for specific criticism, although explicit musical criticism was rarely offered. This may have been difficult for Plant to accept and unsettling for his confidence. After all, the frontman of any band needs to be convincing and to be seen to be convincing. Being one of the three new members, he may also have felt a need to prove his worth beyond doubt. There is scant sign of any orchestrated media campaign to undermine the band or its members, but any such carping reinforced the hurt caused by *Rolling Stone*, giving the band a sense that the press of the day was against them, not for them.

This was not really the case. One of the antidotes to *Rolling Stone*'s cynicism was the radical British magazine *Oz*. Importantly, it was a journal with a much broader cultural, political and artistic brief. Its rock reviewer Felix Dennis wrote: "Very occasionally a long-playing record is released that defies immediate classification or description, simply because it's so obviously a turning point in rock music that only time proves capable of shifting it into eventual perspective. ... Of course, as a result of this album we'll lose the group to the States, and almost certainly within months the *Melody Maker* letters page will headline 'Is Page better than God?'"[8]

There was another side to any insecurity that Plant might have felt. Tour manager Richard Cole suggested later that there were question marks over Plant's continuing involvement in the band after the first US tour, according to Cole because of the singer's inexperience onstage in large venues, his full-on vocal style, and his overtly sexual strutting while still something short of a rock demi-god. Even if there were such thoughts about, no action was taken: the quick and unswerving advance of the band's popularity on both sides of the Atlantic soon rendered such questions counterproductive. The band was functioning well on a personal and musical level; they were rapidly becoming a big act in their own right. Why change? There was little real chance that anyone would have acted upon such thoughts unless Plant's presence was conclusively proved to be detrimental to the band. This was not the case and never would be.

The band spent the month between mid March and mid April 1969 playing gigs in the UK. One of these was in a 250-capacity room at the back of a small pub, the kind of venue that proliferated in Britain and that the band would soon be abandoning for America. In the audience at The Toby Jug Inn in Tolworth, Surrey, an outlying suburb of south London, was drummer Jon Newey, later a successful journalist and publisher.

"It's one of my all-time top-ten gigs," he said recently. "We were squeezed into this back room at the pub and they were using a 200-watt WEM PA system. There had been a long queue to get in outside and the room was completely packed, sweaty, hot – the place was absolutely heaving. They got a fantastic reaction. What they were doing – and it was new for the time – was to take the blues as a jumping-off point, making great re-arrangements, paring it down to the simplest component and then building it up with improvisation and jamming. They were playing 'I Can't Quit You Baby' and 'How Many More Times', but they were playing what I'd call Acid Blues.

"They'd taken the model of Vanilla Fudge, the way the Fudge had used pop songs and soul and slowed them down, extracted the maximum dynamism of these quite simple blues songs, and then played amazing things within that quite simple framework. I was standing three feet away from the stage, which was this platform only about 18 inches off the floor, and we all got it just full in the face. Incredible impact."

Eyewitness Newey felt Page and Bonham were making important steps forward for the band. "Page was combining all these elements – blues, raga, folk music – and applying them to the blues form, at maximum volume. It was like a psychedelic blues approach, even though psychedelia had long gone in London: it had everything in there and it typified that approach at its absolute best. The other thing was that Bonham, like many other drummers of the time, had heard what Carmine Appice had done with the drums in Vanilla Fudge. Appice was so heavy, he laid down such a strong beat, it blew us all away. Bonham built on that: he had that same bottom end, and combined with the blues base in the band it was lethal. All that was really key in establishing Zeppelin in Britain with the fans, because the initial rush of publicity had scared a lot of people into thinking they weren't going to be 'underground' enough. Because that was the circuit they were playing in England: the 'underground' venues. Gigs like Tolworth showed the fans otherwise."[9]

Grant was already putting the finishing touches to their second US tour and broaching the subject of the follow-up album with Page. Taking all this in his stride, Page granted a few interviews with journalists he respected. He told *Melody Maker*'s Chris Welch that he was keen to get back to the States. For one thing, he was "looking forward to playing at the Newport Jazz Festival. It's a great honour because there will be people [appearing] like Muddy Waters and Stan Getz." This spurred him to recall a similar mix on The Yardbirds' last US tour, in spring 1968. "What's so good about the States is that they can mix so many different styles. I saw a concert with Cecil Taylor, who is as far out as you can get, on the same bill with Richie Havens and The Yardbirds.

Before the band went to the States, said Jimmy Page, nobody seemed to want to know them back home. Now that was changing. "I still reckon the States is our main market, though."

That's three completely different styles and they were all accepted by the audience at the Fillmore [West]."[10]

Of Led Zeppelin's emerging style, Page had some equally useful points to make when interviewed by Felix Dennis for *Oz*. "Since recording the album we've changed a lot of the material and the length of the numbers seems to have expanded. One thing that used to get me about Cream was the way I thought they relied too heavily on Master Eric for the improvisations. That's not going to happen with us. Everybody's got something to say and, well, that's what we'll be doing."[11]

Page told *Record Mirror* that he was gratified at the turnaround in British reaction to the band, even though there were few ways for fans to hear the band on radio apart from the unique John Peel show. "It's amazing," he said. "We're working every day now – but before we went to the States nobody wanted to know. And it's not just London – it's all over the country. Very pleasing reaction. I still reckon the States is our main market, though."[12]

Led Zeppelin were now quite comfortably filling their engagements book both for Britain and the USA, playing a gig in Wolverhampton in the Midlands on April 17th before flying out to start their second US tour on the following evening, at the New York University Jazz Festival. They were one of the very first rock bands to appear at formerly jazz-only events, because this was a time when jazz promoters were aware of the waning attractions of jazz for the university and college crowd who had kept the jazz circuit outside of nightclubs buoyant for over a decade. They remained of vital economic value for the patronage they brought jazz artists. Putting Zep on the bill would give the promoters an economic boost and give their jazz artists a considerable audience boost as well. For Led Zeppelin, it was simply another opportunity to reach an audience they were convinced would embrace them because of the quality and passion of their music and the sheer honest commitment they gave to playing it. There was never any shuck or pretence about the band, especially onstage. They were not playing at playing music. They gave their all, every time, and it showed. Their audiences always appreciated that fact.

Peter Grant played a shrewd game in the way he accepted promoters' offers for the band's second North American tour, starting in areas of the vast region that he knew had already taken the band to heart. The US West Coast was given the first dozen or so engagements of the tour proper, after the New York Jazz Festival, starting at the Fillmore West in San Francisco on the 24th.

Following that, with the album continuing to fly out of the shops and the band's morale sky-high, the tour swung out to Hawaii for the first time, touched down briefly in the northern Midwest, then moved on to Boston and New York, two other centres of population already confirmed as partial to Led Zeppelin's message. The upsurge in the band's popularity helped settle for good any feelings of insecurity that Plant might have had about his position. He said: "People really started taking an interest in the other members of the group and not just Jimmy alone. Each of us has a different personality which is now coming to the fore. ... I think the audiences now know each member of the group for his musical ability and for himself."[13]

Tour manager Richard Cole contended that this was the tour on which Led Zeppelin came of age in other ways, earning their name as a band of infamous hell-raisers. "That was the one," he said. "We were hot and on our way up, but no one was watching too closely. ... All the so-called Led Zeppelin depravity took place the first two years in an alcoholic fog. After that we got older and grew out of it. It became a realistic business."[14]

In fact someone was watching: Led Zeppelin were observed at close quarters on this tour by a journalist from *Life* magazine, Ellen Sander. She was a well-known rock writer with strong connections to many of the top acts of the day, from Dylan to The Byrds and beyond, and was well placed to make a dispassionate assessment of the band's position both in terms of their audiences and their impact on the US groupie scene of the day. She placed them in the context of all the bands then struggling to make the breakthrough and working flat out to achieve it.

"They lived and worked and struggled to survive from day to day, from place to place," wrote Sander, "through unspeakable nightmares, just to play music. It was loud, hard, gutsy rock, violent and executed with a great deal of virtuosity. ... No matter how miserably the group failed to keep their behaviour up to a basic human level, they played well almost every night of the tour. If they were only one of the many British rock'n'roll groups touring at the time, they were also one of the finest. The stamina they found each night at curtain time was amazing, in the face of every conceivable kind of foul-up with equipment, timing, transportation, and organisation at almost every date. They had that fire and musicianship going for them and a big burst of incentive; this time around, on their second tour, from the very beginning, they were almost stars."[15]

Page in particular had enormous faith in the ability of American fans to recognise how good his band was. He told an *NME* reporter based in Hollywood: "America made us. It really did. It takes two or three years to build up a reputation in England, but we came over here as soon as we could and when we went back our success had already been heard of over there. ... I didn't have any confidence in British audiences. No confidence at all. That's because The Yardbirds had their biggest success in America, and I just assumed it would be the same for us."[16] This positive American reaction stretched as far as Hawaii, where the *Honolulu Advertiser* reviewer wrote: "Led Zeppelin was the first major British band to appear in Hawaii, and I think most people will agree that we want more. The showmanship exceeded any rock performance here to date."[17]

The tour was a grinding whirl of gigs, with Detroit's Grande Ballroom on May 16th universally elected as its nadir. *Life* journalist Ellen Sander reported the backstage scene. "John Paul Jones appeared at the door, looked into the dressing room full of girls and hangers-on, and closed it. He sulked miserably outside, where fans badgered him constantly. Jimmy Page, inside, with that febrile, forlorn look that brought out perversity in 15-year-olds, sat inside, neither receiving nor giving any invitations. Robert and John, cockney spirits at heart, continued to turn their uproariously vulgar sense of humour on the situation. It was unquestionably the low point of the tour, Detroit: a town as foul as exhaust fumes and as hard as cement."[18]

Atlantic in the United States had released a single from the first album on March 10th to support the tour: 'Good Times Bad Times' coupled with 'Communication Breakdown'. They were the only tracks that really made commercial sense because of their radio-friendly original length and structure. Both Page and Grant took an attitude of studied indifference to this and every other single to come, claiming that their attention was elsewhere – on the albums and on the live work. As if to prove their point, the first record was now certified gold ($1 million sales) and continued to sell well. Naturally, Atlantic wanted to make sure they had the next LP in line for autumn 1969. The band's touring schedule was pretty much flat out whichever country they were in, so they were forced to record on the run and over a period of time. They made a start on 'Whole Lotta Love', 'Moby Dick', 'Bring It On Home', 'Ramble On', 'Thank You', and 'What Is And What Should Never Be', but progress was erratic because studio work had to be snatched between tour commitments.

Richard Cole became closely involved in organising the movements between gig and studio. According to him: "Whenever we had a day off, wherever we were, Jimmy would find an available studio – the Ardent studio in Memphis, the Gold Star studio in Los Angeles – and the band would isolate themselves there from early evening until late at night, adding one more track to the album. ... 'Whole Lotta Love' got an enormous amount of Jimmy's attention in the studio. With Robert's vocal already on the tape, he spent hours building everything else around it. ... Jimmy also worked tirelessly by himself, mixing 'Bring It On Home', then 'What Is And What Should Never Be'. He added 12-string picking to 'Thank You' and a barrage of Gibson overdubs to 'Ramble On'."[19]

The busy mix of live and studio work was doubly hard on Page as he shouldered not only the burden of performing and songwriting – now shared with Plant, who was encouraged to come up with lyrics – but also the arranging and mixing of this material they recorded. When the others could occasionally relax on a day off,

Page was often spending his time in a studio working on another mix or more overdubs. This sometimes meant he would fly from city to city in order to get some sort of consistency of sound from a single studio. "On several occasions," Cole recalled, "Jimmy and I would catch a plane into New York from a gig in Minneapolis or Chicago. I would carry the unfinished tapes on the plane with me, wrapped in foil. We'd grab a taxi to A&R Studios, spend half a day there, and then fly out to the next concert."[20] In fact, between Minneapolis on the 18th and San Jose on the 23rd, the whole band decamped to New York City where they rehearsed and promoted themselves in the daytime and recorded at night.

This was not the way to come up with the best possible results, but their schedules and priorities meant it was the most pragmatic method of delivering a second album. Page was a perfectionist, so it took the greatest toll on him. It was the first time that Cole had been in a studio with Page and, knowing the band's live act very well by now, he was surprised by the difference in the guitarist's attitude to stage work and recording. "He would become much more nervous [in the studio] than he ever did onstage," Cole observed. "No matter how well prepared he was, he rarely seemed completely satisfied. He always wanted something a little closer to perfection. His confidence would ebb and flow. ... It was long, exhausting work, and as much as he enjoyed the creative process, it would sometimes overwhelm him."[21]

According to tour observer Ellen Sander, in Chicago ardent fans in this "heavy Yardbirds territory" were familiar with the group from a previous appearance. Jimmy Page was given a hero's welcome".[22] Prior to the band arriving for a triumphant three-night return engagement in Boston a few days later, she wrote: "Everyone was wrecked, drained, moody, jet-shocked, and almost sick. They were advised that the tour was going extraordinarily well, better than even expected, but it did not seem to affect them, or perhaps they didn't realise the implications of what they'd been through. But each time they faced an audience ... they knew. ... In those few hours the boys would be transformed from tired carping brats into radiant gods. Whatever happened, it never took the joy out of playing and playing well."[23]

The tour came to a jubilant conclusion in New York City at the end of May 1969 with two nights at the Fillmore East, this time as headliners, with Delaney & Bonnie and Woody Herman's Big Band in support. US record-trade magazine *Cash Box* noted that the band "made a strong return to New York. ... They have carried the British bass-drums-guitar concept to an extreme. ... There is plenty of room for dynamics and understatement in the Zeppelin's brand of ultra-hard rock, but the combo

Overleaf: John Bonham onstage at the Bath Festival in England, June 28th 1969.

has forsaken their musical sense for the sheer power that entices their predominantly juvenile audience."[24]

The other biz magazine, *Billboard*, took a similar line, and while they quibbled that "Led Zeppelin are the loudest group around" they had the grace to mention that "this powerful and dominating quartet had its usual standing ovation".[25] That was the paradox that drove music reviewers mad: Led Zeppelin were often not to their liking or taste, but they were undeniably popular.

Nonetheless, the band's personalities were becoming unravelled. Ellen Sander concluded her tour of duty with the band on their final date, at the Fillmore on May 31st. "I stopped in to say goodbye and godspeed. Two members of the group attacked me, shrieking and grabbing at my clothes, totally over the edge. I fought them off until Peter Grant rescued me but not before they managed to tear my dress down the back."

Reflecting on the unresolved ambivalences of her fly-on-the-wall role during this tour, Sander concluded: "If you walk inside the cages of the zoo you get to see the animals close up, stroke the captive pelts, and mingle with the energy behind the mystique. You also get to smell the shit firsthand."[26] Sander cancelled her front-cover feature story with *Life* and her editors backed her. The band were livid: they felt they could do anything within their sphere of influence and get away with it. Sander eventually published her observations four years later in a remarkably even-handed piece of writing included in her book of rock journalism. Even then, Richard Cole claimed in his book, band members and management saw it as some sort of betrayal.

Whatever was going on offstage, promoters had no hesitation in booking the band. A May 31st news item in *Record Mirror* back home even had Led Zeppelin "booked to play a large outdoor pop festival called Woodstock"[27] while the same music paper's following issue had them slated for an appearance in July – supported by B.B. King – in New York's Central Park as part of the month-long summer Schaefer Music Festival. By mid June it was being reported that Zeppelin had been added to the bill at the Atlanta Pop Festival.

Back in Britain at the start of June, the band had to prepare for their first proper UK tour. Before all that, Zeppelin took a well-earned short break at home, interspersed with more work on the new album, again at Olympic in Barnes and also at Morgan studio in Willesden, north-west London. This marked the first time that the band had been able to concentrate on home life or on honing material in the studio without distraction since their formation nine months earlier.

The UK tour was relatively short. There were seven appearances in the final two weeks of June 1969, starting in Birmingham on the 13th, plus a quick dash to Paris for a TV show and two more BBC sessions in London. For many of the UK gigs, Blodwyn Pig and Liverpool Scene were the support acts. The tour programme revealed just how quickly Zeppelin had arrived and how close past scufflings were. Page, quoted at length, talked openly about his session days, pointing out that both he and Jones had come from that scene. "Sessions are great," he said, "but you can't get into your own thing. Both myself and John felt that in order to give what we had to offer we had to have a group of musicians who could lay down good things." He then compared the band once more to his Yardbirds days. "I want us to be raw and basic. That was the whole thing that made The Yardbirds happen. To go into your own thing is fine, but it has to be a form of experimentation that evolves from a basic sound that everyone else knows and relates to."[28]

Most of the concerts in the two-week UK stint got rave reviews across a range of music publications, showing once more that the band's early press reception was mostly positive, from quite early on. *Melody Maker*'s report of the show in Birmingham was typical, the reviewer writing that "Led Zeppelin showed just why they have taken America by storm".[29] Three days later the band made their first BBC radio session of the month, for the Dave Symonds show *Symonds On Sunday*. The host was taking a holiday at the time so Chris Grant MC'd the programme, wittily retitling it for the duration as *Chris Grant's Tasty Pop Sundae*. Zeppelin shared the session duties with Marmalade – a nicely incongruous double bill.

Three tracks surfaced later on the 1997 *BBC Sessions* compilation: 'Communication Breakdown', 'The Girl I Love She Got Long Black Wavy Hair', and Eddie Cochran's 'Somethin' Else'. 'Breakdown' crackles with energy and in some respects benefits from the basic engineering job done by the BBC technicians – although it's not too basic, with both Plant and Page double-tracked. The distortion and edge gained in the process make the song raw and exciting. There is a variation from the LP version where the band cuts the tempo in half (2:01), Page laying down some spare B.B. King blues licks and Plant going into his "squeeze my lemon…" routine – did the BBC know what he was on about? – before cutting back to the routine. 'The Girl I Love' is strung together by a strutting guitar-bass riff very much of the period – Howlin' Wolf via Fleetwood Mac – and is a workmanlike rehash of common R&B parts. Again, it has tremendous presence and the band's sheer excitement at playing together is very evident, lifting a somewhat pedestrian song onto another level.

'Somethin' Else' is perhaps the most interesting performance in that it reveals so much about the band and the roots of its individual members. The arrangement is ad hoc and undistinguished, fast and furious like an encore would be. Indeed it was used on the road that year as an encore, along with many other rock oldies, thanks to Zeppelin's then short list of original compositions. It has a vocal that comes close to pub-band status. Plant happily re-routes the melody line and throws caution to the wind as if he's still appearing with a local Birmingham band rather than a new international phenomenon. Jones's barroom Jerry Lee Lewis piano, boosted too high in the mix and rather unsteady on its fingers, hardly helps matters.

Just eight days later the band were back at the BBC studios, recording four further numbers, this time for Radio 1 DJ John Peel's slot on *Top Gear*. Once again 'Communication Breakdown' was wheeled out, along with 'What Is And What Should Never Be', 'Travelling Riverside Blues' and – as a sneak preview of what would soon be the dominant thread of the second album – 'Whole Lotta Love'. 'Breakdown' sticks to the format of three days earlier, although Plant sounds more at ease. His voice is double-tracked on the hookline and there are two tracks of ad lib vocals during the cut-time passage, revealing a less than 100 percent live source for these tapes. He seems more relaxed with the song, as if his confidence is now at an all-time high. The entire performance is very tight and shows signs of meticulous arrangement, making this their most polished and complete recording from the four BBC sessions of 1969.

'Travelling Riverside Blues', written and first recorded by blues legend Robert Johnson back in the 1930s, brings a new dimension to the band and indicates the way they were thinking when looking for material and angles for the second album then being recorded. Page was not that often to be heard playing slide guitar for an entire song, but he does here, and convincingly. It is also a pleasure to hear him and Jones playing so tightly together on Johnson's original blues lines.

The following day the band were working at Morgan studios in north London on more material for the second album, cutting a track that would remain unreleased, a cover of Ben E King's 'We're Gonna Groove'. As if all that wasn't enough, the BBC had Led Zep back in harness just three days later for an hour-long live special that would wait for broadcast until August, as *One Night Stand*, when the next album was due to be released.

The session was an early test for the BBC's proposed Radio 1 rock concert series. Page recalled proudly some years later that they had helped pave the way for this new radio format. He claimed that Zeppelin and other bands had been complaining for some time to the BBC about playing-times on live shows. "I guess they finally took us seriously," he said later, "because they allowed us to pilot an in-concert show that would allow us to play a complete hour-long set. Our pilot was so successful that it soon became the standard format. That was kind of an important first and I guess shows the kind of clout we had in those days."[30]

At the BBC's Playhouse Theatre in central London the band played a marathon 'Dazed And Confused', Page's guitar feature 'White Summer' / 'Black Mountain Side', 'I Can't Quit You Baby', 'You Shook Me', 'How

Many More Times' and, once again, 'Communication Breakdown'. This last song was beginning to show a few signs of wear, the band pushing to extract more from the structure and riffs than they'd previously managed. The rhythm section remain tight and produce a locked-in groove, but the phrase-ends and breaks show spots of raggedness, while Plant works very hard indeed to inject more intensity into his bluesy lines. The instrumental interlude is played cleanly but seems to hold the number back rather than help it to any new identity.

Better by far are the blues numbers, with 'I Can't Quit You Baby' in particular finding the band at a peak of confidence and playing with impeccable teamwork. Once again, Page's counterpoint to Plant's vocals is not only beautifully executed but entirely apt: there is no showboating for the sake of it, although high spirits abound, especially in the rapid-fire exchanges between Plant and Page. Page's solo occasionally shows signs of raggedness, especially in the 16th-note runs, but much else of what he does shows enormous sensitivity to dynamic range and subtlety of performance. This leads directly back to B.B. King but also builds from what King concentrated on in his guitar playing, showing a variety of phrase, rhythm and shading largely missing from the great bluesman's work after the early 1960s. Page's tone on 'You Shook Me' is razor-sharp and thrilling, his bottleneck slide sounding easy and completely idiomatic. This is a band enjoying their music and a guitarist thrilled with what is going on around him.

By the time Page came to play this version of 'White Summer'/'Black Mountain Side' he had developed it into a solo concert feature with form, drama and narrative content sufficient to take any large audience along with him. He was now performing it on electric guitar, a Danelectro he kept reserved for the job. His statement of the initial theme had become more laden with filigree embellishments, taken from English folk and Indian classical traditions.

The move into the up-tempo section of 'White Summer' in this BBC concert version is faster and more energetic, with Bonham using mallets on his kit (and, later, a pair of conga drums) and Jones supplying a simple bass underpinning, before a solo climax from Page that calls for more quasi-raga techniques of resonating strings accompanying the octave melody. Page's playing is elegant, precise and beautifully weighted, slowing to a brief transitional pause before launching into 'Black Mountain Side'.

Here he uses a more conventional acoustic-guitar technique to state the theme, but moves through other folk styles and techniques to generate a suitable climax in what is, at eight minutes, a long solo outing. It is fair to

Overleaf: The band relaxing at 1969's Bath Festival before going onstage for their afternoon spot.

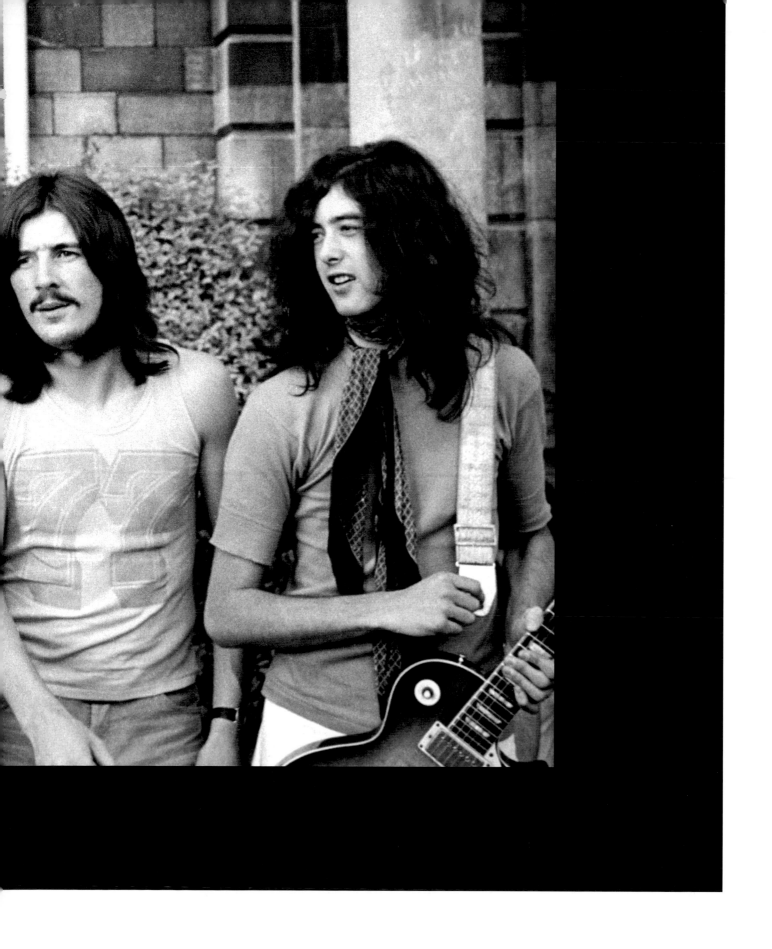

say that no other rock guitarist was attempting anything of this nature onstage or in broadcasts in 1969. The only possible parallel came after this event, when Jimi Hendrix incorporated an extended unaccompanied guitar passage into the coda of his live versions of 'Star Spangled Banner' later that same summer. Hendrix employed scales and acoustic-guitar techniques different from Page's and put them to an entirely different purpose, but they quite possibly occurred to him because Page had first taken the step into this type of concert feature.

With the band in such brilliant form, Page took them into Olympic studios again for further work on the second album. There among other things they added to the backing track for 'Whole Lotta Love'. This piece would come to symbolise not only that album but everything early Led Zep stood for: brutal riffs, sledgehammer drumming, white-hot screaming vocals, sensuality you could almost touch. It was so potent.

All this studio activity was against a background in which Peter Grant's other contemporary success, The Jeff Beck Group, were not only scoring major live successes in the US, but that month, June 1969, had released their own second album on that side of the Atlantic, *Beck-Ola*, as well as an accompanying single, 'Plynth' coupled with 'Jailhouse Rock'. The sheer savagery and weight of sound on this record – especially on 'All Shook Up', 'Jailhouse Rock' and the highly influential instrumental 'Rice Pudding' – showed that Led Zeppelin were not alone in their drive for the sonic boom.

Beck said later: "It was made in desperation to get product out. We just got vicious on it, because we were all in bad moods, and it came out quite wild."[31] The blunt, savagely metallic, bludgeoning riff that was the theme of 'Rice Pudding' was later used by Hendrix in his own 'In From The Storm' as a tribute to Beck, and even today stands as one of the most ferocious pieces of pre-metal-era metal committed to tape. Its floating, free-form second section might just conceivably have had an influence on the emerging shape of Page's own metal anthem-to-be, 'Whole Lotta Love'. By breaking into the US Top 20 that summer, *Beck-Ola* increased the pressure on Zeppelin to get their second album out and retain their new high profile.

Just two more dates remained to be played in Britain prior to the band's third American tour inside nine months and the second of 1969. First there was the Bath Blues & Progressive Music Festival on June 28th, followed the next day by Led Zeppelin's contribution, in tandem with Fleetwood Mac, to the Pop Proms at London's Albert Hall. Both were successful, although their Bath appearance took place during the afternoon. Led Zeppelin were not yet ready to top a blues festival bill sporting Fleetwood Mac, John Mayall, Ten Years After, Colosseum, and Champion Jack Dupree.

The festival was at the Bath Recreation Ground, with the band set up on a small stage that looked more like a village fete marquee than a festival platform. One festival-goer wrote later: "Across the park from the stage was Bath Town Hall, and I always remember the look on Robert Plant's face when he was doing 'Whole Lotta Love'. … During the screech at the end he heard his own echo coming back – so he kept screaming and listening to the echoes. I am sure that this gave birth to the [similar effect on the] album track."[32]

The second date was perhaps a more noteworthy gig for the band, a headlining appearance at London's Albert Hall – two sets, at 5.30 and 8.30pm – as the opening concert of a Pop Proms series running that year between June 29th and July 3rd, preceding the famous classical-music Proms Series. Other artists appearing in the series were Chuck Berry, Family, Fleetwood Mac, Incredible String Band, The Pentangle, and The Who. It was part of the BBC's attempts to ingratiate itself with the audience for non-chart rock that had emerged since the release of *Sgt Pepper* in 1967. That Zeppelin were considered part of this new movement rather than purveyors of headbanging music must have been gratifying to Grant and Page.

Melody Maker, Disc and *NME* were unqualified in their enthusiasm for their Pop Proms set. *NME* noted that Zeppelin "took flight to score a massive personal triumph when they closed Sunday's first night amid incredible scenes and gave the Pop Proms the kind of start the organisers would have been brave to dream of".[33] *Disc* described wild scenes where "there were no less than three encores which ran on even after the power had been cut and Robert had to resort to using his harp. … I haven't seen a band go down so well for a long time".[34]

Nick Logan in *NME* supplied the explanation for this reception. "Zeppelin truly deserved the acclaim – it is boggling that in a matter of months they have achieved such a high degree of musicianship and become one of the biggest crowd-pullers around. Concentrated touring has given them an extra edge in every department and with drummer John Bonham and bassist John Paul Jones laying a solid rear-guard the frontal dialogue between Plant the singer and leader Jimmy Page has developed to a startling and stimulating extent."[35]

In Britain the band had established themselves as a strong live draw, were gaining consistent and high-profile support from the BBC, and enjoyed gushing features, articles and interviews in the music press. They were ready to depart once more to reinforce their lightning-fast ascent in America and finish their second album for Atlantic Records.

Albert Hall, Pop Proms, June 29th 1969. One reviewer said: "In a matter of months they have achieved a high degree of musicianship and become one of the biggest crowd-pullers around."

WHOLE LOTTA NEWPORTS

- NEWPORT FESTIVAL

- 3RD AMERICAN TOUR

- 2ND ALBUM RELEASED

- 4TH AMERICAN TOUR

- CARNEGIE HALL

The Newport Jazz Festival had started out in 1954 as one man's effort to help jazz escape from its dingy, often underworld-linked nightclubs – or the occasional appearance of the music at one of the more dusty citadels of the cultural high ground, such as Carnegie Hall or Chicago Opera House, out of season.

George Wein was a Boston-based promoter who had managed to persuade some well-heeled locals and the Rhode Island administration that a jazz festival at Newport, out in the open in the middle of summer, would be good for business, good for the State's image, and not too much of a nuisance for the well-off citizens who lived or vacationed there. Such festivals were then unknown outside Eastern Europe and France. Newport was thus the forerunner for all the US-based festivals that followed its 1954 debut.

Newport's arrangements worked moderately well until 1960, when a combination of imported teenagers looking for fun – and the all-too-freely-available alcohol that fuelled their idea of fun – led to riots outside and sporadically within the festival. Rather than blame their own lax policing of retailers, the authorities closed the festival early and suspended it for the following summer.

Since the Festival's restoration in 1962, Wein had been especially careful to ensure that the scenes of mayhem – overturned cars, looted shops, National Guard out in the streets with riot gear – would not be repeated anywhere near his festival. But by 1969 acoustic jazz had become increasingly eclipsed commercially by the economic blossoming of rock, which had also become increasingly accepted among younger jazz musicians and listeners. This led Wein to experiment with rock acts at the Newport Jazz Festival. He had not attempted this since 1958, when Chuck Berry had appeared during an evening ostensibly staged as a tribute to the blues and R&B. Led Zeppelin were one of a number of bands approached to appear at the 1969 festival and were happy to accept. They were scheduled to close out the four-day event on the Sunday night, July 6th.

From a financial point of view, the early signs were encouraging. Wein was expecting a total attendance over the four days in excess of 90,000. By the evening of the second day, wrote observer and photographer Burt Goldblatt, "The festival security force of 100 was completely inadequate for dealing with the crowd of close to 30,000, both seated in the park and camped around outside the field. And since both the city and the Festival had ignored the expected influx and had not provided enough security, they were largely responsible for the dangerous situation."[1]

As with many other festivals during this and the following year, the security fences were breached every day and the crowd – paying and non-paying customers alike – were allowed to roam as they pleased. The Festival's first day, July 3rd, was entirely made up of jazz acts such as Freddie Hubbard, Anita O'Day, and Bill Evans. The evening of the 4th saw performances by Count's Rock Band, The Jeff Beck Group, Ten Years After, Blood Sweat & Tears, and Jethro Tull, closing with Roland Kirk. This was a pretty impressive line-up for one evening. As Wein commented at the time, "Rock groups were so anxious to play here at the Jazz Festival that most of them came at their lowest rate."[2]

Saturday 5th saw another mixed programme that included stars such as Miles Davis, John Mayall, The Mothers Of Invention, Dave Brubeck, Gary Burton, and Sly & The Family Stone. During the preparations for Sly's set, the uneasy relationship between the young crowd and Wein's security people disintegrated. Critic Whitney Balliett gave this account for *The New Yorker*: "Several astonishing things happened, and they happened so fast it is difficult to remember their exact order. Sly & The Family Stone were setting up their 20 or so two-ton speakers and amplifiers when a heavy, battering-ram thumping began outside the fence to the right of the bandstand [and] then fireworks, shot from the bluff behind the bandstand, bombarded the audience. It suddenly started raining, and the smell of smoke became unmistakable (the hordes outside, it turned out, had set fire to the grass behind the performers' quarters).

"George Wein rushed onstage and shouted at Sly Stone, asking him, for God's sake, to start playing. He did, and the dam, bulging for two days, broke. Kids, black and white, came pouring through a huge hole they had made in the fence separating the main area of the field from the box seats and the press section. They came like Visigoths, smashing the box railings and turning over chairs and forcing the occupants to flee. They poured into the press photographers' pit in front of the bandstand, filled it, and climbed up on the stage. Police and security guards ran onstage and there was a five-minute melee, with kids scrambling up, reaching the stage, and being tossed back into the pit. The only thing missing was the boiling oil. Sly & The Family Stone roared away, and then Stone, using lots of 'like's and 'man's and 'uptight's, persuaded the massed kids to sit down. All at once some sort of catharsis was achieved, and everything subsided."[3] Such things were happening all over America that year. The love-and-peace ethic that had so optimistically dominated earlier events in 1967-68 began to break down in a welter of stoned justifications of personal self-interest.

On Sunday July 6th, the last day of the event, acts billed included James Brown, B.B. King, Johnny Winter,

By September 1969 the first album was already earning industry awards for strong sales in the USA and in Britain.

Overleaf: The band leaving a record-company event in London during a break between their third and fourth American tours.

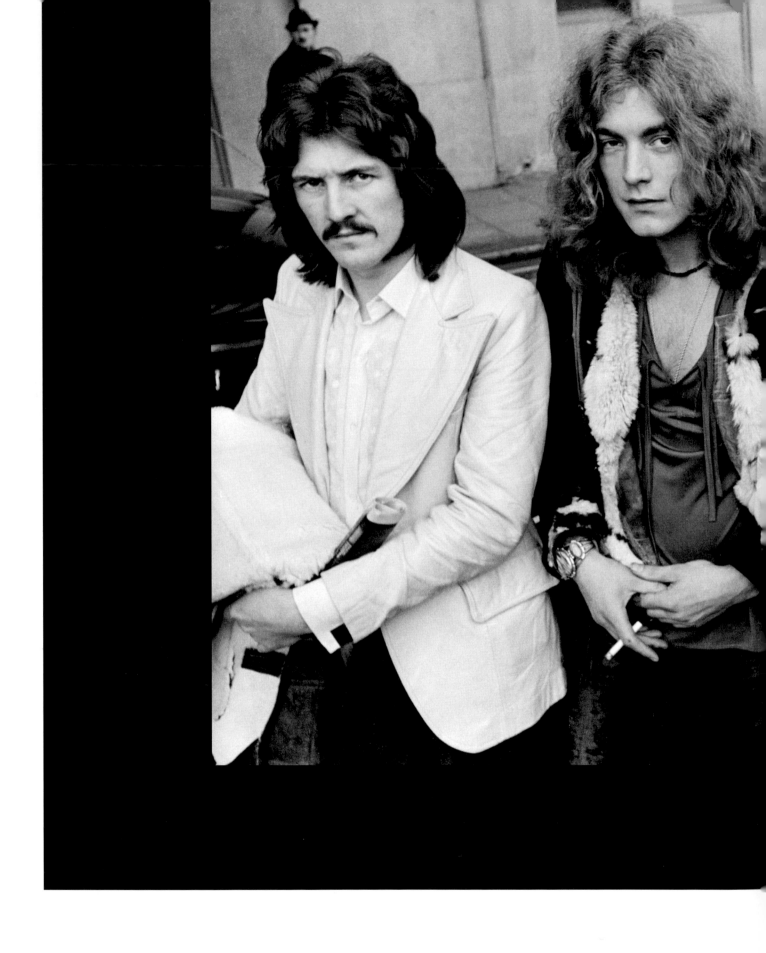

Herbie Hancock, Willie Bobo, Buddy Rich, and Led Zeppelin. By then, Wein's nerves were shredded by the crowd's free-ranging behaviour – he had obviously never been to a rock festival before he'd decided to add that element into his own cultural mix. In an effort to disperse the crowd early and limit any mayhem that might break out at the event's conclusion, given what had happened the previous evening with Sly Stone, he announced to the crowd and on local radio that Led Zeppelin would not be appearing, because a member of the band was ill. This was communicated to Zeppelin's British PR man, Bill Harry, who had arrived at the festival in advance of the band.

After a hurried phone call with manager Peter Grant, who was still travelling to the event, Harry went on local radio to say that the band would in fact be playing. Grant, speaking to journalists afterwards, claimed that Wein's original announcement was made without the band's knowledge or consent. "George Wein panicked," he told *Billboard*. "It was obvious [the organisers] weren't going to get everybody in. ... We came over from England to do the Festival. We were very excited about it. We felt it was progressive musically and would give us a new audience. We feel this [announcement] hurt the act a lot."[4]

Grant insisted that his band appear, even though much of the crowd was already packing up to go because they thought Zeppelin would not be playing. The last act of the entire festival, they came on straight after a short but typically machine-gun-like set by the Buddy Rich big-band. Rich, as competitive a musician and entertainer as ever trod a stage, and a man who by then mixing jazz and pop songs in every set, was determined to upstage the festival's closing act. As usual he played one of his patented marathon drum solos during his last number. *Down Beat* reporter Ira Gitler wrote: "Rich's final solo, in which his sticks became hummingbirds as well as torches, brought the crowd to its feet. It was hotter than the fire with which the crowd outside had tried to burn down a section of the wooden fence at one point in the evening."[5] Whitney Balliett was equally moved, writing that Rich's set "was closed with a long tidal-wave, three-ring, 21-gun, now-damn-it, you-listen drum solo".[6] There is no doubt that Bonham, backstage, would have been drawn to what Rich was doing, both for its sheer technique and its bloody-minded showmanship.

Journalist Chris Welch saw Led Zeppelin play that night. He later wrote that "the show turned out to be one of the most memorable of an already memorable summer. Zep put on a stunning performance, despite all the pre-gig hassles".[7] In a shortened set to accommodate the festival programme, they played 'The Train Kept A-Rollin'', 'I Can't Quit You Baby', 'Dazed And Confused' and 'You Shook Me' – all songs from their repertoire that could fairly be described as blues, and thus in tune with the overall tenor of this "jazz and pop" festival.

Of all the jazz critics in attendance that year who wrote about the festival, only *Down Beat*'s Gitler stuck around after Buddy Rich to check out Zeppelin. He didn't stay for long. "Last came Led Zeppelin which to me was a lead balloon. The distortion of the sound was so annoying on Willie Dixon's 'You Shook Me' that it finished my festival prematurely."[8] So did rock's involvement with Newport. The city elders banned such events in future, insisting that Wein return to a jazz-only programme in future years if he wanted his event to survive.

At a post-festival party, the band mixed with the other acts, including Buddy Rich, in an air of relaxation, until tour manager Richard Cole persuaded a drunk Bonham to get up on a table with him and start dancing very noisily. People began drifting away. Cole and Bonham then emptied the fridge of all its beer, put it in a sack and carted this back to their hotel room. Publicist Bill Harry watched the evening unravel. "We ... looked out in the car park. We could see a bare arse moving up and down. It was one of the group with a girl in a car. We went up into a room and this detective followed us because we had a couple of girls with us. Richard [Cole] slipped him a few dollars and he vanished. So we went into the room and one of the boys went to say something to one of the girls and he was sick all over her."[9]

This was a disappointing conclusion to an event that all the band – and especially Page and Grant – had looked forward to. Thus the third US tour was off to a stuttering start. But other appearances on the East Coast in early July 1969 made up for it as the now unstoppable momentum revealed a special alchemy between fans and band at each appearance. Nevertheless, they weren't going to get anything like a clear run.

Bonham was already exhibiting signs of the out-of-control behaviour for which the band would soon be noted. During the Flushing Meadow Festival at the Singer Bowl in New York City, just a week after the Newport set, Bonham joined some riotous behaviour among no fewer than three British groups present and succeeded in outdoing everyone for outrageousness.

The Jeff Beck Group and Alvin Lee's band Ten Years After were the support acts that day for Vanilla Fudge. Fudge were at their popular peak but close to quitting and going their separate ways. All four members of Zeppelin were in attendance, even though they weren't on the bill. There are many different versions of the events onstage that day, but it is clear that the overall tone of the event was wild. Jeff Beck said later: "It was one of those riotous sorts of day – everyone's energy level was 100 percent and we were throwing things at each other onstage. I threw a mug of orange juice at Alvin Lee and it stuck all over his guitar. It was just one of those animal things. Three British groups in the same place has to add up to trouble."[10]

Later, during the Beck Group's encore with 'Jailhouse

Rock', there was a sudden invasion of the stage by members of Ten Years After and Led Zeppelin, all of whom by this stage were riotously drunk, and none more so than Bonham. The resulting "nine-man jam" has entered rock folklore. Bonham excelled himself by taking over the drum stool mid-encore and altering the beat to that of 'The Stripper'. Rod Stewart, singing with Beck, commented later: "The stage was full of people – we were doing 'Jailhouse Rock' and it was fucking incredible. I finished the whole thing by shoving a mike-stand up John Bonham's arse. ... He got arrested, the cops pulled him off, and I ran away. ... We were all pissed out of our heads. And the Vanilla Fudge couldn't follow it."[11]

Other versions of this mayhem had Bonham coming to the front of the stage and stripping naked as the crowd roared him on. It is also claimed that Peter Grant rushed onstage and rugby-tackled Bonham into the sidestage area, only just saving him from the attentions of the gathering security police. According to Richard Cole, Grant then pushed Bonham into a dressing room and commanded him to get dressed. Cole said that Grant shouted: "If you aren't dressed by the time the police break down this door, you're out of the band!" Grant apparently finished reading the riot act as the crestfallen drummer attempted to find some clothes to put on. "Do you know what you're doing?" Grant asked. "Do you realise that you're jeopardising the future of this entire band by the way you behave? What's wrong with you, John? Are you trying to ruin things for everyone?"[12]

Cole also recorded that Page was disturbed by this bout of idiocy from Bonham. Page, who saw both incidents, told Cole: "Bonzo's got to get a grip on things. He's his own worst enemy. Maybe he's our own worst enemy, too."[13] Given the collective nature of this particular bout of madness, this version of events is probably not entirely accurate. But there is little doubt that, of all those present, Bonham went further and was probably the most inebriated. This pattern would persist. Unfortunately for Bonham, the band's collective will was understandably concentrated on things other than sorting out their drummer's personality problems. The prevailing attitude was that, as long as he continued to keep it together onstage, he was still an asset. He would therefore stay.

The rest of the third US tour – from the Atlanta Pop Festival in early July to the Texas Pop Festival at the end of August – was a confirmation in more than 30 gigs that Led Zeppelin had not just broken through but were now a top-line live draw. Some observers were already prepared to put them second only to Jimi Hendrix in terms of in-person popularity. But their breakthrough was uneven. Journals as far apart as Houston and San Diego wrote about Zeppelin's appearance in their town as if the band was being introduced to their readers. *The Houston Chronicle* was notably cautious, writing baldly: "An English group called Led Zeppelin will be performing in concert tonight".[14]

But Zeppelin's live shows were picking up legions of fans wherever they played. Vanilla Fudge's drummer Carmine Appice remembered that on this summer tour the two bands swapped sets on an almost nightly basis. "[Led Zeppelin] got so big so fast we were on equal billing," he recalled. "We would close one night and they would close another." He underlined the close comradeship between the two bands on that tour. "One night Zep were playing 'How Many More Times' and Page and Plant did that 'ah ah ah' vocal and guitar routine, when Bonzo and John Paul would come in and go, 'Jah dah, digga digga de doo.' ... We'd all agreed to surprise Plant and Page, and instead of Bonzo and John Paul coming in, it was Timmy Bogert and me."[15]

There was no competition between the two bands, who were friends with each other. Fudge had already decided to make this their last tour before breaking up. Here was a tour where one band was looking for the exit sign while the other was on a rocket-propelled journey to the top. It was perhaps prophetic that Zeppelin missed playing Woodstock in August 1969. As chaotic as any festival hailed a success could possibly be, it was arguably the last and biggest celebration of a hippie ethic fast running out of steam, certainly in terms of live entertainment. The generation that had grown up with The Beatles and The Rolling Stones had adopted each new guise that these trendsetters had introduced – including a fascination with the Far East in all its manifestations – but was now so disillusioned with the political and social processes of its own society that the only palliative seemed to be a combination of music and drugs.

The huge outdoor shows – as well as events at the larger indoor venues – had become something of a carnival where the music was part of the drop-out process. Critic Whitney Balliett put his finger on it when watching the crowds mill around him at Newport that summer. "To be sure, some rock – with its handmaidens pot and acid, with its vaudeville exterior, with its shattering volume, and with its unintelligible lyrics – is not meant to be listened to. Beneath its crashing political-social surface, it is designed to provoke a Kubla Khan euphoria."[16]

Led Zeppelin were not primarily addressing this audience. Their fans tended to be a little younger, less disillusioned, more ready to go out for a good time listening and dancing to loud and very exciting music. Some of the music press in America found it difficult to warm to Zeppelin because they were not the target audience. Still, many of the critics, American and British, who actually attended the band's performances, rather than pontificate from the safety of their armchair while listening to the vinyl version, were caught up in the huge energy that Zep in the flesh never failed to generate.

On top of meeting their touring commitments during August, the band – and especially Page – finished work on the second album, finalising mixes, adding last-minute overdubs and production effects, and overseeing final artwork for the jacket. They were under pressure from Atlantic to deliver in good time for the autumn and Christmas market, especially as *Led Zeppelin* was continuing to sell steadily, promising a very warm welcome for any new record from the band.

The second album was completed in August 1969, the masters handed over and the rest left to Atlantic to co-ordinate. In order to give this new effort the best possible chance of success in America, Grant put together a fourth US tour, this time a shorter campaign of just less than a month in October and November either side of the LP's release date. The tour concentrated the band's fire on the major population centres on East and West Coasts, plus the Midwest biggies of Detroit and Chicago and the obligatory visit to Toronto included in any North American tour of consequence. In the meantime, Zeppelin were given an entire month off – something of a luxury for a band that had been in a constant frenzy of touring and recording since the previous December.

During the down time, *Melody Maker* in Britain came out with its annual readers' poll results for 1969, and Led Zeppelin managed their first showing in its ranks. While they did not appear in the Top Group category of the UK Section, their debut album made the ninth and final position in LP Disc (*Goodbye Cream* was that year's winner) and fourth in Brightest Hope, behind Blind Faith, Thunderclap Newman, and Jethro Tull. Oddly for a British band, Zeppelin were voted higher in the International Section, where they made third place in Brightest Hope behind Blind Faith and Creedence Clearwater Revival.

During September 1969 the band and Atlantic watched the pre-orders for the second album pass 400,000 in America alone, while at home in Britain Page and Plant took time to talk to a music press eager to cover in depth the unfolding phenomenon of Led Zeppelin. Both had intelligent and insightful things to say about their own quick success and about the music scene in general. Neither felt that the UK press had been very kind to them, or that British crowds were particularly welcoming: an odd feeling, given their quick, huge popularity there and the generally positive music-press coverage. Page told *Melody Maker*: "Britain is one of those places where you've got to make it. But it's a lot more difficult. Over here you feel you've got to knock yourself out before the people start listening to you, but in the States they listen from the start, and if they don't like you they simply don't come to see you again."[17]

In tune with each other during a dressing-room vigil at The Lyceum in London, October 12th 1969.

Plant, in his first major UK press interview, told *Melody Maker* two weeks later: "Nobody in Britain wanted to know us, but Jimmy told us it'd be different in the States. The first time we went we started off right down the bill on the West Coast, but by the time we got over to the East we were at the top. … I was very nervous when we started off, because everything I'd done previously had been a failure. … This group has really woken me from inertia. Years and years with no success can keep you singing, but it can bring you down an awful lot."[18]

During this short break in the touring schedule Plant gave a number of other interviews. His puzzlement at what he perceived as a cold reception at first in Britain was still noticeable. He spent a fair amount of time comparing British and American audiences, routinely disparaging British crowds in the process. Considering the band's rapid ascension to stardom on both sides of the Atlantic, this seems in retrospect like someone letting off some long-suppressed steam after finally cracking a notoriously tough business.

The contrast between the two band members is intriguing, for while Plant went on at length about his musical origins and tastes, Page talked in detail about the wider music scene, its workings and its trends. For example, he is well aware that Led Zeppelin used a system of promotion for live gigs pioneered shortly before by Mike Jeffery, Jimi Hendrix's manager. Grant and Page grasped early on that what Jeffery was doing for himself and his act was a leap forward in the financing and economics of touring.

Jeffery had realised that Hendrix, then the top US box-office draw for live gigs, was not generating the income he should be. This was because most of the profits were taken by local promoters. In a revolutionary move, Jeffery became his own promoter, using the local man merely as a 'fixer' on the ground, someone to help organise the event and take a small cut of the proceeds. He and his artist took the lion's share of the money from ticket sales and sales at the door – and suddenly Hendrix's tours became enormously profitable. Profitable enough, in fact, to finance his legendary time spent in the recording studio and the building of Electric Lady studios in New York in 1969 and '70, let alone the many Jeffery-led side projects such as concert films.

Grant understood early on the ramifications of this change in the approach to live appearances and, once the band quickly established itself as a draw in its own right, instituted a similar arrangement to that of Jeffery and Hendrix. Zeppelin were demanding – and getting – a comfortable majority slice of the gate receipts, making their touring profitable within a few months of their US debut. Any promoter who wasn't happy with the deal didn't get the act again.

Led Zeppelin, like Jimi Hendrix, were making so much money for all concerned that few passed on the

opportunity to re-book the band, even on reduced percentages.

Page enthused in September: "America couldn't be better for us at the moment. The scenes there are just incredible. The new system is to put groups on a percentage of the gate money, and we drew $37,000 from one amazing gig in Los Angeles."[19] On the last date of that summer tour, near Dallas, Texas, the band had played a festival set for $14,000. Tour manager Richard Cole explained: "We were counting on the second album, finally scheduled for release in late October [1969], to drive our asking price much higher."[20]

Page was well aware that Led Zeppelin were part of a larger development in the contemporary rock scene. He mentioned this in talking to *Record Mirror* the same month, illustrating his views through mention of a band with whom they'd recently been sharing US stages. "If you only concern yourself with your own group, it's difficult to see what is going on outside of that. … I think the underground has now become an established musical form. One of the groups who have helped to do this is Jethro Tull. They present their music with a great deal of excitement, which is what is needed these days."[21]

Page had seen Tull a number of times that summer. At Baltimore's Laurel Pop Festival in July – on a bill including Buddy Guy, The Edwin Hawkins Singers, Al Kooper, Johnny Winter, The Mothers Of Invention, Ten Years After, Sly & The Family Stone, and Jeff Beck – Tull had impressed reporters with precisely the mix of musicianship and stagecraft that Page admired in them. *Down Beat* noted that Tull "provided some of the best musicianship – as well as showmanship – of the evening". Led Zeppelin closed that show and, by contrast according to *Down Beat*, "made a valiant attempt to sustain the level of performance sustained by the Hawkins Singers, Kooper, and Winter, but space sounds, wah-wah effects and soggy drums resulted in a loud but not very moving set". The following night, The Jeff Beck Group's set was "loud and demonstrative, but good nonetheless, and the kids went for him".[22]

The observant Page was learning more than band stagecraft from Jethro Tull. In the earlier *Melody Maker* interview he had mentioned them when discussing Zeppelin's attitude towards releasing singles. "Atlantic put out a single from [our] first album in the States, but it was never meant as a single. Jethro Tull have proved that a good single can get through, so we're going to try it. I don't see any reason why we can't cut a good two-and-a-half-minute track, and a lot of the things on the album are quite short – about four minutes."[23]

Jethro Tull, an 'album band' if ever there was one, had a hit single with 'Living In The Past' in the summer of

1969. Page was talking here about cutting a new single with the band directly after the upcoming October US tour, but events would overtake him. There would be such an overpowering media and public reaction to 'Whole Lotta Love' from the second album that Page and Grant would eventually sanction a single-length edited version of the song for release in the US and other territories (excluding Britain) in November 1969. The single reached Number 4 in the States and was in the charts for 13 weeks. The album, on the other hand, would reach Number 1 on both sides of the Atlantic, entering the charts upon release and in the UK alone charting for 138 consecutive weeks.

That album, *Led Zeppelin II*, was officially released in the USA on October 22nd 1969 and a few days later in Britain. It was certainly a step on from the first. But it was also a reflection of the hectic life the band had been living for the past nine months. As Plant told Chris Welch: "The tracks were done all over the place – in Los Angeles, New York, and London. On one number, [in a hut in Vancouver] I put the vocals on a backing track that had been recorded in Atlantic studios in New York."[24] Page had also decided to use a different engineer to the first record. He explained this some time later. "We went to Eddie Kramer for the second album … . [Later] I consciously kept changing engineers because I didn't want people to think that they were responsible for our sound. I wanted people to know it was me."[25]

The diverse approaches and treatments used on each instrument and track on *II* results from this mixed background and, according to Plant, made for a step forward in variety and breadth. "The band is better because we have been together longer. The excitement is still there, and we also do some quieter things which can be equally effective, as groups like Fairport Convention prove."[26]

The plain numerical title of Zeppelin's second LP was becoming something of a fashion at the time – Chicago and Blood Sweat & Tears would continue the trend. It was perhaps a reaction to the bloated and increasingly vacuous concepts lurking behind the hundreds of themed records made by lesser talents in the wake of *Sgt Pepper*. For lack of pretension it's hard to beat. But the music on *II* is very ambitious.

This is evident from the first piece, the eventual single 'Whole Lotta Love'. While the famous opening three-note guitar-bass riff is as basic a blues riff as could be devised – and close enough to Muddy Waters' 'You Need Love' to have a hundred commentators make the connection – it is positively brooding in its intensity. In more recent times a convincing parallel has been drawn between 'Whole Lotta Love' and 'You Need Loving', a Small Faces number that Steve Marriott and Ronnie Lane had in turn derived from that same Muddy Waters source, the Willie Dixon song 'You Need Love'. Nonetheless,

Robert Plant turns around as the band communicate to a London audience, October 1969.

Marriott and Lane, like Page and Plant, claimed songwriting credits. Eventually in 1985 composer Willie Dixon sued Page and Plant and won a handsome settlement. Whether he ever got around to suing Marriott and Lane is not clear.

In 1995 Paolo Hewitt asked Steve Marriott about the parallel. "Plant was a big fan. He used to be at all the Small Faces gigs. ... He was always saying he was going to get this group together. He was another nuisance. He kept coming into the dressing room, just another mod kid. ... Anyway, we used to play this number and it became a stock opener ... . We did a gig with The Yardbirds which he was at and Jimmy Page asked me what that number was we did. 'You Need Loving', I said, 'it's a Muddy Waters thing.' ... After we broke up they took it and revamped it. Good luck to them. It was only old Percy [Plant] who'd had his eyes on it. He sang it the same, phrased it the same, even the stops at the end were the same, they just put a different rhythm to it."[27]

That riff's dramatic combination with Bonham's drum patterns makes it crackle with brooding energy. Playing a dancing, syncopated eighth-note pattern on hi-hat, Bonham allows himself a set of alternating snare, tom-tom and bass-drum combinations that heighten the drama and vary the impact of the underlying blues riff, giving it a light and shade it would otherwise not have enjoyed. Along with Page's innovative guitar sounds draped over the chorus, this makes for a finely-wrought tapestry of sound and rhythm even before Plant's gripping vocal is added.

With the opening verse, it is clear that the singer has come a long way from the first album in the way he shapes his phrases and produces his voice. He is much more concerned here with injecting point and meaning into the simple words he is interpreting. Plant plays up the sexuality and drama of the lyrics and hints at a sly humour – always part of the black Chicago blues singers' repertoire, but generally scarce among white blues and R&B singers of the time.

The improvisatory middle section of 'Whole Lotta Love' – the part that would be excised for the single version – is magically handled, both in its seamless introduction and the logical flow of the content. It may or may not be a graphic musical depiction of the sex act, and it ultimately doesn't matter whether it is or not, but it has a continuity that all the best musical storytelling possesses. A full two years on from the heyday of psychedelia and its experiments in sound, Page has evoked a soundscape that paints vivid and arresting pictures in the listener's imagination without resorting to tired and conventional guitar-and-riff methods.

The idea of starting the section with Bonham's development of his hi-hat and cymbal rhythms was inspired, because this pulls the listener into the strangenesses of Page's guitar and theremin soundscapes before they are even aware of it. The anticipated guitar solo doesn't really ever arrive; Plant slips in instead and develops what at first is a vocal monologue and then a dialogue with Page's guitar sounds and Bonham's thundering drums.

Page later gave credit to engineer Eddie Kramer in helping him to realise his sound vision. "I told him exactly what I wanted to achieve in the middle of 'Whole Lotta Love'," said Page, "and he absolutely helped me to get it. We already had a lot of the sounds on tape, including a theremin and slide [guitar] with backwards echo, but his knowledge of low-frequency oscillation helped complete the effect. If he hadn't known how to do that, I would have had to try for something else. So in that sense he was very helpful. Eddie was always very, very good."[28]

'What Is And What Should Never Be' has an opening melody line that reflects the otherworldly air of 'Season Of The Witch' in Julie Driscoll's version with Brian Auger & The Trinity. Donovan's song had also been covered by Vanilla Fudge in 1968 in a quasi-rock-opera version undoubtedly known by Page and Plant, and the fetching descending-riff section here carries further evidence of the pair's attention to Vanilla Fudge: the dramatic entry and the nicely judged double-tracked harmony vocals by Plant have a direct antecedent in Fudge's heightened arrangements and vocal lines. The way the song is completed, with a pause and an additional riff section, also echoes the clever arrangements that Fudge were known for at the time.

Not that the influence only went one way. Fudge's last two albums, made after their tours with Zeppelin, are notably more rock-oriented. They feature some brilliant heavyweight drumming from Carmine Appice in the manner of Bonham and brutal guitar riffs supporting raucous singing in homage to Page and Plant. Of course, both bands maintained their own identities throughout the process. 'What Is' is one example where the cross-pollination is at its most noticeable. It is also one of the most imaginative arrangements on Zeppelin's second album.

Another quality that Fudge and Zeppelin had in common was the presence of a fine, creative bass player. Fudge's Tim Bogert is consistently more interesting to listen to than the band's guitarist, Vince Martell, while Jones's inventiveness in the first section of 'What Is' amounts to one of the recording's most enjoyable features. His knack for counter-melody and his rhythmic flexibility pull the listener along and add considerably to the song's mood of a confident sharing of secrets.

'The Lemon Song' is a thinly disguised version of Howlin' Wolf's 'Killing Floor', a blues that Jimi Hendrix had been playing onstage since before his arrival in London in 1966. Zeppelin give it a contemporary edge with the treatments Page brings to his guitar tones. Surprisingly, Jones is not at his best here, consistently playing in front of the beat rather than smack in the middle where Bonham resides, and as a result the bottom end of the rhythm is not as rock-solid as usual with Led Zeppelin. Jones is also very busy and in some places guilty of overplaying.

Page, conversely, has one of his best outings on the album. Clearly enjoying the rough edge of the guitar sound he creates for the Wolf riff that opens the piece, he gets down and dirty in perfect sync with Bonham's driving drums. He also gets off one of his cleanest, most dramatic solos of the period, loose but rhythmically precise and showing an appreciation of Hendrix's technique of building melody and harmony together in a solo – an old blues-guitar idea that Hendrix had radically updated.

Plant gets his moment during the second half of the piece, where Page contributes subtle accompaniment and commentary on Plant's 'squeeze my lemon' monologue. The humour and light-and-shade here is a significant testimony to the distance the band had travelled since their first album, where such interludes had been as uniformly hard-driven (and hard-sung) as the rest of a song. Plant's decision to pay tribute to Robert Johnson's lemon-juice metaphor was not an act of cynical exploitation but a sincere tilting of the hat to a past master. He said a couple of years later: "That line 'squeeze my lemon 'til the juice runs down my leg' was just so indicative of that person Robert Johnson. … It's borrowed, admittedly, but why not? I really would like to think that someone who heard that … would go and listen to Robert Johnson as a result. But I wish I'd written that, I really do. … This Robert Johnson thing was a complete and utter statement."[29]

'Thank You' is Plant's paean to his wife, and on first release it came across as something of a surprise, hinting at an entirely different and sentimental side to both singer and band. A straight pop song that would not have been out of character performed by The Hollies or The Bee Gees, it gave Led Zep fans pause for thought. In retrospect, the tune has not aged particularly well. Its commonplace chords and simple construction leave bare the banal lyrics and commonplace sentiments. Plant would do much better than this in future, no matter how much feeling he packs into what is clearly a heartfelt love song. An interesting by-product of this ballad is that Plant gets as close as he ever would to sounding like Rod Stewart. At least the solo keyboards at the end give Jones a chance to display his versatility and flexibility, while Page's production does as much as possible with the material to hand.

'Thank You' marked the end of side one of the original vinyl LP release, allowing listeners to drift off into a fond reverie before turning over. Dropping the stylus on the beginning of side two brought them back to core Zeppelin values circa mid 1969. 'Heartbreaker' is another modified blues riff with its roots in Howling

Wolf's 'Killing Floor', although the different rhythmic values and a brighter tempo here give it a separate character. This is a lean and mean track, its component parts stripped to the essentials. Once again playing to his strengths, Page gives Bonham the job of keeping the bottom end moving with a spare beat edged along by a busy little hi-hat pattern. In the bridge he uses the darker sonority of Jones's double-stopped bass to support Plant's agonised vocals.

The idea for Page's unaccompanied opening to his solo passage was a good one in theory, but the solo is one of his poorest on any Led Zeppelin record. He frequently stumbles in execution at speed and repeats time-worn fingerboard patterns rather than attempt anything fresh. It is moments like these on the record that presumably prompted him to comment later: "There are so many guitarists around who I think are better than me. … I'm a trifle disappointed with some of the guitar playing on the second album. When I'm in the studio, I really do miss the rapport you get with a live audience."[30] As if to illustrate this claim, Page's contributions once the bass and drums re-enter at speed are more coherent and more elegantly played. The entire band finish the song riffing at speed before a clever edit – reminiscent of the type that The Beatles had used on the side-two suite of *Abbey Road*, released a month earlier – takes us into the pop-song sonorities of 'Living Loving Maid (She's Just A Woman)'.

'Living Loving Maid' is stylistically in keeping with late Yardbirds album songs in its combination of pop and blues sensibilities and the bright, bubbly production values. If the song had more to it melodically or in its lyrics it could have made a good single A-side. As it was, it made it to the B-side of 'Whole Lotta Love' (where it would eventually prompt plenty of airplay after 'Whole Lotta Love' had traversed the US airwaves). Which is about right. If there is any tune that could be classed as filler on an album pulled together in extremis, between and on various tours, this would be the one. It is Led Zeppelin's equivalent of John Lennon's 'Run For Your Life' and Plant's equivalent of 'Polythene Pam'. It was a song that Page later identified as one of the band's weakest, and they never played it live. Which makes one wonder what he thought of the still-unissued Zep version of Sonny Boy Williamson's 'Sugar Mama' from the *Led Zeppelin II* sessions, part of a tiny amount of studio material by the band that remains completed but at the time of writing still in the can.

Much more interesting, both on its own terms and with an eye to Led Zeppelin's own future creativity, is the next tune on *II*, 'Ramble On'. Using a sweet combination of acoustic and electric guitar backing, Page creates overtones of English folk-rock behind Plant's well judged opening verse, allowing the singer to display a considerably wider tonal and timbral range than he had so far on a Led Zep session. Plant moves from melodic

singing that emphasises the considerable expressiveness of his softer, undistorted voice into a higher gear for the chorus, which he delivers with real vocal punch. The contrast is pleasing and also helps the song tell its story – even if the lyrics are a jumble of *Lord Of The Rings* names and romantic pinings. The combination of contrasting moods as well as the electric and acoustic sounds would become increasingly important to the band as their writing continued to develop during the next few years.

The instrumental 'Moby Dick' begins with a riff that could easily have come from a Jeff Beck Group album. It would have fitted well on *Beck-Ola*, for example, alongside 'Rice Pudding', but in fact derives from a Sleepy John Estes guitar line that in itself is generic blues rather than entirely original riff. The riff serves as a full-steam introduction to Bonham's solo drums. 'Moby Dick' would become a staple of Zeppelin's live act through the rest of their career, sometimes stretching to close on 30 minutes. This first effort is not much over four, and is by no means a display of Bonham at his imperious best. The reason is not hard to divine: the performance is made from a series of edits. Bonham explained: "I didn't actually sit there and play a drum solo especially for the record. They just pieced it together."[31] And it sounds that way, for the solo does not flow, has no logical climax, and gives the impression of a few isolated party pieces rather than the coherently argued, often intriguing solos that Bonham was capable of producing onstage.

'Bring It On Home' reminds us of Plant's point, made in a contemporary *Melody Maker* interview, that at the outset of his career he'd done "the whole country blues thing: Memphis Minnie, Bukka White, and Skip James …really deep blues. … My voice really started developing when I was 15, and we were doing Tommy McLennan numbers and so forth."[32] If you listen to a recording of Tommy McLennan's explosive vocals you will immediately recognise the strong link with Plant's blues singing. 'Bring It On Home' is another borrowing from Willie Dixon (and another for which Dixon would later successfully win a royalty settlement).

It starts as an unvarnished tribute to Sonny Boy Williamson and Jimmy Reed through its Page-Plant duo: Plant on vocals and harmonica, Page on mellow rhythm guitar. The song then drives into pure contemporary Zeppelin territory with a punishing unison rock riff from the whole band that immediately transports the listener into heavy-metal ecstasy. Air guitar becomes essential within seconds. But to dismiss it in that way would do the song and its arrangement a disservice, because the amount of detail that Page builds into this track is astonishing. Exquisitely wrought, the piece repays close and repeated listening, especially Page's multi-layered guitar. His

On tour in America for the fourth time, the band consider the view in San Francisco, November 1969.

control of the build-up and subsequent lowering of tension is masterful, allowing a return to the intimacy of the opening blues duet at the song's end. It is a perfect way to finish the band's accomplished second album.

Five days before the record's official US release, Led Zeppelin began their fourth American tour of the year, to give the record the best possible lift-off. The opening night was at New York City's august Carnegie Hall, scene not only of classical music triumphs by everyone from Sergei Rachmaninov to Leonard Bernstein but important showcases by popular-music giants such as Paul Robeson, Harry Belafonte, Duke Ellington, Judy Garland, Dave Brubeck, Nina Simone, Miles Davis, and The Beatles.

Zeppelin, who played two two-hour stints, were well aware of the precedents, with Bonham particularly alert to the fact that when Benny Goodman had introduced big-band swing here in January 1938 – the first to do so as a solo act – the hit of the night had been 'Sing, Sing, Sing', a number that featured a white-hot duet between drummer Gene Krupa and Goodman himself. At times that night Krupa had whipped up a virtual jungle-drums rhythm. Since then, almost every drummer whom Bonham admired had played the place, including, as Chris Welch has pointed out, Joe Morello, whose brilliant work playing the drum-kit with his hands some ten years earlier with Dave Brubeck had first alerted Bonham to such possibilities.

Not only did Bonham have all that in mind, but he was mindful of the drum solo he'd seen Buddy Rich play to an enthralled Newport Festival crowd three months earlier. When it came time to deliver 'Moby Dick' at Carnegie Hall, Bonham played one of his most inspired set pieces. According to eyewitness Welch: "He played for 30 gripping minutes, and flew around the maple Ludwig kit with astounding speed and brute strength. He played with beaters, sticks, and his hands, and never faltered for an instant. But what was truly impressive was the moment he launched into a fast, single-stroke roll on his trusty Ludwig snare drum. It was very much in the style of Buddy Rich – a relentless barrage of accents and rolls that threatened to ignite his sticks. I saw him play many times again, but never with quite such reliance on speed and dexterity."

Earlier, said Welch, "a huge cheer greeted them as Robert ran onstage dressed in black, followed by Jimmy in white satin trousers, John Bonham in a leather hat, and John Paul Jones in red. … Robert and Jimmy between them produced vocal and guitar screams that had the audience wriggling in their seats. … Silence prevailed for Jimmy's sit-down guitar solo. 'He's a masterful guitar player,' a voice breathed in my ear. It was recording engineer Eddie Kramer."[33]

That night, and for the rest of the tour, the band featured repertoire from the new album to alert fans to its arrival on the 22nd. Such co-ordination helped the album

climb within two weeks of release to Number 25 in the USA, and by the time the band were back in England and the tour finished it had risen to Number 2. This was some achievement, considering the contemporary competition. *Blind Faith* was released in September, there was *Abbey Road*, *Let It Bleed*, *From Elvis In Memphis*, Jethro Tull's *Stand Up*, and a couple of months later *Bridge Over Troubled Water* from Simon & Garfunkel, a bestseller that would eventually replace *Led Zeppelin II* after its month in the Number 1 slot and stay there for ten weeks in America and no fewer than 41 weeks in Britain.

The critical reception for the second LP was wildly mixed. *NME*'s Nick Logan described it as "another brilliant album from the remarkable Led Zeppelin."[34] Meanwhile, *Rolling Stone* managed to reach a new low in critical standards by allowing John Mendelsohn to spend his entire review searching for an effective way to use irony in order to damn with faint praise. He failed. For example: "Hey, man, I take it all back! This is one fucking *heavyweight* of an album! OK – I'll concede that until you've listened to the album 800 times, as I have, it seems as if it's just one especially heavy-song extended over the space of two whole sides. But, hey! You've got to admit that the Zeppelin has their distinctive and enchanting

Onstage at the end of 1969 to support the release of the band's second album, Led Zeppelin II.

formula down stone-cold, man. Like you get the impression they could do it in their sleep. And who could deny that Jimmy Page is absolute Number 1 *heaviest* white blues guitarist between 5' 4" and 5' 8" in the world? Shit, man, on this album he further demonstrates that he could absolutely fucking *shut down* any whitebluesman alive, and with one fucking hand tied behind his back too."

At least the band could console themselves that they were not alone in this critical flaying from the new bastion of rock elitism and partiality. Simon & Garfunkel's *Bridge Over Troubled Water* was reviewed in the same issue and pronounced musically bankrupt, the reviewer wondering aloud whether Paul Simon in particular had come to the end of the line of his creative musical ideas.

All this at a time when *Rolling Stone* was happy to spend acres of newsprint on favourites such as Bob Dylan, although the great troubadour was hardly to blame for that. In the same issue as Mendelsohn's review was a 12-page interview with Dylan bringing the reader up to date on his latest movements. The magazine was quite happy to try to find something of merit in Dylan's decidedly inferior output of the period, such as *Self Portrait*. By contrast, that bastion of American musical conservatism, *Down Beat*, neatly and accurately summed up the duality of *Led Zeppelin II*. "As music to turn on with, this is about as good as they come. Just don't stop to think about it."

COUNTESS BITES ZEPPELIN: NOBODY HURT

- 2ND UK TOUR
- ALBERT HALL CONCERT FILMED
- 3RD EUROPEAN TOUR

With the release of *Led Zeppelin II* and the progress of the fourth American tour through to three concluding nights at San Francisco's Winterland Ballroom in the first week of November 1969, the band was looking forward to taking a break during the early winter, away from the long-sustained intensity of their live performances.

But the pressure of success was not ready to let them go so easily. The world's media were now seeking interviews – with Page and Plant in particular, but with anybody else if those first options fell through. The band made careful choices about who to talk to and who not to, favouring media figures who had noted their abilities before it was fashionable to do so.

There was another pressure that had been building since late October but which was not so easy to control. Radio stations worldwide were bugging Atlantic to release a single from the new album. For Atlantic's executives, the decision couldn't be simpler: 'Whole Lotta Love' made for a perfect single. Perfect, that is, apart from being over five minutes long and having a weird, spacey middle section instead of a screaming guitar solo, all of which posed problems for airplay on American AM stations.

First was the problem of length. AM radio was geared for singles of less than three minutes. There had been exceptions in recent years for established acts, such as The Beatles with 'Hey Jude', Bob Dylan's 'Like A Rolling Stone', Elvis Presley's 'Suspicious Minds' (released almost simultaneously with *Led Zeppelin II*), and Jimi Hendrix's 'All Along The Watchtower'. But the unwritten rule was normally hard to overcome. For Led Zeppelin it wasn't an issue: they had little or no interest in the singles market anyway, believing that their natural audience, the people who came to see them at their concerts and who listened to them on FM radio, would be heading straight for their albums for a full-length session rather than the taster that a single provides. But Atlantic were insistent that something should be done.

The US release back in March of 'Good Times Bad Times' coupled with 'Communication Breakdown' as a single from the first album had not been a problem for the band – partly because they were coming from a very low position in rock's hierarchy and were happy to extend co-operation to their new record company, Atlantic, but also because both songs were short to start with and could be transferred to a single without any editing. Their musical integrity would remain intact. The band had even made a promotional film clip for that release. A clearer endorsement of its acknowledged place in the band's scheme of things would be hard to find.

'Whole Lotta Love' was a different proposition. Page and Grant were not entirely against any thought of a single being released, although they genuinely felt it was better to stick to their albums-only position. But the music's integrity came before any other consideration. According to Bonham, the band initially sanctioned the release of 'Whole Lotta Love' as a promo single in the US. "It was only for American AM radio stations to promote the LP and that was a full-length version of the LP track,"[1] he explained to *Melody Maker* soon after its release. Page must have been in agreement with this because he was with Bonham at that interview. Yet events overtook everybody.

Although FM radio in the US was happy to play the full 'Whole Lotta Love' with its other-worldly middle section, AM radio was distinctly jittery. They felt the AM audience would not stick with that section's intricacies and would switch the dial to a rival network. After all, the extended singalong tags on 'Suspicious Minds' and 'Hey Jude' swept AM listeners along with them. Yet the front and back of Led Zeppelin's song was perfect. What to do?

America is not known as the land of free enterprise for nothing, and its entertainment industry is not generally noted for putting taste before commerce. A number of radio jockeys and producers put together their own edit of the song, simply omitting all but a handful of bars of the middle section, and began broadcasting that. The idea quickly caught on and Atlantic soon experienced a chorus of demands from retailers for its release in this form. This put Atlantic in a quandary. They clearly had no objection to the edited version being released – no record company is going to ignore potential sales – but they had a contract that gave the final say to the band. Page was adamant: no edited version, especially no edited version that simply excised the experimental section that he'd worked so hard to create. He and Grant were aware that the argument about the song's length was irrelevant: after all, even in this bowdlerised version it still ran at around four minutes, a good minute or so over the normal AM time limit. It was ultimately a question of artistic integrity, not of playing time.

Grant, in an effort to take pressure off a band still on the road and experiencing staggeringly rapid ascent to the level of supergroup, announced that Led Zeppelin would record a custom-made single in December, after the tour had concluded. This was just a ruse, as Grant later admitted. "I think that was a cover-up. We never went in just to record a single. That was the golden rule. No singles."[2]

As much as anything, Grant and Page saw the entire hoopla surrounding singles – the PR events, schmoozing journos, DJs, and all the rest – as something they didn't want the band to chase. Yet the demand was for 'Whole Lotta Love' and for its immediate release. Perhaps because the edited single was already being aired daily, perhaps because the band were not prepared to take on the entire US entertainment media as well as Atlantic, and perhaps most importantly because fans wanted the single they'd heard on the radio, the edit was reluctantly cleared for commercial release in the United States. It was also issued in other territories, including Australia, where it did phenomenal business and was a jukebox perennial. In the USA alone it eventually sold over 900,000 copies.

In Britain, the local Atlantic office was equally keen to go with the US edit. With the demise of the offshore pirate radio stations and commercial licences for pop radio a few years away, the only British pop-music broadcasting was by the BBC's Radio 1. The BBC was not known for adventurous daytime programming, so Atlantic UK saw the edited single as the only way ahead. But Grant and Page, smarting from their tactical withdrawal in America, refused to sanction a UK issue.

Grant's early-December press release that the band had "written a special number which they intend as their first British single which they will be recording next week" was an effort to placate fans, but although Led Zeppelin did record in England that November, according to Bonham this was the start of work on the third album. Page concurred, though he asserted in the same interview that "we've been writing a lot of new material and we should have a proper single out in January".[3] Just one new song from the November sessions at Olympic studio, 'Jennings Farm Blues', an early electric-guitar version of what later became 'Bron-Y-Aur Stomp' on *III*, has appeared on bootlegs but has never been officially released.

With the edited 'Whole Lotta Love' selling large quantities in the USA and elsewhere, there was little point in making a separate single. It made a great deal more sense instead to look ahead to the third album. Grant eventually faced down local British Atlantic man Phil Carson. "I said, 'Look, we don't do singles,'" Grant recalled. "[Carson] was a bit pushy in those days. I said, 'Have you phoned Ahmet [Ertegun]?' and promptly called him, and there were red faces all round. Our contract stated we had the last say on such decisions."[4] Carson knew he couldn't argue with the terms of the original deal.

The band only ever got close to releasing one single in the UK, 'D'Yer Mak'er', and that was stopped at promo stage in 1973, although from time to time singles would be issued in the USA, Germany, France, Japan, and Australasia as new albums came out. Grant retained his stranglehold at home and concentrated the local Atlantic office on selling albums. As Carson commented later about that initial decision: "History has shown that Peter was absolutely right because, at one point, *Led Zeppelin II* was selling as fast as a single could sell in those days."[5] In fact Grant and his management team continued to have major reservations about the UK market in general, finding its live venues, media infrastructure and obsession with singles charts detrimental to Led Zeppelin's whole strategy.

It wasn't the fans themselves – Grant and the band realised they had a following in Britain every bit as committed as that in the US or Europe. It was to do with the tools the band were forced to use to get across to those fans and the compromises those tools imposed on the band's music. Part of his reasoning about this had to do with what he regarded as the inferior sound and less than ideal circumstances of TV broadcasts such as *Top of The Pops* and other chart-based programmes – a concern he would carry deep into the 1970s. He refused to compromise the band's biggest assets: its sound and its artistic right to play as it pleased. Releasing singles in the UK, he reasoned, would lead a band immediately down that path.

'Whole Lotta Love' coupled with 'Living Loving Maid (She's Just A Woman)' was released in America in the first week of November 1969. The following month saw the publication of the annual *New Musical Express* readers' poll. At the end of the most tumultuous decade in popular music since the 1920s, Led Zeppelin reaped another type of reward for their remarkable industry of the previous 12 months by making their debut in this traditional end-of-year popularity poll.

Although *NME* (like *Melody Maker*) continued to be dominated by The Beatles (Number 1 World Vocal Group and British Vocal Group, polling twice as many votes as The Rolling Stones at Number 2 in both categories) there were the usual anomalies of popular enthusiasm. Tom Jones was best British Male Singer, with Cliff Richard second, while the British Instrumental Unit was won by The Shadows, with Fleetwood Mac second. The Rolling Stones won Best British Disc with The Beatles' 'Get Back' second, Thunderclap Newman's 'Something In The Air' third and Fleetwood Mac's 'Oh Well' fourth. There was no separate album chart.

Led Zeppelin were voted ninth by *NME* readers in World Vocal Group (542 votes compared to over 7,000 for The Beatles at Number 1, and just 28 votes ahead of The Jordanaires) and Number 8 in British Vocal Group. They managed joint third place with Vanity Fare in the Best New Group category, behind Jethro Tull and Blue Mink. Zeppelin could only made seventh in the British Blues Group ranking, just five votes behind Chicken Shack, with Fleetwood Mac, The Rolling Stones, and The Moody Blues taking the top three places. Robert Plant came 15th in the British Male Singer poll. The rippling-out impact of *Led Zeppelin II* and 'Whole Lotta Love' in particular would rewrite these charts to an unimaginable degree during the next 12 months.

The end of the 1960s was coincidentally more of a defining moment for the rock industry than anyone could have expected. The wave of talent and energy that had swept through the 1960s starting with The Beatles in 1962-63 had begun to exhaust itself. In 1969 alone, The Beatles had effectively disbanded (although no announcement would be made until spring 1970). In The

Rolling Stones, Brian Jones had been removed from their ranks and had died that summer, and the memory was still fresh of the disastrous events at an open-air concert in early December 1969 at San Francisco's Altamont Speedway, where a member of the audience was murdered. The Stones themselves were going through a sobering re-evaluation, reflected in part in the music of their darkest, most introspective album, *Let It Bleed*.

As has been said often since, Altamont signalled the termination of the hippie dream that had enjoyed its messy apotheosis just four months earlier at Woodstock. Signalling the end of another type of dream, in November 1969 John Lennon had released 'Cold Turkey', his public confession of his earlier addiction to heroin. Cream and Traffic had foundered, and the band that arose from their ashes, Blind Faith, barely survived its first US tour. Jimi Hendrix, a relative latecomer in this group of superstars, remained the biggest box-office draw of them all in the USA – his absence from Britain was reflected in his poor showing in that *NME* poll – but had not released a new record since autumn 1968.

On the other side of the Atlantic, Motown may have been going from strength to strength, but established acts such as The Beach Boys and The Byrds had witnessed precipitous declines in the sale of their new releases, while early West Coast alternative bands such as The Doors, The Mamas & The Papas, and Jefferson Airplane had already peaked. While their cultural influence remained strong into the early 1970s, these groups' sales never approached the levels of Led Zeppelin's records. Bob Dylan was back, but he was consciously sidelining the role of counterculture leader that had been imposed upon him until his brush with mortality in a motorcycle accident in 1966. From now on he would consciously pursue an altogether more personal vision in his music and lyrics, a process that would reach a peak of sorts with *Blood On The Tracks* in 1974.

Led Zeppelin's emergence – alongside Santana, Jethro Tull, Crosby Stills & Nash, and Creedence Clearwater Revival – was a clear indication that a new generation of bands and fans for those bands had arrived. This was no repeat of The Monkees. John Paul Jones had an idea that it was timing as well as sheer hard work and talent that got Led Zeppelin their break. He told an interviewer that December: "I suppose it's a combination of a good band and the time it broke. Cream had gone, other groups had an even chance of getting in, but somehow we made it."

Although Zeppelin could afford to slow down somewhat in the wake of their fourth North American tour and second album, in fact they took little time off as the new decade began. They were due to play eight gigs in Britain in January 1970, their first tour of any sort at home since mid 1969. Jones explained why. "We don't need to tour England in the new year," he said just prior to its start. "I know everyone goes on at us about our apparent desertion of the country, but if we didn't go to America they'd accuse us of deserting them. After all, they made us what we are and they also buy an awful lot of records. One feels an obligation to Britain in general and, after all, we are a British group, so why shouldn't it be a tour of Britain?"[6]

This in a nutshell explains the dichotomy between Led Zeppelin's apparently single-minded pursuit of American audiences and their appreciation of their British fans. To realise their ultimate career ambitions they had to conquer the American market. To generate the levels of cash needed to finance their plans, let alone whatever lifestyles they may have wanted individually and collectively, the US market was essential. Every major British act of the day was faced with the same choice, and very few indeed chose not to pursue success on the other side of the Atlantic, or consolidate it when it came their way.

Each member of the band gave lengthy interviews to *Disc* that were published weekly to coincide with the live British dates in January. Bonham revealed a degree of self-awareness not always attributed to him in retrospect, admitting that he needed constant stimulation from his surroundings.

"I like people around me all the time – parties, going out, and general looning. I suppose I'm a bit of a noisy person – in fact I'm probably the noisiest of the four of us. … Otherwise I'm still the same person. I enjoy decorating and gardening and I'm still as hot-headed as ever. I'm a bit quick-tempered – I never sit down to think about things."[7]

Bonham also noted with approval the interpersonal balance in the band. "We're not too close, not so that every little thing bothers us."[8] This and the respect they shared for each other as musicians meant that Led Zeppelin did not suffer from the crippling ego storms that did for so many groups who broke through big but cracked up in the process.

Robert Plant, in his *Disc* interview, showed opposite leanings to his friend Bonham. He referred directly to the change in his physical circumstances as therapeutic to his soul, giving him the peace and time he'd craved. "It's exactly what I've always wanted. It gives me room to think, breathe and live. I wake up in the morning and there are no buses, no traffic. Just tractors and the odd pheasant hooting in the next field. I was pretty fed up with humanity in the big cities. … You can walk around London at night and it doesn't matter whether you're the king or the queen, you'll still have a bad time." He also thought that day-to-day living with fame was easier in the country. "If you're popular, everybody wants to know you, so really to me London is a very shallow place. All those

Manager Peter Grant and John Bonham share a joke in Denmark, February 1970.

Speakeasy and Revolution Club people don't want to know you if you're on the way up or down."[9]

Plant had from childhood enjoyed the countryside and living away from cities, and while a good deal of his feelings of distaste for the urban rat-race can be identified as part of the general hippie mindset of the time, there is little doubt that, away from Zeppelin, he was at his happiest with his family out in the country. This impulse would soon prove a key element in the way the band wrote material for their third album.

With the brief UK tour looming, followed by Europe in February-March 1970 and then their fifth American tour taking up most of the rest of March and April, the band had plenty of forward commitments to deal with. Their enthusiasm for playing onstage together and exploring their collective creativity was as strong as ever. As Jones put it: "I don't get bored playing onstage with the band. I don't mind being in the background. I wouldn't like to be out front playing like Jimmy. To be any sort of artist, you have to be an exhibitionist. I am, but not over anyone else in the business. … I would like to think that if we have to stop actually touring, we'll be in a position to make records together, because this particular combination of people turned out nice things, I think. And I've been around long enough to know that few combinations of people actually work."[10]

Grant, despite his qualms about the medium, had been busy brokering a television deal. As *Record Mirror* reported late that January: "A Led Zeppelin TV spectacular has been sold to American TV: filming began at the Royal Albert Hall [and] a special album will be issued to coincide with the screening of the show in the States."[11] Just what shape this proposed spectacular was intended to take is difficult to determine now. Page talked to Chris Welch about it early in February, claiming: "We are working on a film. I don't know if it will ever be shown really, but we filmed the Albert Hall concert and it will be a documentary on what has been going on with the band."[12]

In an uncanny echo of the film project surrounding Jimi Hendrix's February 1969 Albert Hall concert and subsequent European tour, the programme was never completed or broadcast, but the Albert Hall concert of January 9th certainly was filmed: much of it was issued on the band's 2003 *DVD* set. The brief liner notes to that set claim the concert was "originally pro-shot on 16mm film for a BBC TV documentary". But the project was shelved and nothing came of it for over 30 years.

Grant claimed much later that technical problems prevented the film's use. He told Dave Lewis: "We filmed [the Albert Hall] and I think some of the Bath Festival. We did it with Stanley Dorfman and, believe it or not, he used the wrong speed film and it came out too dark. So that was no use."[13] Other comments by Page at the time of *DVD* in 2003 suggested a more confused picture where

business and artistic elements were eddying together in an unsolvable tangle. At one stage they saw rough edits, he said, "and they hadn't captured certain bits, and we thought, 'Is it worth it?' By the time we got to see it we were beyond it anyway."[14] Perhaps with the band developing so quickly at this point – and the coming stylistic shift of new material in the spring – Page's observation about being "beyond it" is the crucial point.

But there were business reasons. As with Hendrix's earlier Albert Hall film, a deal was struck with third parties so that the filming could be done alongside multi-track audio recording. Page would use this multi-track audio for 'We're Gonna Groove' – reportedly from the soundcheck and with additional Page overdubs – to kick off the band's final album, *Coda*, in 1982.

But this was not the sound source for the soundtrack. As Page went on to explain in 2003: "We had recorded and documented via 16mm a performance back in 1970 [at] the Royal Albert Hall. And there was quite a number of disputes over copyright of this material, and in the end it was sold to somebody who acquired it from one of the cameramen. And it was going to be auctioned at Sotheby's and, in actual fact, at the end of the day, we managed to do a deal with the chap [in 1997] to get it back, even though one of the reels managed to go missing! But … you'll understand why it was so important to have this, because there was such precious little Zeppelin [filmed] material."[15]

What eventually appeared in 2003 – well over an hour of concert footage, beautifully shot and in excellent sound – demonstrates perfectly why Led Zeppelin were having such an enormous impact in their live shows. There are 12 complete songs from the Albert Hall in January 1970, with only the band's performance of 'Heartbreaker' missing from *DVD* because one reel of film covering its closing minutes had disappeared. Although the spotlight falls mostly on Page and Plant as the two lead men, there is such a strong chemistry between all four members that you get a real sense of music being worked out and created before your eyes.

The band had song structures and routines through which they would play, but those structures were never a straitjacket. If Page, Jones or Bonham had a new twist to add, it was presented to the other two and pursued for all it was worth. As Jones recalled: "I always used to start the show fairly near the front of the stage, and then during the first number I'd move back and end up underneath John's ride cymbal. That was my favourite place, because

Jimmy Page manipulating the guitar for his own purposes as strings, pickups and frets become one during a live solo.

Overleaf: Onstage in Europe, early 1970. "You had to be on the ball, especially in the improvised parts, because the stuff would change all the time," said John Paul Jones.

I could feel that bass drum, rather than rely on the monitors. And of course I could see John from under the cymbal, because he was on a drum riser and I could look up at him. That way we'd play really tight together."[16] Such close communication, though not unknown in bands of that time, was relatively rare. After all, there were not many bands who were truly improvising together onstage: most were playing a strictly routined set of songs where virtually every note and interpretation had been worked out in advance. Most lead guitarists of the time had pre-set solos that were re-created note for note each night. Led Zeppelin, along with the very best of their peers, were sufficiently gifted, together and adventurous to take risks every time they played onstage together.

To do so required iron-clad concentration, and this level of performance can be seen in the film footage of the Albert Hall date. Jones explained: "You had to be on the ball in those days, especially in the improvised parts, because the stuff would change all the time. You'd have to watch each other for cues. There was a lot of eye contact. Page always looked as though he was looking at the floor, but we'd watch each other's hand movements all the time. There would often be seemingly amazing unrehearsed stops and starts. We'd all go *bang* – straight into it. The audience would think, 'How did they do that?' It was because we were paying attention."[17]

These intense sessions of music-making in front of their audiences sometimes meant they sprang musical surprises on each other that perhaps no one else in the hall would notice. "Lots of things happened onstage to alter the songs," said Jones. "In the fast part to 'Dazed And Confused' John and I would turn the riff round backwards and Pagey would come across and shout, 'What the fucking hell do you think you're doing!' That was good fun."[18]

Plant may be thought of by some as an onlooker during the long instrumental passages when he was not singing or playing harmonica. But that would be to misread his role, as demonstrated conclusively in the Albert Hall film. Plant doesn't spend all his time striking poses and prancing around the stage demanding to be the centre of all attention. He puts on his own spectacle, but his movements and expressions are a reaction to what his fellow band members are playing. His manipulation of the microphone and its cord during Page's solos might be thought of in isolation as a posture, but it is not. He's doing his own version of air guitar in reaction to what he's hearing.

Plant has talked about this a number of times in interviews over the years. Recently he said: "Some of the crucial elements in the performances were those indefinable moments inside the actual music. There was a feeling of reaching and stretching for something that wasn't quite so evident on the records. Playing live was the real jewel in our existence."[19]

On an earlier occasion, Plant revealed that during his first years in the band he often used to stand onstage thinking what a privilege it was to witness this remarkable music making. His movements were a reaction to that music. He underlined the spontaneous nature of his stage presence; although he was being written about as a new rock sex symbol, he didn't see it that way at all. "I don't really know what or how people think about sex symbols. … Really you can't take it seriously. You just get into your music and the sexual thing isn't really apparent to you. It's simply not what you're there for." The audience were people in whom you found inspiration. "Without the audience throwing back vibrations, I just couldn't do it," he commented. "When you're looking into those thousands of faces, it just seems to pour out of me."[20]

The film shows that Led Zeppelin worked very hard at the music, drew their inspiration from each other and the excitement of the crowd, and delivered everything they had to give musically on that particular evening. It also details the very different nature of their act compared to other bands of the time. It is true that Plant would be uninvolved musically sometimes for minutes on end and that, for example, Page would be in the spotlight for long stretches. But he wasn't merely taking a cranked-up guitar-hero solo during those periods. He was constantly interacting with the bass and drums to roll in and out of different themes, sections, riffs, and rhythms, to create different angles to the same music, to change tempo, to inject a huge range of variations on the basic structure that the band toyed with during any given piece.

The musicians were taking enormous chances, working collectively and pulling off some stupendous performances. It was with these methods that they were able to evolve such long and ever-shifting versions of 'Dazed And Confused', 'How Many More Times', and 'Whole Lotta Love'. Similarly, a guitar feature instrumental such as 'White Summer'/'Black Mountain Side' finds Page seated onstage playing his Danelectro, sticking relatively close to the outline of the piece that Zeppelin had been essaying for the past year, but allowing for twists and turns in detail and new phrases and glisses in response to what Bonham, especially, was contributing behind him.

The onstage jams were crucial to Page in developing the germs of ideas he had for new riffs, tunes and patterns that would be used at some future point in new Led Zeppelin songs. It was during this early period of the band's live work that Page made rapid progress with a guitar technique he'd initiated in his Yardbirds days, and which many observers of the day took to be something of a pose: his use of a violin bow.

People with technical knowledge about the structure of the violin and guitar families of instruments will know that bowing a guitar is a completely different proposition to bowing a violin. On a guitar, the strings are not positioned on an arched bridge, and the neck is flat. The arch in a violin bridge means that each string is available to be bowed individually. With the flat bridge of a guitar, only the outermost two strings can be bowed individually: the only other option with a guitar is to bow combinations of notes, from double stops up to complete six-string chords.

Such difficulties had stopped any serious exploration of bowing techniques before Page, as it seemed of minimal use – although Eddie Phillips in British group The Creation also occasionally deployed a bow on electric guitar. The Albert Hall footage shows that Page had managed to turn any limitations into a strength. He concentrates on the sheer colour and texture of the sounds generated by the bow in combination with the electronics available to him and the great sonic weight brought about by extreme amplification.

He may not have been harnessing the power of electronics in the same way as Hendrix, but he was finding his own original path. That it was a serious pursuit he made perfectly clear a number of times. "I'd like to play violin but that's not as easy as it looks," he said at the time. "When I use a violin bow on guitar it's not just a gimmick, like people think. It's because some great sounds come out. You can employ legitimate bowing techniques and gain new scope and depth."[21]

The onstage alchemy that allowed Page to push these experiments with sounds into new areas each night was an important workshop of ideas for the future of the band. Seen from that point of view, Plant's oft-repeated comments about how a single change in personnel at its inception would have resulted in a radically different band make a great deal of sense.

Plant himself is a prime example, for he was one of very few singers not only deeply knowledgeable about the blues, folk music and other forms, but also willing to be spontaneous, to improvise onstage, and always to be on the lookout for new ways to present his contributions to the songs that allowed for a great deal of latitude in their interpretation. In the Albert Hall film this is evident when he scats (uses wordless vocals) in the longer numbers. His game-for-anything attitude is crucial to the success of such songs, as is his ability to react quickly to the changes to a song of the type Jones described. He is quick on his musical feet and is not easily fazed. Not only that, but Plant gets off on the challenge that such situations throw his way.

Plant has self-confessedly had a long fascination with what is often termed 'authentic blues'. Just what music is covered by such a phrase is highly questionable, but Plant enjoyed a deep and genuine love for and knowledge of the blues performers of the 1920s and '30s, as well as the post-war greats such as B.B. King and Muddy Waters. What is much more rarely acknowledged about Plant's own work is that he translates that love into some powerful blues singing and harp playing of his own. The reason is simple and yet not obvious.

Apart from possessing the voice and talent to do these things, Plant learned the vital lessons from mentors such as Robert Johnson, Tommy McClennan, and Skip James. The biggest lesson of all was to express your own feelings and thoughts; Plant had realised that well before his recruitment for Led Zeppelin. In 1970 he claimed: "I always respected Stevie Winwood, I must admit. He was to me the only guy. … [He] was only a little bit older than me and started screaming out all these things, and I thought: 'God, that's what I've been trying to do.'"[22]

Winwood was a huge talent with the rare capacity to express deep feelings from within himself without artifice. Plant could have hardly found a better contemporary soul-mate. So, although others may have found Plant and Page's 'Bring It On Home' some sort of affront to Sonny Boy Williamson, the humour and the sheer sparkiness in Plant's vocals and harp work point to a very different purpose. Plant and Page worked directly from the spirit of the originals and brought their own personalities to bear on them. They were not making slavish, empty copies, but were re-defining how those blues forms could apply to their own age.

Being white boys from England meant that they got plenty of criticism for this – just as Eric Clapton, Steve Winwood and others of that time did. But not from other musicians. Indeed, as with Jimi Hendrix, by the time Led Zeppelin's decade or more as a band had ended, blues musicians the world over were incorporating many of their ideas and techniques into their own playing. Today, whole blues tribute albums have been recorded and released. Back in 1970 it wasn't always evident that such honours would eventually come Zep's way, but the overall level of musicianship in the band was astonishingly high.

All four were particularly widely-read in music and capable of using what they heard in others to good advantage. Page, for example, talked knowledgeably in interviews at this time about music far beyond the rock charts. When asked by Chris Welch whether he was a fan of what was then called jazz-rock and later fusion, he pinpointed the pomposity and lack of sincerity behind Blood Sweat & Tears' music, drawing an unfavourable but entirely accurate comparison with Colosseum. In the same context, he underlined his appreciation of some of the contemporary jazz greats. "I like and understand Eric Dolphy and John Coltrane, but when you get Fred Bloggs blowing away – it doesn't come off."[23]

Perversely, the filmed Albert Hall concert received a mixed live review at the time from Raymond Telford in *Melody Maker*. Claiming that the gig "very nearly met with disaster" he justified this by saying: "From the start there didn't seem to be the excitement that should have preceded a Zeppelin appearance. It took them nearly the whole of their set to get the fires blazing."[24] It is not clear how the writer squared this with his admission that Plant had the audience eating out of his hand by the time they were playing 'How Many More Times' and that they were called back for no fewer than five encores. This was the type of review that drove Plant and Page to distraction.

Plant was able to take a more philosophical view on the whole event some 30 years later. "At the time, one would never have thought that it was reviewable," he told Dave Schulps in 2003. "To look at [the Albert Hall film] now and give it any kind of title or any kind of credence or any kind of reflection is something so far removed from what was happening in those days in 1970. It could've all been over by the fall – it could have been gone. I'd have made a great car salesman."[25]

The rest of the UK tour went ahead to largely good reviews, wide publicity, and high spirits as the second album peaked in the charts on both sides of the Atlantic. Page and Bonham took the chance to get involved in the production of the *Screaming Lord Sutch & His Heavy Friends* album, along with other stars such as Jeff Beck, Hendrix bassist Noel Redding, and session pianist Nicky Hopkins. The only check on all this – and it was serious at the time – was Plant's car crash on January 31st. *Melody Maker*'s News Extra column reported: "Led Zeppelin vocalist Robert Plant was hurt in a road crash on Saturday returning from Mothers Club, Birmingham, where he had been to see Spirit. A mini van and his Jaguar collided and both cars were written off. Plant was taken to Kidderminster Hospital with a badly cut face and smashed teeth, but he discharged himself on Monday and is spending the week at home."[26]

The item concluded with Plant's hope that he'd be fit in time for the last date of the brief UK tour, originally scheduled for February 7th at Edinburgh's Usher Hall, but this had to be cancelled to allow the singer time to recover from his injuries. It was a serious set-back for the band and the first intimation of its members' collective and individual mortality, a full 12 months on from escaping unharmed from the snowbound wastes of Washington state in midwinter when all of nature seemed ranged against them.

Page commented at the time: "Everything has slowed up with Robert's accident. That was a horrific scene. The police came banging at the door with flashlights and asked me if I knew a Mr Robert Plant. When they advised me to call him at Kidderminster Hospital I knew it had got to be serious. I was really worried, wondering if he had the baby in the car. He's still in a bad way and we had to cancel some work, although he said he would appear onstage in a wheelchair. He can't lift his arm above his shoulder and he has a cut over his eye."[27]

The accident extended the relative break the band had enjoyed since the turn of the new year, giving Page in particular time to make progress on ideas for the third album – about which Atlantic executives were already making enquiries. As he told Chris Welch when interviewed at his Pangbourne boathouse, discussing the bother of a non-stop ringing phone: "I was editing tapes yesterday for the next LP, and you need your wits about you for that. There were interruptions all the time which made it a long job."[28]

He went on to reveal just how much thought had already gone into the third Led Zeppelin album, even at this early stage. "We've got a lot of recording to do. ... I've prepared a lot of acoustic stuff for the next album. It's just a matter of getting into a studio. They're all fully booked – it's incredible. We all do a lot of writing in the group and make tape recordings of ideas for songs. I like to get a basic construction together and a number grows from that."[29]

In this same interview Page was concerned about the perception of rock music and his own band's perceived place in what was then being called the 'rock revolution'. He said: "There should be a lot more written about it because pop is going through a very revolutionary stage at the moment. I saw the Jack Bruce film on TV [Tony Palmer's BBC *Omnibus* feature on Bruce, *Rope Ladder To The Moon*] and I was quite amazed. He was tremendous. The whole message was: just listen to the music. That's what it's all about. Many classical people listen to pop music. They realise pop is not just a joke. Critics like Tony Palmer in *The Sunday Times* have helped it all to an incredible extent."[30]

Within a fortnight of completing the Edinburgh leg of the UK tour (delayed until February 17th), a new type of adversity appeared. Three dates into a February-March tour of Europe – a tour diplomatically described by Bonham to the *Gøteborgs-Posten* as "pure charity; the money here is pocket-money compared to what we get in the USA"[31] – the Led Zeppelin bandwagon ran into a roadblock by the name of Frau Eva von Zeppelin, according to Richard Cole "a direct descendent of Count Ferdinand von Zeppelin, the aeronautical legend".[32] She claimed to be guarding the honour of her family name and demanded through the press that the band desist from using 'Zeppelin' in their name while working in Denmark.

The dispute was not a new one; Page's comments to *Melody Maker* the week before the Danish gig imply that the problem had been brewing for some time. He said: "The whole thing is absurd. The first time we played Copenhagen [in October 1969] she turned up and tried to stop a TV show. She couldn't, of course, but we invited her to meet us to show we were nice young lads. We calmed her down, but on leaving the studio, she saw our LP cover of an airship in flames and exploded! So – it's shrieking monkeys now! But she is quite a nice person."[33]

In later years, Jones called her a "bit of a mad woman".[34] Peter Grant, not normally a man to avoid confrontations, this time proposed the simple expediency of playing the opening Copenhagen gig under a different name, for one night only. This led to speculation in the national press about the names the band might use, one of which – Ned Zeppelin – at least made Page laugh. After some confused discussion within the band, Page told the press: "We shall call ourselves The Nobs when we go to Copenhagen." He and Grant had decided that a gig under a joke name like The Nobs would be no hardship.

This turned out to be quite true. The publicity generated by this adroit sidestep was instant and worldwide. It made Frau von Zeppelin's obduracy look absurd and revealed a likeable streak of self-deprecating but witty low-life humour in the band, winning new fans to their cause. It was class warfare with a laugh. The rest of the tour provided the normal high-octane live sets from the band and confirmed their huge popularity in this part of Europe, as well as their propensity for two-hour-plus sets.

There were no more larger-than-life events such as the intervention of Frau von Zeppelin. It was a perfect prelude to the looming fifth American tour, due to start in late March and last a month. It was only to be hoped that Plant, still recovering from his car-crash injuries, would be up to it.

GOT THEM WELSH MARIN COUNTY BLUES, MAMA

- 5TH AMERICAN TOUR

- PAGE & PLANT'S WELSH RETREAT

- HEADLEY GRANGE & STUDIO SESSIONS FOR 3RD ALBUM

- BATH FESTIVAL

As with Led Zeppelin's first US tour, their spring 1970 visit started on the West Coast, with the first date in Vancouver, Canada, on March 21st. It was preceded by press articles emphasising just how big the act had become. *Disc* reported that the band's gross earnings for 1970 would top £2 million – nearly $5 million at the time – and that their first two albums had clocked up no fewer than seven million sales worldwide, with the second album already registering more than two million sales in the USA alone.

The band was news in the local press and broadcasting media wherever they went, prompting obsessive reports about their sudden sky-high earnings, the power of their live shows and the frenzied enthusiasm of the fans. There were even articles about the amount of gear being hulked around, the costs involved and the number of road crew needed to run it. Each member of the band gave multiple interviews, many of them literally snatched at airports, backstage, or anywhere a journalist could persuade them to part with a few words.

This was the type of media treatment The Beatles had been living with since 1963. For all four members of Led Zeppelin, it was of course a new ordeal: not even Jimmy Page had experienced it during his Yardbirds days. Every cliché in the book was pressed into service by a voracious media that had become notably more intrusive and questioning than in the days of The Beatles' rise to fame, including endless speculation that the band was on the verge of splitting up.

This last point particularly annoyed Page, who was justly proud of what he'd fashioned with the band in just 18 months and who knew that there was an exceptionally strong bond between the four musicians. He told one reporter: "There is no reason to split up. There is nothing inherent musically in Led Zeppelin to harm or destroy it. There is variety, great freedom, and no restrictions on the players whatsoever."[1] This was true: the very way in which the band functioned, its internal balance, meant that there really was no reason for them to fall apart through internal dissatisfaction or bruised egos. Everybody was aware that the band was bigger than anything any of them, however talented they may be, could do solo.

Going into their first US tour of the new decade, physically they were running on empty much of the time, given the rigours of the past 18 months. But as ever they were determined to give the best value at their concerts. This in particular was important, considering the accusations of hype that continued to float around them, insinuating that in some obscure way the band were ripping off their fans. Such suspicions were part of a larger malaise making itself felt at the heart of the so-called counter-culture as it splintered and lost heart in the face of its own schisms and attacks from establishment forces in the media and in western governments. Led Zeppelin found the charge both offensive and wrong. They took it to heart and publicly defended themselves repeatedly during this period.

They had come to prominence just as the hippie revolt of the late 1960s was imploding. The enemies of the movement had long ago been identified and rejected, the lines drawn, but now various factions were turning upon each other. As Richard Nixon intensified the war in Vietnam – the one ongoing event that all counter-cultural forces could unequivocally identify as being against – and began his undermining of prominent liberal and left-leaning figures and institutions in the USA, different pressure groups began agitating for their own advancement at the cost of others. Allied to this, especially in America, the recreational drugs of choice for rock stars and middle-class youth moved on from so-called 'soft' drugs such as LSD and marijuana into the much more exciting and volatile realms of cocaine and uppers and downers. There was also a rash of high-profile heroin dependencies. John Lennon's addiction had been the most publicised because of his decision in 1969 to make public his habit as well as his eventual recovery.

None of this came without social and economic cost, the ominous signs of which were becoming plain to see for those who cared to look. Cocaine and the like supplied a much more direct connection – literally – to the underworld that largely controlled those drugs. With cannabis, it had been possible even to grow your own – another part of the hippie dream – and so avoid any association with criminal elements or their offshoots. Cocaine, heroin and its derivatives made that impossible. 'Support your friendly local hood' became the unofficial way of life for scores of people looking for a quick route to ecstasy and social acceptance.

Another acute problem that Led Zeppelin faced in their relations with the music media in particular – especially the self-appointed guardians of the counter-culture – was that they were not paying lip service to fashionable political and social causes in their lyrics or music. Regardless of the fact that Plant had many of the aspirations of the hippie culture in which he'd grown up, the band's music was harsh, fast and aggressive, and their lyrics almost exclusively drawn from the worldly mindset of the blues. On the first two albums the subject matter stuck closely to sex, sensuality, proving one's manhood, romantic love, groupies, and the difficulties faced by people in the easy-come easy-go relationships that musicians have always enjoyed or endured.

None of this touched on the quasi-spiritual, cosmic, mystical, social or even political preoccupations of the counter-culture spokesmen. From this point of view, Led

Julie Felix introduces Jimmy Page on her BBC TV show as "a very talented and special musician" before he plays a solo acoustic version of 'White Summer' / 'Black Mountain Side'.

Zeppelin were deeply suspect to the so-called 'underground'. For their fans, of course, the lyrics spoke of close personal concerns that any spotty youth could understand in a flash. After all, these musicians were mostly only a few years away from their teens themselves. Plant had been just 19 years old at the time of his first US tour back in early 1969.

The music that accompanied these lyrics was a perfect complement, fuelling the adrenalin rush of the entire experience, live or on vinyl. Plant and Page may have been fans of Joni Mitchell, for example, and Plant had long admired West Coast progressive rock, both LA and San Francisco varieties, but all this had yet to filter through into their own creations. So the band continued to be perceived by some as a crude rock circus with too many low-life associations for comfort. The irony was, of course, that this was precisely where rock'n'roll had started its spectacular life, with Elvis's swivelling hips, Little Richard's blatant selling of sex and excitement, and the glowering danger in the performances of Gene Vincent and Eddie Cochran, among many others.

In that respect, at least, Led Zeppelin were the most traditional of 1970s red-hot properties, though few saw it that way. It was perhaps significant that when Page was asked around this time whether he thought Led Zeppelin a 'progressive rock' band, he said: "I've been waiting for somebody to ask me that. I don't know. What we have done is present rock in a different package. We are not a band like [Pink] Floyd, which are really progressive. Maybe our next album will be progressive – for us."[2] It certainly would be. It would usher in an entirely new phase of Led Zeppelin's career.

The fifth American tour, meanwhile, was a success like its predecessors. It was also the first to feature no warm-up acts. Peter Grant had reckoned that the band positively enjoyed being onstage, while they regularly delivered sets well in excess of two-and-a-half hours. So the fans – who after all had come to see Led Zeppelin – were getting real value for money at a time when most headline acts would deliver one-hour sets after the intermission plus maybe a couple of encores. Now with Zeppelin there wasn't even an intermission. The band commanded the stage until they had finished what they wanted to do. According to Richard Cole: "The band felt liberated by Peter's decision. As the sole act on the bill, they would have full control of the entire show. And the idea excited them. Some nights, they felt like playing until morning."[3]

Some of the songs now stretched to something like 25 or even 35 minutes, with an average around seven or eight minutes – three to four times as long as the average pop single. Of all the other acts out on the road in 1970 the only other one capable of delivering such blistering extended performances was Jimi Hendrix, and he just happened to be the biggest box-office draw of the day.

Clearly, both acts were tapping into a real and urgent demand for thrilling and eventful extemporised concerts.

In a synchronicity that was perhaps rather more than coincidence – the two hardly wanted to compete against each other for the same audience – Hendrix began what would turn out to be his last American tour on April 21st 1970 at The Forum in Los Angeles, just three days after Led Zeppelin's own tour concluded in Phoenix, Arizona. A *New Musical Express* news item in early May, while the tour was still gathering momentum, reported: "Led Zeppelin are enjoying fantastic success on their fifth tour here. The itinerary of 26 concerts will gross $1,200,000 for the group. Almost every city they played has been sold out."[4] The band and Grant were quite obviously in tune with their audience's musical needs.

Page might have been liberated by the idea of evening-long sets, but before they'd got into their stride he found he'd lost a prized guitar. Somehow in the transfer between planes getting the band through Canada en route to Boston, a thief had lifted a black Gibson Les Paul Custom from one of the baggage trolleys. Richard Cole had to break the news to Page back at the band's hotel. "He kicked a nearby sofa. 'Richard, this is ridiculous! Do you know how much I love that guitar?' I couldn't recall ever seeing Jimmy quite this angry."[5]

Page was not just throwing a rock star tantrum; he was a serious guitar collector who cherished the instruments he played for their intrinsic qualities. Losing a guitar was like losing a particular voice, given each instrument's distinct personality. Page arranged for an ad to be placed in *Rolling Stone* magazine requesting the recovery of the guitar, no questions asked, but alas there was no response. The depth of his frustration can be gauged by the fact that, as late as 1973's US tour, he would place another ad in *Rolling Stone* asking for the return of the guitar. But the guitar was never returned, mirroring Page's loss of a similar model in Australia in 1967.

The band stuck largely to the first two albums for the tour's repertoire. *Led Zeppelin II* was still very fresh in the minds and ears of most fans, but one or two portents of the third disc did crop up occasionally. 'Since I've Been Loving You' had a few outings, for example. It is indicative of the time it was written that, of the songs that eventually turned up on the third album, this one is perhaps closest to the atmosphere of the first two albums.

But most of the songs were yet to be written, as Plant observed. He told *Melody Maker* at the start of the tour: "We haven't prepared much material yet, but we have got a few things down. And it's all acoustic, folks! You can just see it, can't you: 'Led Zeppelin go soft on their fans' or some crap like that." He also revealed that he and Page had made plans to get away from the stresses and strains of life in the rock lane to write material together after the tour ended. "Jimmy and I are going to rent a little cottage near the River [Dyfi] in Wales where we can lock ourselves away for a few weeks just to see what we can come up with when there's no one else around. The next album will probably come out of that."

Despite the impact of the inevitable long-term tiredness brought about by incessant touring since the autumn of 1968, as well as Plant's accident and recovery, the band were enjoying everything about their gigs and kept their humour intact. As Plant elaborated: "I really enjoy the raving bit, like on 'Whole Lotta Love' I really enjoy watching their faces when I start it, and sometimes I sing the most ridiculous words to it. Then I look at their faces again to see if they've sussed it out, and if they haven't … then I laugh all the more." A rather more equivocal note was struck, however, in the same interview when Plant talked about his ultimate ambitions. "What we've got to do now is consolidate the position we've arrived at, so that eventually we'll be able to say what we really want to say and people will listen to it because it's us."[6]

The tour was a major popular success. Nonetheless it was accompanied by a mixed reception from the media, with some newspaper and magazine reviewers refusing to be caught up in the enthusiasm of the moment, sticking to their own aesthetic stances. Some of the reviews were more convincingly argued than others. On April 14th *The Montreal Star's* reporter went to great lengths to justify his contention that the band was "the most hyped group of them all". He argued: "The volume is turned up high and each note sounds like an avalanche. False meaning is thus attached to each sound; listeners are conned into the belief that because Led Zeppelin are ridiculously loud then they must necessarily play important music."

One wonders what this critic would have made of the premiere of Igor Stravinsky's *Rite Of Spring* or Woody Herman's First Herd in full cry. Volume, for better or worse, is conventionally used to emphasise strong emotion, but this reviewer obviously felt that Led Zeppelin had no emotion to express. "Guitar companies," he continued, "must be pleased with Jimmy Page's work because all he is doing is demonstrating with as much creativity as an encyclopaedia salesman the range of sounds and gimmicks that can come out of an electric guitar. Listening to Page was for me about as satisfying as watching a television picture signal."[7]

The band's extreme volume is beyond question, but the reviewer must have been one of a small handful at the time to find Led Zeppelin's music – and Page's playing in particular – unemotional. Bonham was aware of the high levels of emotional energy buzzing between the stage and the audiences on that tour. He told *The Memphis Free Press*: "You can see the reaction from the audience. They really do get involved. Something sort of very touching; they get very emotional about it, completely involved in a number. They don't just sit there and say, 'We're in the auditorium and watching.' … One reason is that music is

a very big outlet, really, isn't it? At the moment there are a lot of bad things, Vietnam and all these things. A large thing is that they can get to a concert, see a group they really like, and forget everything. … So many groups go out and try to be ultra-cool. I don't dig it. We like to put our whole heart and soul into it."[8]

Bonham also scotched ill-informed gossip about his propensity for breaking drum heads in performance. The rumour had grown because of the colossal sound he generated, the weight of the sticks he used, and the number of sticks he would get through in an evening. Anyone with a moderate amount of exposure to a working rock band will know that a drummer will regularly break a few sticks, not necessarily because he is hitting harder than usual, but because sticks, by their nature and function, take a pounding, and any fault is quickly exposed. Sticks can also get slippery and fly out of a drummer's sweaty hand mid-song, necessitating that the drummer undertakes some eye-catching reaching-around for another stick. From such things, legends of brutal drum treatment can evolve.

Bonham wasn't interested in playing along with such legends. Asked how many drum heads he'd broken on this tour, he replied: "None. You can hit a drum hard if you take a short stab at it and the skin will break easily. But if you let the stick just come down, it looks as though [I'm] hitting it harder than I am. … That snare skin has been on there for three tours."[9] Bonham, who was a great student of the drums and drummers, knew which techniques to apply to get the greatest response from his kit. It was not just a case of hitting the skin. The drums had to be properly tuned for maximum reverberation, the materials they were made of similarly had to be right, and in many cases Bonham, like many other outstanding drummers, imported his own modifications with inner-drum linings and work on combinations of materials. He saw himself as part of a drumming tradition. In the same interview he singled out for special praise drummers from Gene Krupa to Ringo Starr, Ginger Baker to Carmine Appice.

Sceptical critics were not the only dampener on this tour. Page, always alert to social and political trends around him and as observant as ever, noticed a return to a troubled, divisive atmosphere in America. He had last commented publicly upon this when still a member of The Yardbirds, back in 1967. Zeppelin had walked offstage in Pittsburgh because they saw police violence against the audience. They had done so, Page explained, in the hope that it would help restore order. "That seemed to cool the police from running around sorting out the audience, and when we went back onstage after five or ten minutes, there was no trouble. What we're finding so often on this tour of the States is that the relations between police and audience are bad from the start, so it ends up with us having to cool them down."

Page gave an example of a girl who approached him to

allow her to watch the concert backstage "because last time at [Baltimore] the cops tear-gassed the place and I'm frightened of being out there".[10] As with so many other big acts of that time, Zeppelin were having to act as moderators at their own gigs at a time when American society was deeply divided by the changes in its society and an increasingly inglorious and unpopular war. On future tours the band would avoid such violent confrontations by hiring their own concert security, taking the pressure off its audiences. So much for Led Zeppelin being an overhyped band with no thought for the wellbeing of its audiences.

The last three gigs planned for the tour were in Memphis, Tennessee on April 17th; Phoenix, Arizona on the 18th; and Las Vegas, Nevada on the 19th. In Memphis the band got the best and worst that America had to offer them. By day they attended a civic ceremony where they were given the keys to the city. By night, with 10,000 fans in raucous mood, manager Peter Grant had a gun stuck in his ribs by a panicky promoter demanding they stop the show now to avoid a riot. Needless to say, the show went on and there was no riot.

All this tension, plus the rigours of the music-making and everything else associated with a major rock tour, finally took care of an already weakened Robert Plant. The following day, in Phoenix, Plant realised that his voice, after close on a gig every night for the past month, was about to disappear. Despite a horseback ramble in the country to get away from the unhealthy atmosphere of air-conditioned hotels, the backstage areas and other unsavoury urban hangouts, he was advised by a doctor on the day of the Phoenix show to stop singing immediately or risk permanent damage to his voice. Although the concert went ahead as it was too late to notify fans already on their way to the event, the following day's appearance in Las Vegas was scrapped.

With that the tour ended. Everyone was free to return to Britain. Amid press reports that the tour had set box-office records across the States and especially in Canada, the band were ready for an extended break while still on a popular high. With *Billboard* reporting that *Led Zeppelin II* had sold more than two million copies in the USA – only the second Atlantic label album to do so, along with Iron Butterfly's *In-A-Gadda-Da-Vida* – each band member headed for home and family to reacquaint themselves with everyday reality.[11]

That everyday reality had changed radically over the past few months. With the money now at their disposal they had all moved into new homes that more suited their aspirations. Jones and Page remained within a short drive of central London – Page kept his Pangbourne boathouse while Jones moved to Chorleywood in Hertfordshire, to

the north-west of London. Plant and Bonham, meanwhile, both bought farms in the Midlands. Bonham initially tended to take the traditional rock-star approach to owning a farm – that is, leave it to others to run. But Plant took very seriously indeed his role as owner of Jennings Farm (near Kidderminster, about 16 miles west of Birmingham) as the lyrics to 'Bron-Y-Aur Stomp', originally called 'Jennings Farm Blues', would suggest. He was intent on making it work as a farm, producing and personally tending small-scale crops of vegetables for his and his family's use.

Page began to take positive steps to further his fascination with the so-called 'great beast' Aleister Crowley by buying Crowley's former residence on the shores of Loch Ness near Inverness in Scotland. This first public association with the self-proclaimed devil worshipper and dabbler in the black arts was to give the general press a license to run free with wild accusations of similar Faustian pacts by Led Zeppelin members. Some of these stories persist to this day. They have no more grounding in fact than the stories of old Delta bluesmen standing at the crossroads to do deals with the devil for their own access to the alchemy of the blues. Page's involvement with Crowley's writings, life and artefacts, including his old haunts, was more that of a collector and connoisseur than a disciple.

The band enjoyed living fast and loose on the road, as did most of their contemporaries. It is debatable whether some of the more outrageous groupie-related events associated with their name even took place with most of them present. Many of these stories came in Richard Cole's 1993 autobiography that put him squarely in the middle of the mayhem, often only with Bonham as a collaborator. But there is also little reason to think that Zeppelin were any more mild-mannered on the road than anyone else. After all, they were still very young, experiencing tremendous popular success and adoration on a massive scale. They were bound to flex their personal and collective egos. It seems that the least apt to go this route was Jones, who largely preferred his own company and that of personal friends to groupies, other rock musicians, or drug connections.

Back home, none of this pertained. There were better things to do, such as hang out with families and girlfriends. The four individuals who made up Led Zeppelin had unwittingly found a good balance between the closeness a band finds on the road and the ability to leave each other in peace when not working together. Even so, Page and Plant in particular knew that this break in spring 1970 was a special time in the band's development. They were a band of musicians closely wedded to a work ethic that had already brought them staggering success, but they knew that this was the time to ready the material for the next, as-yet-untitled album in a new and untried way.

Jimmy Page in June 1970, looking forward to a rosy future for Led Zeppelin in Europe and the United States.

Plans had already been laid prior to the tour for Plant and Page to meet up after a week's rest and travel together with their respective partners plus Plant's daughter and the family dog to a cottage in rural Wales. There they would combine bucolic rest cures with musical creativity. It was not only an inspired piece of forward planning, but also a tacit acknowledgement of the enhanced role that Plant was now ready to play in the forming of the band's music and approach. This was something that had been coming for a while, but that Plant himself had consciously held back on, not wanting to disturb the wildly successful balance the band had struck at first in 1968-69. While still on the recent spring tour in America he'd told an interviewer: "In the beginning I held myself a long way away from [Jimmy]. The more you get into the bloke, although he seems to be quite shy, he's not really. He's got lots of good ideas for songwriting and he's proved to be a really nice guy."[12]

This congeniality towards one another was a variation on the notions then prevalent in counter-cultural America of getting back to the soil and taking a holistic approach to one's life and career. After so much speed, energy, and eventual sickness, these musicians knew they needed time and space to go on to the next stage. As Plant put it: "Zeppelin was starting to get very big and we wanted the rest of our journey to take a very level course. Hence the trip into the mountains and the beginning of the ethereal Page and Plant. I thought we'd be able to get a little peace and quiet and get your actual Californian, Marin County blues – which we managed to do in Wales rather than San Francisco."[13]

The idea was inspired by friends and role models a good deal closer to home than Marin Country. Plant and Page had long been in close touch with the developments and personalities in the British folk and folk-rock scene; they now wanted to understand more about how they could incorporate the subjects and approaches of Fairport Convention and The Incredible String Band into their own music. Plant felt that "hanging out with the String Band was pretty great, and they introduced me to these teachers who taught Bulgarian scales. It was part bluff and part absolute ecstasy, and the whole Zeppelin thing was moving into that area in its own way, going from 'You Shook Me' to 'That's The Way'."[14]

Plant knew the Welsh cottage well because his family had rented it for summer holidays in his childhood. Called Bron-Yr-Aur (Welsh for 'golden hillside'), the cottage was situated just north of Machynlleth in Powys, central Wales. In a relatively small and long-cultivated island like Britain it was about as far away from the madding crowd as you could get.

That this was to be a working holiday was evident from the start when two Led Zeppelin roadies, Clive Coulson and Sandy McGregor, were taken along to keep domestic things humming so that the musicians and their

partners were free to live, love, smoke some nice Moroccan hash and make music. Especially make music. Plant was aware in advance that Coulson and McGregor would be needed; he knew the cottage had no modern amenities such as electricity, sewerage, heating, or running water, and that given its location and situation it was guaranteed to be cold and damp in spring. Open fires would be essential. Coulson later recalled: "We collected wood for the open-hearth fire which heated a range with an oven either side. We had candles, and I think there were gaslights. We fetched water from a stream and heated it on the hot plates for washing – a bath was once a week in Machynlleth at the Owen Glendower pub."

The two roadies prepared the food, cleaned up and kept the house running, but neither felt taken for granted. "No, everyone mucked in really," said Coulson. "I wouldn't take any of that superior shit. They were wonderful people to work for, normal blokes. They weren't treated as gods – although Pagey was two people: one of the lads and the boss."[15]

There is little doubt that this working holiday was a watershed for Led Zeppelin in many ways. It re-wrote the relationship between the band's major songwriters. It altered for good the very nature of the music they were writing. And it established that their new approach would in fact sustain the band in the long term. Everyone associated with them knew that the pace and catch-as-catch-can approach to making records of the previous year was unsustainable. There had to be a fresh and more measured way of creating new music and so of ensuring their future existence as a band. This was the occasion when they found that way.

Plant had never made any secret of his preference for country life – the more primitive the better – and while Page had always been a city boy, he was very happy to explore new situations, whether it was overseas or in his own country. He saw the new sights and sounds that travel brought as an essential part of the creative process. What worked so well in this rural retreat was the combination of new landscapes for Page with complete peace and relaxation for Plant. They even had the freedom to choose what they did every day, from walking the hills and riding motorbikes along the trails and roads, to doing the fireside thing with guitar and notebooks in hand, harmonicas in pocket. They were a long way from being holed up somewhere in some luxury hotel with nothing to do and nowhere to go.

One particular spot known to Plant, by a small waterfall on the River Dyfi, became a regular haunt for the two working songwriters. Page had brought along his portable tape-recorder so that they would never lose a

Robert Plant: "Jimmy and I are going to rent a little cottage in Wales where we can lock ourselves away to see what we can come up with when there's no one else around."

good idea and could listen to fragments later, analyse them for their strongest elements, and then develop them. Many latter-day portrayals of this songwriting sojourn, conjuring carefree rambles with ideas tossed between the two men, betray a lack of familiarity with the sheer hard graft involved in the creative process. But everyone connected to the band would remember the absence of strain as a distinct contrast to the efforts needed to write and record the previous set of songs for *Led Zeppelin II*.

What is remarkable is the speed with which Plant and Page became attuned to each other's mode of creating songs, along with their compatibility when it came to what they were now trying to achieve and the directions they were looking to go in. Page was completely at ease with writing music on an acoustic guitar. He and Plant worked up new ideas and refashioned tunes they'd already made a start on. 'Jennings Farm Blues', for example, the song they'd started in the studio the previous December, was dismantled and reworked as – appropriately enough – 'Bron-Y-Aur Stomp'. Its new lyrics were a virtual description of what the friends were doing each day: walking down country lanes and singing songs. Another new song, 'Friends', celebrated their coming together at this time, along with their families. It reaffirmed their own strong connections and the band's central position in their lives.

This direct translation of Plant and Page's shared experience to their creative lives was a vital ingredient in their happy collaboration. Before, Page had not been comfortable writing lyrics; his talents and expertise were in other areas. Plant, apart from the direct love-ballad lyrics of 'Thank You' on *Led Zeppelin II*, had stuck pretty close to familiar blues metaphors and images, from 'squeeze my lemon' upwards. Now they were emboldened to move into special interests they either shared or had sympathy for in each other.

Plant, for instance, had a great enthusiasm not only for the West Coast bands that combined elements of rock and US folk – Crosby Stills Nash & Young, Neil Young on his own, and others – but the newly emboldened British branch of the movement. The way that in many instances this was bound up in a celebration of Celtic legends and history suited him exactly. He had a lively and growing interest in myths and legends, mostly of Norse or Celtic origin, and these were interwoven with the more prosaic folk roots of such lyric collections as Francis Child's *English And Scottish Popular Ballads*, which had inspired folk musicians like Joan Baez, Donovan, Sandy Denny and others to explore their own heritage.

Page too was interested in mythology. From an early date he had taken naturally to the role of expert amateur collector of artefacts, from paintings to manuscripts. His research had for some time centred on the life and works of Aleister Crowley. Crowley specialised in arcane and hermetic knowledge, combining these with pursuits more

closely associated with his own emotional and psychological needs and drives, from exploring his sexuality to a rummage around in the power of the blacker arts. This allowed Page too to use the rich and striking folk-myth imagery that Plant had started exploring. Plant, for example, has insisted that the line "we come from the land of ice and snow" in 'Immigrant Song' – written before the forthcoming trip to Iceland in June but with that experience later woven into the lyrics – was intended to have a humorous side, with its hints of Icelandic and Norse sagas pointing up Led Zeppelin's current position as conquerors of America.

It is important to remember that the songs created and worked on at Bron-Yr-Aur were early versions and, in some instances, consisted of incomplete ideas that would later take on new clothing or different directions. Not everything they wrote on acoustic guitar using unamplified voices, harmonica and hand-claps would remain exclusively acoustic in conception. Ideas started and developed this spring included such subsequent *Led Zeppelin III* material as 'Friends', 'Celebration Day', 'Gallows Pole', 'That's The Way', 'Hats Off To (Roy) Harper', and 'Hey Hey What Can I Do' (the B-side to 'Immigrant Song'). Also started were pieces that later became 'Poor Tom', 'Over The Hills And Far Away', 'Down By The Seaside', 'Bron-Yr-Aur' and 'The Rover' on subsequent albums through to 1982's *Coda*.

Additionally, they began work on sections of songs for the fourth album, including 'Going To California' and 'Stairway To Heaven'. 'Stairway' would prove a challenge to Page's creativity for the rest of 1970 as he fashioned each new part. Before the Bron-Yr-Aur experience he'd talked to the press about composing an extended piece, but now he had the patience and confidence to let it take its own form in its own time. Without even factoring in 'Stairway', the list of songs shows how far-reaching was the influence of these weeks on the band's subsequent musical history.

Meanwhile, Peter Grant had not been idle. Not only had he lined up a short burst of live activity in Europe to take care of the summer – two dates in late June, one in Iceland, and the important Bath Festival in England, plus four German appearances in mid July – he also had arranged to continue the filming of the band begun at the Albert Hall in January. The film was to be co-ordinated with the recording of the third album, which at the time was being confidently discussed as a July 1970 release.

With the previous band's gear unceremoniously disconnected to prevent an over-run, Led Zeppelin move into their stride at the 1970 Bath Festival on June 28th.

Overleaf: Manager Peter Grant planned the June 1970 Bath appearance as a spectacular set-piece, later describing it as a turning point for Led Zeppelin's status among UK fans.

Negotiations for the film's broadcast premiere continued as plans for its scope continued to expand. Grant told *Disc*: "A camera team will be travelling with them to Iceland on June 22nd and the whole thing should be tied up within a couple of months. I've already had offers for the film from America and I expect it to be shown in Britain by December."[16]

Later the same month, Bonham elaborated a little more about the film's contents. "It will probably be an hour-long semi-documentary and will include footage from the Royal Albert Hall concert. One of the highlights of the film will be a sequence featuring my four-year-old son Jason playing his drums."[17] The Albert Hall footage had been screened to band members in June. According to Plant: "It was really funny, the expressions with me muttering between numbers, and the terrible faces we made if there was a wrong note. We were roaring with laughter. If that's a representation of us, then it's the best I've seen."[18]

By the time Grant made his announcement about the film, Plant and Page had linked up again with their two bandmates and enthused about their Welsh idyll. There was no lack of enthusiasm for making the next album; it was more a matter of avoiding what had been imposed on them last time because of heavy touring commitments. They took the first step in preparing the material at Plant's Worcestershire farm, where the whole band gathered for rehearsals. This particularly suited Plant and Bonham, who now lived nearby, for they could balance work and family commitments; both had young children. By early June 1970, the band had the first batch of numbers ready to record.

An initial foray into Olympic studio in Barnes, west London, during May saw them start work on 'Friends' and 'Poor Tom', the latter a fine shuffle-beat update of country-blues elements, with one guitar section transforming parts of Robert Wilkins's 'That's No Way To Get Along'. But the four decided it would be much more congenial to record out in the countryside, in a parallel with Plant and Page's Bron-Yr-aur experience. They had Grant's office hunt out a country pile they could take over for a few weeks. They would rent some mobile recording equipment and allow the next album to emerge organically, just as the songs had at Bron-Yr-Aur.

Finally they located and hired a large, rather dilapidated Victorian house called Headley Grange in Hampshire, just to the south of Headley village and some 40 miles south-west of London. Plant fondly recalled it later as "an old workhouse that was supposed to be haunted and have ghosts and that, but it was in fact a tired house. [It] needed some love. And with the tired house and the tired furniture and the peace and the ability to work came an old black dog, who I think was quite deaf but insisted on following me everywhere I went."[19] The black dog would eventually find its own way into Led Zeppelin mythology.

For much of June and July, punctuated only by the spattering of live performances that Grant had booked for them, the band pulled together the majority of the new record in this old, damp, decaying building, savouring the camaraderie that the experience fostered as well as the peace generated by Headley Grange's isolation and character.

After the hardships of the previous set of American concerts, nobody missed the flash and filigree of touring. As Page said one evening while the band and their assistants were gathered around the huge fireplace in the main hall: "This is the way to do it from now on. I feel energised by this kind of place."[20] Jones was not exactly crazy about the location, remembering it later as cold, dank and uncomfortable, but he agreed that the band worked very well together there.

The musicians would fall into jams outside in the open air with any number of instrumental combinations, working up ideas or just enjoying the to-and-fro of collective workouts. They were also becoming very adept at working together in the studio on frameworks supplied by Plant and Page, building each piece with Page's guidance into a completed statement. Bonham would supply not simply a rhythmic accompaniment but rhythmic patterns and developments – as well as the choices of drums used and drumming techniques – and all this would help in establishing the very character and nature of each piece. Jones settled the rhythm and the specific riffs on bass, adding keyboards and other instruments where needed. He also, on occasion, supplied string arrangements. They were all fast workers.

None of the new pieces was in fact finished at Headley Grange, but most of the album took shape there. After that, the Headley tapes were taken to Island's recently refurbished Basing Street studio in north-west London's Notting Hill. The engineer was Andy Johns and the tape operator Richard Digby Smith. Both men were struck by the professionalism and swiftness of the band's working patterns. Johns said: "They worked fast. Pagey was really easy to get on with and I don't ever remember him having an emotional block, not knowing what to do."[21] The rest of the members were equally focused, working always as a team and looking to improve things rather than merely gripe at weaknesses or moan about perceived inadequacies.

The band were certainly working fast in the studio. By late June, just before the Bath Festival, an interview with Bonham was published where the drummer noted: "At the moment we've got ten good tracks laid down, and we have yet to do a couple more. If they turn out OK then we'll stick 'em on the album. The way things are going it looks as though it's going to be a long one. But again it's only going to be a single album. We're not going to do the expected double-album thing, simply because most of these are just padded out with studio leftovers. On the

Zeppelin's albums we only include what we all consider to be our very best material."[22]

Bonham clearly embraced the band's philosophy of uncompromisingly high standards for all aspects of their musical production. In the studio itself, he was often the one to carp about the results of a particular session. Richard Digby Smith said later: "Bonham was the one who'd complain. Always. 'It needs more *thrutch*.' ... But he was a great drummer, ... a naturally fantastic timekeeper and not a trudge merchant; very creative with sound."[23]

That Page was the ultimate arbiter in the recording process was never doubted or even questioned by the musicians or engineers. But that does not mean that Page was dictatorial at the sessions. Jones recalled in the early 1990s: "Generally, he didn't produce us in the studio as musicians. He didn't say, 'You do this, you do that.' There was none of that. We would produce each other, as it were. Especially for overdubs. Jimmy generally became a producer because he spent the longest time on the mixes. But it's not like he was a producer in the modern sense of the term. I would be in the box when he was overdubbing guitar, and he would be there when I was on bass overdubbing. We were both in the box when Robert was singing."[24]

Jones is surely right in this assessment of overall input, but Page was the band's guiding spirit and, with Plant, its major songwriter. These additional factors were important when it came to seniority. There was always discussion and input from all involved, but when it came to a final decision, or a re-think of a song or contribution, it was normally Page who quietly assumed responsibility. Tape operator Richard Digby Smith again: "It was a team effort, but Page had the final say. When Robert was singing, Page would be on the desk; not telling him what to do, working with him; and Robert would simply comply with enthusiasm. [Plant] was a lovely guy, sweet-natured."[25]

Robert Plant was happy to enthuse about the recording sessions to journalists. He told Roy Carr: "We are even using different instruments on some tracks. John Paul plays mandolin and Jimmy is on dulcimer. It'll be acoustic as well as electric, with the emphasis on everyone in the group."[26]

The band's appearance on June 28th at 1970's considerably expanded Bath Blues & Progressive Music Festival had been planned by Grant and Page to be Led Zeppelin's public declaration of loyalty to their British fans. If that was to work, they had to get it right, because no further British appearance was planned for the rest of the year. Grant let it be known that he'd turned down lucrative US gigs in order for the band to play Bath. Considering they'd be playing America extensively later that summer, this was not the huge financial sacrifice he was suggesting it to be.

Virtually the entire band said in the music press beforehand that they were making amends for their lack of British gigs in the past year, when their efforts had been directed towards America. The tone was almost apologetic, with justifications offered regarding their inability to drum up interest from UK booking agents and venues when the band was first formed back in summer 1968. Bonham's chat with *Record Mirror* was typical. "This is home and it's more important to do well in your own country," he said. "In the very early days, I suppose we did lose faith in England. After all that rehearsing, it was disarming to find you couldn't get a gig. It was the Fillmores in America that made us and the kids have been great ever since."[27]

If such interviews – appearing the day before the Bath set – were calculated to guarantee the band a good crowd and a warm response, the tactic worked. A weekend crowd estimated at over 150,000 turned up for the headline acts that on Saturday included an unannounced Donovan, It's A Beautiful Day, Steppenwolf, Johnny Winter, Pink Floyd, John Mayall, and, at dawn on the Sunday morning, Canned Heat. The overrun of time had been appalling and the weather even more miserable, with virtually non-stop rain all day and night. Anyone who was not soaked wet was shivering with cold in a tent or dropping off to sleep as the bands played on. Grant was deeply worried about what this meant for the official Sunday timetable, which started in the afternoon and featured acts such as Donovan (again), Frank Zappa, Santana, Flock, Hot Tuna, Country Joe & The Fish, Jefferson Airplane, The Byrds, and Dr. John.

Grant's meticulous planning for Bath had included his acceptance of an invitation by the British government to represent British rock music at a British cultural festival in Iceland – which allowed the band a short holiday together and a discreet warm-up concert. But now this was in danger of being unpicked by the inadequacies of others. At least the dreadful weather had eased by the Sunday afternoon and the sun broke through for a time. But then who would expect anything else but rain punctuated by sunbursts during Wimbledon Tennis week in England?

Grant had decided early that, with Led Zeppelin as the biggest Sunday draw, they should hit the stage at sunset, which in England in midsummer June is around 8:45pm, although the glow lasts beyond 10:30 at the solstice. He calculated that the effect would be unforgettable for all those present and indelibly imprint the band's set on British consciousness as a defining moment. This had the considerable advantages of finding the crowd awake and ready to rock for the evening, the heat of the day still not entirely dissipated and the band in

Overleaf: Apart from wondering what John's up to, the band consider the future: a third album to finish off and a sixth tour of America.

a good frame of mind; after all, they would not have been kept waiting around until some ungodly hour in the morning. Together with the Festival organiser, Freddie Bannister, Grant calculated that Led Zeppelin would go on between Flock and Hot Tuna.

In the event, the band had good reason to be grateful for Grant's foresight. The nominal Sunday headliners, Jefferson Airplane, didn't hit the stage until well after midnight. By that time, one festival-goer, who'd waited hours for Airplane, the band he'd most come to see, wrote later: "I was suddenly aware just how cold it really was. Perhaps it was the lateness of the hour or the fact that I'd had so little sleep. Perhaps it was the anticlimax after Led Zeppelin's performance. Perhaps it was annoyance at the length of Hot Tuna's set and the consequent additional delay. But to my mind Jefferson Airplane's set dragged. … I sought shelter." Still later, the same fan was snuggled in a tent some distance from the stage. "Drifting in and out of fitful sleep, I was aware of familiar phrases from various well-worn Byrds songs. … The sounds from the stage gently wafted through the tent, finding their only competition in the howling of the wind and the intermittent hammering of raindrops on the canvas."[28] No wonder Grant wanted Zeppelin on at sunset.

His wish was nearly scuppered by the combination of a typical overrun in a busy Festival schedule and a wildly popular set from American progressive rock band Flock. Their violinist Jerry Goodman was a real crowd-pleaser, with flaming red hair and an extravagant stage presence. Goodman would shortly be departing Flock to join John McLaughlin's groundbreaking Mahavishnu Orchestra, a group Page subsequently admired greatly. The crowd demanded two encores and the band was happy to oblige, pushing Grant into paroxysms of nervous rage.

According to Richard Cole, Grant, in direct contradiction of the festival organiser's wishes, ordered Cole and two other Zeppelin roadies onstage at the end of Flock's second encore to begin removing Flock's gear. Cole: "We marched onstage and methodically unplugged the Flock's equipment. 'The party's over,' I shouted at the startled band. Henry and I began moving the drums offstage, and the other equipment followed. The Flock

By summer 1970 Led Zeppelin II had sold more than two million copies in America and the awards came tumbling in.

was shouting at us to stop. So was Freddie Bannister from the wings of the stage. For about ten minutes it was sheer pandemonium on the stage, but we accomplished our mission."[29]

Few in the enthusiastic crowd noticed anything amiss, and it is likely that Cole heightened the drama when it came to writing down the events later in order to set the scene for Zeppelin's own triumph and to downplay Flock's. Ironically, two hours later, Led Zeppelin would do four encores. No one, it seems, tried to get their gear offstage.

Led Zeppelin's set started like a bolt out of a gun with the brand new 'Immigrant Song', the overcoat-and-hatted Page looking like a country landlord with the afternoon off while Plant, in denim and skin-tight T-shirt but with a short goatee beard, at least looked like a rock star. With a fervent crowd willing them on, the band quickly overcame any initial nerves and delivered one of their most inspired sets, mixing old and new repertoire with accomplished ease, keeping the vast crowd's interest firmly fixed on them throughout. One of the reasons for the band's success was the excellence of the festival's 'surround' sound system. As an observer wrote: "My abiding memory is of Page bowing the guitar, then raising the bow and accentuating as the sound bounced along from one speaker stack to the next around the [site]. The sound quality was astonishing … and the band was on top form."[30] Peter Grant later called it "a turning point in terms of recognition for us".[31]

All that was required now was to finish the third album, complete a handful of dates in Germany in July, then prepare for the band's sixth American tour that was set to start in August. This one would support the third album, whose release date was being pushed back towards autumn because of the inevitable delays that overtook such projects. The basic recording had been completed between Headley Grange and Basing Street, but the album remained unmixed and the final song choice was still to be made. On top of that, a sleeve had to be designed and manufactured that would come up to Page's expectations. Much to everyone's chagrin, all of this activity had to be finalised during the new tour, thus thrusting the entire band, and Page in particular, back into the old nightmare of snatching mixing time in studios around America as the tour progressed.

COMING THROUGH SLAUGHTER

- 6TH AMERICAN TOUR

- MADISON SQUARE GARDEN

- 3RD ALBUM RELEASED

- MORE WELSH SONGWRITING

- HEADLEY GRANGE & STUDIO SESSIONS FOR 4TH ALBUM

- 3RD UK ('CLUBS') TOUR

Led Zeppelin's sixth American tour, in August and September 1970, was the band's first as bona fide rock superstars, with all the consequent hoopla and intense media attention. They had two smash hit albums under their collective belt and a third was well on the way to completion and release. Their live act was acknowledged as unique and they were expected to fill auditoriums everywhere they went. They also had a reputation as being fast and loose offstage as well as on.

The resulting expectations meant there was, for the first time, intense pressure on them to match previous achievements. Like every band that survives the initial rush of success and publicity, they were now in some sense competing with their own past. The anticipation of this was in part the motivation for all the consolidation within the band that had quietly gone on in preparation for the release of *Led Zeppelin III* and its supporting tour, scheduled to last six weeks.

There was a lot at stake, but at least confidence was high after the warm-up gigs in Germany. They had been a success, with the band breaking attendance records in Frankfurt. In New York in September Plant and Page even granted a rare press conference to publicise the album and the tour. Footage from this press call would later be made available on the 2003 *DVD* set and shows the two musicians remarkably polite in the face of a barrage of doltishly ill-informed questions from the attendant US media, none of whom sound like music journalists or broadcasters.

But with the album still needing a few overdubs, mixing and final track selection, and the tour about to start, tragedy struck the family of John Paul Jones. His father, professional pianist Joe Baldwin, had been diagnosed in early August with a terminal illness. In shock, Jones wanted to stay with him for whatever time was left. For Peter Grant the decision was simple: the original tour dates had to be re-cast, with the first nine days cancelled – eight concerts in all, mostly concentrated down the eastern seaboard. This included a festival in Boston on August 14th that was to have been headlined by the band. The entire festival was cancelled when Led Zeppelin pulled out. Of those concerts, only the Boston, Cleveland and Detroit appearances were re-scheduled, squeezed in during late August and September.

The band made an effort to put the interruptions to some use. On August 8th *Melody Maker* reported: "Jimmy Page goes off to New York the beginning of next week to do the final mixes on the new Led Zeppelin album entitled *Led Zeppelin III*."[1] In fact he only started the work in New York. According to engineer Terry Manning, Page contacted him about finalising the album in Ardent Studios, Memphis, where Manning was based. Page and Manning had known each other back in the Yardbirds days and Manning knew how the guitarist liked to work in

the studio. Although the album was completed between dates in the opening weeks of the tour, Manning and Page worked quickly and efficiently together, Manning able to read the producer's every reaction to what he was hearing. Manning recalled years later: "He would do a sort of rocking back and forth of his shoulders when the mix was coming into the feel area he desired."[2] Page finally signed off on the final mixes on August 24th, a rest day in the original schedule, and the next day travelled to Nashville to slide back into the tour in a show there that evening.

Back at the gigs on the rearranged itinerary, the band was greeted enthusiastically by fans, although some of the new songs from the as-yet-unreleased *Led Zeppelin III* had a mixed welcome. Page talked about this mid-tour to an American journalist. "We've started doing the acoustic things onstage and it's been going off well, especially here [in Los Angeles]. Some places, though, it's been a bit of a shock. I relate it back to the period after we'd done the first album, but the second one hadn't come out, [and] the reaction was a bit cold, really. ... A similar sort of thing has happened with the acoustic things, for the moment, there not being any association. The audience is hearing them fresh and there have been mixed reactions. They've always gone down OK, but you get the feeling that people prefer to hear the heavier stuff, which is a bit of a mistake because there's a lot you can give, and the best thing is to show them what you can do altogether. ... We always give as much as we've got to give that night. When it comes to encores, we'll go on and on and on if they want to."[3]

On August 17th, the second date of the re-arranged tour, in Hampton Beach, Virginia, the band encored with the A- and B-sides of their first single, but mixed new with old by debuting 'Immigrant Song', 'That's The Way', and the solo 'Bron-Yr-Aur' (a piece not released on album until 1975). They also played 'Since I've Been Loving You', premiered on the spring tour but also to be released on the new album the following month. However, the disruption and sadness caused by the death of Jones's father continued to dictate events. The timing of the Cleveland concert on the 26th had been hastily brought forward to allow all four band members to fly out that evening and attend the funeral in England. Impressively, they were back into the schedule by the 28th. But the loss was felt throughout the band and its entourage.

As on the previous American venture, Led Zeppelin stuck to their policy of being the only band on the bill at their self-promoted concerts, while at weekend festivals – such as the Winnipeg Man Pop Festival on August 29th – they were headliners over their old rivals Iron Butterfly and a host of lesser names. Echoing the rain and damp of Bath in June, Winnipeg in August became so cold, wet and windy that by early evening the day-long event had to be adjourned from the Stadium to the local Arena. At least Led Zeppelin, the last act of the night, sent everyone home with happy memories of a fine set.

With Jones juggling his professional responsibilities and personal grief, the band managed to complete their commitments with exemplary professionalism. They all attempted to bolster Jones's spirits in various ways: Plant, at the September 2nd Oakland concert, drew the crowd's attention to his bandmate's organ playing on 'Since I've Been Loving You', saying proudly that Jones played both keyboard and pedals. "He's doing it all at once," announced Plant to the crowd. "It's not easy, but he certainly pulls it off well."

Two nights later, the band delivered a memorable extended set to 20,000 fans at The Forum in Inglewood, Los Angeles, then decamped to the city's Troubadour club where Fairport Convention were playing (vocalist Sandy Denny by this time was long gone from the line-up). The two bands were on very friendly terms and, according to those present that night, the musicians jammed for over three hours together onstage, all of them recorded. The tapes were apparently confiscated by Grant and have yet to surface.

Whatever the hurdles and the expectations, the tour was a big money-spinner. The band did not go out for less than $25,000 per performance, and at the crowning Madison Square Garden shows in New York City on September 19th – a matinee and an evening set, though the matinee was only 75 percent full – they grossed a cool $200,000, according to *Billboard*.

Peter Grant had invited ex-Yardbird Chris Dreja, now working in New York, to see the band play at the Garden. It was his first experience of ramped-up rock. Years later Dreja told Chris Welch: "I went to meet Zeppelin in their dressing room and they were charming, because they realised they owed us a hell of a debt. ... I went out on the stage and heard the band blasting through some huge PA system to an audience of thousands, and I was just astounded at the magnitude of it all. In two years the whole scene had changed. We never had those powerful, sophisticated PAs to interpret that music." Dreja was aware that Page had gathered around him a band of very different personalities compared to The Yardbirds. "Everybody in the old band was a pretty sensitive, complex person. We were all a bit stiff-upper-lipped. We didn't even revel in our fame. We were terribly low key. We shied away from being stars."[4]

The tour brought a perceptible shift in the way that many of the local concert reviewers perceived the band onstage. From Milwaukee to Honolulu, they noticed a greater degree of relaxation and ease, especially from Plant and Page. In Honolulu, where Zeppelin played two shows, they were appraised as "more human and relaxed now. ... Plant seemed especially perceptive about what was going on around him. He stopped the show twice for emergencies, something which they probably would not have done the first time they were here."[5]

But Jones's admirable fortitude in honouring the restructured tour came at a cost, and the strain finally showed. Jones was a resilient, upbeat and independent spirit who normally kept himself at a distance from the offstage horseplay of the rest, and understandably he withdrew somewhat for the rest of the tour in order to get through intact. Even tour manager Richard Cole noticed something different. "On the flight back to London ... John Paul was seated next to me. Zeppelin's Rock of Gibraltar, he got the job done. On this tour more than the others, he tended to keep to himself. Maybe he was trying to back away from some of our lunacy. Perhaps he just enjoyed his own company more than ours."[6]

That the band – its individual members included – had survived in such good shape could to a great extent be credited to manager Peter Grant. His insistence on getting the priorities right and never putting the interests of the band or its music second in any situation had paid off. As Plant said just prior to the tour's end: "As much credit goes to us, it goes to old Peter as well, because he goes all round the States with us, everywhere we go, when he could just sit in the office in London. He's been a big part of the thing."[7]

On Saturday September 19th, the date of the final gigs of the tour in New York City, the annual *Melody Maker* readers' poll was published back home. Led Zeppelin came first, displacing The Beatles, now at Number 2, who had not failed to top the poll since 1963. But this was not the only major event of that week. The previous day's London evening papers had screamed the shock headlines that Jimi Hendrix had been found dead in a hotel room in Notting Hill, west London. The times were a-changing indeed.

Five days into the following month – and a day after the death of another hippie icon, Janis Joplin, this time from a heroin overdose – *Led Zeppelin III* was released (again, it appeared a little later in the UK). Pre-orders were in six figures and it was confidently predicted to dominate the end-of-year charts. But it had been a struggle to get it out in time for the pre-Christmas market. The problems came mostly from the complex cover design that needed meticulous managing, as did everything about a Led Zeppelin album.

Rock writers bestowed generally positive if qualified approval on *Led Zeppelin III*. Some critics got it immediately; many found it a puzzling departure. In a world ruled as much then as now by expectation and musical conformity, any minor deviation from the past by a top-selling band was viewed with mystified suspicion in the mainstream rock press, while a repeat serving of last year's model on this year's album was generally dismissed as an artist merely repeating things and trying to live off

Overleaf: Jimmy Page and tour manager Richard Cole arrive in Honolulu, Hawaii, for two dates in September 1970 during the sixth US tour.

old triumphs. Only a handful of revered musical gods of the time – Dylan, Lennon, The Grateful Dead, Zappa, The Band, Neil Young, Joni Mitchell – escaped such treatment and were reviewed on their own terms.

Lester Bangs, who seemed always to have somewhat enjoyed his own bewilderment at liking Led Zeppelin, quipped in *Rolling Stone*: "I keep nursing this love-hate attitude towards Led Zeppelin. Partly from genuine interest and mostly indefensible hopes, in part from the conviction that nobody that crass can be all that bad. ... In fact, when I first heard the album, my main impression was the consistent anonymity of most of the songs – no one could mistake the band, but no gimmicks stand out with any special outrageousness, as did the great, gleefully absurd orang-utan Plant-cum-wheezing guitar freak-out that made 'Whole Lotta Love' such a pulp classic. ... Finally I must mention a song called 'That's The Way', because it's the first song they've ever done that's truly moved me. Son of a gun, it's beautiful. Above a very simple and appropriately everyday acoustic riff, Plant sings a touching picture of two youngsters who can no longer be playmates because one's parents and peers disapprove of the other because of long hair and being generally from 'the dark side of town'. The vocal is restrained for once - in fact, Plant's intonations are as plaintively gentle as some of The Rascals' best work."[8]

Meanwhile, perhaps in order to sustain their implacably anti-Zep stance, or perhaps in sheer malice, *Rolling Stone*'s editorial people finessed the honest ambivalence of Bangs's review by running a large photo of Plant alongside, accompanied by the extraordinary caption: "Coming round for the third and maybe last time." Three cheers for impartiality. Given this, it becomes easier to understand why, some time later, Page resorted to welcoming the crowd at a San Francisco appearance in the following manner: "It's good to be in San Francisco [cheers]. I like San Francisco [more cheers]. You have an important newspaper based here in San Francisco [boos]. I don't like that paper [greater cheers]. It's called *Rolling Stone* [enormous booing]."[9]

Chris Hodenfeld in his review in *Strange Days* had a similar sense of bemused wonder to Lester Bangs. He concluded: "It's good that Zeppelin are playing like they want to be listened to (not just heard, but listened at). It is really about the best direction they could have gone in, and, probably not surprisingly, they've not lost any of their raucous crazy-action in the translation."[10]

Page himself didn't see *III* as a perfect album, but he thought it a very important one. "The only fault I find in it," he said that October, "is that there aren't any really long tracks. I'd like to have got one long track on it, but as it was we had 14 tracks to choose from, and to get a cross-section of what we were doing at that point we had to select very carefully, and a lot of good things had to be left off because of it only being a single album."[11]

Another reason for the album's mixed reception was the record sleeve over which so much time and effort had been expended. Its incongruity was noted at the time by some reviewers. Hodenfeld said: "This slice of hot wax, however, is a bit like its jacket. Very sleek, some traces of humour, and a lot of different things going on at once."[12] As opposed to the first two records with their simple, striking images and bold, virtually timeless design, this was very much of the moment, reflecting a taste for pop and trash culture that was fashionable in art circles as the new decade dawned. Bangs in *Rolling Stone* felt moved to refer to Marvel comics when confronted by the new album's jacket. The cover was cluttered, confusing in pictorial content, had a gimmick – a moveable card disc inside the front gatefold sleeve – and suggested the preoccupations of a Top-40 British singles band like T.Rex or Sweet rather than the album-based all-round rockers that Led Zeppelin believed themselves to be. Considering the intense pride that all four musicians felt over their achievements on the record, the jacket seems, even today, to be a missed opportunity.

Page later confided his own lack of pleasure in that sleeve design. "A disappointment," he told Brad Tolinski. "I'll take responsibility for that one. I knew the artist and described what we wanted with this wheel that made things appear and change. But he got very personal with this artwork and disappeared off with it. We kept saying, 'Can we take a look at it? Can we see where it's going?' Finally, the album was actually finished and we still didn't have the art. It got to the point where I had to say, 'Look, I've got to have this thing.' I wasn't happy with the final result: I thought it looked teeny-bopperish. But we were on top of a deadline, so of course there was no way to make any radical changes to it."[13]

Plant felt that the new album reflected a new maturity in the band's outlook on the world, as well as its music. He told *Record Mirror* that spending so much time in America, seeing and living through the things they'd experienced there, had changed them all and made them aware of the importance of standing up and being counted. "We've been to America so much and seen so many things we don't agree with that our feelings of protest do reflect in the music," said Plant. "America makes you aware of the proximity of man's fate. You see so much that is great, so much that is terrible. The rush, the hassles, the police, people may say we make bread but in some cities it's so rough at concerts, the audiences are scared to come. ... I've come around to another way of thinking now. A while back, we were upset because we didn't get much early help here at home. Times were not too good when we started. Now I can see it in a different

Robert Plant with ex-Fairport Convention singer Sandy Denny at an awards event. Later, Denny would sing on 'The Battle Of Evermore' on the band's fourth album.

way. I want to play more at home. Britain has so much that America doesn't. I could never move from here."[14]

Heard in that light, the opening track of *Led Zeppelin III*, 'Immigrant Song', has its ironies amid some mordant humour. The galloping-horses-going-to-war riff and drum pattern hark back to elements of the guitar-drums riff of Hendrix's 'Little Miss Lover', but Plant launches into a banshee howl that has repeatedly been compared to an invading horde of Goths straight from Valhalla. In fact it hails from an altogether more cheerful clime. These are the opening measures of the melody of 'Bali Hi' from Rodgers & Hammerstein's musical *South Pacific*. Plant's subsequent lyrics transfer the action from an idyllic Pacific island to a "land of ice and snow", but this does not deflect the jubilation at the core of the song.

These immigrants are celebrating their arrival, not bemoaning their fate, telling tales of invasion and conquest that dominate the history of pre-Norman-Conquest Britain, when those isles were subject to progressive waves of invasions from Angles, Saxons, Danes, Vikings, Jutes and more. The Celts who had once lived all across the country were pushed progressively west and north, and in the end controlled only Scotland, Wales and Ireland. The attractions of the "green land" Plant sings of were clearly too much to resist for these particular immigrants.

The piece is short – 2:23 – but full of drama and colour. Page's layers of guitars and production techniques bring natural climaxes to the piece before the outro and give the song a continual sense of forward movement. There is also a kicking, rising bassline in the turnaround (first heard at 0:44) that helps lift the tune to a different level of energy. It was an obvious single, and was released as such in the States, its brooding power and sheer sonic scale not best translated to AM radio but carrying a punch on FM. It peaked in the US *Billboard* singles chart at Number 16 and stayed there for ten weeks: a good effort for a band with no interest in the fate of singles.

The next song, 'Friends', more than any other on side one signalled the huge shift in emphasis in the band's music since *Led Zeppelin II*. It is based on an acoustic guitar pattern that owes more than a little of its inspiration to Steven Stills's 'Carry On', the opening track on Crosby Stills Nash & Young's *Déjà Vu*, released that March. Zeppelin's song quickly develops an entirely original flavour with its lacings of haunting vocal melodies, Indian-influenced strings, and ambiguous harmonic centres, typified by the rising pattern of stop-chords used as an end-of-verse cadence. These trace out a diminished C scale later reflected by the course of the string melody, all evoking an air of mystery and wonder against an energetic rhythm backing.

What makes the piece leap further into vivid life is the beautiful other-worldly vocal line that Plant develops unexpectedly over the top of this swirling musical alchemy. Considering the previous recorded history of the band, this vocal line seems to come from a parallel universe. Plant uses his customary blues intervals, but he is working more as an improvising musician might, pulling in notes from beyond the home key and relocating them as an unsettling counter-melody that only heightens the sense of a band delivering a new message. Other techniques underline this. Page uses a phalanx of acoustic guitars – including 12-string – to paint the initial scene before hand-played drums enter, pointing to one of the main inspirations for the piece: Indian classical music, but seen through the distorting mirror of each musician's individual interpretation of those ideas.

There are 50 seconds of instrumental introduction here prior to the vocal entry, and Plant's role is not constant, allowing the underlying musical mix to dominate. The spare, held-note arrangement for a small string section (scored by Jones) is entirely appropriate, emphasising the bittersweet mood of the song and underlying the simple but heartfelt message of the lyrics.

More than three years on from George Harrison's 'Within You Without You', there is a sure touch here in the way that Zeppelin assimilate other elements into Western song forms and a sense that the self-consciousness of Harrison's pioneering efforts in creating an East-West hybrid had long fallen away. 'Friends' is without doubt a little masterpiece. The only flaw comes with a rushing in tempo by the guitars towards the end, making things sound a mite breathless rather than serene as the climax is reached.

As usual with his meticulous approach to recording, Page had been looking to improve the way he could record his acoustic guitars and had found it through using a limiter, a device that minimises sudden volume leaps and increases perceived overall loudness. "I used an Altair Tube Limiter. I'd got that from a chap called [Dick Rosmini] who'd recorded an album called [*Adventures For 12-String, 6-string And Banjo* on Elektra in 1964]. I'd never heard an acoustic sound quite like that. I bumped into him in the States and asked him how he got his recorded sound, and he said the whole secret was the Tube Limiter. It was so reliable. We even used [later] it on *In Through The Out Door*."[15]

'Friends' segues into 'Celebration Day' with a swirling keyboard oscillation and again marks something of a departure from previous Zeppelin songs. Although it has roots in Elmore James and even 1930s blues slide guitar, there are hints of funk rather than simple blues or R&B in its rhythm guitar parts and 8/8 fatback beat. This recalls a similar hybrid that Jimi Hendrix was reaching for independently at around the same time in his song 'Freedom', which shares the 8/8 beat pattern. In this context, Page's B.B. King-derived guitar fills sound oddly

□ **Jimmy Page onstage in 1971 with his Gibson Les Paul guitar.**

anachronistic. In lesser hands the contrast would not work, but Page's precision and grace of execution compel admiration. Plant's semi-spoken verse emphasises the funk-like feel, while the hookline turnaround is pure inspired pop. Plant is singing "My my I'm so happy" and the band sound exactly that as they work effortlessly as a team to deliver the song's message.

'Since I've Been Loving You' sounds well-greased in this version – apart from Bonham's squeaky bass-drum pedal. Zeppelin had been playing the piece live all through the spring US tour and had properly settled on what to do. A slow blues in 6/8 of a type they'd already mastered, this one is particularly intriguing in its demonstration of how the band has evolved as a functioning unit since the first two albums.

With the addition of Jones's keyboards – this time a Hammond B3, with Jones supplying the bassline on its pedals – 'Loving You' reaches back to the informal but closely structured studio jams that Al Kooper and Mike Bloomfield put together for their 1968 album *Super Session*. The level of interplay between the instruments and the way they link with the vocals suggest a real four-way conversation. From that point of view, this is not merely a showpiece for Plant's keening vocals but a full-scale display of Led Zeppelin's telepathic interplay within the modern blues form.

Page's guitar solo midway through uses different scales and lines than the normal Chicago-based ideas he'd normally select, instead echoing the long-limbed augmented blues lines that Hendrix had used on similar material back in 1968 in his jams with Steve Winwood and others. Page's playing has the freshness and spontaneity of discovery and the formal balance within a larger piece at which he always excels. Bonham's emphatic but unflashy drumming underlines the quality that is the keynote of this entire seven-minute piece.

'Out On The Tiles' comes as a throwback after the first four tracks, emphasising the noise-plus-riff-plus-rhythm matrix – the riff idea came from Bonham – that was Led Zeppelin at its most basic, raw and exciting on the first two albums.

A few years later Page used this specific track to explain how he achieved this signature Zeppelin sound in the studio. "Close miking and distance miking," he explained, "that's ambient sound. Getting the distance of the time lag from one end of the room to the other and putting that in as well. The whole idea, the way I see recording, is to try and capture the sound of the room live and the emotion of the whole moment, and try to convey that. ... Consequently you've got to capture as much of the room sound as possible."[16]

Page's guitar sound (and Jones's bass tone) is extraordinarily muddy and downhome on the verse here. Only the chorus – an optimistic, rising melody that is a clever variation of the verse, jubilantly sung by a double-tracked Plant – identifies it as part of the new Led Zeppelin sensibility. One aspect of the arrangement is important for its indications of future Led Zeppelin interests. On the turnaround between verses (at 0:25 and 1:42) the band cut a beat and turn the entire beat around, starting the riff in an entirely unexpected place. Exactly who came up with this little shift is unknown, but it pre-dates the kind of thing they would extend on 'Black Dog' by six months. Given the gestation of 'Black Dog', it could have been either Jones or Bonham.

'Tiles' closed the original side one of the vinyl LP. The average Led Zeppelin fan of 1970, starting into side two still bewildered by all the changes and innovations on the first side, would have been scratching their head in confusion at the acoustic folk-rock of the first two minutes of 'Gallows Pole'. After all, when there was an uptempo, riff-based song to deliver, in the past Led Zeppelin had used electric guitars and the driving drums of John Bonham. But not now.

'Gallows Pole' has an interestingly hybrid history, for it comes from the pre-war black folk-blues tradition of Leadbelly and The Mississippi Sheikhs rather than the Delta blues of Robert Johnson. There were close ties not only with white folk and protest music of the 1930s and right up to Zeppelin's day, but also with the Celtic and Anglo-Saxon folk-ballad tradition that supplied so many mid-century folk singers with their repertoire, from Joan Baez to Len Chandler, Sandy Denny and beyond.

'Gallows Pole' was a British-sourced folk lyric re-applied to a common scene in the Southern States during the 19th and 20th centuries. A convicted criminal pleads at the gallows in the hope of a last-minute reprieve by offering money or other favours to the authorities. This notion had appealed greatly to Leadbelly, a man well used to singing for his own personal salvation – he sang himself out of prison on two separate occasions. Leadbelly popularised this particular folk tune in the 1930s on records and in live performance. It stayed in the folk repertoire after Leadbelly's death in the late 1940s, and Page came across it in a version by 12-string guitarist Fred Gerlach, who recorded it for the Folkways label. Page said: "We have completely re-arranged it and changed the verse. Robert wrote a new set of lyrics. That's John Paul Jones on mandolin and bass, and I'm playing the banjo, six-string acoustic, 12-string, and electric guitar. ... I did the pedal-steel guitar and that's Robert doing the harmonies as well as the lead."[17]

Plant may have re-worked the lyrics, but the basic

John Bonham as ever relentlessly driving the band forward, pictured here onstage at Southampton University on March 11th 1971.

Overleaf: Led Zeppelin in their element, communing and communicating onstage at Southampton, March 1971.

meaning has not shifted and many of the details are still in place. This is his first effort at telling a dramatic narrative through lyrics, and while he clearly has some distance to go to match the gripping intensity of Leadbelly, who sweeps the listener up in the narrative suspense of the scene, he convincingly establishes the desperate mood of the piece. The tension is also built by the progressive way the accompaniment swells from single guitar to an array of instruments, all worrying away at an insistent two-note rhythm. The last instruments to enter are banjo, electric guitar, and drums after two verses are completed, and they punctuate that Morse-code riff to the end, where Page comes riding out of the ensemble with some pleasing blues melodies.

Page's solo at this point is notable for its close imitation in sustain and timbre of a violin played in the folk-blues style, almost as if the experience of hearing Jerry Goodman of Flock at Bath had inspired him to bring this sound into the band's repertoire. This last section is a touch overlong, with its unvarying nature beginning to pall before its end, but Zep otherwise manage an effective updating of this old hanging song.

'Tangerine', up next, dated from Page's Yardbirds days and started life as a Relf-Page co-composition, 'Knowing That I'm Losing You'. That original song was recorded in New York by The Yardbirds early in 1968 but rejected for release by Epic Records. According to Greg Russo in his book on Yardbirds history, the music was all by Page and the lyrics by Keith Relf. Russo said: "Page used nearly all of Relf's words with the exception of the title line, and it became 'Tangerine' with a sole Jimmy Page writing credit."[18]

The vagaries of copyright registration aside, it must be said that it hasn't entirely made the transition to Led Zeppelin from The Yardbirds' 'Still I'm Sad' and 'Heart Full of Soul' idiom – Relf's voice may also have better suited its mock-Tudor stylings. There are touches too of the type of arrangement (and subject-matter) used effectively on Mickie Most's Donovan sessions in the Yardbirds years when both Jones and Page were still hired hands. The song's construction and overall tone is very much that of 'lost love' ballads from 1966-68, with Plant's treble-tracked vocals towards the end of the piece evoking the mournful air of a lovestruck pop star, but without a great deal of inspiration behind them. In this way, at least, the song betrays its roots.

The artificiality of 'Tangerine' is underlined by the relaxed, easy beauty of the next number, 'That's The Way', another acoustic piece. The simple acoustic guitar and mandolin patterns of the first four minutes make much of an unresolved major 7th chord and the absence of drums, in the process maintaining a great intimacy of communication. Plant's vocal and his lyrics sustain this too, directly addressing the listener in a conversational style as if they are part of the song's story. Plant uses his

softest voice for almost all of the song's lyrics. There is a wistful edge to the music and the words, implying that the singer has accepted a situation he would rather was otherwise. It's a beautiful composition, and though it has no stylistic overlap with Neil Young, its air of intense, bittersweet romance evokes the Canadian's approach and impact.

'Bron-Y-Aur Stomp' has the wide-eyed, jubilant humour and joie de vivre that Bob Dylan's early comic narratives possessed, although its mood is more pastoral and its aim to celebrate rather than to poke sly fun. Again the accompaniment is folk-like, with Page using his own customised string tuning, the rhythm firmly two-beat, as Plant celebrates the joys of the country in a song that is close to conjuring fireside jams among folk musicians of any era. The introduction is shared with an arrangement of the old folk song 'The Waggoner's Tale' made by one of Page's favourite guitarists, Bert Jansch. Page explained: "That's an acoustic bass, not a double bass: it's like an acoustic guitar with a [bigger] body. John Paul took all the frets out and he plays it acoustically. This has got the rattling of the kitchen sink – we've got everything in it! We even overdubbed Bonham on castanets and spoons."[19]

The final track on *III*, 'Hats Off To (Roy) Harper', is a defiantly low-key affair, an acoustic duet between Page and Plant based on the old blues number 'Shake 'Em On Down'. That was written and first recorded by Bukka White in 1937 and had been a sizeable hit for the bluesman at the time. White also re-recorded it for guitarist John Fahey's Tacoma Records on his 'rediscovery' in 1963. A Columbia LP reissue of all White's pre-war recordings for the company had appeared in 1970, transferring his original performance onto vinyl for the first time. Such an enthusiastic blues fan as Plant would no doubt have been aware of this, as well as White's '63 remake.

The idea to include such a piece on the album came from a blues jam that Plant and Page had enjoyed one night at Bron-Yr-Aur where, according to Page, they'd run through a number of old blues songs. They updated the arrangement and added modern sounds by messing with vocal amplification, and recast the title to publicly acknowledge their fellow musician and friend Roy Harper. It is not the pair's best blues performance, being too unvaried, despite some convincing singing from Plant. Page tries with his guitar part to make up in speed what it lacks in light and shade, and this is initially gripping, but it becomes merely frenetic as the track progresses. We are three minutes into the performance before the 12-bar pattern of the original is observed, thus breaking at last the drone that has been the song's fate until then. With the final sounds of Page's slide guitar at

Jimmy Page relaxes backstage at Manchester University, March 19th 1971.

the conclusion, the album comes to an oddly downbeat ending, almost as if the band had wanted to underplay its overall impact.

Considering the bold, confident opening statement of 'Immigrant Song', this was a rather puzzling place to end. The band wanted the listener to take away a very definite impression after concluding side two. Was this the future for Led Zeppelin now? Not, it seems, according to Page. He was already developing his plans for the next LP. "This album," he said at the time, "was to get across more versatility and use more combinations of instruments. The next one will be just one long track on one side with these combinations of instruments: mandolin, banjo and so on. It would last about 25 minutes with instrumental sections. It's still in the planning stages."[20] One aspect of *III* rarely mentioned is the relative scarcity of set-piece solos by Page. It is almost as if he had consciously decided to avoid such things after the fireworks on the first two albums; this was to be a record that celebrated the collective talents of the band working together rather than one hotshot guitar soloist.

Led Zeppelin III was released into a record market gearing up for Christmas 1970 with some serious rock contenders from both sides of the Atlantic. Over the summer the big story had been the release of the *Woodstock* movie, and the triple-album highlights from that festival had topped the US charts for a month. During the autumn there were many big-selling heavyweights jostling for attention and sales: *Cosmo's Factory* (Creedence Clearwater Revival), *Get Yer Ya Yas Out* (Rolling Stones), *New Morning* (Bob Dylan), *Paranoid* (Black Sabbath), *Atom Heart Mother* (Pink Floyd), *Mad Dogs & Englishmen* (Joe Cocker), *After The Goldrush* (Neil Young), *Stephen Stills*, *Emerson Lake & Palmer*, *Sweet Baby James* (James Taylor), and *All Things Must Pass* (George Harrison). In early January, John Lennon's first post-Beatles studio album, *Plastic Ono Band*, was released. In the face of such competition, Zeppelin's new album reached Number 1 and sold spectacularly at first, but eventually made less of a sales dent than its predecessor. It remains the lowest-selling album from the classic Led Zeppelin studio canon, its radicalism proving a long-term problem for the band's less adventurous fans.

The first single, 'Immigrant Song', made it to Number 16 on *Billboard*'s chart that December, but had less overall impact than the iconic 'Whole Lotta Love'. The band decided to make 'Immigrant Song' rather more

collectable than their other singles by adding a B-side not on the album. It was 'Hey Hey What Can I Do', a medium-tempo ballad with some pleasant mandolin accompaniment to a rather uncommitted Plant vocal and a less than inspiring melody line before the singalong end-chorus. It revealed shared folk roots with Rod Stewart's 'Maggie May' and was a perfect B-side curiosity that languished in obscurity until included on the four-CD *Led Zeppelin* compilation of 1990 and the ten-CD *Complete Studio Recordings* set of 1993.

An out-take from the time, 'Poor Tom', had to wait for release until 1982's *Coda*. It is a superior re-treading of an old quasi-minstrel folk song of the type Leadbelly would have loved to play back in the 1930s. Bonham's train-style drum beat is perfectly accompanied by Page's glittering acoustic fingerpicking, while Plant, revelling in his country-blues role, conjures wonderful images through deft phrases, sly inflections, and some delightfully light harmonica accompaniment. Perhaps it was one acoustic track too many for *Led Zeppelin III*, but a piece of this quality hardly deserved such a long wait to be heard.

With the album out in the world and doing well, the band's thoughts turned to its successor. There was no US tour to contemplate, so Zeppelin had an opportunity to plan and write new material at their leisure. In a vote of confidence for the direction they had all taken during 1970, they decided to follow roughly the same path as they had for *III*. First, Page and Plant went once more to Bron-Yr-Aur in Wales for relaxation and a chance to work on some new and not-so-new ideas. It was a shorter visit than the one in spring and served mainly to get the creative ball rolling. Again, the ideas from the cottage, along with those provided by Jones and Bonham, were taken to the full band at Headley Grange in November, where they were thoroughly rehearsed. Then complete backing tracks were recorded there, using the mobile equipment they'd become used to working with on the previous album.

At the same time, entirely new ideas emerged from these sessions. Jones talked to *Disc* during the rehearsals, saying: "It's better to do it all the way we do now because you haven't got so many distractions. We've done a good deal: [we've] broken the back of it, and recording starts this month. But rather than waste a lot of studio time thinking of the riffs and lyrics in the studio, we decided [Headley Grange] was definitely the best place to get the numbers down before we went there."

Jones also talked about the teamwork that exemplified Led Zeppelin's approach to making music. It would, he said, have been possible for any one of the four musicians involved to be protective of their own ideas, or to go off and embark on a solo project – after all, this is what happened in many bands. But none of the four ever felt the need or the point. "I suppose we're all capable of

Sorting out tonight's set. Jimmy Page: "We always give as much as we've got to give every night. When it comes to encores, we'll go on and on and on if they want to."

Overleaf: A date on the band's 'back to the clubs' tour designed to restore their street cred in Britain, here at Nottingham Rowing Club on March 21st 1971.

putting a trademark on an album, marking just one person, but none of us are so narrow-minded. That wouldn't be the group, and the group's always played what comes out, and what comes out goes down. If it sounds good to everybody, then it's played."[21] Of the songs they treated in this way, 'Misty Mountain Hop', 'The Battle Of Evermore', 'Black Dog', and 'Stairway To Heaven' would later find their way onto the band's fourth album.

By the close of December 1970 the band had completed initial recordings on the mobile at Headley and were ready to move to Island's Basing Street studios in London again for overdubs. Page later told an interviewer that every track except 'Stairway To Heaven' was recorded by the band at Headley Grange, while Page and Plant did the overdubs at Olympic studio in London.

After the strongly acoustic emphasis of much of the third album that had required Bonham in particular to show great restraint and discretion, much of the new material gave him especially wide scope to develop the music's character and style. Years later, Jones felt this strongly. "He had a lot of input into the riffs we played, more than he was credited for, I'd say. He would change the whole flavour of a piece, and lots of our numbers would start out with a drum pattern. We'd build a riff around the drums."[22]

Ironically, as Led Zeppelin were working hard to make their next recording project a wholly memorable one, the music press in Britain was full of rumours of a split. This was not the first time; someone, somewhere simply decided it was Led Zeppelin's turn again. The usual round of firm denials were made, with Grant's PR man Bill Harry announcing to *Melody Maker*: "There are no plans for Led Zeppelin to split up. And there are no plans for any member of the group to work with any other artists. The group have all been joking about these rumours, but they are upset at the way they are being spread by people who claim to be close to the band. We'd like to know who these people are and how they get their information."[23]

The rumours were all the more puzzling given that the previous week both *MM* and *NME* had carried details of all the dates on a newly-announced Led Zeppelin tour of Britain and Ireland for March. It was to take a unique form, concentrating on the kind of small British venue that the band had not played since late 1968. There were a number of reasons for the move, but they can all be traced back to the band's desire to be taken seriously as a musical unit and to be seen as a group of people with a social and political conscience. All four musicians in the band took what they were doing very seriously. They felt they were giving value for money in all they did and were stung by criticisms aimed at them from their earliest success onwards that described them as an overhyped industry confection, a money-making machine betraying the counter-cultural dream.

They felt that double standards were being applied. Figures such as Bob Dylan, John Lennon, The Grateful Dead, and The Doors had all made a lot of money over the previous few years, but few called their integrity into question. Somehow their millions had not sullied their creative vision. With Led Zeppelin, people continued to suspect their motives, especially since many commentators had made a point of drawing attention to the contentious issues of songwriting and copyright assignations on the first two albums in particular, where old blues pieces had been re-fashioned and the songwriting claimed by Plant and Page. The nasty stench was difficult to disperse.

Zeppelin's move to acoustic on the most recent album, the continuing diversification of their creative efforts, and this latest decision to go into the smaller venues all point to a group of musicians with an urgent need to prove to their contemporaries, and to themselves, that they had credentials as good as anyone else. Whatever happened, once the tour had been completed they could hardly be charged with the crime of exploiting their fans, or anyone else for that matter. There was little chance that such a tour could make a profit.

Peter Grant also saw it as an astute move. The band had not played live since the previous October, and by the time March arrived that would amount to a five-month lay-off, the longest since the band had formed. A small-gig tour would rekindle their enthusiasm for live work, allow them to get close reaction to anything new they might want to try, and also prepare them for more extensive tours into Europe and America later in the summer of '71.

Prior to that, however, the band completed the recording for the fourth album in February. Plant confirmed mid-month to *Melody Maker* that "the next album won't be called *Led Zeppelin IV*. We'll think of something else. So far we've got 14 tracks down, and we did quite a bit with a mobile recording truck down in Hampshire. ... We've been able to experiment with drum sounds by using just one microphone and things. At times it sounds like early Presley records drumming."

During the rest of the interview Plant revealed the existence of "a nice ten-minute thing 'Stairway To Heaven', which starts off acoustically and just builds up," and also a version of Leroy Carr's 'Sloppy Drunk', with Page on mandolin and Plant himself on guitar – thus fulfilling his long-held ambition to record on the instrument. Plant thought it was a song where "you can imagine it being played as people dive around the maypole". He mentioned that they'd recorded "enough for two albums, but we won't put out a double album. People can appreciate a single album more because there's only eight tracks as opposed to 16".[24]

With the music down on tape, all the band had to do to finish their fourth album in just over two years was to select the tracks and mix and master them. Led Zeppelin were still producing high quality music at a phenomenal rate. Indeed, it is remarkable just how much of their classic recordings occupy such a very short space of time. Only the delay of the fourth album until autumn 1971 disguised their prolific work rate at the time.

Meanwhile, there was the British/Irish tour. Page talked to journalist Keith Altham about what was being now billed as 'the Back To The Clubs tour'. Page lamented the fact that the original fans of the band were now just specks in the vast crowds they usually played for. He felt a degree of responsibility towards those fans who had helped get them past the initial stages of their career. "We are playing the Marquee for exactly the same amount as we did in the old days as a thank you to those promoters and audiences alike. ... We will establish contact with our audience and re-energise on their reaction while they will have a chance to see a group in the accepted tradition."[25]

He entered a plea to the promoters to do the right thing by the fans and sell tickets on a first-come first-served basis, and throughout the interview stressed the philanthropic side of the exercise. He told the press that "if they expect red-carpet treatment then my advice is don't bother to come. Because they are taking up valuable space which someone who really wants to hear us would otherwise occupy". He also let it be known that at least one of the shows would be played for the benefit of the charity Release, an organisation that helped young drug-abusers combat their habits.

The reality of the tour, when it got underway in Belfast and Dublin, was sobering – even if the band and their fans found the music as exciting as ever. The Belfast audience was volatile and enthusiastic: they were privileged to be the first audience anywhere to hear 'Stairway To Heaven'. Page afterwards pointed out that it was different to the recorded version – which no one at that point had heard – because Jones had tracked on recorders to the introduction to the song "which we can't reproduce onstage, but the acoustic guitars came off well".[26]

The English segment of the tour, taking up most of March 1971, turned out to be something of a mixed blessing for a band now used to the luxuries and comforts that their status and income had bestowed upon them. While the crowds were uniformly enthusiastic and the band responded to their excitement by delivering superb sets, mostly through amplification that was expertly handled and crystal clear – something of a miracle in its own right, given the small venues and their normally atrocious acoustics – some of the dressing rooms and backstage areas were as rank as they ever had been back in the 1960s when all four band members were still scuffling for a living in such places. Still, not all the dates were in clubs. There were university halls and larger dance venues

as well, and while the dressing rooms here were not vast, they were not the glorified toilets that graced most clubs.

Uniquely, there is official aural evidence for the sound of the music played on this UK tour. The tour was completed by an appearance on April Fool's Day at the Paris Theatre in London especially for BBC radio and John Peel's *In Concert* show (Led Zeppelin had played the pilot concert for this series back in 1969). The broadcast followed just three days later and, limited by time, a number of songs were not transmitted. Remarkably, one of those was the brand new 'Black Dog' from the as-yet-unreleased fourth album. Only in 1997 did this and two other songs, 'Since I've Been Loving You' and 'Thank You', receive an official release on the *BBC Sessions* CDs, alongside the concert as broadcast at the time.

Page had commented during the tour that the band found themselves playing shorter and tighter sets, and the playing times of some of their big set-piece numbers such as 'Dazed And Confused' and 'Whole Lotta Love', with its attendant medley, were noticeably reduced from some of the 1970 epics. The starter on the radio set, 'Immigrant Song', preserves a fiery Plant vocal settled into a staccato riff that is more prominent and more aggressive than the studio version. It is also faster, making Jones's bass runs in the turnaround an exciting blur of articulation. Page's solo, as so often with him, is more fluent than in the studio, his ideas connecting up logically and the phrases sounding like natural extensions of each other. His attack is also finely judged.

'Heartbreaker', following without pause, is a celebratory rave, allowing the band some high-spirited showing off, especially Page with his unaccompanied spot. 'Since I've Been Loving You' keeps much to the shape of the 1970 live takes, though if anything Plant delivers an even more highly charged vocal than before. The piece continues to show evidence of evolution in its treatment, with its blues form allowing the musicians to shape it as they wish.

'Black Dog' suffers through the limitations of the BBC technology of the day, the overwhelming bottom-end thrust of the studio sound absent. Jones attempts manfully to put as much character into his bass patterns as he can, whatever presence has been sapped electronically from his and Bonham's sound. But although the song – completely new to this audience – retains its brutalism and urgency, its sheer sonic impact is largely missing. Despite that, Page's solo is full of verve and attack and has a precision of execution that his studio version does not match. This being the BBC, the audience applaud politely at the song's end.

'Dazed And Confused' in this rendition remains an aural depiction of hell-fire experienced by the troubled love-struck (or lust-struck) narrator. The highlight is Page's long violin-bow solo, given a second dimension by the echo chamber attached. Page goes for more single-

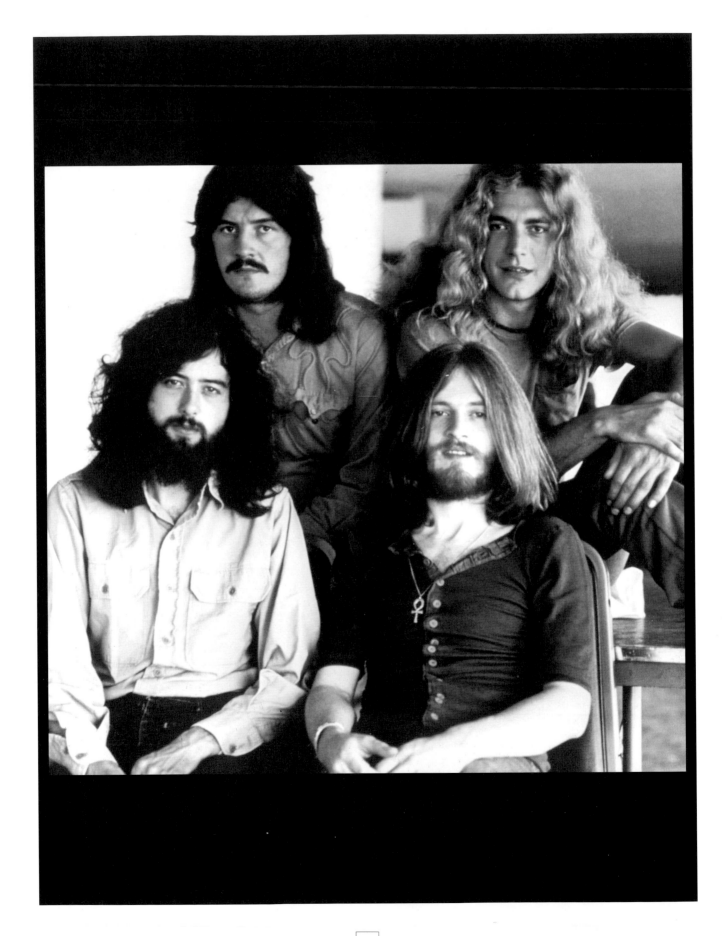

line patterns than normal, resisting the urge simply to go for great splashes of amplified arco colour. This has its benefits in the way he builds up an intriguing musical narrative, an eerie subterranean odyssey that comes close to anticipating the entire story of Genesis's *The Lamb Lies Down On Broadway* by three years and telling it in just a few minutes. After that, the entire band sounds like quicksilver for the rest of the number.

To follow that onslaught with the broadcasting debut of 'Stairway To Heaven', live onstage, was a considerable act of bravery or confidence, depending on your point of view. The slow-picked guitar beginning, leading to Jones's organ accompaniment and Plant's vocal, is a particularly exposed place to be, and there are a few points where someone falters briefly: Plant delivers a nervy opening verse but settles on the second; Page too takes a while to fall into the song's spell. But by the time the famous "makes me wonder" passage comes around, all is well and the rising sense of wellbeing is almost palpable.

When the descending chords make their appearance – a sequence used by many since their first outing in Dylan's 'All Along The Watchtower' – Page launches into his solo and there is a different sort of excitement, an almost visceral sense of adrenalin-rush power and energy that only live performance can deliver. By this point the band are sure that their performance of this new piece has been a major success. Not that the polite applause from the BBC audience at the end – virtually identical to the clapping after every other song – would have been a clue at the time.

Another new song – the third in a row at this concert – comes next. 'Going To California', also destined for the fourth album, pushes the band's acoustic side even further forward, its conversational mix of mandolin and guitar bringing a fireside intimacy to this most public of events, a radio broadcast. The self-deprecatingly sly humour of the piece is another welcome departure for the band; although Led Zeppelin are most often associated with unsmiling, full-on metal riffs and a huge, huge sound, the individual members were not given to taking themselves too seriously and the humour in their music is often overlooked.

To follow this with 'That's The Way', from *Led Zeppelin III*, was to consciously follow the acoustic mood and extend it to more than simply an interlude within the general onslaught. The band were making a statement about how readily they could shift from style to style and achieve authentic inspiration and expressiveness. The deftness of touch in this piece is impressive, given that so many bands at the time resorted to sentimentality or sheer bathos when it came to presenting balladry or less aggressive emotions, their lumbering style unable to achieve the delicacy needed to find the right balance within this different genre. Led Zeppelin did not have that problem once the material from Bron-Yr-Aur was written, learned and disseminated.

The band wound up the BBC show with a 20-minutes-plus 'Whole Lotta Love' that delved into the medleys now such a feature of the live set. Here is another aspect of the band's light-heartedness, their enjoyment evident as they run happily through old rock and blues numbers in a rave-up that recalled the fun of the best Yardbirds days.

Fun may not be the first word that comes to mind to describe what Zeppelin had onstage, but the music tells that story unequivocally. (The official 1997 *BBC Sessions* issue of the 'Whole Lotta Love' medley from this performance was edited by Page so that he could fit it onto the CD: four old rockers were left in – 'Boogie Chillun', 'Fixin' To Die', 'That's Alright Mama', and 'Mess O'Blues' – and three taken out – 'Honey Bee', 'The Lemon Song', and 'For What It's Worth'.)

The performance – and broadcast – was concluded with 'Thank You', which receives an interpretation a good deal less maudlin than the original on *II* and is all the better for it. Bonham thunders away below and the instrumental passages are given a power and drive missing on the album. While the melody and lyrics, especially those of the bridge, still smack of 1967 whimsy – and Plant sounds tentative and out of tune in places – the addition of a scorching Page guitar solo is a definite plus, as is Bonham's madfrenzy drumming in accompaniment.

The band's task (and tour) completed, Peter Grant in particular was gratified with the result, even though he knew before they started that they would be lucky to cover their costs. To him, the bonus in credibility was incalculable, for it quietened any criticism of the band as a unit only interested in money and fame. They had demonstrated the hard way that they cared about their fans, their homeland, and their continuing musical growth. There was no need to repeat the exercise in the immediate future. Next up was the mastering of the forthcoming album and the largest European tour they'd yet undertaken. Summer 1971 looked pretty good for Led Zeppelin.

Surrounded by the warm glow of success, the band know there is plenty still to come: yet more international touring and a fourth album.

ALBUM?
WHAT ALBUM?

- MIXING 4TH ALBUM
- 7TH AMERICAN TOUR
- 1ST JAPANESE TOUR
- BOMBAY VISIT
- 4TH ALBUM RELEASED

After the successful conclusion of the Return To The Clubs tour in March 1971 there was a brief pause in live work while Jimmy Page took the multi-track tapes of the fourth album to Sunset Sound studio in Los Angeles, which he had been told possessed the latest mixing and mastering facilities. He took regular Basing Street engineer Andy Johns with him.

Working consistently, the two spent the majority of April in L.A. perfecting the mix and its subsequent mastering. Unexpectedly, something went wrong. Sunset Sound, a justifiably famous studio complex with state-of-the-art equipment used by all the top acts at the time, had more than one studio in the building. Because they were only mixing, Page and Johns plumped for the smaller Number 2 studio to save on cost: a prudent decision in light of the known facts.

With a minimum of fuss, the job was completed to Page and Johns's satisfaction and they took the finished quarter-inch master back to Britain. What no one had allowed for was the brighter speakers and different acoustics in Studio 2 compared to the places in which they'd recorded, and that there was a mismatch between the tape machines at Sunset Sound and at Olympic in London, where the band heard the finished album for the first time. A problem more common than generally acknowledged, it meant that the timetable for the album's early release was in disarray. They would have to start mixing from scratch. This led to a confusing succession of mixing sessions in various London studios.

Two tracks, 'Black Dog' and 'Stairway To Heaven', were mixed at Island in Basing Street, with five others finished at Olympic. The only track whose Sunset Sound mix survived through to the released album was 'When The Levee Breaks'. Although Johns was present for almost all the mixing sessions, the necessarily piecemeal process of fitting this work around summer tour dates and his own commitments, plus the inevitable loss of confidence stemming from the Sunset Sound disaster, led the engineer to cede his place in front of the faders to the experienced George Chkiantz for 'Battle Of Evermore'.

A process that the whole band had hoped would be unified and quick had, through mischance, become drawn out and fragmented. With some European live work in June and July and a seventh US tour starting in August, the initial hopes for a new album in this period continued to recede. This was hardly ideal, but there was no option. To complicate the already tricky changes they were making to the schedule, soon after the remixing was finally completed the quarter-inch master for 'Four Sticks' was somehow lost, according to Plant. They had to give the track a final mix, for the third time, and then add it to the proper master sequence. Plant commented later in the year: "The whole story of the fourth album reads like a nightmare."[1]

The European jaunt consisted of a handful of dates in Scandinavia and a single concert in Milan, Italy. On July 3rd, as Zeppelin prepared for the Milan show, ex-Doors singer Jim Morrison died in the bath of his Paris hotel room, thus signaling the end of another skewed 1960s dream. Meanwhile, the crowds for the Zep gigs were huge, but 1971 continued as a year beset by unrest and violence at concerts, sometimes due to the nature of the crowd, sometimes to external political and social events that had little or nothing to do with the music. At that stage in rock's history, concerts were perceived as a convenient theatre in which to act out some of the basic dramas afflicting Western society. Throughout America and Europe in 1970 and 1971 the potential for violent confrontation was always lurking, with so much mistrust between youth and authorities.

In Italy, confrontation between political and cultural factions was intense. Unfortunately, the Zeppelin concert on July 5th at Milan's Vigorelli Velodrome became the scene of the latest pitched battle between police and gangs of rock-hurling political agitators. *Il Milanese* said in its report the next day: "The outcome would have been worse if the police department, remembering the sad consequences of past incidents, had not prepared in advance for such an eventuality."[2] This meant that over 2,000 police were present before the first note was played. According to the newspaper, the trouble started on the streets outside the stadium, with tear gas fired at demonstrators and troublemakers who were reported afterwards to be chanting leftist songs and slogans. About 30 minutes prior to the band's set, tour manager Richard Cole recalled, a series of loud explosions at the back of the Velodrome announced that the trouble had moved inside.

Led Zeppelin decided that they would take to the stage anyway, in the hope that the music – the reason the fans were there in the first place – would calm the situation. Unfortunately, according to Cole, by then "the riot squad was flexing its authority by wildly swinging batons and tossing tear-gas canisters into the crowd. Choking, coughing, panicky kids fled in all directions – including toward the stage."[3]

As the band played, the situation quickly spun out of control as people sought refuge onstage and backstage from the batons and the tear gas. After a canister exploded yards from the stage, manager Peter Grant took the decision to abandon the concert. The band ran backstage and, with the help of various Zeppelin road crew and ancillaries, found shelter along with Grant and Cole in a first-aid room. They stayed there until it was safe to emerge. They eventually left the Velodrome under heavily-armed police escort. It was the last Italian concert Led Zeppelin ever played.

With that nightmare out of the way, the band returned to Britain and something of a summer break: they had close to a complete rest from Zeppelin activities for a month. A US tour would kick off in mid August and a couple of nights at the Montreux Casino early that month were the preparation. Otherwise they were close to six weeks away from touring. Page continued to stay on top of the fourth album's slow progress toward its delayed release, but the other three went back to their families.

Problems and arguments over the new album's final identity ran all through the summer and into autumn 1971, with Zeppelin's team and Atlantic in New York at odds over what Page wanted for the jacket design. Of course it would be another gatefold sleeve, as befitted the band's status. But apart from that there was little agreement. Page had not taken kindly to the widespread criticism of *III*'s cover art and had decided that, this time, it would be devoid of easily categorised images and words as *III*'s had been full of them, from the title onwards.

Page felt that the final artwork for the third album bore little relation to his original ideas and this had led to its misinterpretation. In a bid to avoid a repeat of this, he and the band decided they were going to aim for allusion and enigma. He and Grant told Atlantic that they wanted no words at all on the cover, inside or out. In November 1970 The Byrds had released an album called *(untitled)* after it had been erroneously ascribed that non-title, something the American group saw not only as a stroke of fate but also very amusing. Page and the rest of Zeppelin, however, were serious about what they hoped to achieve.

Initially they even wanted to avoid a catalogue number, but eventually conceded the impracticality of this notion. No one would be able to order or deliver the record, especially if it carried no title. Of course, The Beatles had been down this road in 1968 and had found the logical answer – an all-white outer sleeve with merely "The Beatles" embossed on the cover next to a unique serial number for that copy. On the inside cover were pictures of the four band members and a list of song titles.

The following year, John Lennon had released two albums with no words on the front sleeve and only minimal information on the back: *Two Virgins*, additionally sold in brown paper bags, and *Live Peace In Toronto*, with a picture of a small white cloud in a blue sky. Lennon's first post-Beatles LP, *Plastic Ono Band*, had only the title in small print on the bottom left-hand side of the reverse sleeve, while Paul McCartney's first solo effort, released in 1970, simply had his name on the back of a gatefold sleeve. As an indication of how much the popular music scene had evolved and speeded up, it had taken The Beatles five years and ten albums to dispense with all identifying marks. It had taken Led Zeppelin a little over two years and just three albums. But such elegant simplicity as the design for the title-less Beatles double-album could not be repeated without widespread accusations of Zeppelin running out of ideas if they had to borrow from The Beatles to design their record jackets.

Besides, such minimalism was not so fashionable in

1971 and was not really to Page's taste. By then he was deeply involved in his researches into magic, esoteric knowledge and folk mysticism. He wanted this to be reflected in the sleeve design. With his firm belief that 'Stairway To Heaven' would be perceived as a defining moment for the band, and with the song's words awash with Plant's own folk-myth imagery, the cover had to convey at least a flavour of such concerns.

The album designers were briefed and given the raw material with which to work: a photo containing a painting of a faggot-gatherer that hangs on the interior wall of a demolished house against a background of slum clearance and tower blocks in Eve Hill, Dudley, in the Midlands. For the inner artwork there was an even more specific reference to Page's interests in the esoteric tradition through a dramatic portrayal of the Tarot card Hermit symbol.

Only on the inner sleeve that held the record itself would any wording appear. On one side were the lyrics to 'Stairway To Heaven', with an engraving of a mystical scholar reading from an ancient volume nearby. On the other side of the inner sleeve were the song titles in order of performance and the necessary credits.

Also on the inner sleeve were the four symbols that emerged after Page asked each member of the band to pick his own identifying symbol. Page later claimed that this idea for the album came in stages. After he'd finally decided against a record with no identifying marks, he suggested to the others that they put just one symbol on the inner sleeve. This quickly became four symbols, most obviously because there were four musicians and this was the fourth album. Everything was tailored to suggest the idea of 'four' as central to the record without this being explicitly stated. That was why Page was annoyed later when a few over-zealous fans and commentators started using his own symbol – 'Zoso' – as the album's name: it explicitly denied the unity and balance he perceived as the core of the record's identity.

Just as the all-white untitled Beatles double of 1968 eventually became universally known as *The White Album*, Zeppelin's fourth in the absence of an assigned name was eventually bestowed the unofficial titles of *Four Symbols* or *Led Zeppelin IV* by fans. What the band members call it remains conjecture. What is beyond conjecture, however, is that it was still not ready for release by the time they flew out to begin their seventh US tour in mid August 1971. Just before, they played two nights at the Montreux Casino in Switzerland, something of a novelty for all concerned. It was a venue closely associated with the Montreux Jazz Festival during the 1960s and '70s, and *Sounds* commented that "dinner jacketed diners mixed with Led Zeppelin fans".[4] So began a long slog of about six weeks of live work, with their first Japanese tour tagged on the end and just five days' break between.

Led Zeppelin arrived just two weeks after the major

musical event of the season, George Harrison and Ravi Shankar's Concert For Bangladesh, which had taken place in New York City on August 1st. It had created a great deal of publicity and large amounts of money donated towards the rebuilding of the country devastated by floods and storms. The cause was a major talking-point, establishing that rock music could actively contribute to lessen the burden of unfortunate people. Within the rock music world, however, the excitement came from seeing Harrison onstage along with his friends Eric Clapton and Bob Dylan. Dylan had not been on a stage since 1969's Isle of Wight Festival. As a public-relations splash this was impossible to top, and Zeppelin didn't even try.

Once more the tour stuck mainly to the two coasts, with exceptions including Chicago, the Texan dates, New Orleans, and St Louis. It was very extensive and in some ways the most fraught to date, with its share of unpleasant incidents. Discomfort with the very idea of being on the road began to set in among the Zeppelin camp. Even though the fourth album was trailed heavily at every concert, it remained stubbornly not ready for release. In the event, it would appear until November – a good two months after the end of the US tour, during the band's second UK tour of the year.

This particular American tour seems to have been remembered more for the confrontations between the band, its entourage and the rest of the world than for the music played. A defining incident came right at the beginning, in Vancouver. Tour manager Richard Cole and manager Peter Grant were ever vigilant for unauthorised recordings of the band's concerts, and especially so at the beginning of this tour when new material from the unreleased fourth album was to be premiered.

They spotted a man close to the stage making no attempt to hide what looked like a microphone, attached to a portable tape recorder, held up towards the PA system. Cole and members of the road crew picked up the man and threw him on the floor. Then they smashed his equipment to pieces, telling him if he wanted a recording he should go to a record shop like everyone else.

But this was no bootlegger. He was a local government official, part of a team attempting to monitor the band's decibel level. The man lodged a complaint that night and the Vancouver police arrived at the stadium before the show had concluded. Grant somehow smoothed over the incident, promising to replace the broken equipment and persuading the official to drop his complaint. The police decided not to take their enquiries further and, after a report in the *Vancouver Sun* the following morning, the assault stayed out of the mainstream papers, although the music press picked up on it. It was a warning, if anybody wanted to acknowledge it. But no one much did.

By autumn 1971 the band's members were all individually wealthy. Management had organised a solid

protective shield between them and the outside world that operated on any tour. The means of enforcing that protective shield were rarely questioned. In the moral vacuum that exists for the length of any tour little is done to curb impulses to excess that any member of the touring party might have, road crew and all. As Richard Cole expressed it: "We didn't give a fuck. The doors had to open now. If they didn't, we'd break them down. And that was it. We made our own laws. If you didn't want to fucking abide by them, don't get involved."[5]

Musicians on tour had operated in moral vacuums for decades, and for all sorts of reasons. Chubby Jackson, bassist with the Woody Herman Herd big-band back in the 1940s, said: "Down deep, we were all harmlessly nuts. We had to get up on a bandstand nightly, daily, and entertain people who had looks on their faces – like they all looked the same. So just to do that, when we were off the bandstand, we'd say, 'Damn it, let's entertain ourselves.' And that's how a lot of the fun really started."[6] For Jackson, 30 years before Zeppelin, the fun was there onstage and offstage and centred on the band's efforts to keep morale high while on the road. If it wasn't kidding around, it would be drink and drugs. He saw more than one colleague to an early grave through overdoses.

For 1970s rock bands there was more at stake, so the fun tended to be after-hours and away from the stage itself, where their money and fame could provide a controlled environment and a modicum of protection from the consequences. Led Zeppelin had no moral purpose in going out on the road and playing long tours, being only part of a wider picture in rock where excess and indulgence was not only condoned but encouraged.

Yet it is hard to escape the feeling that in such an artificial world of false values, wild and reckless behaviour could easily blur the borders with quasi-criminal brutality and, more worryingly, obscure the early manifestations of emotional disturbance that would be so damaging later. John Bonham's unchecked and often random acts of outrage – allegedly shitting in fans' shoes and the like – suggest an expression of deeper problems than mere horseplay. But nobody in the band's otherwise aggressively protective entourage was paying attention. At that time, especially in the USA, there was a sense of violence in the air and a feeling that the violence could turn against the band.

Richard Cole later remembered this seventh US tour as the one where they had more death threats from anonymous nutters than any other. The police were routinely informed but no arrests were ever made, thanks either to efficient security screening or the random luck of keeping the freaks at bay. None of this helped the band's sense of isolation and paranoia when dealing with the outside world, or their sense of balance when even the mildest confrontation arose.

Peter Grant, like many successful managers before

and after, developed a close and effective team-mentality. This came partly through a healthy sense of paranoia – "nobody likes us and we don't care" – that has helped countless different teams over the years. There will always be moments when the paranoia spins out of control, especially when booze and drugs, unlimited power and complete unaccountability are added into the mix. Yet Bonham, back in England just prior to the new album's release, told Chris Welch: "The American tour we did was good in actual fact. … We played really well and had some great things happen. … I think I enjoyed it more than any other tour of America. You see, we had a lot of time at home to think, and we grew a lot closer together. … We all came out of ourselves and everybody played well and we are really happy!"[7]

It was an important tour musically, especially for Page and Plant because they were taking a risk putting their new material – 'Black Dog' and especially 'Stairway To Heaven' – to their audiences without prior warning. It was the ultimate test for the material and one not taken lightly by any popular group at the time. The band were looking for an enormous vote of confidence and a confirmation of trust from their fans. That this confidence and trust was forthcoming from the audience on this tour was a vindication for Page's music policy.

A typical Zeppelin set in autumn 1971 had a certain shape, reaching a first climax around half way through with 'Dazed And Confused'. There would follow some more low-key songs, then a gradual build-up to the second climax, centred on the 'Whole Lotta Love' medley. Most of the following would be present: 'Immigrant Song', 'Heartbreaker', 'Since I've Been Loving You', 'Black Dog', 'Dazed And Confused', 'That's The Way', 'Going To California', 'What Is And What Should Never Be', 'Moby Dick', 'Whole Lotta Love', 'Rock And Roll', 'Communication Breakdown', and 'Thank You'. The last two were encores, while any two of the others would sometimes be rested from one night to the next in order to keep the set fresh for the band.

This set 'shaping' was similar to what the band had developed when they'd played music from the first two albums: a fiery beginning, a big blues ballad, then back to a mid-way climax of epic proportions. What amounted to a second 'half' was even more accentuated by autumn 1971 with the introduction of the acoustic numbers from the third and fourth albums, almost like a collective gathering of breath and senses before the final aural assault and battery of 'Whole Lotta Love', 'Rock And Roll' and the encores. It showed just how shrewdly Page understood dynamics and pacing and how the band worked to a clear plan and pattern, however spontaneous their interpretation of any song might be on a given night. Still, the sheer length and pace of the tour and their own nightly efforts proved draining.

By mid September and the end of the American tour,

the band's energy levels and spirits had sagged. According to local reports in Honolulu, the Hawaiian concerts were uninspired. "The music was limp and uneven during all but a small part of the evening," the *Honolulu Star-Bulletin*'s reviewer wrote. "It was obvious that these guys were not into what they were doing. Rhythms were off, Plant's vocals were relatively impotent, and the overall cohesion and enthusiasm was missing. … You couldn't help but get the impression that these guys were tired and looking forward to the end of the evening."[8]

Yet they were still not in a position to head home. After a week away from concerts, resting in Hawaii with their wives and companions, they flew into Japan for an intense itinerary of five concerts in six days. Since The Beatles had performed in Tokyo in 1966 audiences there had craved live rock acts, and Zeppelin were following in the footsteps of many top bands. They arrived in Japan as 'Immigrant Song' lodged at Number 1 in the singles charts, a lucky omen given the song was now entrenched as the band's opening concert number. Despite the demand, live concerts by top acts were still a relatively unusual occurrence, and each Zeppelin gig was sold out. Audiences were ready to give unqualified support.

Two concerts at Tokyo's famous Budokan Hall – where both The Beatles and Bob Dylan had played their first Japanese concerts – were followed by a special commemorative concert in Hiroshima, one of two Japanese cities devastated by atomic bombs at the end of World War II. The concert raised money for victims of the blast, many of whom still suffered from the effects of radiation decades after the event. It was a success on every level, with Zeppelin's members given the Hiroshima Peace Medal to recognise their humanitarian gesture in helping to raise funds. It was a rare official endorsement of the band's ability to achieve much when they put their collective energy behind a project, and showed Peter Grant in a humanitarian light the public seldom saw.

Other kinds of individual energies of a mindlessly destructive variety were well in evidence on that tour. Carnage was visited upon the Tokyo Hilton by John Bonham and Richard Cole wielding Samurai swords, wrecking two hotel rooms and butchering an entire corridor. The band's reward for this night of fun was a life ban from the hotel for the entire entourage.

Another prank directly affected the music, with the band for the first time in its career compromising the quality of its performance in order to indulge an in-joke. They asked the head of Atlantic Records UK, Phil Carson, to appear onstage with the band in Osaka under the pretext of helping out on bass – Carson was a professional-standard bass guitarist – while Jones was on keyboards. Carson did his duty, only to find the rest of the

Overleaf: Led Zeppelin onstage at The Forum in Los Angeles on August 21st 1971.

band disappearing to leave him alone onstage. What the Japanese audience thought of such a schoolboy prank is not clear, their impeccable manners stifling any catcalls or boos, but the whole caper was received with bemusement. Everyone involved with the band realised it had been a bad miscalculation and the exercise was not repeated.

It is bizarre that the band agreed on such a stunt in the first place, and shows just how strung-out on touring they were by this last set of concerts. Richard Cole claimed that the band were routinely consuming vast quantities of liquor, although it seems Cole and Bonham regularly out-drank everyone else. In Tokyo one night, he claimed proudly, the entire band drank staff and geisha girls quite literally under the table. They began increasingly to slip between using legal and illegal drugs. "We might have also snorted some cocaine except we couldn't get it there," wrote Cole, "[because] it seemed to be taboo in Japan. Yes, alcohol was still our primary substance of choice, but elsewhere, we had begun using cocaine more frequently, simply because it was so available."[9]

Happily, the tour was concluded without anyone arrested or killed, and the band was rewarded with a well-earned break. Jones, Grant and Bonham headed straight for Britain, Jones and Bonham to their families and Grant to the office to co-ordinate the release of the new album. He had a November UK promotional tour to put in place for the LP, but also had to plot a schedule for February 1972 and another visit to the Pacific rim, this time to Australia and New Zealand.

Plant, Page and Cole decided to return home via Bangkok, Thailand, and Bombay (now Mumbai), India. The band had only a cult following in those countries at the time and could indulge in tourist-type things without being recognised – whether it was shopping trips, whorehouses, or checking out the local music. Well, almost. Their noisy presence in a Bangkok brothel attracted the attention of two young sailors from Liverpool who couldn't believe who they'd stumbled on, thousands of miles from home. So much for anonymity.

A taxi driver showed them the different sides of Bombay away from the normal haunts of white tourists, including brothels, music shops and the poorer discticts, and talked to them about life in India for ordinary people. On the last evening there they even had a meal at his home. But for Page and Plant, if not Cole, the point of the visit to Bombay in particular was accomplished between recreational activities. During their stay at the Taj Mahal Hotel they put out feelers to local musicians.

Plant later remembered it in cavalier style. "The upper class Indian, and the Anglo-Indian – the people that are clamouring and grabbing the Western idea – will grab it enough to open a discotheque in sunny Bombay where you have six million people sleeping on the street every night. … You have a disco around the corner called the Slipped Disc."[10]

Reynold D'Silva and his friend Yusuf Ghandi, then living in Bombay and part of that city's rock scene, recalled that Plant and Page came down to the Taj Mahal's genteel disco, The Blow Up, and immediately decided it was too flashy and formal. The Zep musicians made enquiries about other places worth visiting and the local driver took them to another club, The Slip Disc, at Apollo Bunder on Bombay's waterfront.

Yusuf Ghandi, then working there as a DJ, was taking a breather outside between sets when he saw Page, Plant and Cole arrive. "It was a members-only club," said Ghandi, "a real rock'n'roll type place: great atmosphere, grotty, full of smoke, low-life, everything. We had a bouncer on the door and he wouldn't let Plant, Page and Cole in. At that time there were many problems with drugs and hippies trying to get into places like that and most clubs were employing bouncers to keep them out. I was standing outside and I noticed these three English guys talking calmly to the bouncer, trying to persuade him to let them in. They were dressed in cool suits and had long hair, and I knew hippies didn't dress like that, so I thought well, they could be rock stars. I walked over to see if I could help.

"I asked what was happening and [Richard Cole] introduced me to Plant and Page. Of course, I immediately knew that they were from Led Zeppelin – we were all fans of the band from their records – and persuaded the bouncer to let them in. I said that I'd take responsibility for them and tell the owner what was going on. We went in and they immediately liked the atmosphere. Robert Plant saw the scene, smelled the pot in the air, took off his coat, threw it on a seat, and said: 'Back to sanity at last!' Slip Disc had a live band and the DJs like myself played real rock, not bubblegum like the DJs at The Blow Up."

The band playing that night was The Velvet Fog, whose singer/guitarist Naresh Mansukhani and bassist Xerxes Gobhai were friends of Ghandi. Without too much effort from Ghandi and his awe-struck friends, Plant and Page were persuaded to sit in with The Velvet Fog. Plant later remembered the whole thing as somewhat farcical, but Ghandi had a different slant. "Page borrowed Mansukhani's guitar and they played two numbers with the drummer and bass player. The crowd were really responsive. Then they went back over to where they'd been seated and relaxed again. They stayed for the evening. … It's funny, but the owner hadn't realised who they were: he asked what was going on when they went up onstage – 'Who are these guys and why are they sitting in?' Of course, once he knew he was ecstatic. He went over to them and asked them to play again. They declined. He offered them free beer if they would! Of course, they just laughed."[11]

A few days later, Page and Plant went back to London. They felt like their mission was accomplished: they had already toyed with the idea of making some music in India with local players and wanted to see whether this was a realistic possibility. After a few days scouting and making enquiries, they'd discovered it was. The seeds had been sown for the following spring's Bombay sessions.

In Britain in October 1971 the band were finally able to start preparing for the release of the long-delayed fourth album. They had finished the music more than half a year earlier and the mixing was completed prior to the summer tour. The band had been through an entire spring, summer and autumn's worth of touring with no new LP to trumpet. The strain was showing. One biographer later quoted 'insiders' who called it "the most internally fraught period the group had experienced."[12] Perhaps this was a major reason for the particularly unhinged behaviour on tour that year.

As September changed to October, the artwork for the new album was finally completed to everyone's satisfaction and the record put into production. The record was issued in the USA on November 8th. A few days later it was in British stores, just a month after Cat Stevens had released *Teaser And The Firecat* and Marc Bolan's T.Rex went to Number 1 with *Electric Warrior*, and a week after John Lennon's *Imagine* LP hit the top spot. It took the rest of the month for *IV* to overhaul Lennon and make it to Number 1 in Britain, but by mid December *Electric Warrior* was once again at the top, boosted by its latest single, 'Jeepster'. Rod Stewart's 'Maggie May' was the biggest single of the autumn, closely followed by Slade's 'Coz I Luv You'. Led Zeppelin's album entered a rapidly changing British market which, with the sudden rise of Glam and its offshoots, was already vastly different to the one they had originally expected for the record.

On the other side of the Atlantic, 'Maggie May' had made Rod Stewart a major solo star, with the album *Every Picture Tells A Story* reaching Number 1, while Cher had re-activated her career with 'Gypsys, Tramps And Thieves' in the singles chart and Isaac Hayes delivered a new urban sound in 'Theme From Shaft'. John Lennon's 'Imagine' single only made Number 3, although the album went to the top. *Shaft* was another chart-topping LP at the time, followed by *Santana 3*, and Sly Stone's *There's A Riot Goin' On* was the Christmas Number 1 album. Carole King's follow-up to *Tapestry*, called simply *Music*, took over the top slot in the new year. The separation between UK and US record markets was becoming increasingly apparent as the 1970s got underway, despite the previously close links. From now, fewer new acts would successfully span both British and American charts. It would take the advent of disco in the late 1970s for the two to re-engage once more.

Like every other Led Zeppelin album, the fourth one starts with a big-boom-bang to make the listener sit up and pay attention. This time it is 'Black Dog', which was created through collective sessions on a Jones bass riff. The bassist said he'd come up with a long, complicated riff after a visit to Page's house where they were listening to Muddy Waters's *Electric Mud* LP from 1968.

On the way home, Jones had turned the riff around and inside out in his head. He came up with a clever pattern that turns back on itself more than once, crossing between time signatures as it does. As this is a blues, there are a number of other possible sources beyond Muddy Waters. In 1959, the groundbreaking jazz musician Ornette Coleman made his second album as a leader, *Tomorrow Is The Question!*. On it, he recorded one of his own blues compositions, 'Turnaround', based on an unbroken, complex and rhythmically asymmetric line that constantly repeats and rephrases itself, disguising the easy going 12-bar blues form lurking underneath. Ignored at the time of its release, it later became the Coleman composition most often played by other musicians. A man as musically sophisticated as Jones, who had a specific interest in modern jazz, could easily have used a memory of the piece to mentally juxtapose against the *Electric Mud* riff, sparking a similar line of musical enquiry in a very different stylistic context.

The 'Black Dog' riff was such a complex piece of band playing that they quickly decided in rehearsal to locate the vocal line elsewhere. The obvious place was in a call-and-response form – something as old as the blues itself but recently given a very sharp contemporary edge by Fleetwood Mac in 'Oh Well', a Number 1 single in Britain in 1969 and a song that shares part of its bass-and-guitar riff with 'Black Dog'. Another recent call-and-response hit was 'Cold Turkey', John Lennon's 1969 exorcism of heroin that pitched his voice, accompanied solely by Ringo Starr's drums and Klaus Voorman's simple bass, against a wall-of-sound guitar figure from Eric Clapton that more than adequately represented the screams of pain associated with a heroin cold turkey.

Led Zeppelin's take on the form is quite different in effect. For a start, Plant was not about to write lyrics dealing with heroin withdrawal or talking to god. In this honest-to-goodness supercharged blues, he would concentrate on traditional blues themes: love, lust, and the whole damn thing. "Hey, hey, mama, said the way you move / Gonna make you sweat / Gonna make you groove." This is Muddy Waters territory: confident, swaggering and passionate, but given a young-man sex strut as only Plant could at the time.

One of the great paradoxes of good music is perfectly illustrated by the opening riff after Plant's first stanza: the way that apparent complexity can arise from simple ingredients. The riff is a tangled and self-referencing line that implies a 2/4 metre, suggesting a drum pattern that would give a cut-time snare backbeat. But we don't get that pattern. The metre is extended to twice the implied length, to 4/4, giving the effect of a single giant breath held as the entire riff is articulated against a slow-motion drum beat. It's easy to illustrate just how weird this makes the 'Black Dog' riff sound: just imagine the riff of 'Oh Well Part 1' played with a Bonham long-metre drum beat underneath. It would have the same distended but dramatic effect.

To add to the shock value, an extra beat in the guise of a pause is added between Plant's unaccompanied vocals and the start of the riff, thus placing the riff section back-to-front rhythmically, even though it is in 4/4. When the first bridge section of the song is reached (0:42), again there are no vocals over the riff – and this time it plunges into a time signature as remote from mainstream rock as anything Captain Beefheart or Frank Zappa had devised. The undisguised 5/8 metre makes for an odd number of beats in the bar, turning the backbeat around each time if Bonham wanted to follow the shape of the bar lines. For quite a while in rehearsal this had failed to fall into place.

Jones explained: "I told [Bonham] that he had to keep playing four-to-the-bar all the way through. ... But [in the verse turnaround] there is a 5/8 rhythm over the top. If you go through enough 5/8s, it arrives back on the beat. Originally it was more complicated, but we had to change the accents for him to play it properly."[13] The sum effect is that, for a short few bars in the bridge, Bonham is playing on the opposite side of the beat to the bass and guitars, before two measures of odd time become even time again and the beat reunites all three players on the same side (0:49). The resulting tension is almost exultant, electrifying the listener. No matter how many times you hear it, your ears are torn in two as you try to follow both sides of the beat through the turnaround. The eventual merging at its end is a tremendous release and consummation of the song and the band's energy. What doubles the excitement is that this is played by all concerned with maximum attitude and swagger.

Suddenly in the bridge (0:52), Bonham bursts into the double-time we'd expected all along – although he still doesn't add the backbeat – as the bass and guitars move into a simple pedal tone to which Page adds a decorative tail while Plant glides in and out with "oh yeah" phrases. The band moves on (1:04) to the verse repeat, "Eyes that shine burnin' red / Dreams of you all through my head", the main riff, and a potent "ah-ah ah-ah..." Plant-led pause. Then into a bludgeoning two-note riff (1:40) that, again, is rhythmically inside-out and asks Bonham to place the usual snare emphasis instead on the bass-drum while he shadows the bass-and-guitars riff with his sticks. It is close to a bolero in its off-centre swing, but the sound is so brutal you'd never associate it with Latin dance .

Back to the verse (2:04) and a complete recapitulation and development of the entire structure – except that some guitar harmony is added, and when it comes to the two-note riff, Page takes a solo (3:36) in place of Plant's urgent half-words, while Plant mutters, sighs and shrieks in the background. Page has said that there are as many as four guitar tracks on this recording, layered to give the requisite texture and depth to the punishing sound.

Page was by no means the first to build up many layers of guitars in this way but, in the wake of Hendrix, he was by far the most imaginative in the use of the technique within a rock band. His arranging and production gifts bring great depth of sound and colour to the banked guitars, buttressed by the gigantic sound extracted from Bonham's drums and Jones's firm but huge bass sound. Jones never allowed his sound to become diffuse, a mere blur in proceedings, but neither did he go for a clipped, toppy sound that would have robbed the band of its bottomless depth and a proper mesh with Bonham's drums. In songs such as 'Black Dog' his sound did much to give a perfect aural balance and clarity to the music.

Oddly, given that it is one of the most brutally exciting pieces Zeppelin ever created, Page's Telecaster solo at the close of 'Black Dog' is not one of his best. Perhaps it's because he has to solo over a tricky rhythmic base, or maybe, as he has repeatedly explained since, it's because he tightened up in studios. He begins here with a repeated rising triplet phrase in mid register that has plenty of energy but no sense of movement and it sits uneasily with the back-to-front rhythm underneath. Next he moves to a crotchet variation in a higher register, then a series of longer bent notes that seem to search for but fail to find release. More repeated patterns bring him back to the original triplet riff and a collection of typical Page blues phrases that sound less a result of inspiration as of sitting in the studio doing overdubs and waiting for the solo section to end. Perhaps in going for speed and precision Page misses the opportunity to really take off and just glide over the turbulent rhythms beneath him.

Such reservations are swept aside by the swashbuckling entry of the second number, 'Rock And Roll', on a surging cushion of Bonham 8/8 boogie. If you've savoured the wild-eyed frenzy of Little Richard's original 1950s recordings you'll recognise the source of the drummer's incredible rhythmic push: 'Keep A Knockin'. That had a similar drum madness, topped by Mr Penniman screeching "Keep a knockin' but you can't come in / Come back tomorrow night and try again."

Led Zeppelin preserve Richard's manic energy and adrenalin rush but fashion the song into something of their own. Given the almost sombre complexities under the apparently straight blues structure of 'Black Dog', this simple boogie blues form comes as a whoop of joy and release. Every member of the band is at absolute full tilt and it's virtually impossible to listen to this song without a smile on your face, such are the high spirits involved.

The musical inspiration may have come straight out of Little Richard – though it's worth remembering Fleetwood Mac's concert version of 'Keep A Knockin'' in 1970 – but the hastily improvised lyrics from Plant stemmed from the shuffle-boogie blues tradition of artists like John Lee Hooker and Elmore James. Page's solo on this more traditional rock piece is much more successful than on 'Black Dog', packing in both technique and excitement while exhibiting real verve in the execution, especially in the stop-time bars at the turnaround (2:13).

The crunching end of 'Rock And Roll' leaves us completely unprepared for the fade-in of the next piece, 'The Battle Of Evermore'. It is one of Zeppelin's most beautiful and elusive songs. Originally conceived by Page as an instrumental, it testifies to the brilliant versatility of all four musicians. Plant, recognising the need for a second voice, showed impeccable taste in choosing Sandy Denny, the ex-Fairport Convention singer and one of the most haunting vocalists of her generation.

Plant uses his natural tenor voice in the verses, rarely pushing it hard, showing a firm understanding of the ballad-singing voice most often used in folk. Denny responds with a pure singing tone, especially in her response passages where she sings alone. It is a unique event in the recorded history of Zeppelin to hear the band with another voice. Only in the unison passages with Denny does Plant use his driven falsetto or a coarse timbre and blues scoop on the note. The blend is remarkably successful and much more subtle than it first seems. The song has rarely attracted comment beyond the fact that Denny appears on it, or that the lyrics are derived from Plant's immersion in *Lord Of The Rings* and the myths and legends of Scottish border wars, obsessively portrayed by earlier generations in songs and poems.

Even by the late 18th century there were collections of these ballads, with Percy's *Reliques Of Ancient English Poetry* of 1765 one of the first and most influential. They formed a cornerstone in the development of the British manifestation of the Romantic movement, especially in Scotland, where war and witchcraft often mingled in the work of writers such as Sir Walter Scott and James Hogg. 'Battle Of Evermore' is perhaps overshadowed by the more immediate beauty of the song that follows it on the album, but it has a haunted longing that becomes increasingly powerful on repeated listening.

That longing is located as much in Jones's mandolin playing as in the words or the melody. Page has often disparaged his first attempts at composing on a mandolin, dismissing them as the kind of thing any guitarist swapping to the instrument might first play. The chord sequence may well be common in mandolin circles, but the driving rhythm (buttressed by an acoustic guitar) and the unworldly ambience and sense of space of Page's production makes the music almost pictorial, as if Plant and Denny are singing around a camp fire on a "darkling plain".

Many bands subsequently took 'Evermore' as a cue to dive off into ever more grandiose depictions of mythological heaven-and-hell conflict, but few have noted the key to this song's success. It is beautifully understated, combining a fierce emotional strength with enigmatic understatement. Both qualities are everywhere in evidence on Sandy Denny's own records – check out 'Bushes And Briars' from 1972's *Sandy*, for example – and those she made with Fairport Convention, so there is little reason to doubt that these were the qualities Plant wished her to bring to the session and the song.

After the beguiling 'Evermore' and its drastic change of pace from the first two tracks, 'Stairway To Heaven' is introduced by Page's solo guitar. It is a perfect segue as the troubled intimacy of 'Evermore' gives way to the warmth and peace of 'Stairway'. As a composition it is something of a patchwork quilt, but it has been so nimbly worked over by composer Page that all the joins are seamless, with the musical story compelling in its logic and forward motion. Jones recalled that 'Stairway' and 'Evermore' were the only two songs brought to the Headley Grange rehearsals in anything like complete form, the others all emerging from the collective efforts of the four musicians. Both are ballads that tell a story and 'Stairway' in particular is in a form that was unlikely to have emerged from band sessions.

Like Lennon & McCartney's 'A Day In The Life', it has an overall scheme, rising from slow ballad to dramatic crescendo and resolution, passing through several developmental stages on the way. Page's most brilliant and daring arranging idea was to leave bass and drums out until half the music had been performed, thus opening with an unaccompanied guitar progression that has a pastoral mood.

Guitarist Randy California from West Coast band Spirit often mentioned that this opening guitar pattern sounded "exactly like" his instrumental, 'Taurus'. California's explanation for the parallel was that Zeppelin opened for Spirit on their first American tour. Some commentators have also noted a similarity in part of the song's chord structure to 'And She's Lonely' by The Chocolate Watch Band, another group with whom Page shared a stage, in California during his Yardbirds days.

Page may well have been intrigued by the beauty of the finger-picked guitar chords that link the different sections of 'Taurus' together and may have played around with the chord progression over the years. 'Taurus' begins with the same four chords against the same descending lower line, but then goes to a rather awkward resolving chord before returning to the top of the progression. Page's version supplies a simple but much more elegant and emotionally satisfying two-chord resolution that is also more in tune with the peaceful air of the opening section of 'Stairway'.

Page's opening chords are subtly fleshed out by Jones on organ and a bank of overdubbed recorders, sustaining and expanding the pastoral atmosphere here. The sense of idyll is confirmed by Plant's lyrics, which are a considerable departure from average Zeppelin subject

matter – or indeed the average rock band's subject matter. Here we are closer to the concerns covered in songs by Fairport Convention or Donovan. In fact, for the first time Plant's approach to his lyric writing in this piece approaches the economy and intensity of line and image associated with the best songwriters or ballad poets, just as Donovan's had three years earlier in his remarkable but subsequently neglected solo half of *A Gift From A Flower To A Garden* (1968). As with Donovan's acute and shimmering observations of nature in 'The Lullaby Of Spring', 'Starfish-On-The-Toast', and 'Isle Of Islay' – accompanied by fingerpicked acoustics such as on 'Stairway' – Plant had moved on from straightforward narration and the stark depictions of emotional or sexual states that had until then been his preoccupation. Now he reached for allusion.

The parallels between Donovan and Plant do not stop there. Donovan occasionally wrote evocations of medieval and classical legends, including 'Atlantis' and 'Guinevere', a remarkable portrait of the famous fictional figure in the moments before her fateful compromise. While Plant's readings eventually led him to different myths and legends, the pursuit was the same. Donovan was signed to Mickie Most and both Page and Jones had worked on his sessions, aiding familiarity with his ideas. In that sense, the first third of 'Stairway' is something of a throwback, invoking the innocence of that initial hippie explosion.

Plant places his first character – the woman buying her place on the stairway – in the kind of enchanted land familiar to us from fairy tales and popular legends, where innocence has to triumph over error and bad intentions through pure instinct. Each challenge in the song is a challenge to instinct: the piper, the two roads, the songbird, the voices of those who stand looking, nature itself. These have to be correctly interpreted by the characters in the lyrics and, ultimately, by us.

This is an old tradition in balladry, with one of its most glorious and epic poetic incarnations occurring in Edmund Spenser's *The Faerie Queene*, first published in the 1590s and wholly concerned with breathtakingly written depictions of moral and ethical dilemmas and their just resolutions. Plant, a modern man, was not working to a specifically Christian programme, but is well within the Islamo-Christian humanist tradition, especially when he declares "and it makes me wonder". Life makes you wonder. Finding the path through it lasts a lifetime. The first four verses, all accompanied solely by guitars and recorders, have the same rhyme and syllable scheme, with each a variation on the initial poetic idea of choice and the preservation of innocence and instinct.

At the conclusion of the first two verses there is a

bridge section (2:15) made up of luminescent A minor sevenths in banks of 12-string guitars and organ pedal tones, laying a tapestry of music over which Plant musingly sings his "and it makes me wonder". Then the verse-bridge pattern is repeated, only this time the verses have extra guitars and some soft organ harmonies added.

With the introduction of the next section of the song and Bonham's entrance (4:20) the verse pattern changes and the meaning shifts too, reflected in the augmented arrangement, although the musical structure remains essentially the same. There are two verses that directly address the listener, who is now being asked to deal with the same questions earlier addressed to the Lady and the singer himself. These verses, underpinned by Bonham's assertive but precise drums, are set to a rich major progression that conjures a sense of exultation and purpose, set either side of the meditative sevenths of Plant's "and it makes me wonder" refrain (4:45).

Then the entire song is abruptly interrupted and taken in a different direction (5:33), musically and lyrically. The change is dramatic, as if Page felt the join between the middle and last sections was too intrusive to disguise: better to make a merit out of necessity and have a tricky stop-time fanfare-like passage of guitar-bass-drums to signal the movement to the concluding part. This fanfare is repeated before Bonham settles into a slightly quickened tempo and a rock-steady 4/4 beat. The quickened tempo was deliberate, as Page made clear in 1991. "What I wanted was something that would have the drums come in at the middle and then we'd build to a huge crescendo. Also, I wanted to speed it up, which is against all musical … I mean, that's what a musician *doesn't* do, you see?"[14]

Page begins his solo over a three-chord cycle first made famous in Dylan's 'All Along The Watchtower' and later appearing in hundreds of (mostly lesser) songs. Intriguingly, the man who created a hit single out of Dylan's song, Jimi Hendrix, used this progression for his own meditative ballad 'Hey Baby (New Rising Sun)', a song dealing with subjects closely related to Plant's in 'Stairway'. Dylan's chord pattern awoke deep emotional and creative responses in many artists at the time.

The harmonic underpinning of the last section certainly brought an outstanding response from Page when it came to the guitar solo. It is one of his greatest, for reasons that are not hard to pinpoint. It has an easy pace, rhythmic variety, passion and lyricism, and a natural, almost casual storytelling element that all the best recorded instrumental solos possess, from Louis Armstrong onwards.

He went back to a Fender Telecaster from his then customary Gibson Les Paul because the Fender has extra bite to its sound and allows him more legato than usual. Unusually, he recorded the solo without wearing headphones to hear the backing as he played, preferring

Onstage during the seventh American tour, more noted by many observers for a series of confrontations rather than the music the band played.

instead to have the playback on big monitor speakers in the studio room.

Engineer Richard Digby-Smith remembered that session. "We played him back through them as loud as possible, and he just leaned up against the speakers with a cigarette hanging out of his mouth and rattled out that solo."[15] Richard Cole watched Page working alone at night at Basing Street studio "using the Telecaster and building guitar track upon guitar track until he had the powerful instrumental harmonies he wanted. He recorded three different guitar solos, none of them similar, and finally chose the one he thought was best after agonising over them in the studio late one night." The freshness and spontaneity of this approach is another reason for the solo's success, along with the rich melodic possibilities that Dylan's minor progression offers to the soloist.

With the conclusion of the solo – itself a kind of second introduction to the concluding section – Plant re-enters (6:45), this time in classic Zeppelin battle-cry mode, double-tracked and wailing as he delivers the last verse of the lesson. Many observers have wondered at the let-down of the last line – "to be a rock and not to roll" – but it is clear that Plant wanted a joking pun to end and a nice allusion to the central dilemma of the lyrics: being true to one's instincts and yet not falling into any one of life's many snares before climbing that stairway.

In a sense, although the final reiteration of the image of the Lady climbing the stairway to heaven gives a satisfying musical resolution to the entire performance, and brings us full circle as required, a more tantalising end would have been achieved if that tag had been left off and the song had finished with Page's screaming, ascending lead-guitar notes after Plant's "rock and not to roll" line. But then the song would not have had the huge emotional consummation at its conclusion that made it so dear to an entire generation of rock-music fans. It evokes the age-old question: which has primacy, lyrics or music?

Decades later, Jones could declare 'Stairway To Heaven' to be one of his favourite Led Zeppelin tracks, and for all the right musical reasons. "I'm not talking about its being successful in commercial terms, but successful in that everything worked well and fell into place. Everything built nicely. ... Both Jimmy and I were quite aware of the way a track should unfold and the various levels that it would go through. We were quite strong on form. ... I suppose we were both quite influenced by classical music, and there's a lot of drama in the classical forms. It just seems natural for music to have that, as opposed to everybody starting and just banging away and finishing. That's part of song structure. It's also part of pop music."

With Plant's unaccompanied vocal at the end of 'Stairway', side one of the vinyl album came to an end on an unassailable peak. What could the band possibly do on side two to sustain the quality? Their answer was to do

something different and not compete with themselves. Most of the second side is a shift back to traditional Zeppelin style and values, group efforts that evolved through the four working on ideas, mostly at Headley Grange the previous winter.

'Misty Mountain Hop' is a case in point. Starting with a swaggering riff played on keyboard, guitar and bass that simulates the walking-through-the-park that Plant sings of in the first verse, it tells in almost whimsical fashion the story of a bunch of hippies lying around smoking dope in a park and then getting busted for possession. The song title is a reference to *The Hobbit* (a popular thing to do that year, with Marc Bolan writing 'The King Of The Mountain Cometh', a reference to the same *Lord Of The Rings* topography) and a sly play on words regarding one's usual state after smoking dope. Plant, needless to say, was pro-cannabis; the police were not (and still aren't). Nothing much changes.

The drum sound on 'Misty' is outstanding, a huge cavernous whack that resonates in your head long after the track has finished. Otherwise, it's other production details that stand out: the double-tracking and treatment of Plant's voice; the clever combination of instruments to buttress the riff; the raw edge of Page's guitar.

The next track, 'Four Sticks', is the weakest on the album. It was a Page idea and another exercise in unusual time signatures as in portions of 'Black Dog', but not so much a riff-based piece as a piece that wouldn't exist without the riffs stringing it together. As far as 5/4 riffs go, it's not much further on than Dave Brubeck's vamp in 'Take Five' (1959), the first hit song in 5/4. Bonham flails away with four drumsticks (hence the title) to keep up the impetus, but he sounds uncomfortable all the way, sticking like glue to the pattern and not free enough within the time signature to be able to play with it at all.

Jones recalled that Bonham simply could not get his head around this rhythm pattern and wasn't helped by the fact that Page "couldn't actually count what he was playing".[16] Neither could Bonham, said Jones. This meant they couldn't analyse how Bonham could put the beat together and then execute it – they could only think in phrases and hope they'd land on it sooner or later. By the time they'd got a couple of acceptable takes it was left at that. The song was never attempted live for fear that it would come apart at the seams.

During the bridge there is a shift to 6/8 and the perspective opens up a little as the band settle into a more natural swing with more interesting shading and emphases. The final bridge brings into play some pleasant keyboard effects from Jones and a fine climbing motif, but it remains undeveloped and the song goes back to the straitjacket of 5 time, sounding unfinished in the same way as George Harrison's 'Not Guilty': an idea with potential that is never fully realised. The whole structure of 'Sticks' hangs on the flair of the drummer, but he is simply keeping up with everybody else. It remains a studio-bound exercise rather than a musical success.

After that mild discomfort, 'Going To California' seems to flood the room with light. It is an unabashedly beautiful mid-tempo acoustic song, and while some feel it owes a considerable debt to Joni Mitchell it bears very little stylistic resemblance to her songwriting style, her typical chord progressions, or even her subject matter.

Page delivers some superb and understated acoustic guitar fingerpicking which, as always where Page the producer is involved, is beautifully recorded with a full but sparkling tone. Once more in his lyrics Plant manages to deftly combine a touch of whimsical (and self-deprecating) humour with some quite moving and obviously heartfelt lines about a yearning for the type of uncomplicated living and loving he seems to think come naturally to Californians. Or perhaps he is remembering his numerous visits to the state and the times enjoyed, for there is also in the yearning a wistful touch of nostalgia, even when describing long stretches in "a big jet plane", his nod to Mitchell's big yellow taxi.

Jones's mandolin picking on this track adds a wonderfully pastoral touch, and indeed the entire guitar-mandolin accompaniments – there are no drums or bass – once again recall Donovan rather than stylistic models from further afield. It is a real gem of the album and a triumph of wry understatement, something not often associated with Led Zeppelin but a frequent part of their artistry from *III* onwards. The only drawback is its isolated position between the big booms of side two sequencing.

Moving from this idyll to the sturm und drang of 'When The Levee Breaks' is an awkward juxtaposition, and it may be that the two pieces could have benefited from a swap, allowing 'California' to conclude the album. It's over 30 years too late and well past 20 million copies sold to change anything now, but it would have showcased 'California' better, just like 'Stairway' on side one.

'Levee' is a stupefyingly heavyweight barrage of sound centred on the piledriving force and simplicity of Bonham's slow, remorseless backbeat. Page and engineer Andy Johns had concentrated on that drum sound when mixing this track, working it up to a monolithic density that suggests the sort of imaginary storm and half-darkness that leads to levee-breaking bad weather.

The mobile at Headley Grange allowed the band to repeatedly take advantage of the building's varied and resonant acoustics in the most unlikely settings. Page recounted later that it gave them the solution for recording 'Levee'. "We tried to record that in a studio before we got to Headley Grange, and it sounded flat. But once we got the drum sound at Headley Grange, it was like boom! And that made the difference immediately. … We set the drums up in this main hallway, and they sounded so good that we said, 'We're gonna use this.' And we set up a stereo mike, just up the stairs. There actually

was a bass-drum mike set up, but it didn't get used because we already had such a balance of sound. So what you're hearing is the sound of the hall with the stereo mike on the stairs, second flight up."

The simple guitar and bass figures played by Page and Jones are derived from a classic 1929 Memphis Minnie McCoy blues, which explains the deep delta-blues feel of the composition. Page's excellent and sympathetic slide-guitar work has similar delta roots, almost becoming a second voice, while Plant puts down one of his most varied, controlled, and expressive raw blues vocals with traditional country-blues subject matter: the lament of the poor who are subject to the forces of elemental nature.

The almost surreal soundscape captured on this long track (seven minutes and more) perhaps hints at the rather different overall sound that Page and Johns aimed at during their stint in Sunset Sound studio, for this was the only mix salvaged from that initial attempt. It is fascinating to speculate what 'Black Dog', in particular, would have sounded like if the original Sunset Sound mix had succeeded. Yet 'Levee' also suffers from too few ideas added to the ingredients as the minutes tick by, compared with 'Black Dog' and its companions on the first side. This characteristic at least it shares with 'Four Sticks'.

With the bone-crunching conclusion to 'Levee', the fourth Led Zeppelin album comes to an end. While side two's four songs don't quite add up to a fulfilment of the expectations built by side one, it is a remarkably consistent achievement with enough true peaks of attainment and sufficient overall vision and coherence as a musical statement to stake a claim not only among the very best that Led Zeppelin produced, but among the best of the 1970s. It is a great deal more consistent than John Lennon's *Imagine*, for example, an album with sublime peaks but truly embarrassing troughs, or *Sticky Fingers*, the engaging but generally lightweight Stones 1971 follow-up to their previous studio album, *Let It Bleed*.

With the new Zeppelin album at last on sale in stores worldwide and a November/December UK tour lined up to drive it home to the fans for Christmas, it seemed that the band would finally be able to complete the story on a long-drawn-out saga. In a sense that was true, for Led Zeppelin were now free to play in concert whatever repertoire from the four albums they chose and to plan unhindered for the future.

But *Led Zeppelin IV*, with its sleeper 'Stairway' seeping into the consciousness of the youth of the western world, would ensure that nothing would ever be the same again. The band had unwittingly set a benchmark against which they would forever be measured. Like the lyrics in the song about the worlds of innocence and experience, almost overnight the band moved to a position where they would live in the shadow of their past achievements. They would also have to deal with the consequences of the stresses and pressures of extreme fame.

PERFORMING PIGS AND MEMORIES OF LAUGHTER

- 4TH UK TOUR

- AUSTRALASIAN TOUR

- BOMBAY RECORDINGS

- STARGROVES & STUDIO SESSIONS FOR 5TH ALBUM

- 8TH AMERICAN TOUR

- L.A. FORUM & LONG BEACH SHOWS RECORDED

The final tour of 1971 corrected what the band felt was an error of judgement earlier in the year with their Back To The Clubs tour. Although the media and fans had generally approved, the band and their manager felt that it had been a largely meretricious exercise. They were better off sticking to larger venues where ticket demand and other basics – acoustics, safety issues and the like – could be properly addressed.

The new British tour began in the north-east of England in Newcastle upon Tyne on the evening of Armistice Day, November 11th, and was originally announced as just eight concerts, concluding at the Free Trade Hall in Manchester on the 24th, but eventually was extended over a month. There were still fewer appearances than in the densely-booked overseas tours, where a gig a day was normal. Most of the concerts were planned to have Led Zeppelin as the sole act, but some were much more elaborate affairs.

Demand for tickets was so ferocious that every concert sold out within 24 hours of its confirmation. The initial Wembley Empire Pool show sold out in 54 minutes. People were queuing outside booking offices all night to secure their tickets. Grant felt secure enough about the demand to add extra dates in Manchester and London and pick up concerts in new cities.

As word spread about the outstanding nature of the new record it became evident that Led Zeppelin were the hot rock ticket of the season, turning the tour into something of a triumphal progress. What T.Rex had become for British teenyboppers, Led Zeppelin were for the next generation up.

The opening show at Newcastle had the audience baying for more after two-and-a-half hours of music, the band kicking off with 'Immigrant Song' and 'Heartbreaker' before moving through a set similar to that of the last US tour. According to reviews, the concert was marred by the infamous acoustics of Newcastle's City Hall, but the crowd didn't seem to care. By the time the band had reached Wembley on the 20th, they were in top gear.

Zeppelin had planned something special for the Wembley shows: they featured an old-fashioned parade of groups plus extras: trapeze artists, trampoline stars, and performing pigs in policemen's helmets (the pigs apparently refused to do anything – a clear case of stagefright according to Grant). All were hand-chosen by the Zeppelin team.

Other bands on the bill were Bronco, Stone The Crows, and Maggie Bell, in an event that lasted over five hours. Again the Zeppelin set echoed those of the US tour: it was beautifully paced and included fine renditions of slower numbers such as 'Going To California' and – a rare outing – 'Tangerine'. The quieter sections were rotated from venue to venue, with Liverpool for example treated to 'Gallows Pole'. By the end of the British tour the band felt that, after all the travails of getting the fourth album out, they were ending 1971 on a high. As a special bonus, they were all home in time to celebrate Christmas with friends and family.

In America, where the release of *IV* was not promoted by a tour, the initial reviews were mixed but mostly generous, with *Billboard* and *Creem* both striking a positive note. The album failed to reach the Number 1 slot, which at the time was the exclusive property of Carole King, whose *Tapestry* had spent a total of 15 weeks at Number 1 in the USA. But the Zep album's steady sales, in America and throughout the world, eventually kept it in the charts not just for months but for years, making it the band's biggest-selling record. Meanwhile, 1972 was already earmarked for Zeppelin's first Australasian tour as the band's horizons continued to expand.

The only action in the Zeppelin camp over the new year of 1972 concerned the grudging clearance first of 'Black Dog' and then 'Rock And Roll' as singles from the fourth album for US release. Neither did spectacular business, but at least they gave the album a continuing presence on AM airwaves in the absence of a touring band.

Bonham was by now well established in the country with his family; he'd bought a farm during 1971 and built a house close to Stourbridge in the Midlands, about ten miles west of Birmingham and a convenient drive away from Plant. The initial move to a farm was not exactly the fulfilment of a long-time wish, but the drummer grew into a new domestic role.

Bonham, a practical man with some experience on building sites in pre-fame years, oversaw restoration and construction on the property with a practiced eye and later took a real interest in breeding Hereford cattle. His focal points during life away from the band became the farm and his family – his son, Jason, born in 1966, was to become a gifted drummer. He also developed a passion for exotic cars.

Jones too was completely taken up with home life when not on the road. He and his wife had three children and they lived in Rickmansworth, Hertfordshire, just north of the London suburban spread. Jones, always a busy, motivated man with a close-knit family group and a circle of friends largely away from the band, by now had a home studio and was hardly at a loose end in Led Zeppelin's downtime.

During the fourth album's long gestation, Page had finally moved from his Thames-side Pangbourne home into an altogether more sumptuous location in Sussex. (The following year he also bought Richard Harris's tower house in Kensington in London's West End.) The new country residence was Plumpton Place, an 18th century estate remodelled by Edwin Lutyens with its own extensive man-made grounds. An early project was to convert part of the attic into a home studio, while the increased space allowed Page to store and display his ever-expanding collection of guitars, fine art, esoterica, and arcane writings. The following year Page added Richard Harris's tower house in Kensington in west London to his holdings.

In February 1972 they started their first tour in Australia and New Zealand, flying out via Bombay and Singapore. Indeed Singapore had been intended as the location for the opening concert, but someone on the ground had not done their research. Some years earlier the Singaporean government had introduced a ban on male hairstyles that reached below a shirt collar at the back. The government had decided that long hair on males was a contributing factor in juvenile delinquency and the lowering of the nation's morals, and had taken appropriate action.

Led Zeppelin were not even allowed off the plane, and with the idea of a short back and sides for the band not even worth mentioning, they flew on to Perth in Western Australia to begin the tour there instead. Things would not get off to a brilliant start there, either.

Of the four, only Page had been to Australia before, with The Yardbirds in 1967. During the intervening years much had changed both internationally and Down Under. A conservative government was embattled on many fronts, including the deeply unpopular Vietnam War, and took an aggressive stance towards what it considered degenerate youth culture. On top of that, some state governments were of a conservative cast, none more so than that of Western Australia – the state where Led Zeppelin arrived.

The state's agents liked nothing more than to mount extensive operations against incoming celebrities in the hope of a high-profile drug bust. This gave them the perfect reason to deny that particular celebrity the chance to enter the country and fulfil their tour obligations. Led Zeppelin were a band whose reputation preceded them – long hair, loud music, stories of degenerate behaviour in America – and they were given the treatment. Surprisingly, no one seems to have tipped them off that this would happen.

Upon landing in Perth the band, like every other arrival by plane from abroad until the end of the century, were sprayed with disinfectant on board like cattle being deloused. Led Zeppelin then made their way to their selected hotel. After settling in and resting, they prepared for their debut in Australia the following day. First came an interview on local Perth radio where Page, Plant and Jones talked about a wide range of Zeppelin-related topics. Page was asked about the idea behind their set list. "We're sort of into a lot of things, and trying to present as much as we can, really," he replied. "It's not always easy, but we're trying to get a cross section of what we do and

what we've done. That's basically [it]: we do a little short acoustic section where we try and show people that we're not a bunch of animals."[1]

On the evening of February 16th they began their first concert, at Subiaco Oval in Perth, in front of 8,000 paying customers and hundreds of fans who had entered illegally by cutting a hole in the fence. There were another 4,000 outside and the situation was tense.

When 100 fans mounted the stage and began dancing, Plant attempted to defuse a violent police reaction by speaking directly to the crowd to cool it and not cause unnecessary trouble. Somehow a major incident was avoided and the concert was completed to wild enthusiasm. Later that evening members of the band, out on the town and looking for entertainment, dropped in on a Perth night club and jammed onstage, playing old rockers like Elvis's 'Teddy Bear' and Buddy Holly songs. Early the following morning, however, police raided the band's hotel in search of drugs. Finding none, they left disgruntled and without apologising. Richard Cole recalled Plant commenting: "If they had waited a day or two, we might have had something!"[2] Welcome to Australia.

Normal Australians, especially those who liked rock, extended a genuine welcome to the band. After all, tours from bona fide megastars, rather than has-beens or would-bes, were still rare in Australia in early 1972. The country had yet to become part of the regular rock touring circuit and instead relied heavily on local releases of overseas albums or local live acts. A major advance had come the year before when The Kinks had toured Australia, supported for the biggest gigs by a Melbourne band, Daddy Cool.

The Australian band had just broken through as a top-selling local act and actually upstaged the British band in Melbourne and Sydney – the first time any local could remember such a thing happening. From that point on, touring acts were no longer met by supine audiences who would accept any old rubbish served up in the name of entertainment. However, groups that gave their all received a heartfelt response. Led Zeppelin had more than succeeded in Perth and would continue to do so for the entire tour

There was still the usual litany of problems to deal with. In Adelaide, the next tour stop, bad weather washed out the initial date for the outdoor concert, forcing a 24-hour postponement. The band delivered a long and committed set of music on February 19th, almost identical to the one in Perth, which itself was close to the running order used on the last US and UK tours. 'Bron-Y-Aur Stomp' had crept in to freshen up the set a little. Once again, however, there was violence between police and fans.

Eight thousand people saw them play in Adelaide, one of whom was Martin Armiger, a distinguished musician, film-music composer and novelist. He said: "I was actually outside the Adelaide Tennis Courts for most of Led Zeppelin's concert. I spent the first half hour up a tree with a distant view of the stage. I got through into the outer on a friend's pass-out in time to hear a long acoustic set of Page and Plant (almost an entr'acte, with them sitting on the front of the stage) which struck me as ultra-musical, very Celtic-folky, and deliberately anti-rock'n'roll in stance – in the same way Traffic were anti-rock at the same time as being huge rock stars. Their way of picking out a connection between folk and rock forms was interesting. Then they cranked up the rhythm section again, [and] some of Plant's wailing left me cold, [but] Page was a strange marvel. I remember the sound was big and somehow empty in the middle, with a booming bottom end and this very precise patterned filigree all around."[3]

According to press reports, the first half of the Melbourne concert in Kooyong Stadium on the 20th was under-amplified (hardly something normally associated with the band) and consequently many in the vast outdoor audience struck up conversations, only occasionally checking what was happening onstage. This hardly endeared them to Plant in particular, who more than once asked the crowd to shut up and listen. But it wasn't until after both the short acoustic set and an enforced ten-minute break waiting for a rainshower to pass over that the band at last found the right volume and the crowd was completely captivated.

Afterwards, Plant commented: "Perth, I think, was the best we've played yet – we'd just landed and we were full of Bombay and Singapore. ... [Melbourne] was warmer. You could see the people and you could see the colours. Everybody was grooving and everybody was smiling. ... That was about the first outdoor afternoon concert we've done for two years."[4]

Following the sole concert in New Zealand, in Auckland, Zeppelin flew to Sydney, where a vast crowd – 26,000 according to one source – gathered to watch them perform at Sydney Showground on February 27th for another afternoon concert. On 2003's *DVD* there is black-and-white footage, including sound, of the band playing 'Rock And Roll' here, with the four musicians looking lean and dangerous onstage and the performance sounding fast, tight, and hungry. The energy pouring from them and the precision with which they articulate that energy is stunning. The crowd's response is enormous at the song's end.

Footage of the band's performance of 'Immigrant Song' (with the sound supplied from a 1972 Long Beach concert) emphasises the sheer impact the band has onstage as they command its entire length and depth and Plant in particular reaches out to commune with his audience.

After one more concert, in Brisbane two days later, the band returned to Sydney to stay at the fashionable new Siebel Town House in Potts' Point, a small, ultramodern hotel with commanding views of the harbour, situated next to the red light district of King's Cross. There they rested and enjoyed themselves at the beginning of March before preparing to fly back to London.

The tour had been a major popular success and a good financial move, but Plant and Page had not yet finished their overseas dalliance. While Jones and Bonham returned to London – Bonham's wife Pat was heavily pregnant with their daughter, Zoe, delivered successfully that April – Plant and Page flew to Bombay for some relaxation and private musical experiments. Both men, but especially Page, had long been fascinated by the idea of East-West musical fusions. Page had been to the sub-continent a few times before and both had investigated the country the previous October.

There had been considerable planning for this Bombay visit: although the pair enjoyed a number of impromptu jams, their prime objective was a recording session that certainly was not a loose affair with a handful of locals. The studio date was a serious attempt to work on pre-existing material with a large ensemble directed by one of India's most prestigious and respected musicians, Vijay Ragav Rao.

Plant and Page quickly renewed their acquaintance with the Slip Disc disco. This time, they were expected not only by some musicians and fans but also the Slip Disc's management. Years later, musician and writer Nanu Bhende, who was present the night Page and Plant visited, recalled the scene. "One afternoon, in the winter of 1972," said Bhende, "I got a call from an excited Ramzan, the owner of Slip Disc, the happening discotheque and live-band showplace of our time. He told me that Robert Plant and Jimmy Page of Led Zeppelin were in town and are to visit the Slip Disc and perform that evening, so please get there as early as I could. If only you could imagine the excitement and turmoil that took place for the next few hours.

"Good news sure travels fast, and as we waited for the arrival of our rock icons we prepared for their performance with a last-minute check on the music equipment available. Those were the tough days of import control and we had really poor stuff that was scrounged and smuggled with the help of relatives from abroad and rich benefactors. We were hoping that this would not mar the enthusiasm of the rock superstars who were used to the very best.

"It had been decided that Xerxes Gobhai, the talented bassist from Human Bondage, and Jameel Shaikh, the drummer from my band, would back them, but nobody had any idea what they would perform. There was just no time to get into any details, as anything would do for us music-starved fans. And before we knew it, Led Zeppelin

Bombay-style were announced to the audience. Jimmy and Plant got into the groove from the word go as they launched into 'Rock And Roll', the hit from *IV*, and the audience went wild! They followed that with an extended blues where their stay in Bombay seemed to feature a lot. 'Black Dog' followed and before we knew it, it was all over. They must have been onstage for a maximum of 25 minutes and we savored every second of that."[5]

Later, a group of exhilarated and eager young DJs and musicians drove the band around Bombay. According to Richard Cole, Page had a portable tape recorder with him and made recordings of street musicians, as on previous occasions. Slip Disc DJ Yusuf Ghandi and his friends introduced them to some of the musicians they would use on the forthcoming recording session.

"The best group in Bombay at that time was called Human Bondage," Ghandi asserted. "They were a blend of Indian classical music and rock. They did make an album or so later on, but they hadn't recorded then. The guitarist was Suresh Shottam. We took Page and Plant to a friend's house after the bazaar where Suresh was, and Page was very impressed by him. Suresh had a Fender Mustang guitar – Fenders were very rare in India then – and Page was amazed at this. He said to Suresh: 'Do you want to sell your guitar?' Suresh replied: 'No – it's the only one I have.'"[6]

Six months later Page would refer in an interview to an unnamed guitarist he'd met in Bombay. "[He] was really good. I mean he would have held up very easily [here in Britain]. He played the sitar for six years, and he's adapted from that. But it wasn't like raga rock, more like [John McLaughlin]. Yeah, it was very good indeed, a very competent musician. He frightened me to death by saying: 'Oh, I practice for at least eight hours every day,' and you could see that he did, too. He played sort of classical guitar too, but not Bach: things that were like Bach structures but his own inventions. But he was getting no market whatsoever because they didn't understand."[7] This was quite clearly Shottam. The Indian guitarist would later move to New York to further his career.

After a few days looking around Bombay and soaking up the local atmosphere, Page and Plant hired a local studio while Vijay Ragav Rao assembled an informal orchestra of local musicians. Rao was a multi-talented musician, a fine flute player, a composer and conductor. He could perform traditional Indian classical music but also turned out Western compositions and wrote for the popular Bombay film industry. An outstanding talent, in the late 1970s he relocated to America for a few years and conducted the studio orchestra for two of Frank Sinatra's late albums, *Trilogy* (1979) and *She Shot Me Down* (1981), often referred to as the last great albums Sinatra made.

Rao was exactly the sort of man to pull together a session such as Plant and Page planned. Able to call on the top players from both sides of the East-West musical divide, he put together an ensemble – including guitarist Suresh Shottam – designed for the job. It has been said since that this was the Bombay Symphony Orchestra, but that was certainly not the case. The Bombay Symphony Orchestra was a thriving concert orchestra founded by conductor Zubin Mehta's father Mehli in 1935. It was equipped for playing Western classical repertoire and could not have supplied the kind of musician that Page was looking for. Rao would have assembled professionals mostly from the Bombay studios – something he regularly did for other projects – and it is possible that this informal ensemble was dubbed 'the Bombay Symphony Orchestra' as a light-hearted joke.

The ensemble, directed by Page, Plant and Rao, recorded experimental versions of 'Four Sticks', suitable because of its rhythmic sophistication, and 'Friends', which was in sympathy harmonically and melodically with Eastern musical ideas. George Harrison had already enjoyed some success with similar projects using Bombay musicians: his soundtrack music for the film *Wonderwall* was largely recorded in Bombay in January 1968 using local players and vocalists. Page and Plant probably felt that Led Zeppelin had an equal chance of pulling something off.

But Plant commented later: "It was very hard for them to cope with the Western approach to music."[8] Not only that, but this was the first time the two men had attempted to have their songs performed by players other than those in the band. They were not used to communicating their ideas to large numbers of musicians about whom they knew very little. So the experiment was stored away as something 'interesting', and the music has never been officially released.

Plant and Page, along with Cole, returned to Britain and a short break before it would be time to consider sessions for the next album. The two musicians were happy to be interviewed back home, both conscientiously trying to answer some of the more familiar questions that came up about the fourth album. Plant told *NME*: "Music is very much like a kaleidoscope, and I feel that particular album was just a case of us stretching out. It was a very natural development for us. I like people to lay down the truth. No bullshit. That's what the feather in the circle was all about."[9]

Page, attempting to explain to *Disc & Music Echo* some of the fundamental ideas behind the album's cover, wandered into his ideas about the confluence of magic, music and morals. "My house used to belong to Aleister Crowley. I knew that when I moved in. Magic is very important if people can go through it. I think Crowley's completely relevant to today. We're seeking for truth: the search still goes on. Crowley didn't have a very high opinion of women – I don't think he was wrong. Playing music is a very sexual act, an emotional release, and the sexual drive comes in along with all the other impulses. ... At least as musicians we aren't doing any environmental or moral damage. In fact the musicians can ask some of the ugly questions that politicians don't want to answer."[10]

The band were refreshed from over a month spent largely away from their professional lives. Plant, like bandmate Bonham, welcomed a new baby into his family in April, his son Karac. That same month Zeppelin gathered at Stargroves, Mick Jagger's property in Newbury, Berkshire, along with the Rolling Stones mobile studio. These were the first formal band sessions since February 1971, more than 14 months ago. Page told Ritchie Yorke: "We had no set ideas. We just recorded the ideas each one of us had at that particular time. It was simply a matter of getting together and letting it out."[11]

The band initially sought the relative comfort of Stargroves in preference to Headley Grange as they pooled creative ideas to see what was on the table for the fifth album. As with the February 1971 rehearsals, most of the songs were fragments at the start. 'D'yer Mak'er', for example, was little more than a simple doo-wop feel that Bonham enjoyed playing. Jones's 'No Quarter' and Page's 'Rain Song' were the exceptions. They had rehearsed 'No Quarter' during the fourth-album sessions but put it aside for further development, and there is evidence that an even earlier version was tried at the first Headley Grange rehearsals for Led Zeppelin III. A brooding piece dominated by Jones's keyboards and Plant's plaintive vocals, its content lends support to the idea that Jones first started it shortly after his father's death in 1970. He said later: "It just came about sitting around the piano. Using various effects. I knew instantly it was a very durable piece and something we could take out on the road and expand."[12] There had been a considerable wait before that became a possibility.

The band attempted to inject as much spontaneity and fun into these sessions as possible, using the mobile to record in different locations in the house and its grounds, including out in the garden, as they looked for new ways to capture drum and vocal sounds as well as new contexts to inspire jamming and song development.

Engineer Eddie Kramer was a veteran of Zeppelin sessions (he'd done work on II) and Jimi Hendrix's latter-day work. He was with the band at Stargroves and recalled a carefree atmosphere. Yet Stargroves alone was far short from being enough. For a start, there were problems with its acoustics, according to Plant. "We went down there and got a few things together, but the sound in the place wasn't as good recording-wise as we'd been able to get in that weird place, Headley Grange. ... That was a bit of a deterrent really. Nevertheless, there was quite a bit [put] down there – immediate stuff laid down straight away, and maybe we'd put the vocals on in the studio."[13]

Eventually the band felt compelled to undertake a comprehensive series of re-recording sessions on this material, replacing below-par sections and brightening the disappointing sound as much as they could. With Page as the instigator and quality-control expert, they continued to strive for the best possible results, unafraid to wait until those results arrived.

As with previous albums, recording was shifted around a number of locations, with Headley Grange, Olympic, and Island studios all playing a part in the final line-up for the album that eventually became Houses Of The Holy. Richard Cole remained impressed by the band's concentration and dedication during these sessions. "This time around, there was not the fast pace of the debut Led Zeppelin effort in 1968 ... but the mood was never lackadaisical, either. Jimmy demanded that the final product have decimal-point precision. For that reason, we finally moved into Olympic studios in London. In a more formal studio setting Zeppelin became a lot more accomplished."[14]

The tracks started at this time included 'The Song Remains The Same', 'The Rain Song' (possibly carrying an early title, 'Slush'), 'Over The Hills And Far Away', 'The Crunge', 'Dancing Days', 'D'yer Mak'er', 'No Quarter', 'The Ocean', 'Black Country Woman', 'Walter's Walk', 'The Rover', and 'Houses Of The Holy'. Out-takes from previous album sessions during 1970-71 now included 'Poor Tom', 'Bron-Y-Aur', 'Down By The Seaside', 'Night Flight', and 'Boogie With Stu'. All this was easily enough for a double-LP release. Yet work proceeded disappointingly slowly. 'Walter's Walk', a fiery riff-laden rocker, would eventually be put to one side, lying dormant until 1982's Coda. It could easily have held its own on the upcoming Physical Graffiti where so much of the overspill from Houses Of The Holy would end up. But then we might not have had 'Hots On For Nowhere' on Presence, for the guitar riff in the bridge of 'Walter's Walk' provided the turnaround riff in 'Nowhere'.

Page and Jones in particular spent much of May 1972 in various recording studios attempting to work each track up to completion, but it would take months of further overdubbing, re-recording and adjusting by the whole band, individually and together, before the final choice could be made and the masters prepared. Page's initial wish for a June 1972 release to coincide with the next US tour was quickly abandoned as he realised that there was a mountain of work to do and decisions to be made.

Then there were the usual debates and questions about the jacket. Ever since Led Zeppelin III this had been a traditional area of delay, confusion and conflict for the band, its designers and the manufacturers, as well as the record company. This album would be no exception.

So Led Zeppelin went out on their third American tour in a row with no new album to promote. Try as they may, as they took more time and care over each new recording project, they found it simply impossible to marshal all the different and opposing forces involved in producing an album in time for a specific tour. Still, this seemed to have little impact on their popularity as a live act, and with 'Stairway To Heaven' well on its way to iconic status on turntables and FM radio airwaves in America, by summer 1972 there was little sense of the band lagging behind in its achievements or relevance to the music culture of the day.

This eighth American tour, although similar to so many of its predecessors, was important as a watershed in professionalism. In America rock was changing swiftly, moving out of the sometimes charming, sometimes infuriating chaos of the post-hippie era into the streamlined professionalism of the mid and late 1970s. It was no accident that manager Peter Grant was one of the first to look for suitable innovations.

With ample time to prepare for this tour, Grant had thought through the most pressing areas of concern. One was the cash take from the concerts. He resolved his ambivalence about the band's share of the take by insisting that, from this tour onwards, all American concerts yield 90 percent of the take to the band, 10 percent to the promoter. With a band as hot as Zeppelin, this was agreed with relatively little fuss. The greedy promoters dropped out of the picture while those who knew they still stood to make money even on 10 percent of the gross were the ones whom Grant knew he could trust. His confidence in the band's ability to generate income was fully justified: all the concerts sold out within days of the tour being announced, with little or no need to advertise.

The other difficulty was to make the tour easier to negotiate, physically and emotionally. There were two main problems: the mode of transport around such a large country; and the need for a better liaison between band and media on both sides of the Atlantic. As ever, band members were touchy about their perceived lack of positive column inches to reflect their undoubted achievements. They were resentful of the ease with which other bands and personalities dominated the headlines, especially in the fashion-led and claustrophobic music press.

The Stateside favourites for 1972 when it came to British groups were The Rolling Stones, touring the USA that summer for the first time since 1969, and The Who, a hardy perennial live act. Both hoovered up acres of newsprint about their activities, especially after the Stones released *Exile On Main Street* that spring. Although Led Zeppelin's dog-in-the-manger attitude had softened a little since the largely positive reception for the fourth album, they could still be prickly. Set within a context of management that thrived on adversity and the group spirit that such a style engenders, it meant there was little prospect of a resolution through neglect and the passage of time.

Both questions were settled to the band's advantage.

For transport, Cole was commissioned to hire a private jet and found one at a good price. He and Grant had been very concerned at the number of death threats the year before, while their recent experience of poor end-of-concert security in Australia had made them determined to put a seamless escape operation in place for each arena. To that end they hired an ex-Philadelphia cop, Bill Dautrich, who went ahead to each venue and arranged the proper police escort for their cars before and after the gig. Cole said: "Every member of the band knew in advance the route he'd be taking from the stage to the limos at the end of each concert and which car was his. ... Usually within 30 seconds the limos were moving, and when they hit the top of the ramp the sirens would begin blaring, continuing for most of the ride back to the hotel or airport."[15]

With transport and security sorted out, they next answered the question of press and media relations by hiring B.P. Fallon as the band's official PR. There had been no one working in that role since Bill Harry. Fallon was an Irishman with excellent rock credentials. He had been a radio DJ and had worked at The Beatles' Apple record company before moving to Island Records, helping to publicise such acts as Traffic, Free, and Joe Cocker. Immediately before Grant contacted him, Fallon had been responsible for the huge wave of publicity in Britain that had accompanied T.Rex's rise to chart dominance in late 1971. Marc Bolan had even written him into the lyrics of 'Telegram Sam', the fastest-selling British single of early 1972.

The band and management didn't need much convincing that Fallon would be quick enough on his feet to handle the complexities of Led Zeppelin's media relations, but he was brought on board with little or no time to prime press and radio prior to the tour's commencement. Acting quickly, Fallon helped arrange for *Melody Maker* to send reporters over for part of the tour and to watch the Long Island concert midway through, which resulted in firsthand reports of record-breaking attendance at American venues and the universally impressive crowd reaction to the band's standard set.

Prior to their arrival in America, the band played two European warm-up gigs in late May – in Amsterdam, Holland, and in Brussels, Belgium – where they performed excerpts from the recent recording sessions, debuting the rhythm from 'The Crunge' within 'Dazed And Confused', for example. When the US tour proper got under way, 'The Crunge' would continue to crop up from gig to gig, but the only other regularly featured new song from the unreleased album was 'Over The Hills And Far Away', which would eventually be released as a single by Atlantic US (with 'Dancing Days' on the flip side) to coincide with the follow-up US tour in March 1973.

In Baltimore on June 11th the band celebrated

outselling Elvis Presley in Buffalo, New York, the night before, where they'd been forced to lock 3,000 ticket-less fans outside as they tore through their set. At Baltimore's Civic Center they incorporated two Presley hits into their 'Whole Lotta Love' medley, 'Heartbreak Hotel' and 'I Need Your Love Tonight', causing the crowd to smile and join in the fun.

Fun and laughter were clearly important to Plant during this tour, for he often referred to it in his chats between numbers. A few nights later in Uniondale on Long Island, New York, he ad-libbed for the first time: "Does anybody here remember laughter?" after the line: "And the forests will echo with laughter" during 'Stairway To Heaven'. This would quickly become a concert staple, challenging Led Zep audiences to rise to the occasion and not get too embroiled in the high seriousness of what, after all, remained an entertainment.

The band hit the headlines for more than musical reasons when a Vancouver concert had to be cancelled due to fan unrest and threatened violence. There had been ugly scenes the previous August, and as soon as trouble started, the Vancouver police department refused to oversee the concert, forcing the promoter to cancel. This could have led to cancellations throughout the tour, so Grant arranged for all tickets purchased for the Vancouver concert to be honoured by an additional date in Seattle, about 120 miles to the south. It was an imposition greatly appreciated by the band as well as the fans, as it gave Zep an extra day at one of their favourite American hotels, the Seaside Inn on the waterfront in Seattle. Every TV set from the suite of rooms booked by the band was thrown into the sea from the hotel windows – an act of vandalism happily paid for by Grant before they checked out. He even offered to cover the expense of another set thrown into the water should the hotel manager himself feel like joining in.

The gig at The Forum in Inglewood, Los Angeles, on June 25th was a highlight. The band's repertoire that night was typical of the set they played on this tour, although the seven encores demanded by a wildly enthusiastic crowd was something of a record even for them. The full set was: 'Immigrant Song', 'Heartbreaker', 'Over The Hills And Far Away', 'Black Dog', 'Since I've Been Loving You', 'Stairway To Heaven', 'Going To California', 'Tangerine', 'Bron-Y-Aur Stomp', 'Dazed And Confused' (incorporating on this occasion music from 'The Crunge' and 'Walter's Walk'), 'What Is And What Should Never Be', 'Dancing Days', 'Moby Dick', and 'Whole Lotta Love'.

According to eyewitnesses the medley during the last song included snatches of 'Everybody Needs Somebody To Love', 'Boogie Chillun', 'Let's Have A Party', 'Hello Mary Lou', 'Heartbreak Hotel', 'Slow Down', and 'Going Down Slow'. This tour provided American audiences their last opportunity to hear this extended medley – for the 1973 US tour the band would play a slimmed-down rendition concentrating mainly on 'Boogie Chillun'. The multiple encores that followed the main set started with 'Rock And Roll' and went on to 'The Ocean', 'Louie Louie' (featuring a spine-tingling Page solo), 'Thank You', 'Communication Breakdown', and then, as the band tried to wind things down for the end of an exceptionally long evening, 'Bring It On Home' and, lastly, Eddie Cochran's 'Weekend'.

Those who witnessed the Forum performance thought it one of the band's absolute live peaks, with Plant in better voice than he had been on the last two tours and the rest of the band giving absolutely every last drop of inspiration to the music. It was nights like these that were turning Led Zeppelin into legendary live performers, while still at the top of their game and the number one live draw worldwide.

Decades later, Page came across the original multi-tracks of the recorded Forum show while he was preparing the Led Zeppelin *DVD* set for release. He combined the best of them with tapes from the June 27th Long Beach show to produce the triple-CD set *How The West Was Won*, also released in 2003. From the Forum, Page included 'Black Dog', 'Over The Hills and Far Away', 'That's The Way', 'Dazed And Confused', 'Moby Dick', 'Whole Lotta Love', 'The Ocean', and 'Bring It On Home'. His own comment in the CD inner sleeve was simple and conclusive: "This is Led Zeppelin at its best."

Listening to the zip and precision in the L.A. Forum 'Black Dog', it's hard to argue with Page. Taken faster than the studio version, it converts the sheer weight of sound and measured execution of the original into a remarkable flight of speed and action, a coiled spring of energy. Page plays little different in his solo, but the added thrust of his live guitar sound helps sustain it better. 'Over The Hills' comes alive when Bonham enters, bringing a razor sharpness to the rendition and inspiring Plant to a great, howling vocal.

When all 25 minutes of 'Dazed And Confused' is digested, the first thought is how far this band has come from the careful arrangement on the 1968 studio original. The same building blocks of the song are still in place but everything has been expanded, re-interpreted, ratcheted up in daring and expression. There is a lot more space for invention.

Uniquely, Zeppelin manage to stick to their collective approach when it comes to extemporised playing. They sustain the forward momentum of the sprawling piece and avoid that awful tedium of most rock bands' extended work where the listener is simply waiting for the latest torrent of an overheated soloist's notes to expire so that the melody might re-emerge.

Page is a great technician as a guitarist, but his forte is not the improvised melodic variation of most blues and rock guitar soloing. He finds other things to do with his facility, many of them colouristic: the guitar bowing, the use of echo chambers, the completely free-time sound-painting. Some of these are related to his interest in Eastern music, while many ideas are designed to heighten the impact of the rhythm section when it's pummelling away at a riff or a rhythmic pattern.

However, the most salient characteristic of Led Zeppelin in their extended performances is their firm grasp of the overall form of the piece and how to keep a sense of drama, of light and shade, running through the performance. They expertly wield elements of surprise and contrast to re-introduce excitement and expectation into a piece as one section segues excitedly into the next. Bonham accomplishes a similar feat on his own in 'Moby Dick', this version lasting just under 20 minutes.

'Whole Lotta Love' from the Forum concert comes in at just over 23 minutes and again demonstrates the sheer joy that Jones, Bonham and Page generate through their quick-fire rhythm changes, their chases and their patterns. It's an astonishingly tight working unit with no hint of daylight between them. When they enter the medley, the focus is on accurate but barnstorming recreations of the original boogie, rockabilly and western-swing feels – 'Boogie Chillun', 'Let's Have A Party', and 'Hello Mary Lou' – plus the downhome blues of James Oden's 'Going Down Slow' in which Page takes one of his most masterful blues solos, full of beautiful touches and perfect control. 'Heartbreak Hotel' and 'Slow Down' are missing from the official version released on *How The West Was Won*. The edit-point comes about 12 minutes in as Plant sings "well…" unaccompanied at the conclusion of 'Mary Lou', only to acknowledge applause and start 'Going Down Slow' instead. That "well…" is of course the famous first word of 'Heartbreak Hotel'. Perhaps there were copyright clearance problems blocking its inclusion?

Of the Forum encores, just two make it to the official release: 'The Ocean' and 'Bring It On Home'. 'The Ocean', dedicated to the waves of Zeppelin fans present at every concert worldwide, was a highly appropriate encore, its uneven, pummelling riff and high-spirited lyrics a perfect extra for the audience that night. A good-natured but rather rambling 'Bring It On Home' ends the CD and almost ended the encores that night for a crowd that just didn't want to go home at all.

Just two days later, the band ripped into a similar concert at Long Beach Arena, and while the sound captured on the *West Was Won* CD is just a little less bright and the band marginally less razor-sharp than the Forum gig, it is still an overwhelming experience. From the set played that evening, Page extracted for the 2003 CD the opening 'Immigrant Song', 'Heartbreaker', 'Since I've Been Loving You', 'Stairway To Heaven', 'Going To California', 'Bron-Y-Aur Stomp', 'What Is And What Should Never Be', 'Dancing Days', and 'Rock And Roll'.

The prominence of Plant's vocals on 'Immigrant Song' is welcome, his articulation of the lyrics something of a revelation after the embedded mix on the studio version. Page's long unaccompanied solo on 'Heartbreaker' is one of his happiest: well articulated and full of sly humour as well as stunning guitaristic effects. His follow-up solo with Bonham and Jones pounding behind him switches between crowd-pleasing stuff – fast runs going nowhere in particular, for example – and solid kick-ass chording that makes the whole selection red-hot in tandem with the bass and drums and wildly exciting. The audio of this performance was synchronised in 2003 with film footage of the Sydney version of the song and appeared on the Led Zeppelin *DVD*.

'Since I've Been Loving You' finds the band back in familiar blues territory but playing with admirable relaxation, Page again judging the light and shade of his work to perfection. His opening chorus is simply one of his best on tape, while his obbligatos to Plant are a delight. 'Stairway' opens with a beautifully measured guitar-Mellotron duet that has the band finding the right stately tempo rather than rushing, as live performances of ballads so often do.

Jones plays with particular melodic fluency on the Mellotron after Plant's entry (and the temperamental 'tron stays in tune for once). The Mellotron was a peculiar invention that seems electronic but in fact verges on the mechanical. It was a tape-replay keyboard, used by The Beatles to great effect in the 1960s and then overused by others to diminishing returns. It was superseded by synthesiser innovations early in the 1970s, but its unique other-wordly sounds remained captivating if used properly.

In the recapitulation Jones switches to Fender Rhodes electric piano and the tone darkens as Plant paints the scene of the forest echoing with laughter. "Remember laughter?" he adds, the line now a fixture. In the second section, Page's solo is aggressive and the band noticeably speed up in response, and while this is not usually something helpful to a performance, it ups the drama and tension as the musicians work out a little rising link riff to embellish the three-chord cycle beneath Plant. It is a very impressive transfer of a studio classic to the stage, involving just four musicians.

'Going To California', delivered to a Californian audience, is full of sun and warmth, with Plant particularly plaintive and convincing. Jones, on electric guitar alongside Page's acoustic, plays in a different style, closer to country players, keeping up a continual commentary on Plant's vocals and meshing perfectly with Page, keeping his figures mostly to a single fretboard position but making the instrument sing. 'Bron Y Aur Stomp' continues this bucolic canter at an increased tempo and with the crowd clapping along, evoking visions of a hippie-style barn dance.

'What Is And What Should Never Be' traces some interesting roots not so evident on the studio version. The opening verse links with soul-jazz chords and rhythms of the mid 1960s as used by Grant Green, Kenny Burrell, Jimmy Smith, and others. Of course, the other half of the song is classic Zep thunder and the contrast is pleasing, as is the long pause prior to the solo that has the crowd yelling their appreciation. The solo itself is slide guitar, dreamy and frenetic by turns. It is a well-judged performance played with a good sense of dynamics by all four musicians.

By contrast, 'Dancing Days', shorn of its recording studio overdubs, comes across as a simple rock strut reminiscent of Free and The Rolling Stones. This is 'All Right Now' and 'Brown Sugar' territory, apart from the deliciously discordant opening guitar figure. It is excellently played, packing a hell of a punch, and throws down the gauntlet to any band claiming raunch but failing to deliver onstage.

The last rendition from the Long Beach concert is the encore, 'Rock And Roll'. This steamrollering performance shows the gap between what Zep would be doing by the time of the live album *The Song Remains The Same* (recorded 1973) and what they were regularly delivering in concert in 1972 and before. Plant, for one, is fresher-voiced and still capable of delivering strong, transfixing vocals in his upper register – something notably missing by the time of the 1973 Madison Square Garden concert that was used as a major source for *Song Remains* and the subsequent film. Page's solo on this is joyous, technically devastating, and awesomely coherent. All the pressure is off and he's really enjoying himself as the crowd goes berserk. It's the perfect way to finish an outstanding gig.

Such concerts could only be regarded as a triumph for a band that prided itself on its dazzling live music-making, with the focus where it should be – on the music itself and the fans' enjoyment of that music. Yet an interview they gave *Melody Maker*'s Roy Hollingsworth after a similar triumph in New York showed they were still a long way from achieving satisfaction at the way in which they were perceived by the wider public.

Jones in particular forcefully made the point that other groups – The Rolling Stones, Jethro Tull – got better press than them and didn't deserve to. "They say Jethro Tull are brilliant onstage; well, they do the same bloody thing every night, the same gags, everything the same. Each of our gigs is treated differently, we don't have any set religiously-rehearsed thing. And what you've seen tonight has been happening for years."[16]

Plant amplified such complaints. "Our egos have been hurt," he said, "they really have. For some reason, English critics have never told the truth about us. For some reason they've been out to get us, a bit. So things are clouded over and nobody gets to know what's really happening."[17]

At least Plant's moan was closer to the truth of the matter. Zeppelin wanted their media egos massaged and were intent on throwing their toys out of the pram if no one listened. Their problem continued to be that, by and large, no one did.

Zeppelin's barnstorming concerts were taking place against a backdrop of widespread media indifference to this eighth US tour in contrast to The Rolling Stones' magisterial progress through their celebrity-laden 1972 US extravaganza. This might well explain some of the bitterness that the band members were feeling.

Back in Britain shortly after the conclusion of the jaunt, Bonham told *NME*: "Look, we've just toured the States and done as well as if not better than the Stones, but there was hardly anything about it in the British press. All we read was the Stones this, and the Stones that, and it pissed us off, made us feel what the hell, here we are flogging our guts out and for all the notice being given to us we might as well be playing in bloody Ceylon. Because the kids in England didn't even know we were touring the States."[18]

Bonham's diatribe was not entirely accurate: both *NME* and *MM* covered the tour while it was in progress. Perhaps he was more incensed at the lack of US media coverage than he admitted. But the band felt that their total commitment to onstage performances and their fans deserved much more coverage than they were getting. After all, the Stones, even by 1972, had become as much a part of the burgeoning celebrity circuit as they were a rock'n'roll band, with Jagger, his wife and famous friends more a talking point than any of the music they played. Jagger had even commissioned a film to be made of the tour, *Cocksucker Blues*, to commemorate the band's first US tour since the disastrous 1969 effort that had culminated in the Altamont murder. Bonham had either forgotten that Zeppelin had meanwhile toured the US seven times and in the process become less of a newsworthy event, or didn't care.

Bonham indirectly made the point about celebrity in the same interview, commenting that there was no chance that anyone in Led Zeppelin would ever be allowed to go on an ego trip. If they did, he felt, "They'd probably get their bleedin' gear torn off their backs, thrown into the sea of something equally unpleasant." To the drummer, that put Zep in a particular camp of rock groups.

"There are some bands who do this kind of thing, with the result that the kids go along for the sake of going to a concert and not because it's an event." They are likely to become real enthusiasts for the music and go and pick up all the albums that band has made. This, he thought, was what happened with Zeppelin. "For instance, our second album is still a strong seller. This seems to happen mainly in the States, where the kids are starting to back-track on all our albums."[19]

With the eighth US tour drawing to a close in late

June, the band had three engagement-free months to look forward to. After that, it would be more or less solid work from October 1972 right through to mid January 1973. While the rest of the band returned to their families and a private life that had been on hold for most of the year, Page continued to oversee the painfully slow progress on the fifth album.

He also accepted a commission from film producer Kenneth Anger to write the soundtrack music for Anger's short film *Lucifer Rising*. Page later told an interviewer he'd been working hard on the music. "I wanted it to sound timeless in a way, not to sound dated by anything. I used a synthesiser on it but I tried to use it in such a way that it didn't sound like a synthesiser, just that all the instruments didn't sound like what they ought to sound. You don't quite know what it is at any point."[20] Page started this project with considerable enthusiasm and was genuinely pleased with his progress on it. In the event, as Led Zeppelin affairs once more impinged, time slipped by and the job became a distraction more than a commission.

WHERE'S THAT CONFOUNDED BRIDGE?

- 2ND JAPANESE TOUR

- MIXING 5TH ALBUM

- 5TH UK TOUR

- 4TH EUROPEAN TOUR

- 5TH ALBUM, HOUSES OF THE HOLY, RELEASED

The band's success in Japan in 1971 and Page and Plant's growing appetite for far-flung travel suggested that a quick return there would be a good idea. Those earlier dates had largely amounted to novelty, when curiosity as much as anything else had brought the band to the country and the fans to the band. After the novelty of the year before, when curiosity as much as anything else had brought the band to the country and the fans to the band, this time Zeppelin's impact on local fans was instant. All available tickets to their seven concerts sold out within a day or so of their announcement.

The Japanese tour was concentrated on just the largest urban areas, including two concerts each in Tokyo and Osaka. The shows were notable for the continued introduction of material from the latest recording sessions. The first Tokyo Budokan concert, for example, featured not only 'Over The Hills And Far Away', a staple of the last US tour, but also 'The Song Remains The Same', 'Dancing Days', 'The Rain Song' and, once again, 'The Ocean' as an encore.

It was as if the band were relaxed enough about playing Japan, far away at that time from international media attention, to try out their newest material on a virgin audience. Budokan also saw a re-shaping of the now standard Led Zeppelin set, with 'Immigrant Song' relegated to encore and 'Rock And Roll' replacing it as the storming set opener. This reorganisation placed the running order close to what the band would use on their 1973 American tour supporting the eventual release of that fifth album, *Houses Of The Holy*.

The Japanese tour proved a major success for the band, increasing Zeppelin's profile there. It was a step forward in their loosely-defined ambition to be popular in every country in the world, even if no one was sure of the purpose of this ambition.

According to tour manager Richard Cole, a brief stop-off in Hong Kong during the tour led to the band's collective introduction, by accident, to heroin. As Cole described it later in his book: "With the passage of time, Zeppelin continued to become more enamoured with cocaine. Not that we had forsaken alcohol. But people were constantly offering us cocaine and it seemed silly to say no."[1] Cole had asked an acquaintance to find them some cocaine during the Hong Kong sojourn and the contact came back with heroin. He didn't bother telling the band, all of whom were violently ill within a few hours after sniffing the drug. An isolated incident that no one enjoyed, perhaps, but unfortunately for all concerned it would not be the end of their heroin connection.

At the end of October 1972, Zeppelin returned to Montreux, Switzerland, where they had enjoyed playing at the Casino 14 months earlier to a relatively small audience in a beautiful setting as a prelude to a major tour. Since that last show the Casino, a venue enjoyed by many jazz, blues and rock musicians, had burned down in December 1971, leaving the town without a suitable venue for occasional concerts. The destruction had been lamented by Deep Purple in their worldwide hit 'Smoke On The Water', a Number 4 single in America in June 1972. Sentiment aside, it was clear to the town's burghers that Montreux needed another music hall, and by the summer a new place, The Pavilion, had been completed.

This was the venue in which Led Zeppelin appeared for two nights late in October. They brought their own sound system and team, playing to a capacity audience of 2,000 and delivering a set very close to those of the just-finished Japanese tour. Opening with 'Rock And Roll' and 'Black Dog', they included four tracks from the unreleased fifth album and concluded with a 'Whole Lotta Love' that expanded greatly on the band's current penchant for Elvis Presley covers.

Melody Maker's Chris Charlesworth, along for the gig, enthused: "They just have to be the best heavy band [Britain] has produced." Later that trip Robert Plant talked to Charlesworth about their current music-making. He had some intriguing points about their medleys. "It comes spontaneously. After the opening sequence I just start a song and hope everybody will catch on. I did 'Let's Jump The Broomstick' once, but we often put in ['Let's Have A] Party', which is a really good one."[2] As usual with Montreux appearances, Zeppelin's set was recorded by Swiss radio, but none of this music has ever been made available, even on the virulent bootleg market.

The band spent as much time as possible before the start of a major tour of Britain and Europe attempting to finish the selection process and the final mixes for the material recorded for the fifth album. They also had to decide what they wanted for the jacket. This meant choosing a title, if there was to be any title at all, so that the designers had something to work with. It had to be resolved quickly, for the British tour would trigger a bout of road-fever longer and more intense than anything they had previously undertaken. Apart from a month off in late spring, they would tour almost continually – Britain, Europe, America, in that order – until late July 1973.

Accordingly, the album running was agreed after sustained deliberation and debate and the record given a title. This, as far as Atlantic was concerned, was a huge step forward: *Houses Of The Holy* was a riot of description compared with what Page and the boys had provided so far: *Led Zeppelin I, II, III* and that untitled one. The only problem was that in the horse-trading that went with the finalisation of the song line-up, the title track had been bounced from the record as too similar to 'Dancing Days', already earmarked as a B-side for the first single off the album as well as a key album track.

Plant talked about this process to Chris Charlesworth while in Montreux. "In between gigs we have always got studio time booked so the albums become a continuous thing. If we keep going into studios, a wider spectrum of stuff comes out of it. Already there's enough material recorded for the next Zeppelin album, but problems with the sleeve have held things up. Now it looks like January will see its release. ... There's a track on this new album called 'The Crunge' and it's really funny. It's something we would never have imagined doing. Numbers like this are really good because if you carry on just on one plane you just repeat yourself." Of course, many fans are quite content if their favourite band does indeed repeat the formula until it runs dry. But any act with a modicum of spirit and creativity eventually pushes at the boundaries – and Led Zeppelin were no average band and did not deal in modicums.

They were no more average when it came to the perennial problem of dealing with the press and its inevitable demands for access. Plant talked to Charlesworth about the band's idea of acceptable intrusion. "If you want to do it, you can keep up with everybody else and get your name in the papers as often as you can. That's done initially because artists like Elton John or T.Rex have something that is good and people have to be made aware of it. In England ... it wouldn't be very hard to get our names in the papers if we went about it the right way, by throwing our doors open to everybody in the press. 'Do come up to the farm and see Robert Plant milking his goats' would get us in, but ... we don't want to have to keep up to that pace. People will soon remember us when they come and see us."[3] Such is the difference between someone who looks upon fame as a means to an end – making music to the best of his ability for as many people as possible – and someone who sees fame as an end in itself.

Needless to say, the British rock public turned out in force for the end-of-year tour, provoking sell-outs within days across the entire schedule from the end of November to the end of January 1973, with a break for Christmas and the new year. Page was definitely up for the tour. He told one interviewer in mid November: "A British tour to some groups comprises a few dates around England; you know, a few key dates. But we're going to Wales and Scotland: Edinburgh, Glasgow, Dundee. We wanted to play Ayr Ice Rink, which I remember playing years back, but we couldn't get it. ... [Kings Hall] Aberystwyth holds about 900 or even less and it's going to be so good to do."

Page wanted to balance the altruistic impulses and intimate atmospheres of the early 1971 Back To The Clubs tour with the realities of ticket demand and the need to play at big venues, at least in major urban centres. It was this part of his adventurous spirit that pushed him to such commitments. All the same, he made the point that on the last American tour the set lengths had got out of hand. This band simply loved playing together: onstage virtually nightly for a month, they had been "playing an average of three hours every night, sometimes more than

that, and it was really doing us in". So they were trimming the set and sticking to what he called "all the more important ones"[4] so that the set lengths were not so impossible. After all, no group on the circuit came anywhere near this amount of music for an evening's concert entertainment.

Just days before the tour started, Page talked to Keith Altham for *NME*, revealing a previously unsuspected admiration for Frank Zappa and for John McLaughlin's new Mahavishnu Orchestra, but concentrating once more on the music critics. Complaining that these people had no idea how much hurt they could inflict through bad reviews and snide remarks, he claimed: "It's only quite recently I have been able to get a better perspective on their relative significance. ... I've realised now, though, that one or two exceptionally offensive remarks won't harm a group or a career. It'd only be serious if the general consensus of opinion was against us. ... I don't really want to talk about critics, but they're a sore subject with me. If they want to get their teeth into something, why don't they attack some of the appallingly bad situations there are within mass media – like BBC Radio 1."[5]

The first show was, like the previous tour, at the City Hall in Newcastle and was generally agreed by the band to be something of a warm-up, although the fans gave them a rapturous reception and many critics extended the palm of friendship and admiration for their sheer musicianship. One report noted that the band had delivered four encores "which the audience had simply screamed, clapped, stood and begged for. Honestly, the scenes after [they] had left the stage were amazing. The crowd was like starving rats who'd have done anything for another slice of rock."[6]

Once again these four men were proving themselves to be a superbly functioning unit with a total commitment to what the band could achieve. As Page claimed after the concert: "There are four minds at work, not just one; everybody's coming up with ideas all the time and we can all handle anything, so there's no reason why we shouldn't tackle anything. We do like to do everything ourselves, if possible."[7]

The Glasgow concerts were disturbed by an incident in which the band's publicist, B.P. Fallon, was badly beaten-up by irate fans who had been sold counterfeit tickets and were looking for a scapegoat. In response, the band decided against encores that night, provoking disgust in some of the fans present, who felt they shouldn't have been penalised for someone else's problems. So what is an encore? Is it an extra, bestowed by the performer as a thank you to an appreciative audience? And if there is a break in that link on any given night, why should there be encores? With the band delivering an average of two-and-a-half hours a night, no one could realistically declare themselves to be ripped off.

The tour rumbled on around Britain, gathering plenty

of music-press attention and a typical flurry of for and against letters from fans and detractors, the latter coming up with ever more unlikely objections to the band's concerts. One sad *Melody Maker* correspondent even managed to describe Bonham's playing at Manchester's Hardrock as "bashing away at leather suitcases and dustbin lids".[8] To complete the simile, perhaps cloth ears were the start of his problem.

After Birmingham, the band had a few days off, just enough to notice the major pop media event of the pre-Christmas season. Back in March, inspired by Led Zeppelin's success the previous November, T.Rex had given two sell-out concerts at Wembley's Empire Pool. In 1972, Marc Bolan's new group had enjoyed remarkable success, chalking up hit after hit and becoming widely proclaimed as the biggest thing in pop since The Beatles. This had of course been said many times since The Beatles had broken up, but Bolan had good cause to believe the propaganda: he was provoking the sort of hysteria in his fans unseen since 1966.

Although he was never to make a sustained impact in the USA, Bolan's boogie-type rock was a hit just about everywhere else in the world, with 1972 his peak year. The Empire Pool shows were filmed by Ringo Starr, a great fan of the band who did a deal with Bolan so that Apple Films would produce the project. By September the two men had edited the final work and by Christmas it was being shown in cinemas to ecstatic fans. Running at just 65 minutes, it was a brilliantly-shot collage of exciting concert footage, a group of fey, amusing and unscripted fantasy vignettes, and assorted general looning. Both Starr and Bolan claimed to be fans of Federico Fellini, and the great Italian director's influence from films such as *Satyricon* are easy to spot, though nobody seems to be taking themselves too seriously in the process.

There was a direct reference to Zeppelin. During a Mad Hatter's Tea Party sequence (shot in the gardens at John Lennon's Tittenhurst Park) Bolan hands the butler a piece of paper from his hat. The butler strides off, turns to camera, and reads the poem written on it. Called *Union Hall*, it refers to "the chosen ones" and contains the lines "Beatles, Stones, Zep, Rex and all / Keep on rockin' at the Union Hall." This reference, plus the fact that *Born To Boogie* came before Zeppelin's own efforts at a concert film with fantasy vignettes and was a success, makes it a likely trigger for Peter Grant's decision that the same thing should be done for Led Zeppelin in the future.

The first half of the UK tour finished with two nights at North London's vast and draughty Alexandra Palace, a venue rather neglected then and rarely used for rock, but by necessity brought into the fold by the decision of the Albert Hall's management's to ban all further rock concerts at the venerable venue after one riot too many. The Palace may not have been the ideal venue, but Zeppelin won glowing reports from the UK press for both shows there, providing their own perfect prelude to the Christmas break. They could look back on their achievements in 1972 with satisfaction, even if they remained frustrated over their records. In a rock world rapidly shedding its late-1960s clothes and shaping the new looks and sounds of the '70s – reflected by the rise to prominence in Britain of the androgynous David Bowie and in America of Alice Cooper's music-as-black-theatre – Zeppelin were as central to the music's present and future as they had ever been.

The band members individually welcomed 1973 at home with their families. Batteries re-charged, they played the second leg of the UK tour without major mishaps, although Bonham and Plant suffered a car breakdown on the way to the first gig of this leg, at Sheffield on January 2nd. They arrived late and Plant caught a cold, necessitating the cancellation of the original Preston and Bradford dates, rearranged for free days later in the tour.

Once again the crowds responded enthusiastically to what they were hearing at the concerts as Led Zeppelin continued skilfully to weave together old and new. 'The Rain Song' had its UK debut on this tour, and Jones's keyboard work was much admired. The band were taking advantage of their increasingly diverse material to branch out further onstage, with the highly versatile Jones in particular given the room to develop his varied musical presence in the band. He continued to be a puckish interviewee, for example when *NME*'s Nick Kent asked about his bass-playing influences. "I was asked this question some time ago on KSAN Radio and I answered 'Mozart', which seemed to put the interviewer off so much that he never really recovered," said Jones. "I think I also said that I like Tamla Motown bass players as well, which seemed to disgust him even more."[9] As a fine bass player unperturbed by fashion, Jones knew well that both Mozart's and Tamla Motown's basslines were spectacularly good and a great place to go for musical inspiration. But that did not stop him enjoying the DJ's bemusement.

With the British tour successfully concluded and Zeppelin triumphantly reasserted at home as a premier live act, the band had February to themselves prior to their European campaign. But the new album – still not officially announced with a title, although it had been confidently expected in-store by mid January – suffered yet more delays. It would not now appear before the band had left for their early-March concerts in Scandinavia.

This time the delays were down to problems in matching the colours of the jacket's original artwork with those that came off the printer's press. This is a relatively common problem that can result in a disastrous loss of

Opening a British tour at the end of 1972, Jimmy Page said of their live work: "We can all handle anything, so there's no reason why we shouldn't tackle anything."

tone and clarity on the finished product. Zeppelin's new design was nothing if not demanding on the printer. The colour registration on the new jacket had to be perfect for it to have the impact the band wanted, and it took a lot of work to achieve an acceptable result. Page told one scribe that the jacket "was supposed to be a work of art"[10] and care lavished on it suggests that he meant this literally.

The jacket was the first of the band's to be designed by the trendy Hipgnosis company and was revealed along with the music and the album's name, *Houses Of The Holy*, on its US release on March 18th (and, as usual, some days later in Britain). Like its predecessor, it was conceived across the entire expanse of both sides of a gatefold. Again, there were no words on the front or back, with written information relegated to the inner sleeve that held the actual disc. But in a stylish concession to marketing and sales people, the band allowed Hipgnosis to include a paper band that slipped over the entire jacket, with the record's title emblazoned upon it. Peter Grant said: "My big artistic input on that album was the wraparound band which we put on to shut Atlantic up. ... [I] got the idea from those lavish books that have wraparound covers."[11] The inner sleeve repeated the record's title and – for the first time on a Led Zeppelin record – reproduced the lyrics for all the songs. The typeface chosen for the inner sleeve title was from this point on associated with all things Zeppelin. The type's Viennese Secessionist and Symbolist stylings suggested an association with high art and esoteric beliefs that appealed to the band's aspirations.

The highly sophisticated artwork on the inner and outer jacket modified two dramatic photographs of what seems to be a prototypical pre-Christian Celtic mountain landscape. On the outside it was peopled by naked children, while inside an übermensch was practising sacrificial worship at a ruined battlement. The images gave the strongest suggestion yet that Page and Plant's interest in legend, mythology and esoterica was beginning to help form their overall notion of what the band and their music was about. Still, it is hard to believe that this notion had reached a point of coherence with an overall philosophy behind it. Page and Plant, the two band members most closely involved, were intelligent and articulate young men, but there is not a great deal of evidence to suggest that they had more than the normal dilettante's interest in such knowledge and practises.

Singer Michael des Barres, a friend of Page's at the time, saw Page's interest in the occult as part of his self-conception as the ultimate rock star. Just like Marc Bolan wearing ermine robes, a king's crown and an orb and sceptre for photo sessions, Page was into the

Robert Plant at Newcastle City Hall, December 1st 1972. When the band finished, wrote one reviewer, "The crowd was like starving rats who'd have done anything for another slice of rock."

paraphernalia of it all. "I used to go down to see Jimmy," said des Barres, "and he'd pull out [Aleister] Crowley's robes, Crowley's Tarot deck – all of the Crowley gear that he'd collected. I thought, this is great! It was all so twisted and debauched, their whole thing. That's what Jimmy represented to me. I don't know what I represented to Jimmy. I always thought that Jimmy liked me because I happened to say 'Rimbaud' at the right time."[12]

While this self-image may seem preposterous today, in an era when ideas of rock's power to do anything much apart from entertain adolescents and tired old men have long been abandoned, it must be recalled that nothing is conceived in a vacuum. In early 1973, rock was still thought by cultural commentators to possess the potential to change the world for the better, or at least to aid an aspiration to deeper cultural resonances than 'Hello Mary Lou' enjoyed in its day. Bob Dylan was still a visionary, The Band and Van Morrison dealt with the human condition, The Who were halfway between *Tommy* and *Quadrophenia*, Pink Floyd had perfected the art of enigmatic utterance. Coming up fast on the outside, David Bowie had delivered the mock-opera of *Ziggy Stardust* with its complaint about "five years, that's all we've got" and was less than a year away from "this ain't rock'n'roll, this is genocide!" over the opening measures of *Diamond Dogs*. Whether the music inside the monumental artwork edifice containing *Houses Of The Holy* actually mirrored its concerns was a moot point at this stage. Meanwhile, there was a European tour to play.

The tour lasted most of March and a few days into April 1973, revisiting old haunts, including Denmark and Sweden, and undergoing another sustained belt through Germany, where Zeppelin's fanbase was huge and hugely loyal. There was the additional pleasure of a tilt into France, a country so far largely ignored by the band.

As usual, Zep travelled with the minimum of personnel. Always a tight ship with a fiercely loyal road-crew built up by Grant and Cole over many campaigns, the band shied away from the travelling circuses of hangers-on that accompanied many of the big-name bands of the day. They preferred the freedom that such privacy bestowed and the opportunity to relieve the pressure of exhausting day-to-day engagements.

The Scandinavian concerts were not among their most memorable, judging by the reviews, but the long swing through Germany and into Austria was warmly received, as were the new songs from the still-unreleased *Houses Of The Holy*. Fans were well aware that Zeppelin were a band that always gave 100 percent in their music, and their appreciation was evident. Like all successful performers, Page knew that real fans – as opposed to fashion victims who pick up and drop performers according to what they are told to like – are quick to spot a lack of effort or conviction in a performance. "We only perform if it makes us happy and we enjoy it," he told the

German magazine *Bravo*. "Every concert we do is very serious: it doesn't matter if there are 50 or 10,000 people there. If we were to see our concerts [merely] as part of some job, then we would be out of business very fast. The fans would turn their backs on us."[13]

On March 16th Led Zeppelin played their first ever concert in Vienna. At the Stadthalle they concentrated more than usual on their earlier repertoire and set a fast pace; even their acoustic number that night was the sprightly 'Bron-Y-Aur'. By the time they reached France towards the end of the month they were in high spirits and delivering the goods nightly.

The first French concert was on March 26th in the southern town of Lyon. Grant and Cole's inspection of the 12,000-seat stadium normally used for basketball and other indoor sports quickly revealed that security was virtually non-existent, so they asked for backup from the French office of Atlantic Records. Benoit Gautier, an Atlantic executive, attended and helped quell rowdy fans who were lobbing empty wine bottles onto the stage.

Staying on for the rest of the French sojourn, Gautier quickly noticed the unusual closeness of the band and its road crew. It seemed to him more like a fraternity of like-minded people than a touring band and its lackeys, which was more commonly the case then with rock bands. He found some of the road crew more than ready to fight rather than talk their way out of a tense situation and often encouraged in this attitude by Cole and Grant. It made for a constant sense of menace and brooding protection around the four musicians, who consequently were free to live on tour with a very low level of outside interference or interaction unless they specifically required it. This attitude had served the band well in their hard-working and rapid rise in status, but Grant and Page were both aware that, whatever its benefits, this overly defensive, withdrawn stance was no longer in step with what the band needed in order to advance their career. They were working on the best way to move from that position before the French part of the tour was finished.

The band played a successful date in Nancy's Parc des Expositions, deep in Vosges country, one of the most beautiful regions of France, but some of the party antagonised local police after some horseplay that bordered on hooliganism. Bonham was implicated, causing Gautier to observe: "He had no natural defence against being manipulated, and nothing to protect him. ... The roadies would start to push him to do something, and he'd go crazy. He would throw drinks or dump food on anybody if Jimmy told him to."[14] The business was sorted out without too much loss of face either by the band or the Gendarmes, and the following day Zeppelin were free to complete the handful of concerts left on the tour.

However, they enjoyed an unexpected break when two further provincial French concerts were cancelled after the local promoter pulled out, leaving them to enjoy the long-anticipated release of the record and to plan what to do with the free time. Rather than merely return to London for the interim, Grant decided to push on to Paris where they could extend their stay at the famous George V hotel. This was not an idle whim. He had decided the time was right to upgrade the band's public relations, which had withered since B.P. Fallon's injuries in Glasgow the previous December, leaving the band unrepresented and with a new album to promote. After asking around his industry friends, Grant phoned a Los Angeles-based PR company mostly involved in film work, Solters Roskin & Sabinson. He made contact with senior partner Lee Solters and asked him to come to Paris to meet the band and talk about what his company could do to improve what they perceived as a poor relationship with the music press and the media in general.

Solters, who concerned himself with the world of Hollywood stars and heavy movers, brought along the head of the firm's rock'n'roll division, Danny Goldberg, a man in his early 20s and very much in touch with the currents of the US music business. Solters and Goldberg arrived in Paris in time to catch the band's second and last Paris concert on April 2nd – the last date of the European tour – and then meet with them all at the George V hotel the following day. According to Cole, who was present at the meeting, Solters summed up the band's current media impasse. He was accurate and pulled no punches. "Your music is taking a back seat to a lot of negative publicity about your offstage life, and that offstage image will require some rehabilitation. Because you've shied away from most interviews for so long, all the press has to go on are the rumours about your maniacal behaviour. We've got to mainstream you and change that outlaw image. We also have to let the population at large know that you're accomplished musicians, not savages."[15]

Solters had hit all the right buttons. None of this would have mattered if the band's members were genuinely uninterested in wider acceptance for their substantial musical achievements. Many rockers, especially of the heavy variety, were proud of being outlaws in their own eyes and had no interest at all in rehabilitation. But Zeppelin's band members, especially Plant and Page, had long moved on from that and yearned for wider recognition, not only of their talent but of their increasing sophistication and worldliness.

This has been a well trodden path for entertainers and celebrities of all descriptions since the dawn of time. Led Zeppelin were only the latest arrivals at the door of wider acceptance. What Solters had suggested as the solution to their problems would have been completely unacceptable just 12 months earlier, when the entire band were still actively hostile to the media in general. But they had learned the lessons of 1972, when they were comprehensively upstaged by The Rolling Stones in media adulation if not in concert gates and revenue. Now they were willing to listen and to shift their stance if it gave them what they wanted.

The deal was effectively sealed when it became clear that Goldberg, who they knew would be their key liaison man, had once written for *Rolling Stone* magazine. The history between that media organ and Led Zeppelin was, to put it mildly, one of mutual mistrust and antagonism. The fact that Goldberg not only came originally from the enemy's camp but could suggest ways of winning that enemy over made him a shoo-in for the job. With a deal agreed in Paris, Grant, Page and Goldberg spent a great deal of time in the weeks prior to the start of the next US tour, due start early in May, plotting their rapprochement with the music media. This would centre on the musical qualities of their live shows and the perceived advance in their music represented by *Houses Of The Holy*, a few weeks old and already breaking records for pre-orders.

Paradoxically, just as Grant and the band began in earnest the job of cleaning up their image and making their operation altogether more professional – as Plant said to Goldberg, "we're businessmen now" – there were signs that the long-term pressure of their position in the rock firmament and the demands of fame and touring had brought a coarsening effect to more than just Bonham, who for some time had been behaving badly on the road.

Benoit Gautier had quickly become aware of this during his week or so with the band in France that March. He said later: "It was obvious that some of them were using drugs, but they were very discreet. They never asked for grass or anything: they mostly asked for legal things, mostly girls. Prostitution is legal in France. They wanted good booze, nice parties, and amusing people. ... Robert was a truly nice person. He never harmed anybody, had good manners, was always smiling. ... The wisest guy was John Paul Jones. Why? He never got caught in an embarrassing situation. He would always show at the very last minute for anything. You'd never even know where he was staying. ... He was the most mischievous in the band. He was the kind of person who enjoyed mind games. ... He was so smart and could have been the most vicious and dangerous of all of them; he wasn't, but he could have been. ... I thought he was brilliant. He could do any other job and had a great sense of a practical joke."[16]

Most worrying were the signs that Page might no longer be the completely disciplined professional, a role he had been proud to assume until then. Gautier said: "Jimmy was the mastermind of it all, and seemed very much in control." But the French record-company man observed another side. "When I saw Jimmy doing cocaine one day I was totally shocked. He didn't seem like that kind of guy. And not only was it shocking that it was Jimmy, but that he would show that side of himself. That was the first time I ever saw Jimmy lose control."[17]

Not that Page saw it that way at the time. A couple of weeks later he told a British journalist that he would give up if being in the music business was simply a business, or if he ever succumbed to ego-tripping. "For me, personally, the music's more important. I'm such a different person offstage and onstage. I think it's the spontaneity, really, for me. Going out there and something comes out of the guitar that never came out before. ... [Also] it's a good time to write on the road, because you start getting into this pace, especially if you're really condensing tours like we do. ... If you put that same pace into writing, obviously you're going to get a totally different pace. That urgency which you're not going to get at other times when the mellower things come out at home. So it's good to get both."[18] The new developments observed by Gautier would have a major long-term effect on the band and its music, but for the moment such things were only noticed by insiders.

As for the music newly available on *Houses Of The Holy* in good time for the US tour in May, it had been recorded at an earlier time in the band's history, before circumstances had begun to coarsen their sensibilities to the point reached when Gautier observed them in France. Oddly for such a forward-looking album, *Houses Of The Holy* starts with a song based on a guitar pattern that Page had first played when still in The Yardbirds. 'The Song Remains The Same' (originally titled 'The Campaign') begins with the same fanfare chords used by Page for the introduction to 1967's 'Tinker Tailor Soldier Sailor', which was written by Page and Yardbirds drummer Jim McCarty and featured Page's earliest recorded work with the violin bow on his guitar.

'Song Remains' is the first Zeppelin piece to begin at a breakneck tempo; others before had broken into fast tempos at various points along the way. The band keep up this pace for the entire introductory section, which lasts well over a minute and features not only some spectacularly shimmering multi-guitar overdubs but also a wonderfully locked-in bass and drums pattern.

Much comment has been made since about the Eastern flavour of some of the accompanying guitar sounds and of Plant's singing on the track, especially in the later parts. The guitar sounds at times like a tambura, sometimes a sitar. Plant's first entry is folk-based and very warm in its expression; later (3:08) he comes in at the top end of his range, using a pentatonic-scale melody that has some blues in it but also much in common with the melismatic lines of Indian singing. In that tradition, a melody is often extended unexpectedly past its normal termination point, providing an extra thrilling dimension through the suspense of its flickering musical journey.

The Eastern flavour is even more explicit when Plant sings the verse that begins "All you gotta do now..." and

Overleaf: For some time now Zeppelin's concerts had included an acoustic interlude.

ends in an extraordinary weave of semitones high in his range. This is a direct imitation of Indian reed and vocal music and provides great excitement as the song builds to its climactic end. It is also a first, for the band and for rock, because this is no mere grafting of alien musical figures from another culture through the use of ethnic instruments – a practise that Page in particular loathed – but a proper assimilation of its musical methods into a rock format. The Bombay experience of 1972 had paid off.

The entire piece is a dazzling display of everything that Page does best on a guitar and with the recording studio, from the brilliance and depth of sound on every instrument through to the carefully considered guitar parts spread across many layers, extracting varied colours from the basic fabric of the song. The change to half tempo when Plant enters at the verse section ("I had a dream…" 1:26) is simple but arresting. His slightly recessed and heavily treated voice is given a new quality, as if it is functioning as an additional instrument rather than with the traditional rock role of cheerleader.

After this verse, the song repeats its structure so far, with Plant adding another verse of lyrics ("California sunlight…") instead of more guitars. Then a cadential figure in triple time (beginning at 3:43) allows the band to use a turnaround and channel straight back to the top rather than go through the half-time verse section again. In this way the band not only steams into the final passages at full tilt, but the song naturally picks up momentum for the sudden arrest at the full vocal chord that ends it. A perfect construction perfectly realised.

The beginning of 'The Rain Song' announces something new on a Led Zeppelin album: the carrying of themes and motifs through from one song to another. Page has indeed talked about 'The Song Remains The Same' starting life as a prelude to 'The Rain Song'. "It was originally going to be an instrumental: an overture that led into the 'The Rain Song'. But I guess Robert had different ideas. You know: 'This is pretty good. Better get some lyrics – quick!'"[19] This confirms the impression that the entire first side of the original vinyl release – 'Song Remains The Same', 'Rain Song', 'Over The Hills And Far Away', and 'The Crunge' – forms an informal suite. Each song shares certain devices and themes that make a type of progression. It contrasts strongly with the static and unrelated patchwork that the second side offers.

'The Rain Song' begins with a cascade of arpeggio'd guitar sound that immediately links it to 'The Song Remains The Same', and while the specific chord progression is different, it has a similar cyclic form. The rhythmic figures also echo the first song, as if this is the minor-key variation of that piece's optimism. The little guitar decoration Page uses in the second part of the verse is a variant of the fills he uses in 'Song', and in turn a basis for similar decorations in 'Over The Hills'. Plant's first verse – mentioning spring, sunlight, growth – contains lyrics that echo 'Song Remains The Same', with its references to California sunlight, Calcutta rain, and everything small needs to grow.

Plant's later recollection of that song's genesis suggested he knew that this was something special. In a sense the lyric goes from the universal – the idea of the world-song that underpins 'Song Remains The Same' – to the personal – with 'Rain Song' referring to a relationship going through the pleasure and pain of growth. Page's beautiful setting for these lyrics is enhanced by Jones's use of the Mellotron, here lending the requisite touch of mystic awe to a gentle love song that widens out into a larger statement about everyone's love. Page's guitar obbligatos are allowed to float in and out at will, lending a sense of space and peace not normally present in Led Zeppelin songs. Two verses go by without any vocals, for example, and without any blazing guitar solos. As such, the song as a mood piece sits midway between Hendrix's 'Drifting' of 1970 and Brian Eno's 'Becalmed' of 1974.

As the song progresses (it's quite long at well over seven minutes) there is a chance that the mix will be over-egged when Jones's piano tinklings are added to the Mellotron, guitar, bass and full-power drums that mark the major divide about two-thirds into the piece. For a moment or two, things get dangerously close to sanctimony, as if The Moody Blues had crashed the party. But Plant's vocals make a decisive rescue, injecting a raw, bluesy edge and a feeling of sheer need that cancels any tendency to blandness. The gentle let-down at the end thus becomes a perfect landing.

'Over The Hills And Far Away' comes next. The title was first used by the English composer Frederick Delius in the 1920s, and both pieces share a similarly uplifting feel. Zep's song starts in the same key as 'The Rain Song' and begins with a guitar pattern that sounds like a cheerful variant of its opening, as well as another way around 'The Song Remains The Same'. This connection is emphasised by Page's use of an acoustic guitar to state the opening riff. The song picks up the theme of 'The Rain Song', speculating about the singer's position in life and love and how he embraces what the world has to offer. So we go back to what 'Song Remains' was about, presented in a new way and another light.

A snaking guitar-and-bass riff enters, introducing the next section and allowing Bonham to unleash his drums properly for the first time on the album. Plant follows suit by opening his throat and screaming the lyrics, but they aren't the usual honeydripper blues stuff. He is still dealing with his wanderlust and his wonder at the world, and the instrumentation is a clever balance of riff, rhythmic breaks and punctuations, carried along by

Jimmy Page talks to an interviewer at the band's offices in London around the time of the release of the fifth album, Houses Of The Holy.

simple chord structures that allow for Page's imaginative arrangements. The arrival of his guitar solo, over another variant riff and a key change, allows the song to step up a gear and the excitement to increase before Plant delivers his final version in the original key and back over the original snaky riff. The development of the riff patterns is a pleasure in itself, maintaining interest throughout, no matter what the rest of the song is doing, and almost incidentally providing a sense of movement and progress, thereby following the song's theme of search and discovery.

Those riffs also provide the link to 'The Crunge'. The interest in this simple piece comes mainly in the playful rhythmic patterns that Page, Jones and Bonham create together, paying tribute to the phenomenal James Brown sex-machine rhythms but also tearing at those same rhythms and distorting them into something completely separate and typically Led Zeppelin. The little rhythmic units that the band work with here also echo 'The Song Remains The Same' and help tie this informal suite of pieces together more completely.

'The Crunge' is clearly a bit of fun. Plant's sly tongue-in-cheek lyrics play with James Brown themes and at the end even ask us to smile at the song's search for a 'bridge' or second section – one of James Brown's favourite onstage ploys and a great way to increase the tension. Jones retained a great affection for this song, later commenting: "The Crunge is brilliant. [It's] very tight, really, when you think about it. It's one of my favourites. All the synthesiser lines were done monophonically from an old VCS-3. Bonzo was also very interested in Stax [and] Motown."[20]

Contrary to the idea that 'The Crunge' was a one-off jam, some months later Plant talked of the difficulty he had in writing its lyrics. "Bonzo and I were going to just go into the studio and talk Black Country through the whole thing – you know: 'Ahh bloody hell, how you doin', you all right mate?' – and it just evolved there and then at the end of my tether. It came out."[21]

Many commentators have found 'The Crunge' a lumpen, humourless imitation of soul music, but that is to miss the point. Its tribute is affectionate, as was 'Hats Off To (Roy) Harper' back on Led Zeppelin III. They are not trying to outdo James Brown or prove they can be blue-eyed soul boys. They are being Led Zeppelin and bringing their own unique blend of instruments, lyrics and attitude to some great riffs, and in doing so they prove that metal can swing, especially when Bonham is the man behind the drum kit.

Unfortunately, the second side of Houses Of The Holy does not live up to the uniformly high achievement of side one. The ability to sequence a record so that it flows is one of the more arcane talents in the record industry; the

Jimmy Page attacks his Gibson Les Paul with a violin bow, a technique that dated back to his Yardbirds days.

lack of flow here indicates that there had been so much discussion about which songs to use from the pool they'd created in early 1972 that the final choice was an unedifying compromise to satisfy individual tastes that does not hang together as a set. It is not merely that there is a great deal of stylistic territory being covered, from old-fashioned Zep ('Dancing Days', 'The Ocean') through progressive rock ('No Quarter') to cod-reggae-cum-50s-revival ('D'yer Mak'er'). Only one piece can be described as inspired, either in conception or performance. That song is 'No Quarter', which is placed in a no-man's land between 'D'yer Mak'er' and 'The Ocean'. More like the devil and the deep blue sea.

'Dancing Days' kicks off with a full-on, slashing riff that raises the hairs on the back of your neck and promises much. The band are in a fabulous mid-tempo rocking groove and Page works wonders with his slide-guitar semitones – again an Eastern influence on what is a basic boogie blues pattern. But the melody line is disappointing. Plant sticks to his middle register and sings mostly in a restrained monotone during the verse, using small-interval variations that paint a strangely subdued emotional picture, jarring with the perky background and the words themselves, which are lively and full of little jokes. Plant's melody is centred on a different scale to the band, lending a further sense of detachment. The song deals with summer, love and high spirits, but manages to undermine its own mood and end up feeling a little uneasy in the process.

The next piece, 'D'Yer Mak'er', breaks the mood of the album and comes across as a false move and the first real failure of Led Zeppelin's recording career. This was a particular favourite of Plant's at the time, and while it is abundantly clear that no one involved in its creation wanted to treat it too seriously, a sober assessment at the time would have relegated it to the also-rans.

Clearly Plant's enthusiasm got it onto the record. He told Zig Zag in 1973 that he considered 'D'yer Mak'er' "a lovely song", adding: "So many people rip us off for it in England but I don't know what they expect us to do. I expect us to be very serious and very conscientious about everything we do, but it is a nice song. We had just laid down 'The Song Remains The Same' which is a real belter. … It was about 5.00am and I had been hoping for a long time to do something like [it]. … It was born then and there."[22]

There are so many problems with the piece it's difficult to know where to start. The rhythm simply can't make up its mind what it is: 1950s pastiche (what Page is playing); cod-reggae or ska (what Jones is playing, on bass and piano); or lumpen heavy rock (what Bonham is thrashing out). On top of that, Plant sings a set of lyrics that are devoid of content, relying on his coy interpretation to bring humour and irony to a song that refuses to take off. But coyness will not make this one fly:

such themes of teenage angst only work when the vocalist (boy or girl) is utterly, passionately sincere. Think of *Grease* for an invocation of romantic angst that works.

The song had problems from its inception: even the tired title, a hoary old play on words, reveals how witless the entire idea was. As Jones recalled about the recording: "John was interested in everything except jazz and reggae. He didn't hate jazz but he hated playing reggae – he thought it was really boring. When we did 'D'Yer Mak'er' he wouldn't play anything but the same shuffle beat all the way through it. He hated it, and so did I. It would have been all right if he had worked at the part – the whole point of reggae is that the drums and bass really have to be very strict about what they play. And he wouldn't, so it sounded dreadful."[23]

By drawing attention to Bonham's failure to come to grips with the very basis of the song, Jones is being overly generous to everyone else's role in this failure. They'd have been better off doing an Elvis cover if they wanted a few laughs on the album; at least it was something they could all do superlatively well. Jones told another interviewer: "It just makes me cringe a bit. It started off as a kind of joke, really. It got into a reggae rhythm and we put it down. I wasn't happy with the way it turned out; it wasn't thought through carefully enough. … I'm a great fan of reggae, actually … but … to my mind it didn't work at all. I know Robert really likes it. Even in the band, people have different opinions about the songs."[24] At the time Plant pushed hard for the song to be released as a single: it would have been a more appropriate fate, allowing it to be quietly dropped from the album line-up in favour of one of the many held-over tracks.

'No Quarter' at six-and-a-half minutes is the second longest song on the record and a piece that Jones had originally presented to the band for development over a year before its eventual completion. It is the most coherent and weighty composition on the second side. There have been suggestions that its beginnings could have been linked with the death of Jones's father in 1970, and its melancholy would tend to bear that out that idea, though Plant's oblique lyrics don't deal with the subject.

In fact it's not clear what Plant is dealing with, apart from a depiction of men coming home from war in some northerly country – Vikings, perhaps, or others from Norse and Celtic legends. The music meanwhile tells its own articulate story and is packed with drama. It once more underlines the now obvious fact that Led Zeppelin were far from a one-dimensional heavy rock band. Page comes up with some telling guitar touches, including a nice tilting of the hat to Hendrix when he quotes Jimi's 'Hey Joe' turnaround riff in the introduction, a part of the song that, when repeated, forms a sort of tag to the chorus.

Jones's keyboard work is kept simple and stark and works well as a result, especially in the passages where Bonham drops out. In a remarkable improvisatory instrumental section that starts around 3:05, Page uses his solo passage (from 3:57) to play answering phrases from two different guitar tracks. This section gets as close to jazz as Zeppelin ever did, with Page and Jones in particular playing with great sensitivity, swapping phrases and feeding each other different ideas to respond to. Page helps to sustain the mood and create the feeling of a chorus of instrumental voices in between Plant's vocals through this subtle interweaving of guitar lines and chords.

'The Ocean' begins with a virile, oddly-phrased and captivating Page riff in 7/8 that neatly turns the beat around and immediately announces a deep Zeppelin groove. The sound is somewhat recessed, perhaps a result of its initial recording at Stargroves, so while the song has a classic construction of alternate vocal and non-vocal passages, the purely instrumental portions don't quite have the kick normally associated with the band.

Plant's lyrics are some of his most effective, drawing a neat parallel between the pleasure he gets looking out on an ocean of water and an ocean of faces, but his singing is at times a little pinched, his voice strained, although this may be the effect he was aiming for. The most effective part of the song comes through contrast: a pause in the sledgehammer riff allows Plant to use a quiet baritone chant (a variant on Page's initial riff) to build up from an almost whispered base and re-introduce the bridge. The two-beat walking ending to the song suggests that no one wanted to end it with a simple recapitulation of the opening, which would have left it curiously undeveloped – so we get a good but hardly memorable Page solo over doo-wop chorus phrases from Plant, who adds an "it's so good" as the band hit the concluding chord. It's an upbeat way to end the album but not the most memorable conclusion the band had managed up to then.

This was the album that was unleashed on the world in March 1973. It is a flawed collection that, while it broke new ground for the band in many ways and in part was a major achievement, ultimately betrayed its long gestation period. It is hard to escape the feeling that if it been released closer to the unfolding success of *Led Zeppelin IV* the line-up of songs would have been different and more tightly co-ordinated. The feel may well have been different, too, for there is a palpable air in the songs towards the end of the album of a band who have arrived, big-time, and are surveying their domain.

It's not that the music is lazy or self-indulgent, apart from the misfire of 'D'Yer Mak'er'. It's more that the band members are no longer novices trying to prove their worth, but experienced stars with a very different outlook on life. Just how different that outlook was would be revealed by the course of events in the following years.

> **Jimmy Page told an interviewer: "For me, personally, the music's most important. I'm such a different person offstage and onstage."**

VIEW FROM THE TOP

- 9TH AMERICAN TOUR
- MADISON SQUARE GARDEN FILMING/RECORDING
- PLANS FOR ZEPPELIN DOCUMENTARY FILM
- HEADLEY GRANGE REHEARSALS FOR 6TH ALBUM

Led Zeppelin's fifth album, *Houses Of The Holy*, made it to Number 1 on both sides of the Atlantic. In Britain it had to wait for Alice Cooper's *Billion Dollar Babies* and a Hits Of The Sixties compilation to pass through before making the top for two weeks. Zep's album was in turn succeeded by The Faces' *Ooh-La-La* and David Bowie's *Aladdin Sane*, though none of them out-performed Elton John's February 1973 release *Don't Shoot Me I'm Only The Piano Player*, the biggest-selling album in the UK that year.

In the States, the LP took longer to get to the top, arriving there in May and spurred eventually by the momentum generated by Zep's ninth US tour. Elton's album had also reached Number 1 for two weeks in early March, succeeded by Eric Weissberg's *Duelling Banjos*, soundtrack to the hit movie *Deliverance*, which was at the top for three weeks. After this, early April saw another soundtrack hit the top, Diana Ross's *Lady Sings The Blues*, followed by Alice Cooper, then Pink Floyd's *Dark Side Of The Moon*, which somehow had missed Number 1 in Britain but still became a mammoth worldwide seller. *Houses Of The Holy* finally made it to the US Number 1 in mid May, staying there for two weeks. Zeppelin were in turn supplanted by The Beatles' 67-70 singles collection.

With a US tour approaching, 'Over The Hills And Far Away' was released in America as the album's first single, coupled with 'Dancing Days' as a B-side. *Houses Of The Holy* received mixed reviews the world over as writers found different things to praise and condemn, but no one declared it the masterpiece that sales and expectation demanded.

Plant expressed his distaste for the mixed reception in interviews published during April 1973 before the start of the tour, but Page managed to keep a cooler head. "I don't really care," he told *NME*. "It doesn't really make any difference. I'm deaf to the album now because we made it such a long time ago, but I know there's some good stuff there." He mentioned the fact that 'The Crunge' and 'D'Yer Mak'er' were "just a giggle" but he also showed an awareness of the album's shortcomings. "The rock'n'roll is in all four of us," said Page, "and onstage that's what comes through. In fact we had two tracks, one called 'The Rover' and another unnamed, that we were going to use, both of which were really hard rock. We'll possibly use them next time."[1] 'The Rover' would indeed make it to the next album, but it would be quite a wait.

Plant continued to lead from the front with press engagements in the build-up to the tour. The guitarist told *Sounds* the same week that Plant "wrote all the lyrics" on *Houses Of The Holy*, which he said was one of the reasons for the consistency of the subject matter on the record. Page also talked about why the band had been slow to release the last two albums. Quite simply, they'd been working so hard.

"I'm sure people aren't aware of this," Page told Rob Mackie. "I'm sure they think we sit on our arses all day long, but we don't. All I know is I haven't stopped for three years. ... I haven't had a holiday since the group started. There's just so much going on as far as studio work, or rehearsing, or touring. Then again, there's songwriting as well."

He also mentioned the subject of unreleased songs. "Yesterday, actually, I was playing some tracks I haven't heard for years, and sometimes the tracks that haven't gone on [the records] are better than the ones that have. Sometimes you think: 'Well, that bit's all right, but this bit isn't. Why don't we re-write it and shuffle it around?'"[2] With so much fluidity in the band's activities, and with four strong personalities to be catered for, one can understand why Page should find himself in that position from time to time.

The US tour was broken into two sections, the first half swallowing May 1973, followed by a month's break for most of June, and then more or less the whole of July back on the road. The tour would be something of a watershed for the band in a number of ways, for they were no longer relying on their music and stage act alone to put across their message. New PR man Danny Goldberg was on board for much of the trip, arranging interviews and drumming up publicity both locally and internationally. They had decided to upgrade their live act to incorporate a sophisticated light-show, start wearing less hippie-ish stage clothes (Page in particular took this idea to heart, having special clothes designed for himself), and increase the visual impact of the band.

Additionally, they decided to film their appearances at Madison Square Garden in New York City at the end of the tour in late July, when they presumed they would be at their peak of playing and exposure. The tour was their longest ever and, prior to its start, a leak to *Rolling Stone* magazine had manager Peter Grant expecting it to be the biggest-grossing US tour of all time, exceeding $5 million. The item was duly published. Grant saw this simply as the opening shot in his campaign to have the band recognised as the biggest act of the day.

There were long work-out rehearsals, turning soundchecks into mini-concerts of their own, during which the band fooled around with fun remakes of old rockers that they'd always enjoyed playing together – 'Round And 'Round', 'Shakin' All Over', 'Nadine', 'School Days' and the like. But they also worked up some of their own material that had not appeared on any

John Bonham working hard on his 'see through' Ludwig Vistalite kit onstage at The Forum in Los Angeles on May 31st 1973.

Overleaf: Enjoying the California sunshine in June 1973 during Led Zeppelin's ninth American tour.

Zeppelin album yet, including 'The Wanton Song', 'The Rover', and 'Night Flight'. Two of these dated back to 1970-71; 'The Wanton Song' was more recent. All three would later be brought to completion in the studio in time for the sixth album, 1975's *Physical Graffiti*. The length of time in which the band allowed some tunes to mature is another indication of the care with which they approached every new recording project.

Led Zeppelin started this biggest tour yet with what they hoped and expected to be a blockbusting concert, on May 4th 1973 at Atlanta's sports stadium, where they were hoping for 50,000 fans to turn out. The hopes were fulfilled and the crowd, sweeping past the stadium terraces and onto the sports field to be closer to the band, were completely unfettered in their appreciation of the music. The concert lasted close on three hours, starting with 'Rock And Roll' and moving through the updated set that the band had tried out on the recent British dates.

The newly introduced light-show added drama and a sense of occasion to the music and the performers. 'No Quarter' was introduced to the American public with a stage full of dry-ice smoke. It was an immediate hit and would remain in the band's set for the rest of their career, a lasting tribute to Jones's expertise on keyboards. By the time 'Dazed And Confused' arrived, the onstage effects extended to smoke bombs, lasers, and cannon shots. This was Led Zeppelin in a new guise, using showmanship American-style to completely captivate an American audience. It worked.

This show and others like it on the tour did indeed turn out to be the biggest-grossing rock events for a single act in American showbiz history up to that time. Whatever had happened the year before with The Rolling Stones, Led Zeppelin were now hot news, making Danny Goldberg's media-relations job a good deal easier. *Circus* reported in a sort of half-unbelieving ecstasy: "When the [Atlanta] concert was over and Zeppelin headed for Florida in their Falcon jet, they were told that the 49,236 customers who had seen them that day had been the largest crowd ever assembled for a rock concert in Georgia's history. The holders of the previous record? The Beatles. ... Said Jimmy Page: 'Our minds were blown'.

"Yet the Atlanta concert was only a foretaste of what was to happen the next day in Tampa, Florida. Early Saturday afternoon, police estimated that a crowd of 90,000 kids had surrounded the new Tampa Stadium. By six o'clock, 62,700 of them had packed into the Stadium's field and bleachers – including an estimated 6,000 gatecrashers."[3]

These momentous events were news not only for the music papers but also for the dailies on both sides of the Atlantic. Cold, hard cash figures like those Led Zeppelin generated on this tour were even of interest to *The Financial Times* back in London. As tour manager Richard

Cole recalled later: "Thanks to the sell-out crowd [in Atlanta] the band was $250,000 richer than they had been at the start of the day. But that was only the beginning. The crowd at Tampa Stadium the next night – 56,000 people – shattered the single concert-attendance record set by The Beatles at Shea Stadium in 1965."[4] Cole was quite right about this, but he failed to point out that the Beatles crowd had been kept confined to the stadium seats and that Zeppelin, generating $310,000 compared to The Beatles' $300,000 that night, were grossing less in real terms thanks to eight years of inflation. But it still looked good in print in all the dailies, and the band celebrated the fact that they were unquestionably the biggest live act of the day in rock – although Elton John was in hot pursuit.

The first leg of the tour wound its way through many Southern towns and cities, building up momentum and giving the band and crew ample opportunity to indulge in wild on-the-road behaviour. In New Orleans, even the normally in-control Jones passed out, drunk, in a hotel room with what he thought was a pretty young woman, only to be told by the members of the entourage who retrieved him the next morning that in fact he'd been drinking alone with a transvestite. The transvestite also passed out eventually in the same room and woke some time later to find himself abandoned.

While they were in New Orleans they were treated to a special event at Cosimo's studio by Atlantic boss Ahmet Ertegun, who lined up a collection of New Orleans music legends to perform for Zeppelin, including Professor Longhair, Art Neville and The Meters, and Snooks Eaglin. The band, and especially Plant and Page, were overwhelmed by seeing some of their boyhood heroes play especially for them, and on home turf too.

From the Royal Orleans Hotel in the same town, Plant talked to a female interviewer about the buzz he still got from the live show every night. "As long as there's a face looking up at me, ... as long as there's a face that knows what I'm doing, it could never be boring. It's the ability to make people smile or just to turn them on one way or another for that duration of time. And for it to have some effect later on. ... I like them to go away feeling the same way you do at the end of a good chick, satisfied and exhausted." It was a subtle point he was making to her there.

The following week the same reporter's published interview found Page in loquacious mood. Lisa Robinson quoted his ideas for changing the performance every night as he explained that the band had always functioned in that way and with good reason. "No matter how efficient [a band are] musically, I think once you know what's coming – and that refers to anything you can get into – it becomes a bore. And if we were like that, our LPs would have all stuck in the same sort of groove, more or less. But as all our minds are alive and still working, that's why we go through these changes."

Asked why he didn't have a second guitarist in the band to help out with the music, Page was clear about his reasons. He dismissed out of hand the idea of having a mere rhythm guitarist to keep things going while he whipped up a storm over the top. A twin-lead setting as he'd briefly enjoyed with Jeff Beck back in Yardbirds days would perhaps be tempting, he mused, but "I don't think it would be right, because it's more of a challenge to try and get it with just what we've got. That's the thing, really: if we can keep it together ourselves, and just play … we should be able to orchestrate anything on our own".[5]

Page and Plant's excitement about playing live ran right through all four members of the band and clearly provided the impetus and energy that translated itself every night onstage into an overwhelming musical entertainment. The crowd fed off their music and they in turn fed off the crowd's enthusiasm and love for the music.

Plant in particular appreciated this bond, feeling it gave him something special to build on. "I used to hate America," he told *Zig Zag* the day after a concert at The Forum in Los Angeles, as the tour turned westwards. "Well, I didn't hate it, I was just frightened to death of it for a long time. Then the last two tours have proved to me that I have grown up enough to see that there is a lot of goodness here, and there's a lot of people who are truly the beautiful people … I mean the tremendous rapport that we have developed with audiences over here. It isn't a 'Whole Lotta Love' rapport, it's like the 'Stairway To Heaven' type rapport. We walked on last night … and 18,000 people were there, and there were about 16,000 lights burning, glowing among the crowd. You walk out there and you are filled with something fantastic, and you play your balls off and they give you what you give them."[6]

Plant spoke later to *NME* from Los Angeles during the last days of May. "In this band we're very lucky that everybody is more enthusiastic as time goes on. There is no fatigue or boredom musically at all. There's a bit of boredom when you're stuck in Mobile, Alabama, or places like that," said Plant, not bothering to add the rest of Dylan's famous line. "A few lamp standards may fall out of the windows – things like that – but we move on and we keep playing that music."[7]

In L.A. at the Continental Hyatt House hotel (nicknamed The Riot House), away from performing, the band had long done much more than throw lamps out of hotel windows. This time around there was a reporter from a British national newspaper to write about the shenanigans. *Sun* reporter Bob Hart wrote an article that made the band's hotel antics front-page news. He'd long suspected that some of the antics were staged for him and other reporters in order to guarantee strong coverage. But what he didn't write about was the band's increasing use of cocaine, which had been the rock-star drug of choice in America for a number of years. Years later, Hart related: "There was an English girl who was the coke lady. This was so that nobody else ever carried or touched coke. She would apply the coke with the little finger of her right hand, then follow that up with a sniff of cherry snuff and, as a final touch, she'd dab the nostrils with Dom Perignon [champagne] 1966."[8]

Whatever was fuelling the band – music, drugs, booze, girls – they kept it up right through to the two L.A. Forum gigs at the end of May and start of June that crowned the first leg, making an indelible impression on everyone who came across them en route. But problems had arisen as they arrived in Los Angeles when Page sprained his hand on a wire fence while signing autographs at the airport. The first Forum date had been postponed to give him time to recover. Never in the rudest health, Page took longer than that. In fact he claimed afterwards that by completing the first leg of the tour he delayed a full recovery from the damage to a finger ligament for over a month. In the immediate future he had to struggle against his injury for the LA and San Francisco gigs.

Bootleg recordings of the May 31st Forum concert – scheduled on Bonham's birthday – reveal that Page managed to overcome his injury and complete the usual marathon set in good spirits and with few lapses in technique. The set-list was a variant on the usual, including 'Misty Mountain Hop', 'The Song Remains The Same', 'Rain Song', 'Dazed And Confused', 'No Quarter', 'The Ocean', and a 'Whole Lotta Love' pared down from the extravaganza of the year before. Between 'The Ocean' and 'Whole Lotta Love' Plant conducted the crowd in a singalong 'Happy Birthday' to Bonham. That celebration was followed in private by a lavish birthday party thrown by local radio station KROQ. Rock stars and other personalities attended (including a happy George Harrison) and all enjoyed the decadent fun. *Deep Throat* was shown on a video machine for those interested and the entire troupe minus Grant ended up in the swimming pool.

Meanwhile there were gigs to play to finish the first leg. Even with his finger causing discomfort and less than properly mobile, Page helped the band deliver at Kezar Stadium in San Francisco's Golden Gate Park. One observer called it the best live set he ever witnessed. During a long day's music with The Tubes and Lee Michaels also playing, and after a lengthy and not exactly inspiring opening solo acoustic set by Roy Harper, Led Zeppelin set about their San Francisco performance like men inspired.

Sun journo Bob Hart related that the backstage area was lavishly laid out with barbecue food, drink and refreshments, but the band and its entourage were ushered by promoter Bill Graham into a smaller office.

"He showed the guys to another little room where there was a table bearing a large pile of a certain white substance."[9] After indulging in this they were certainly ready to deliver to the folks of San Francisco, starting with a barnstorming version of 'Rock And Roll' and continuing for another two-and-a-half hours. Hart was particularly impressed by Bonham's drumming. "I think people tend to forget the impact of John Bonham: that drive and that incredible attack that he gave them. He was almost knocking people over in the first five rows with his ferocity."[10]

The first half of the tour concluded in L.A. with the postponed Forum appearance on June 3rd, the band on a high even with Page's injury, and the crowd joining in the atmosphere. Plant was inspired by what the band had achieved, in spite of physical set-backs and the fact that his voice was not in great shape throughout the tour. He was in high spirits when he talked to journalists about the band's future and what they might yet achieve. He told *NME*: "I would like to create something now and be part of the creation of something now that would be valid for years to come. ... Something like a mammoth stairway which takes in a lot of the mood of the group. It's my ambition to write something really superb. ... Last night when all those lights were there, that was a spiritual allegiance. You walk out there and they're going: 'Yeah, we know you can do it,' and with that sort of thing tucked inside your belt you can only go from strength to strength."[11]

The band in fact went from Los Angeles to all points west and east for a month's rest and recuperation. It was originally planned as a time for complete relaxation, but in fact they needed all that time and more for Page to recover the full workings of his damaged finger. He also had time to think about the Gibson guitar stolen in 1970 and place an ad in the *Rolling Stone* issue of July 19th asking for its return. As with earlier ads, he got no response.

Chicago was the venue for the two concerts that started the tour's second leg in July 1973. The band had reconvened there on the 6th. After some unnerving experiences flying from gig to gig in their small private jet on the first leg, Grant had ordered Cole to find a bigger, more stable aircraft during the break. Within a few days he located a 40-seater Boeing 720B that had been refurbished especially for hiring to rock stars and bands for tours. It was called *Starship* and until then had been

Robert Plant and friend at the infamous Hyatt House in Los Angeles, June 1973, a hotel known then to the rock'n'roll fraternity as The Riot House.

Overleaf: Jimmy Page in Seattle, June 1973. "I think it's the spontaneity, really, for me. Going out there, and something comes out of the guitar that never came out before."

used for one-off events. Cole managed to negotiate a price for the July leg of the tour: $30,000, or $10,000 per week. Among other things, it allowed Cole to reorganise the band's accommodation during tours because they could now pick specific bases for a collection of concerts and fly back to that one base for a few nights in a row, minimising the disruption caused when it was a new town every day.

Naturally one of Grant's first reactions was to alert PR man Danny Goldberg to this new travelling arrangement to maximise the publicity value, not only among the world's rock press but also the general media. Led Zeppelin, like Caesar's wife but in a very different context, had not only to be the biggest and most extravagant in the world, but had to be seen to be. Publicity was now essential. In the event, when the band and its entourage finally met up with *Starship* at Chicago's O'Hare airport and a bunch of hacks in tow, they even managed to upstage Hugh Hefner's not inconsiderable private jet, parked alongside. It was a perfect pitch in the game of celebrity one-upmanship and a moment to please Grant in particular – especially when in subsequent years The Rolling Stones and Elton John followed in their footsteps and used the plane for their own US tours

Within a few days of the Chicago concerts, Page and Grant had decided to activate an idea kicking around in one form or another for a couple of years, but which had started to crystallise since the release of T.Rex's concert movie *Born To Boogie* last December. Grant wanted to make a documentary film about Zeppelin. He felt that the three nights forthcoming at Madison Square Garden would be the ideal time to shoot some verité footage.

Earlier in the year there had been serious discussions with Joe Massot, a friend of Page who had been talking informally to band members about a concert film since the 1970 Bath appearance. Those notions had been killed by Grant, who wanted a name film-maker for any Led Zeppelin film project. Massot had been involved in shooting the 1971 hippie rock western *Zachariah*, a cult hit but hardly something to recommend him to the big time. Indeed Grant felt Massot didn't have the necessary gravitas. After all, Bolan had used Ringo Starr and the professional Apple film unit and had jammed with Ringo and Elton John in Apple's Saville Row studios, adding footage of the jam to the film. Massot couldn't compete.

Midway through this latest US jaunt, Grant changed his mind, aided by the fantastic response for Zeppelin at every concert, the media coverage they were generating, and the sense that history was being created every day. If they didn't act quickly, the 'right moment' might be lost, perhaps forever. With Grant's knowledge of the film world virtually zero but his need now pressing, he fell back on the only film person he knew.

Grant rang Massot on July 14th and informed him that he was to be in place with a film crew and ready to

shoot at Madison Square Garden between July 27th and 29th. No contract: just Grant's word. Thus started a saga that would swallow a small fortune and the best part of four years before anything was put before the public.

With Page and Grant behind him, Massot hired a crew and arranged to shoot the three nights of music and a few offstage moments. The problems began here. While Ringo Starr and his team had shot two complete T.Rex concerts in one day, they used a film crew of five cameras, worked out all their angles in advance, and made sure that both concerts were shot in their entirety, with adequate camera overlap. Massot and his team didn't manage to do this.

Few of the band and crew had any idea what was going on and had no faith in the hastily-assembled film crew. It was not their province. They couldn't even understand why they were being asked to wear the same stage gear for the three nights at the Garden. As Richard Cole wrote later: "Robert thought [Massot] was kidding. 'Is he a filmmaker or a fashion consultant?' he asked me. [Grant], too, was getting nervous. 'Do you think they know what they're doing?' he asked as we watched the crew at work."[12] As it turned out they didn't, not exactly. Yet Grant never stopped to consider bringing in a producer with the relevant experience to ensure that the basics of documentary film-making were in place.

During the Madison Square Garden concerts there were other things to worry about. To tie in with the filming, the performances were recorded on audio multi-track for a possible movie-soundtrack album release in the future. With the band quite aware of what was going on around them, this was a huge risk to take. Would they get performances of sufficient stature after the record-breaking tour that had preceded them?

Their entrance onto the Madison Square Garden stage suggested very different expectations from previous Led Zeppelin concert tours, as did the band's attire. Even Plant, the eternal self-confessed hippie, wore a fetching powder-blue puffed-sleeve blouse-like shirt; Bonham had on a sequined black T-shirt; Jones was in an extravagant *commedia dell'arte*-type jester's jacket; while Page closely echoed the type of outfit that had accompanied Marc Bolan's triumphant live progress around the UK in the last two years. Page certainly embraced the notion of glitter stage-gear in his own personalised way. The extracts of the concert that appeared in the movie *The Song Remains The Same* and Zeppelin's *DVD* collection portray visual feasts and impressive extravaganzas, noisily adored by the audience on all three nights.

But the eventual release in 1976 of the double vinyl LP soundtrack *The Song Remains The Same* to coincide with the movie of the same name suggests, even with its inserts and edits, that this was a concert (or series of concerts) at the end of a long and punishing tour. Plant's voice, in particular, is in indifferent shape compared with the recorded concerts from 1972. The album reveals a number of patching edits, even of single notes and whoops or sounds from Plant, made in an effort to improve his live contribution. Yet Page later found good things to say about the performances on a set that is still mostly shunned or ignored by all but the most devoted Zep fans. He told one interviewer: "I think there is some really serious bow playing on the live album. I remember being really surprised with it when I heard it play back. I thought, 'Boy, that really was an innovation that meant something.'"[13]

The song line-up on the *Song Remains The Same* album follows the typical 1973 Led Zeppelin concert set quite closely: 'Rock And Roll', 'Celebration Day', 'The Song Remains The Same', 'Rain Song', 'Dazed And Confused', 'No Quarter', 'Stairway To Heaven', 'Moby Dick', and 'Whole Lotta Love'. There are songs missing in order to cram it all into the space available; other songs they played included 'Black Dog', 'Misty Mountain Hop', 'Since I've Been Loving You', and 'The Ocean', all later released on the *DVD* of 2003. But the double-vinyl did track the overall concert shape.

The record starts badly with Plant in poor voice on 'Rock And Roll', unable even to get into the correct register for the opening verse. Although the band itself sounds tight, the sound quality is muddy, recessed and confused compared with the clarity and depth they'd achieved over on the West Coast for the 1972 live takes. Things do not improve much on a splashy but untidy 'Celebration Day', although Page's quote from Jeff Beck's 'Plynth (Water Down The Drain)' from the 1969 album *Beck-Ola* is a nice touch.

'Song Remains The Same' is spiced with imaginative Page moments where he manages successfully to approximate the bank of guitar sounds on the studio original and also comes out with small additional felicities. But Plant can't put the weight behind his vocal to really stamp his authority on the piece. This is an example of one of the tracks where his vocal line is patched. Yet that rhythm section is indomitable.

'The Rain Song' is more successful, allowing Plant to build a different mood and use another aspect of his vocal cords. Once again, Jones contributes sympathetic Mellotron backgrounds and blends superbly with Page's mellow guitar. 'Dazed And Confused' in 20-minutes-plus length provides plenty of room for the band to demonstrate their individual and collective dexterities, and somehow the rawness of Plant's voice is not so much of a problem on such a basic blues-riff piece. They continue to develop the independent live character of 'No Quarter' here, and the increasingly sympathetic crowd who know it from the album version listen in rapt attention as Jones is given the major instrumental role usually in Page's hands onstage.

'Stairway' is introduced by Plant as "a song of hope"

and the crowd recognises the guitar intro instantly. Plant delivers one of his most consistently convincing performances of the evening on a ballad where he can save his voice and pace himself. As a complete performance this is perhaps superior in pacing and precision to the Long Beach concert recording of the previous summer, marking one of the few times that one of the 1973 concert recordings improves on those of a year before. Nonetheless, Page's long solo is possibly a little too long.

'Moby Dick' is 'Moby Dick', an event that remains impressive and admirable but more an audio-visual treat rather than something to be listened to repeatedly on an LP or CD. 'Whole Lotta Love', used for most of the tour to wrap things up in a shortened form, again catches Plant a little short in the vocal department. His voice is surprisingly thin, while the band, true to their determination to cut down this number, clock it in at around 15 minutes, running through 'The Crunge' and 'Boogie Chillun' but not indulging in the extended medley of the 1972 dates.

In retrospect *The Song Remains The Same* soundtrack album reveals a band fighting fit for these concerts, with the exception of Plant's clearly ailing vocal cords, although on its release in 1976 the record was roundly dismissed. Perhaps it had missed its moment. Issued in 1973 it would probably have been welcomed by fans with the tour's sounds still swimming around their heads.

The tour concluded at the end of July 1973 with those three nights in New York City, after which the band could disperse to their homes and families and watch the world's reaction to their achievements. They had been touring on and off since October of the previous year and desperately needed a long break. They could not continue to move at such a pace indefinitely if they were to survive as a fully functioning band with a long-term future. Page acknowledged this when he told an *NME* reporter in New York: "It's been an incredible tour, but we're all terribly worn out. I went past the point of no return physically quite a while back, but now I've gone past the mental point. I've only kept gong by functioning automatically. ... We're going to take it easy for about two months and then I expect we'll start work on a new album."[14]

But they didn't escape New York so lightly. On the evening of the last Madison Square Garden concert, over $200,000 in Led Zeppelin cash was removed from the overnight safe in the Drake Hotel where the band and its entourage were staying. Tour manager Richard Cole had placed the money there the previous night and was the one who discovered it missing the following day. His first response was to tell manager Peter Grant and then with his road crew search all the suites in the hotel booked to the band to 'cleanse' them of possible illegal substances in preparation for the police search that would inevitably follow. The band were told of the robbery later that evening.

Even with the FBI involved and Cole passing a lie detector test, no progress was ever made to find where the money went or even who took it. There was speculation that it had to be an inside job of some kind – hotel staff or Led Zeppelin staff – but that's what it remained: speculation. The case hit the papers worldwide and ensured a fitting scandal for a send-off at the tour's end, but as Page told a reporter: "It had reached a point where we really couldn't care too much. I mean, if the tour had been a bummer, then that would have been the last straw, but it wasn't. ... I've had far worse situations than that on the road."[15]

The band used the rest of the summer and early autumn of 1973 as a time for individual recuperation with their families and friends, re-establishing themselves as people who could sustain a peaceful domestic life. In the midst of this, according to Grant later, Jones decided he wanted to quit the band. A homebody at heart, he was sick of the treadmill of touring and just wanted out. "He told me he'd had enough and said he was going to be the choirmaster at Winchester Cathedral," Grant commented later.[16]

Jones later corrected that impression. "The choirmaster thing was a tongue-in-cheek joke I made to some journalist who made more of it than it was. It is true, however, that I did consider leaving after our American tour in 1973. I'd just had enough of touring, and I did go to Peter and tell him I wanted out unless things were changed. There was a lot of pressure on my family, what with being away so long. ... Things had to change, and they did, so it quickly blew over. I trusted Peter to put it right."[17] Grant had given Jones the time and attention to talk through all his concerns about the band and then asked him to go away and think again. With the air cleared, Jones decided to stay on.

Shortly after this, each of the band members was asked to give some thought to the film project. Grant and Page, in consultation with film-maker Joe Massot, had decided that Massot ought to shoot a sequence with each of them individually. Harking back again to the formula of the T.Rex *Born To Boogie* film, the two decided to follow in Marc Bolan's whimsical footsteps and include fantasy vignettes that would summarise each band member's distinctive characteristics and ideas. In principle this was a sound idea; in practice it became one of the project's biggest hurdles, because there was no theme or unifying spirit behind each sequence to provide any sense of continuity. There was also a conspicuous lack of humour.

The band – plus Grant, who decided he should have his own vignette – had time and space to each dream up a sequence capturing how they'd like to be portrayed. The ideas were then slowly cobbled together. Jones recalls that

Overleaf: Playing to an enormous crowd at the Kezar Stadium in San Francisco's Golden Gate Park, June 2nd 1973.

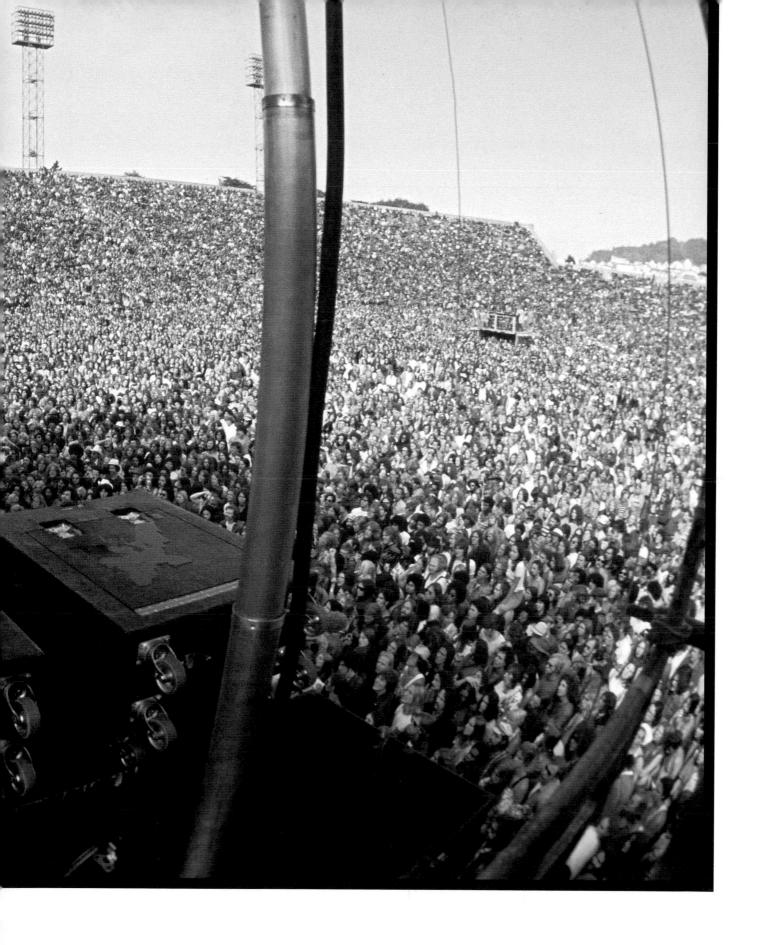

he originally wanted to "use an old film, *Doctor Sin*, which had all these horsemen crossing the marshes, and have me added in at the end. Turns out the film was owned by Disney, so I had to do all the riding myself, which was hilarious really, as I can't ride that well."[18]

The scenes were dangerously close to home movies and amateur dramatics, but if handled properly they might have added a personal dimension to the overall plan of the still-unnamed project. As autumn gave way to winter 1973, filming progressed in fits and starts and the film shot of the four band members ranged from idle boastfulness to the lightly pastoral. In addition to this relatively benign activity, Page was beginning to make plans for new songs and possible new recording sessions later in the year. He also continued to work on music for the short film project *Lucifer Rising* for Kenneth Anger.

The other three, by contrast, were content to recover their composure away from the madness and pressures of American touring schedules. Plant said a few months later: "When I come home from a tour, I feel like a fish out of water. I have to get reacquainted and readjusted. I sit down and I say, 'Oh, this is where I live, that's the door, there's the stairs, up there's the bedroom, outside's the horse.' I'll admit it's nice to maintain this equilibrium. Not having to push yourself into it. Now, having been back from America since August, I feel like I'm very normal again. I just push away the emotion of the road trip until it's needed again. ... But I think I'll always see the Continental Hyatt House as beauty in its own way."[19]

By November 1973 the band had sufficient musical ideas worked out in embryonic form to re-deploy to Headley Grange once more for rehearsal and workshop sessions to knock the material into shape. Even at this relatively early stage, Page was confident that this time, after many hesitations, he was ready to compile a full

At New York City's Madison Square Garden in July 1973 at the end of a long American tour. The band's three concerts at the Garden were filmed and recorded for The Song Remains The Same.

double-album of new material and re-worked leftovers from previous recording projects.

Page said: "The last album was difficult to get into because it was so complex. We used intricate rhythm patterns and hid a lot of ideas in the lyrics. The next one will still have complex songs, and will have an acoustic guitar piece based on a solo I used to do with The Yardbirds during a song called 'White Summer'. But most of the album will get back to something people think we've been drifting away from – straightforward rock'n'roll." Page's predictions about the sixth album would prove to be reasonably accurate, although his acoustic number would be quietly dropped from the song list as the sessions progressed. Plant, present at Page's house when the interview took place, got somewhat carried away when he chimed in: "What we talk about is creating something as notable as Beethoven's Fifth. Not just something that would still be remembered in 50 years, but something so mammoth that it would last ... forever."[20]

Plant's understandable hyperbole aside, it looked as if 1974 would be a busy and fulfilling year, especially as these last months of 1973 saw the expiry of the original recording agreement with Atlantic Records. Grant had, as always, anticipated this change in their relations with Atlantic by some months and had been discussing with Page in particular the idea that the band should start their own record label. After all, The Rolling Stones had been running one for a few years now.

The band went to Headley Grange for rehearsals aware that whatever emerged would be on their own label. Not only that, but they had agreed with Grant that whatever set-up they put in place should not just be a vanity label for Led Zeppelin but a proper record company, signing and promoting real talent that they personally believed in. Shades of the troubled Apple Corps, perhaps, but if anyone spotted the similarity at the beginning of 1974, no one was worried enough to point it out.

TAXING CONCERNS

- SWAN SONG RECORD LABEL FORMED

- MORE FILMING FOR DOCUMENTARY

- HEADLEY GRANGE & STUDIO
  SESSIONS FOR 6TH ALBUM

- RESHOOTING CONCERT FILM
  FOR DOCUMENTARY

In January 1974, Led Zeppelin's manager Peter Grant and Ahmet Ertegun of Atlantic Records made a joint statement announcing that the band would be forming their own as yet unnamed record label and that Atlantic would be distributing this label exclusively worldwide. The announcement came after weeks of often tense negotiation between the two men. There was a lot do be done to establish the new company – thinking up a name, for one thing – before they opened their offices and began working on projects and signing new artists. Although Page and Grant remained the prime movers behind the project, it was important to hire talented and competent staff to make sure each aspect of its operation reflected and maintained the band's commitment to quality.

Such attention to detail had previously been the source of major friction between Atlantic and Zeppelin, but it had raised quality levels on the band's releases – whether it was the correct cutting of the metal master for a record or the upgrading of the manufacturing process of the vinyl discs. Grant and Page demanded – and eventually got – the best possible service whenever they noticed any slackness. It would have to be the same for the new label. But first of all it had to be named.

As late as April 1974, Plant was saying they still hadn't made a decision. "We went through all the usual ones, all the ones that twist off your tongue right away, like Slut and Slag: the sort of name one would associate with us touring America. But that's not how we want to be remembered. We want something really nice."[1]

By May, the machinery was in place in America and was coming together in England. The name for the label was Swan Song, chosen by a most circuitous route. Page and Plant were sufficiently aware of the story about swans singing just prior to death that they felt at ease making jokes about it, ignoring any dark portents inherent in the name. After all, 'Led Zeppelin' itself was chosen with thoroughly British black humour, so why shouldn't Swan Song be equally able to defeat such expectations?

The name was introduced in New York City upon the opening of the American arm of the company. In Britain it took a little longer to get business up and running because Grant had taken the opportunity to end his long-term production relationship with Mickie Most. Grant relocated his London office to Chelsea and seriously considered making it the base for all Led Zeppelin business when he was not working from home at his 16th-century country manor house, Horselunges, at Hellingly, Sussex. The formal production split from Most allowed Grant and Page the opportunity to reorganise their publishing. They formed Joaneline Music Inc to publish future Led Zeppelin songs.

This internal rearrangement of the band's business along with the on-off film project kept all the band occupied and left them little opportunity or desire to go back on the road. In addition to these two time-consuming projects, the band had gone back to Headley Grange in earnest during February to begin refining the songs and ideas they'd put together in rough form just before Christmas.

This time they took Ronnie Lane's mobile studio with them. Even this presented a surprise delay. Soon afterwards, Page revealed: "It took a long time for this album, mainly because when we originally went in to record it, John Paul Jones wasn't well and we had to cancel the time. … Everything got messed up. It took three months to sort the situation out."[2] This rarely mentioned break in the familiar recording pattern due to Jones's bad health may well have coincided with his deliberations over whether to leave the band.

The band's hiatus was enforced against the unsettling background of an energy crisis in Britain during the winter of 1973-74, triggered by the OPEC oil-price hike. The whole country was plunged into chaos as the government of the day introduced emergency legislation to slash power consumption over the winter. From January 1974 this led to power cuts and compulsory three-day working weeks. To make a bad situation worse, the coal miners' union had imposed an overtime ban a month earlier and finally came out on strike early in February.

This was a full-scale crisis for Britain, only partially resolved by a mild winter and the government losing a February election. Although these events passed relatively undocumented in rock music, Paul McCartney at least fashioned something from the wreckage with his resolutely cheerful song 'Power Cut', which appeared on that year's *Red Rose Speedway*. Most recording studios were closed as unpredictable power supplies made it risky to attempt such work. Down at Headley Grange, with their own generator, the Zeppelin crew were not quite so vulnerable, but there was no possibility of transferring to other studios until the crisis was resolved.

As usual by this time with Zep recording programmes, the material was a combination of old and new ideas. There was now a considerable backlog of unreleased material from previous sessions, plus ideas that had never been finished to anyone's satisfaction. One of those was a long untitled instrumental piece dominated by acoustic guitar and with occasional vocal interjections that Page had been tinkering with since 1971. In an interview around this period he identified it as something he'd been developing out of the old 'White Summer' piece he'd recorded with The Yardbirds and played on early Zeppelin tours. By the time it got to Headley Grange in early 1974, the work was still without a title or a settled form and close to 20 minutes in length. After one particular take was finished, an observer suggested it might be called 'Swan Song'. The piece has remained unreleased but the title was moved from the instrumental, first as a potential name for the next album and, eventually, to the new record company.

Plant felt that by the time the band assembled at Headley Grange for the new sessions they were in a golden period of creativity and esprit de corps. "It was a really fine time," he told Dave Schulps years later, "and a fine moment. I think that, for a while at the time of *Physical Graffiti*, we were right on top of it. We weren't looking for hits, we didn't give … very much thought to whether or not success was an issue. It was just: we were really quite prolific. Tunes like 'The Wanton Song' and 'Trampled Under Foot' and 'Custard Pie', these things could just appear as great little diamonds just sparkling, and fantastic moments. There was such freedom and coherence between the players. And I would just gambol, … taking a bit from the blues, adding a bit of innuendo – a bit of humour for 'Sick Again', you know? Just making some kind of camp social commentary of the times."[3]

New songs worked up in rehearsal or presented in various stages of completion at Headley Grange included 'Custard Pie', 'In My Time of Dying', 'Trampled Under Foot', 'Kashmir', 'In The Light', 'Ten Years Gone', 'The Wanton Song', 'Sick Again', and the long piece eventually called 'Swan Song'. Older material later included on the sixth album made up approximately half the project.

It was time for the band to take stock of all their music, past and present, work it up to the best of their collective abilities, then release it into the world. As with past albums where they had started off at Headley Grange, there was much cross-pollination of ideas. Bonham and Page, for example, came up with the monster riff that dominates 'Kashmir' and made a demo of it together. Other pieces from previous sessions remixed this spring at Olympic studio in London and earmarked for the next album included 'The Rover', 'Walter's Walk', 'Houses Of The Holy', 'Bron-Yr-Aur', 'Down By The Seaside', 'Black Country Woman', 'Night Flight', and 'Boogie With Stu'. 'Walter's Walk' was not resurrected at this time and stayed in the can until 1982, but the band overhauled all the others during the long work-out at Headley Grange and they were eventually included on the resulting double-album.

In late March 1974, Plant told one interviewer he was optimistic that the album could be ready by late summer. But, he added, "We haven't yet got around to our six-month decision on covers yet." They were still finalising song selection and Page was overseeing the mixes, but all else was done. "Over a period of three weeks, we managed to spend at least three days a week actually recording – you know, between various calamities: the Roy Harper gig, highs and lows, and all the rest. But we got eight tracks off and a lot of them are really raunchy. We did some real belters with live vocals, off-the-wall stuff that turned out very nicely."

Plant explained their working methods down at Headley Grange. "I think our music is more of an excitement thing – it has to be impromptu. You know, it just drops out of your mind – it falls out of your head and onto the floor and you pick it up as it bounces. That's how we work. But what else would you expect? We hire this recording truck and trudge off to some cruddy old house in the country. The last thing you'd expect is the music to fall right into place. But it does. We even spent one night sitting around drinking ourselves under the table telling each other how good we were."

Plant was sufficiently enthused by the entire process of recording this new set of material that he admitted this might be the time that Led Zeppelin allowed a double-LP to emerge. Challenged on the likelihood of that turning into something of a vanity project with more than its fair share of filler, Plant made the obvious comparison. "In my opinion, The Beatles' *White Album* was great. I'll agree that it takes a long time to get into – there was just too much of it at first for you to assimilate everything. That came later, and when it did, it was good." This prompted a word or two of caution from Plant to writers who might all too willingly rush to judgement on Zep's next. "I sometimes wish the critics would wait for three months before reviewing a new record. Take a little time and get into it a bit. I know in my own mind if I'm satisfied with the way the music and lyrics fit together. But the full effect of every track doesn't come through for a long while. … Page and I, in particular, are extremely critical of ourselves. But there are times when you can overdo that."[4]

In the meantime, work on the film had not been going so well. All four musicians and Grant were complete novices when it came to the mechanics of making a film, but they were demanding about the type of film Joe Massot was to make. Massot had originally thought of broadening out the semi-documentary from a simple concert picture with interviews into something a little more ambitious. This had appealed to Grant and Page, especially the idea to film vignettes allowing band members to assume a character of their own choice. The choices they made would reveal much about each of them.

Massot said: "We wanted to show them as individuals, but not in the traditional way with interviews. They wanted more symbolic representations of themselves. All the individual sequences were to be integrated into the band's music and concerts."[5] As mentioned, the obvious precedent was 1972's *Born To Boogie*, but Marc Bolan's film had its own rock lineage, however much the T.Rex star referred to Fellini as his inspiration. Ringo Starr's gorilla outfit in one vignette leads directly back to *Magical Mystery Tour*, while his cameo as a tramp in *A Hard Day's Night* from 1964 was the first rock fantasy vignette. So Led Zeppelin were hardly breaking new ground.

The project would nonetheless have worked perfectly well if there had been a general acknowledgement of the basic tenet of film-making: the director calls the shots.

But in a band like Led Zeppelin, where Grant and Page had the decision-making power, this was never a realistic option. Brian Epstein let Dick Lester get on with it for *A Hard Day's Night* and *Help!*. The Zep film might have worked if there had been someone in the band with a film background or acting experience or talent. Or even the advantages of having a script beforehand. The subjects themselves needed to understood the tedium of shooting a film before they started on it. Endless re-takes of the same shot are required, normally for technical reasons unrelated to the actor, who has to be able to just shrug off such things, put ego to one side, and maintain concentration.

Another problem was that communication was difficult when the band was not recording or in rehearsal, spending most of their time scattered to their homes and families. Jones for example seems not to have even been involved in the decision to include personal vignettes. He later claimed: "Somebody said: 'You've got to do a fantasy sequence,' and I thought: 'What?'"[6]

Some of the ideas were quite ambitious and technically impractical. Page, for example, wanted an individual sequence shot at night where he climbed a steep slope to be confronted by a cloaked figure who revealed himself to be Page as an older man. The scene was shot in winter when the nights were freezing. Page quickly became exhausted as he climbed the mound again and again for retakes, while the crew had trouble achieving correct registration on the film because of the night shoot that Page had demanded. Day-for-night was not something he had managed to get his head around prior to shooting.

With all the individual sections shot by early 1974, it was left to Massot to begin the new year by editing the thousands of feet of Madison Square Garden film into something coherent before adding the individual sequences. By spring he had presented a rough cut to Grant and the band. The screening was a disaster and Massot was quickly removed from the project. He said later: "They finally came to a preview theatre to see the 'Stairway To Heaven' segment and started to fight and yell when the film began. They thought it was my fault Robert Plant had such a big cock. It took them another year to recuperate."[7]

Grant had already been talking to an Australian film-maker, Peter Clifton, and in March 1974 persuaded him to take over the project. Grant arranged for Clifton to meet up with Joe Massot and to view the rough cut the band had seen. According to Clifton: "It was a complete mess. There was no doubting Joe's talent, but he was in deep waters with this filming attempt and he did not have the strength to push the band members around. None of the material he had captured on 16mm or 35mm actually created sequences. There were a few good shots but they didn't match up, there was no continuity, and no cutaways or matching material to edit or build sequences."[8] Perhaps someone ought to have taken a professionally detached look at *Zachariah* before hiring Massot.

Clifton agreed to take on the film, but with the condition that he create a new script and that new footage was shot to link the film properly, creating the cutaways and other essential sequences that would allow the film to tell some sort of coherent story. He had Grant's full backing and, at least officially, the support of the band and road crew. However, it didn't take him long to realise that a difficult salvage operation was going to be made much worse by the conditions in which he had to work. "To be honest, the guys weren't terribly interested in the film. It was more Peter's idea."[9]

This was a fatal flaw. Projects in part based on fantasy and whim that have less than enthusiastic backing from the subjects themselves don't usually turn out too well. Whatever the shortcomings of *Born To Boogie*, for example, the energy and enthusiasm of Bolan and Starr for the project is never in doubt for a moment. Almost everyone concerned with that movie talked of it being "incredible fun" to make. This certainly wasn't the case with Zeppelin's epic.

Yet with Grant's backing, there was little doubt that the film would eventually be finished, although Grant's ignorance of the film-making process and the band's disinclination to pull together on the project meant it was unlikely to emerge unscathed from its muddled beginnings. But Clifton plugged on. "He was incredibly good to be around because if you had Peter Grant on your side, then you had no problems," Clifton recalled later. "He gave you that extraordinary sense of security that I don't think anybody else has ever given me. And that's what he gave to Jimmy, because he loved him. … They were very close, and it was like Jimmy needed Peter and Peter loved Jimmy. So having Peter on his side made him realise he could make anything happen."[10]

Months went by with Clifton up to his neck in footage, sorting through what could and could not be used and planning the extra shots he would need to organise. Not until the end of 1974 would everyone be in a position to plan the orderly completion of the film with the extra shooting. Meanwhile, there was an album to complete and a record company to launch.

Grant had managed to lure the band's press liaison man Danny Goldberg away from PR company Solters Roskin & Sabinson and gave him the job of running the American side of the fledgling Swan Song label. Finding a head for the UK arm proved more troublesome. After a couple of false moves – ex-Zep publicist B.P. Fallon was the A&R man for a short while – the job went to Abe Hock, a Los Angeles record exec, but he lasted no more than six months. Then Grant hired Alan Callan, who had known Page since Zeppelin's beginnings.

A double American launch for the label was held at

The Four Seasons in New York City and the Bel Air Hotel in Los Angeles in May 1974. A visibly frail Groucho Marx came along, as did Bryan Ferry. By then the first acts had been signed to the label and plans were well underway for the first releases. Soon after the New York launch, Grant articulated the label's initial aspirations. "We just want four or five acts that we could all add something to."[11]

Those four or five acts came together more quickly in the US than in Britain. Bad Company were a band of old friends of Zeppelin's, including vocalist Paul Rodgers, and they signed with Swan Song in America but – due to old contracts with Free – with Island Records in the UK. The first single, 'Can't Get Enough', was a hit on both sides of the Atlantic in June 1974 but for different labels. Bad Company's self-titled debut album had the same dual identity. This was not uncommon: as far back as Cream and The Beatles, records had come out on a different label on each side of the Atlantic, and only with the increasing proliferation in the 1970s of recording deals that required world rights rather than specific territories did a more integrated release pattern emerge. Even then, there would be some world class acts on a whole raft of labels across different countries.

Other artists signed to Swan Song included Maggie Bell (an old friend of Grant's from her days fronting Stone The Crows), Dave Edmunds, and The Pretty Things. Both Page and Plant were long-time fans of the Pretties, one of the best bands of the first wave of British Invaders in 1964, although they had never quite broken through to the bestseller ranks. They had been through many incarnations, and in 1967 created one of the most important – and overlooked – LPs in 1960s pop, *S.F. Sorrow*. Since then they had trod a hard road; the Swan Song deal marked a giant step back into the rock limelight.

Roy Harper was an artist whom Plant in particular wanted signed to the new label. Plant, Page and Bonham had recently demonstrated their solidarity with Harper by appearing at his concert at the Rainbow Theatre in north London. Plant had even MC'd the occasion. Jones later played bass behind Harper at a summer Hyde Park concert. But somehow conditions were never right, Harper never completely happy with what was on offer, and the deal was eventually shelved.

Plant was proactive in Swan Song affairs, recognising a chance for the band to become more than a one-trick pony. "Jimmy and I were in a position to buy both Sun Records and Chess," he revealed years later. "They were both for sale, and we took it to the guys and said: 'We can take these labels and return them into mainstream popular music.' But it was a lot of dough and they didn't consider it to be a goer."[12] Grant in particular was opposed to such a move. The idea was quietly dropped and the opportunity slipped away.

Meanwhile, the launches of Swan Song in the USA,

especially the trip to Los Angeles for the entire Zeppelin troupe, had for the first time brought home to them the true consequences of the New York robbery of the previous summer, where $200,000 in takings had disappeared. As a matter of course such organised trips carried their own insurance cover in case of incidents, losses or other problems. To travel abroad, and especially in America, without adequate insurance cover was simply not an option. However, with the loss of so much cash, Zeppelin's premiums were suddenly hiked and the conditions attached to any insurer who would consider them became much more troublesome.

As Swan Song's Alan Callan observed during the 1975 tour, the insurance companies would insist on "guards outside every hotel and dressing room door, and you have police escorts on your cars to and from gigs. Eventually what happens is you isolate the musicians from the rest of the world. You stop them interacting, even among themselves. They can't knock on each others' hotel room door and say: 'Fancy a walk down the street and getting a pair of jeans?' If one of them is injured then the tour is cancelled and everyone has to get their money back."[13]

This kind of isolation was not such a problem for Jones, as he had long been a loner on the road, often not even staying on the same floor as the rest of the band in an effort to distance himself from their shenanigans. But it made their stays away from home a lot less fun than they used to be. Thankfully, on this particular label-launching junket, there were no concerts to play, only a sprinkling of interview commitments and a lot of leisure time. The band received an invitation to meet Elvis Presley, which they accepted with alacrity. Even the biggest live act in the rock world were awed to meet a rock legend like Elvis in person and were not above asking for autographs – for their families. Elvis, in turn, got their autographs – for his daughter. From my house I can see your house.

With the launch of the label and the quick rise to chart-topping status by Bad Company, it seemed that Led Zeppelin and their management would enjoy another year of growth. Sessions for the next album were complete by the end of May 1974, and during June the press were told by company sources that mixing and editing would probably be completed that month. Work was indeed concluded on the mixing, editing, and sequencing of tracks, but there was still a very long way to go before the double-album would see the light of day. The album jacket design had yet to be commissioned, and it soon became evident that Page and Plant had very different ideas about that aspect.

In the background, the film project staggered on, with Clifton now aware what he needed to complete the footage. The problem as he saw it – and as he repeatedly explained to band members and Grant – was that most of the Madison Square Garden footage was on 16mm and the quality deteriorated when it was blown up to 35mm. Massot had shot some 35mm footage but, as Clifton said later, "He only used 400-foot reels, because he was shooting with handheld cameras. That meant that there could only be one three-minute take at a time. And 'Dazed And Confused' was 27 minutes long."[14] Grant could see the problem. "They filmed three nights at the Garden and never got one complete 'Whole Lotta Love'."[15] In order to link all these passages and use some of the musical highlights of the concert by sync-ing the audio to the visual image, he needed to film the band afresh playing those songs. It would take months to organise.

During the summer and autumn, Page also attempted to complete his music for Kenneth Anger's *Lucifer Rising* and allowed Anger to use the basement of his Kensington house to edit the film. He flew out to join in the fun on Bad Company's tour of America in September, appearing onstage with them in Austin, Texas and in New York City. By that time, America had seen the long-running Watergate crisis come to a conclusion, with President Nixon resigning in early August to be replaced by the accident-prone Gerald Ford. Not that Page or anyone else in Zep had been following events too closely. Interviewed in New York by Lisa Robinson for *NME*, Page talked about what he'd been doing lately. "I've been working really hard on the LP and a bit on the film. The album should be out around October, hopefully. Then I'll be able to really work and finish up the film."[16]

Page's cavalier attitude to his personal work schedule irked the irascible Anger in particular, who had been working intermittently on *Lucifer Rising* since 1967. Anger had continually run out of money (and sponsors) for the project and had braved endless delays before even meeting Page; now he could see yet another false dawn. He spoke later about his involvement with Page. "Even though he gave me a room to work in his house in London, and the use of the editing console that was used for the Led Zeppelin concert movie so that I could use the equipment to work on *Lucifer Rising*, he was never around; wouldn't return my calls. He had only completed 28 minutes of music when it arrived."[17] It would have been difficult for Page to have done a great deal more at that point. While Anger had shot around four hours of footage, he'd only been able to complete half an hour's worth because of constant monetary constraints.

Late in 1974 Page showed the Anger film to Peter Clifton, who was working on the Zep film; Clifton too judged it to be around a half-hour long at that time. But he was mortified by the subject matter and couldn't wait for it to end, even though he thought the music fitted well and was quite evocative. Page and Anger continued to work on the project, and even opened an esoteric bookshop together for a while near Kensington High Street in west London. But the relationship would eventually fail. Anger later claimed, among other things,

that Page's interest in the occult was "not that serious. He's interested in collecting, whatever that means, but he's proven to me that he doesn't have a serious interest in Crowley by the manner in which he's related to this situation. Also, he has everything in a bank vault."[18]

Page and Anger somehow managed to maintain a fitful partnership until a work-in-progress showing of the 30-minute 'fragment' in New York in 1976, after which Page's soundtrack was removed and the relationship gradually fell apart. The aptly-named Anger commissioned a new score from other sources, claiming that Page had failed to deliver a full soundtrack. "Everything just dried up. He's fallen into a trap that's an occupational hazard of the rock industry, I guess, but I think it's an utter disaster for anyone with a serious interest in the occult. I've never known it to be creative. A lot of people have been involved with it, but they'd be better off if they hadn't been."[19]

Just what Anger expected of Page has never been made entirely clear. Page certainly extended considerable help to Anger when no one else was interested, but Anger could hardly have expected him to prioritise the film project over Led Zeppelin, for example. There were also plenty of other distractions in the guitarist's life at the time. Page was enjoying a particularly tangled love-life in the latter part of 1974 that spread across whole continents and involved broken hearts and intrigue – none of which was conducive to him being at his most productive.

The entire Led Zeppelin contingent attended the launch party for The Pretty Things' first Swan Song album *Silk Torpedo*, held at Chislehurst Caves in Bromley, south-east London, on Hallowe'en night, October 31st 1974. It was one of the band's most debauched outings on British soil, with gallons of booze, food fights, strippers dressed as nuns, nude women playing the part of sacrificial victims, and all manner of unrehearsed events. The music press attended in force, giving The Pretty Things more publicity than they had enjoyed in a decade.

Something else came out of that evening, as Plant later related. Zeppelin had not played onstage together for well over a year. "I realised I really missed the unity of the four of us. I realised that, above everything else, above record companies, above films, we were Led Zeppelin. … From that moment on we started rehearsing and getting into full gear."[20] Plant told another reporter: "I didn't start Swan Song to make more bread. I mean, what are we going to do with any more bread? I live in a modest way. I live on the borders of Wales with people I've known for years. I'm sentimental. … I'm not a sensible, thoughtful person, but I love the feeling of togetherness with people. I love my work, which is communication on a vast level."[21]

But the two big Led Zeppelin projects of the moment – the film and the new album – were moving at a snail's pace. By early December, Page felt sufficiently confident of the double-LP's imminent release that he'd slipped a white-label preview copy to Nick Kent. Kent wrote an exclusive track-by-track preview for *NME*, concluding that it "does contain some of Led Zeppelin's very finest moments and then again the album's tonal density is absolutely the toughest, most downright brutal I've heard on record in well over a year. It could easily end up in the same pantheon as the band's first and fourth works, a good country mile above the second and third. One thing's for sure – for sheer aural ferocity, *Physical Graffiti* can eat *Houses Of The Holy* for breakfast".[22] But fans would have to wait another three months to buy a copy.

There was a breakthrough of sorts on the film when director Peter Clifton finally convinced Grant and the musicians that they would have to perform onstage in the same outfits they'd worn at Madison Square Garden the year before so that he could shoot the essential connecting material on 35mm in order to complete the movie. This shoot was eventually arranged in complete secrecy, to be staged in parallel to the band's late-1974 rehearsals for a new-year tour of America that would kick off the band's year-long exile abroad.

There were two reasons for the exile: the tour would support the planned release of the new album, now titled *Physical Graffiti*; and a prolonged absence from UK shores would avoid the exceptionally high rate of tax paid then by top-earning British residents. The tax problem had been gathering momentum for a considerable time but until very recently had not worried Grant or anyone else. It came as something of a shock, as tax difficulties often do. Grant later claimed that "we were only told about three weeks up front. Our accountant Joan Hudson told us of the massive problems we would have if we didn't go."[23]

The album was, according to the US Swan Song press release, to be released "shortly before the tour begins", but artwork problems would once more push back the release date At this stage the tour dates were announced to start on January 18th 1975. Also in November, Page told Nick Kent, invited down to Liverware, a dilapidated rehearsal studio in Ealing, west London, that the Zeppelin film was "nearing completion, though we don't have a title or distributor yet. I've yet to mix the soundtrack, and the final editing hasn't been completed … but now it's starting to get there. We've finally got a distinct framework. For a start the fantasy scenes do seem to relate to individual numbers the band play".[24]

Page could now say such things with confidence because a proper shooting script had been agreed and the extra footage had been shot by Clifton using special techniques that enabled him to synchronise their movements with the original soundtrack. After that, it was a matter of editing between the new footage and the three nights' worth of original stock from Madison Square Garden. Clifton said: "I got them all on the stage together in their outfits and they suddenly realised they were back onstage together for the first time since Madison Square

Garden. They started playing 'Black Dog' just for me and we all got such a shock. They were so hot and tight and fuelled up with you know what. There had been a huge argument just minutes beforehand and then suddenly they began playing, and it was an extraordinarily electric moment between them."[25]

Jones remembered another side to these proceedings. The filming took place during rehearsals, so some nights were to be filmed while others were not. He and the others were later accused of being un-co-operative when it came to wearing the Madison Square Garden gear for the filming sequences. "It was a massive compromise," he claimed later. "We never knew what was happening. … I'd ask if we were filming tonight, but be told that nothing was going to be filmed so I'd think: 'Not to worry, I'll save the shirt I wore the previous night for the next filming.' Then what would happen is that I'd get onstage and see the cameras all ready to roll. Nobody seemed to know what was going on. It was frustrating."[26] Equally frustrating was that, just before they agreed to the extra band footage, Jones had radically restyled his hair: "I had to use a wig, which caused some laughs."[27]

With the shooting behind them, the band welcomed 1975 with their two customary warm-up concerts, in The Netherlands and Belgium, refining the set-list and making sure that songs from the new album would work properly in concert. Backstage in Brussels on January 12th, Plant gave a friendly interview to *Old Grey Whistle Test* presenter Bob Harris in which he talked about the as-yet-unreleased *Physical Graffiti*. He said it had taken "three or four months" to record and that there had been "no one continuous period" where they'd polished off the whole thing.[28] Things seemed to be working for the band rather than against them after what had been a difficult and testing year for everyone. But it was not to last.

In the week between the Brussels concert and their departure for America, Page suffered another injured finger. This time he inadvertently caught the third finger on his left hand in the hinge of a carriage door as he was leaving a train at London's Victoria Station on the way to a rehearsal. "It's the [finger] that does all the leverage and most of the work," he told *NME*, "and it really came as a blow because I just couldn't play with it."[29]

With the tour just days away, Page had to devise a way of playing Zeppelin's stage repertoire without pressing that finger into action. He improvised a two- and three-finger fretboard technique and slowly managed to introduce it onstage. Some pieces, however, would not adapt to the limitations and had to be quietly rested. 'Dazed And Confused' was a victim of this cull because the piece required Page to bend strings forcefully and use considerable finger strength in the process. As a substitute the band brought in 'How Many More Times', a song they had not played live for nearly four years. But the tour would go ahead.

WHOLE LOTTA GRAFFITI

- 10TH AMERICAN TOUR FIRST LEG
- 6TH ALBUM, PHYSICAL GRAFFITI, RELEASED
- 10TH AMERICAN TOUR CONCLUDES

By the time of Led Zeppelin's tenth US tour in January and February 1975, their bad-boy reputation preceded them. The previous November, NME's Nick Kent had relayed gossip from US magazine *Popswap* about the sexual proclivities of various rock stars. Kent quoted unnamed groupies about Page: "Girls, he's into everything. Those who've tried it say it's an experience they'll never forget."[1]

With such high expectations on every level, the band arrived in America amid a blizzard of publicity. Even *Rolling Stone* sat up and took notice, attempting to make up for some of the lost years between them. The magazine went so far as to send out a reporter on the road with the band. The journalist was Cameron Crowe, who joined a phalanx of journalists that included Lisa Robinson for *NME*.

Crowe's piece resulted in a front-cover feature in *Rolling Stone*, the first in the band's history. It appeared in March, timed to coincide with the new album's release. In grand *Rolling Stone* style, it loosely told the entire history and pre-history of Led Zeppelin and its four members, just in case by 1975 anyone reading the article may have missed this information elsewhere. Apart from the absurdity of that imposition from above, Crowe managed to obtain some insightful quotes from Page and Plant.

This time Zeppelin were touring the US in parallel with their old rivals Jethro Tull, who were playing five shows at The Forum in Los Angeles to a total audience of 92,000. Zeppelin were confidently predicted to gross $5 million on the two legs of this tour and all tickets for both legs were reported as sold out within 24 hours of their official availability. This was clearly the age of stadium rock and the fans loved it.

However, all was not well in the Zeppelin camp. Page was suffering impatiently with his damaged finger, as he told Crowe. "I have no doubt the tour is going to be good, it's just, dammit, I'm disappointed that I can't do all I can do." Crowe watched as Page beat a fist quietly into the palm of his damaged hand. "I always want to do my very best and it's frustrating to have something hold me back in the set the very second I'm able to play it. We may not be brilliant for a few nights, but we'll always be good."[2]

Plant too was in less than brilliant shape, coming down with a cold during the three late-January Chicago shows. Surprisingly, reviewers also criticised the overall sound quality, an area where Grant and Cole spent huge amounts of time and money in an effort to make sure it was top-notch throughout. With the poor amplification system effectively nullifying Page's efforts and swallowing the weakened Plant, the concerts were some of the least distinguished in the band's generally glorious live career.

The three Chicago shows revealed the choices for a revised set, with 'Sick Again', 'Trampled Under Foot', 'In My Time Of Dying', 'The Wanton Song', and 'Kashmir' mixing well with the opener 'Rock And Roll', 'The Song Remains The Same', 'When The Levee Breaks', and 'Stairway To Heaven'. 'Stairway' was positioned as the finale. Things could only improve for the band, but at least Plant had enjoyed a major highlight while in Chicago. "I've already had the biggest turn-on I could imagine, and that was going to watch Buddy Guy and Hound Dog Taylor last night," he said. "I mean, really: the blues isn't dead. Al Green is great, but underneath all the shim-sham, there's a town called Chicago."[3]

In Detroit the band delivered a set that was the template for most of the rest of the first leg of this tour. They played 'Rock And Roll', 'Sick Again', 'Over The Hills And Far Away', 'The Songs Remains The Same', 'The Rain Song', 'Kashmir', 'No Quarter', 'Trampled Under Foot', 'Moby Dick', 'Stairway To Heaven', 'How Many More Times', 'Whole Lotta Love', and 'Black Dog'.

As Plant played these long sets with a weakened constitution, his condition continued to deteriorate and his voice suffered accordingly. After the Indianapolis date, the band agreed that the flu-ridden singer needed at least one concert cancelled so that he could recuperate. The St Louis date on January 26th was pulled; the next concert was not until three days later, by which time the touring party hoped he would be over the worst. Even with the luxury of the *Starship* aircraft in which to relax while moving around the country from venue to venue, the band had to limp through most of this first leg of the tour. In addition, there were self-inflicted problems arising from long-term bullying and generally disreputable behaviour by certain troupe members.

While Plant recovered in Chicago from his flu, the rest of the band flew to Los Angeles on the *Starship* to relax away from the Midwest winter. Journalist Chris Charlesworth witnessed a memorable knees-up on board the plane as they escaped the snows of Chicago. "All the way to L.A. we got roaring drunk and sang old English songs with John Paul [Jones] on an electric organ. Peter Grant loved it. ... He was singing 'Any Old Iron' and 'My Old Man Said Follow The Van'."[4]

Later during the same journey, Bonham was drunk, out of control and unchecked. He assaulted a stewardess, saying he was "going to have her".[5] She started screaming. Whether he would have gone ahead and raped the woman will never be known, because Grant intervened, hauling him off the terrified girl and away to a private cabin. The dichotomy in Bonham's behaviour was becoming ever more pronounced during this tour. Journalist Lisa

John Paul Jones and his trusty Fender Jazz Bass, onstage at the Market Square Arena in Indianapolis, January 25th 1975.

Overleaf: Backstage life during the tenth American tour, which ran in two sections from January to March 1975.

Robinson, travelling with the band at the time, wrote later: "When Bonzo was sober, he was a sweetheart – articulate and a gentleman. Drunk, particularly during a full moon – a nightmare."[6]

But no one in the band was prepared to tackle Bonham head-on about his problems. Understandably, the assaulted stewardess took some time to be talked around by a solicitous Page, but eventually she agreed to let the incident drop. Somehow, even with a *Starship* full of music journalists, Grant kept the lid on the story and it didn't leak to the papers. It is difficult to imagine such tight control of a similar incident today.

As Plant began to recover from his flu, Bonham suffered a stomach infection that sapped him of his power and lowered his spirits. The only bright spot came as the band hit New York City and Madison Square Garden. Page's finger was beginning to heal sufficiently for the band again to play 'Dazed And Confused'. The song's title was a little too accurate for their current state.

Page in particular had been affected by the physical problems that had hit him and Plant. The whole point of touring for Page was the sheer pleasure he felt onstage with the band. When that was impaired, it was all too easy to feel despondent. As he told *Rolling Stone*: "I love playing. If it was down to just that, it would be utopia. But it's not. It's aeroplanes, hotel rooms, limousines, and armed guards standing outside rooms. I don't get off on that part of it all. But it's the price I'm willing to pay to get out and play. I was very restless over the last 18 months where we laid off and worked on the album."[7] Plant's revelation last October, when he realised just how much he'd missed playing with the band on tour, seems to have had a corresponding echo in Page.

After successfully negotiating three nights in New York, the band played a last date in St Louis on February 16th, making up for the original concert cancelled when Plant was too ill to sing. Band and fans felt that this was on a par with the preceding Nassau Stadium concerts as the best Zeppelin had to offer in this first leg of the tour. The return to form coincided with Plant regaining his health and Page's steadily improving finger. A particular highlight – preserved on bootlegs – was the pairing of 'The Song Remains The Same' with 'The Rain Song'. After St Louis, the band took a ten-day break in warmer climes to repair the personal and physical damage suffered so far.

While they were out of the country between the two legs, the *Physical Graffiti* double-album was released to an expectant rock world on February 24th 1975. The culmination of a year's work, it was designed to make maximum impact on every level. The jacket art was a complete change from any previous Zeppelin offering. There was a photograph of typical New York City brownstone terrace houses, taken in Greenwich Village. Window cut-outs in the front revealed the band's name, while the back had the same brownstone block at night with blinds drawn.

Inside the package, those blinds were on inner sleeves that also listed the titles of the tracks on each vinyl disc, plus a run-down of where they were recorded and who engineered each one. The track titles were rendered using a technique introduced in the early part of the 20th century by the Dada and Surrealist art movements, pitting different typefaces and sizes against each other to create unequal, energetic, active words that seem to speak to the viewer. Apart from ironically anticipating the typographical approach of punk, now only a year away and which added only a newsprint context (the *Never Mind The Bollocks* jacket, for example), this gritty design seemed more like Rolling Stones territory than Zeppelin's familiar myth-and-legend-chasing style.

One of the most striking aspects of the jacket design was the appearance of a series of photographs of people and objects in the windows once the inner card sleeves had been removed. They touched upon a set of very American icons and a range of bizarre images. Also there were the obligatory shots of the band members, but their collective presence also reached back to the jacket of *Sgt Pepper's* and could not have been conceived without such a model.

Where The Beatles' sleeve had been a surreal but straightforward depiction of people they admired and wanted as 'members of the band', the motley crew on *Physical Graffiti*'s sleeves were depicted with a large slice of irony, as if the mid-1970s rage for kitsch had infected Zeppelin. There were images of Elizabeth Taylor as *Cleopatra*, a still from *The Wizard Of Oz*, four stills from Queen Elizabeth II's coronation service in Westminster Abbey, the famous man-on-the-moon photo, Jean Harlow, Lee Harvey Oswald, a still from a Busby Berkeley extravaganza, King Kong, paintings by Dante Gabriel Rosetti and Leonardo da Vinci, and mid-century shots of strippers. Physical graffiti indeed.

The concept was perhaps a calculated attempt to appeal to American fans and critics. If that was the aim, it worked, for *Physical Graffiti* entered the US charts at Number 3 before hitting the top spot and staying there for six weeks. In those charts, March 1975 had opened respectably enough with Bob Dylan's *Blood On The Tracks* at Number 1. This was chased away for one week by Olivia Newton John's *Have You Never Been Mellow* which, thankfully, was relieved of the burden of being US Number 1 album by Zep's new release. Six weeks and millions of copies later, *Physical Graffiti* ceded its pre-eminence to *Chicago VIII*. Later that same summer, Elton John's *Captain Fantastic & The Brown Dirt Cowboy* was at the top for seven weeks, making it the year's best seller. As *Graffiti* sat at the top of the US charts, all five previous Led Zeppelin albums re-entered the lower regions, confirming that Zeppelin were the band of the moment.

In Britain things were slightly different. The album hit Number 1 in mid March, taking over from Status Quo's *On The Level*, but it was displaced after just a week by Tom Jones's *Greatest Hits*, which lasted a month before conceding to The Stylistics' similar compilation, the UK's biggest seller of the year. After that it was The Bay City Rollers with *Once Upon A Star* followed by Paul McCartney's *Venus & Mars*. The record's impact was similar to its contents. As Plant noted later: "*Physical Graffiti* was spectacular. It had a lot of good songs and a lot of visitations to different musical areas."[8]

The band chose to rely on the strength of the songs and performances themselves to impose a sort of organic order on the double album. The opening piece, 'Custard Pie', harks back to the band's 1968-69 roots, with a modified Bo Diddley beat dressed up by some worthy harmonica accompaniment from Plant and spidery Clavinet work from Jones. It's a basic piece of music that takes its structure and chorus from the old blues 'Shake 'Em On Down' and relies on the muscle of the pumped-up rhythm section for strength. But it has no great distinguishing features, either among Plant's lyrics or the workmanlike arrangement.

Plant's urgent vocal betrays wear and tear on his vocal cords and a reluctance for his larynx to do as he asks. This is the first sign of the change in his voice that occurred between 1972 and 1973 as the years of touring and high-volume blues shouting exacted its toll. Page had also made adjustments to his sound, some of which he felt later were less than ideal. In 1991 he said: "The amp sound on [*Graffiti*] isn't one of my favourites. It was all right at the time."[9]

'The Rover' makes a deeper impact from the start. It began back in 1970 but its recording was largely completed in 1972 during *Houses Of The Holy* sessions. Plant's voice is therefore fresh, flexible, and volatile, his sense of complete control in direct contrast to the opening song. The strutting, pumped bass-note rhythm on the verse anticipates many American rock and pop fashions of the later 1970s and demonstrates just how devastating a bass-and-drums Jones and Bonham remained.

Page lays down a whole range of imaginative riffs and effects on his guitars, exploring the wah-wah and phase effects pioneered by Jimi Hendrix and Jeff Beck. He comes up with a series of musical sculptings quite thrilling in their contrasts and sudden beauties, again draping sophisticated and brilliant arranging ideas over a simple composition as he does habitually when Led Zeppelin are at their best. As he said at the time: "I may not believe in myself, but I believe in what I'm doing. I know where I'm going musically. I can see my pattern and I'm going much slower than I thought I'd be going. I can tell how far I ought to be going. I know how to get there; all I've got to do is keep playing. That might sound a bit weird because

of all the John McLaughlins who sound like they're in outer space or something. Maybe it's just the tortoise and the hare. I'm not a guitarist as far as technique goes. I just pick it up and play it. Technique doesn't come into it."[10]

Page was being a touch ingenuous in his comment, but the important point was that he is always thinking across the entire range of a song, not merely about his own narrow instrumental concerns. That is very clear on this compact, dynamic song that is full of colouristic adjustments from guitar to guitar track, providing maximum character. At a little over five minutes, it doesn't have the unevenness that a longer version might have suffered, and which causes problems for other *Graffiti* tracks. Needless to say, this would have been an infinitely better track to have included on the second side of *Houses Of The Holy* than 'D'Yer Mak'er'.

The next song, 'In My Time of Dying', provides an example of the bloated effect of an overlong performance. It was taken from a gospel piece made famous by one of Plant's heroes, Blind Willie Johnson, who recorded a classic version in 1927 under the title 'Jesus Make Up My Dying Bed'. It had also been memorably performed by a very young Bob Dylan on his first album back in 1962. It starts brilliantly, with great drama and expectation built with a hushed beginning. Page's softly stroked and beautifully articulated slide – a telling rearrangement of Johnson's original guitar line – harks all the way back to the delta. Then Jones and Bonham arrive.

After a complete verse with the rhythm section and without vocals, the original unaccompanied slide returns, this time with Plant entering to deliver the gospel theme: going down slow but heading to heaven. "Jesus, come and make up my dying bed," sings Plant. Page and Jones play in perfect partnership as Plant continues with a third verse, delivering music of great tenderness and warmth, like a praying chorus to Plant's solo plaint.

These opening three verses take up the first three-and-a-half minutes of the performance, after which a completely new riff and tempo is set, again taken from traditional blues figures but given tremendous muscle by the Zep rhythm section. Plant drifts over the alternating riffs, his voice a touch buried in the mix, then Page steps forward for a slide solo which is fleet and eloquent under Bonham's railway-train chug that provides incredible momentum.

The tumbling turnaround riff used through this mid-tempo section is brilliantly nailed down by Page, Jones and Bonham with the type of wild-eyed enthusiasm and verve that underscores all their best blues work. After a repeat of this section, a bridge emerges, to indifferent effect, taking the band back to the descending riff and then a variant on the opening patterns. This time the whole band is on board and Plant is deep into his testimonial-style blues preaching. It's time to go home: Plant is singing about being taken home. But the track,

now over eight minutes long, doesn't finish. The tag – for that is what it has now become – stumbles on as Plant improvises blues phrases and traditional "save me" lyrics at length, adding nothing to the performance apart from time. The joys of repetition, as Prince put it. Or vamp 'til ready.

At last, after more than ten minutes, the end comes with a suspended chord over which Plant fails to finish the phrase "Take me to my dying bed," substituting "car" instead after a long pause while others talk behind him. The track isn't stopped clean: a bit of studio chat is left in, further undermining the unity of the performance and reminding us forcefully that this is, after all, just a recording session. Page himself explained that he left this in to show that they were a working band, after all. We're reminded every time we hear the track. With this, side one of the original vinyl LP ended.

The jaunty, optimistic 'Houses Of The Holy' opened side two of the original vinyl album. It finds Plant once again in possession of his complete vocal equipment, for this is another leftover from the Stargroves sessions of 1972. The song has a typically powerful, coiled, patented Zeppelin heavy blues riff that ties it all together like a piece of artfully shaped wire, set to the walking pace at which this band excelled. In the second verse, Bonham even applies the cowbell beat that helped make Free's 'All Right Now' such a compelling strut.

Plant's lyrics are insinuating and clever, a sort of sweet rock'n'roll seduction routine, and his move to the high pitched yelps at which he was so good comes across as sheer exuberance, entirely fitting the song's happy theme. Page's vigilance as a producer is also in full flight: he spotlights Plant's whoops with a touch of echo, immediately removed for the next verse. This is the attention to detail we expect from him but get from few others of his contemporaries.

To its detriment, however, the contrasting section that the song cries out for never arrives. Once Plant's vocals are finished, the riff starts up again and is here to stay, Page taking one of his less remarkable short solos while the track fades as if no one knew quite what to do next in order to develop the piece to a logical end. This is probably the reason why it stayed off its eponymous album, but it is disappointing that the band still couldn't finish the job when they revisited it for inclusion here.

Next up is 'Trampled Under Foot', notable again for some innovative guitar sounds that Page described as "sort of backwards echo and wah-wah".[11] It's another Zep

A typical day on board the infamous Starship, the aircraft the band used for travelling between gigs in the United States.

Overleaf: Making productive use of the soundcheck before Led Zeppelin's appearance later that day at the Coliseum in Greensboro, North Carolina, on January 29th 1975.

strut with an urgent, nagging quarter-note riff carried by both guitar and Clavinet. The track is a good old-fashioned pedal note thump, with everyone enjoying its brutal edge, but it is perhaps situated in the wrong place on the record, coming after 'Houses' and its similar strut rhythm.

All the counteracting riffs and the breaks supplied by the rhythm section keep listeners alert in this rich and rewarding if over-hooked composition, but Plant's recessed vocals don't exactly impose themselves. This is mostly because there isn't much of a melody line, more a series of interjections and exclamations in the tradition of James Brown, but with the voice pulled back so far in the mix (something Brown would never have done) their impact is greatly reduced. At least the funky keyboard solo from Jones keeps everyone up and dancing.

It is thus with something approaching relief that we are rewarded with a shaped melody we can all hear properly on 'Kashmir'. Page had long been interested in Arabic as well as Indian music: during a 1974 *Crawdaddy* interview between William Burroughs and Page, the novelist had urged the guitarist to explore Morocco and other Arabic-African centres. Page and Plant did eventually go there and, to this day, Plant regards southern Morocco as a magical place. In 2003 he said: "'Kashmir', from my angle, was written on the road to Tan-Tan in southern Morocco, just off the Atlantic coast. It's a place where your mind can really dance and where your imagination is way open. After a while all the stuff you've ever thought about has gone and you've got this whole different place; it's giving you a door into a whole different view."[12]

Peter Grant heard an early demo of 'Kashmir' made by Bonham and Page. Years later he recalled: "It was fantastic. Funny thing is when it was first finished it was decided it was a bit of a dirge. We were in Paris and we played it to Atlantic and we thought it was a dirge, so Richard [Cole] was dispatched to Southall in London to find a Pakistani orchestra. We put the strings on and Jonesy got it all together, and the end result was just exactly what was needed. He was a master arranger."

Zeppelin's epic was originally titled 'Driving To Kashmir'. It is a study in repetition and stasis that makes no attempt to develop its themes. It draws inspiration not just from scales often used in Indian and Arabic music but also the type of startlingly colourful arrangement and scoring used by composers such as Ravel and Borodin in similarly exotic-themed pieces where they needed to suggest forward momentum. The obvious parallel is Ravel's *Bolero*, a composition Page had long ago demonstrated that he knew through his guitar-laden rearrangement of it for Jeff Beck back in 1966. Ravel's piece is a rhythm-dominated study in narrative without any form of musical development, gathering tension and momentum through orchestral heightening and

embellishment. This is, of course, an ideal way to give the impression of travel and arrival, which is the experience 'Kashmir' has to offer.

The single major chord of the verse in 'Kashmir' is vitally coloured by semitone steps played by the strings, giving different flavours and colours for each step and creating a cumulative effect of suspense. The resolution through a little guitar flourish doubled by strings (0:53) at first promises resolution but in fact just brings us back to the beginning of the cycle of tension. Around 2:12 a contrasting section arrives which is equally static, being a simple bounce between the tonic and its octave by guitar and strings in an off-beat pattern – a variant of the underlying bass pattern in the first section – that works against Bonham's drums.

There is only one other section to the song, bathed in Mellotron and settled on just two chords. It enters on two separate occasions, first at 3:22. This brings at least a brief change in tonality and allows Plant to alter his vocal line, but the song soon reverts to the initial pattern. When this second pattern finally returns (6:37) it has its own type of irresolution, the climbing Mellotron figure allowing no further development. This is no relief from the remorseless heightening of suspense as it repeats and repeats like a recurring line of wooden fence-sticks alongside the road on an endless journey. The fact that 'Kashmir' fades on this vamp demonstrates that Led Zep were intent on depicting that journey, not the arrival. In this sense, at least, the original title was perhaps closer to the final depiction.

Throughout all of this, Bonham's huge, rock-steady beat keeps a consistency of texture and theme and becomes the true focus of the piece. It was his idea to have the two metres of the verse working against each other to provide a tension that has no release, for when it comes back to metric unity, it immediately moves off again. Unchanging but very dramatic in its cycles of repetition, it allows listeners to conjure their own image of the imaginary place depicted in the song.

It could be argued that 'Kashmir' ultimately lacks enough variety in its orchestration and dynamics to maintain interest for its nine or so minutes in the way that *Bolero* does. But it is a brave and imaginative shot at a new type of form through repetition taken from Eastern music and applied to rock. Perhaps the imperfections give it a vulnerable charm that *Bolero* doesn't share.

'In The Light' opened the second disc of the original vinyl set. Its suspended-time opening once again calls up an image of the East through the combination of Jones's keyboards and Page's guitar drones. This time there is a more specific sense of morning in an Indian setting, the instruments depicting a vocalist or a sahnai player wailing a haunting melody over a peaceful, expansive A tonic.

With the arrival of Plant's double-tracked voice the mood is confirmed by his quasi-mystical lyrics ("in the light you will find the road"). In accompaniment, Jones contributes a rising arpeggio similar to that supplied by tambura players in Indian classical music, adding to the Eastern impression. As the full band is introduced, the R&B ethos of a heavy riff meets the Eastern flavour of an exotic scale, creating a different kind of tension through the contrast provided by Page's return to blues intervals. Jones later expressed pride in this section. "You can always tell my riffs from Page's," he said, "because mine have got lots more notes and are linear. His are chunkier and chordier. ... 'In The Light', during the verse – that's a riff of mine. I leave the seventh ringing. Page doesn't do riffs like that. In fact, anything with chromatic movement would be mine."[13]

At 4:10 the release from this tension comes in the bridge, where a confident A major fanfare with a stately descending bassline allows Jones's keyboards and Page's guitar to accentuate the positive, almost as if the light is bursting from the song as well as the sky. The Beatles loved this particular progression and it has been used by virtually every rock artist since, but Led Zeppelin manage to dress it up so nimbly that it sounds wonderfully fresh. At the bridge's end the song is recapitulated in compressed form, ending with the celebratory major feel and a fade during which there are some effective multi-tracked guitars and delayed echo. Once again the track is very long: close to nine minutes and therefore longer than 'Kashmir', which is usually thought of as the epic on *Physical Graffiti*. The introductory section alone of 'In The Light' lasts for almost two minutes.

After the scale of 'Kashmir' and 'In The Light', the solo-guitar piece 'Bron-Yr-Aur' effects a small but delightful lift in the atmosphere, like a spring shower. It has a simple cyclic form and is solely fingerpicked, making it sound to some extent like a connecting piece between two larger works, but that takes nothing away from its charm. Unfortunately, this leftover from the days of composing for *Led Zeppelin III* doesn't connect too well at its close: 'Down By The Seaside' is a sufficiently jarring contrast as to be a complete stranger.

The intoxicating lazy-days ramble of 'Seaside' would have been better kicking off an album side and setting its own opening mood. It develops well: after a couple of minutes of ambling on the strand, remembering the pop styles and attitudes of the early 1960s, an urgent mid-tempo riff enters, before returning to that past idyll. Written back in 1970 and recorded in time for the fourth album – the youthful vigour of Plant's voice is notable – it was kept in reserve until this record.

Perhaps Plant's determined efforts to invoke the slightly askew country-rock style of Neil Young were judged inappropriate for that more unified collection. Even on *Physical Graffiti*, his Young-like twang is not entirely at peace with its larger surroundings. At least on this expanded canvas there is plenty of space for such a well-constructed amble. It is a pity that some of its impact is drained by its positioning.

'Ten Years Gone' wound up the third vinyl side. A sophisticated and heavily-worked-at composition, it carries echoes of the chord progressions and guitar glissandos favoured by John Lennon and Paul McCartney. The twin-guitar line first heard at 0:32 suggests the opening guitar figures of 'Band On The Run' while the progression suggests 'Dear Prudence'. 'Band On The Run' is also echoed, in Page's guitar solo. But there is a great deal more to the song and its composition than Lennon or McCartney pastiches.

It has a complex form, a real sense of narrative even without the deeply personal story Plant is telling in his vocals, and a masterful development of the instrumental arrangement by Page and Jones. In a classic arranger's move, they subtly build the mood and augment the instrumental textures to give the ear something fresh and delectable each time a section of the song's structure is repeated. This is clear from the introduction, which is no mere scene-setting but an exposition of the first group of themes in preparation for Plant's vocal entry.

Plant's lyrics are spare and simple, allowing the music to do as much work as the words. His delivery is also restrained, a quality that the tune needs if it is not to be driven into the ground by overemphasis. The climax he reaches, with his voice coarsened and the emotions exposed, is fulfilling because the song is then allowed an appropriate decrescendo, moving back through the sections already played and with a concluding, resigned vocal verse – but this time with richer instrumentation, sumptuously intersecting backing guitar lines, and a firm underpinning from Jones and Bonham.

Page's guitar solo just prior to Plant's climactic vocals ("did you ever really need somebody") is strikingly elegant in line and attractive in tone, its sustain allowing Page to create aching melodic shapes that connect neatly with Plant's lyrical melancholy. The song is, again, not short – it runs for over six-and-a-half minutes – but its careful construction means that there is no sense of superfluity, with every phrase and section having a logical and satisfying place in the tune's scheme. Easily one of *Physical Graffiti*'s most impressive achievements, 'Ten Years Gone' is also one of the band's career highlights.

The final side of the original vinyl release started with 'Night Flight'. This is a happy, simple rock song, originally recorded by the band in January 1971 at Headley Grange. It tells cheeky tales of lovers' escapades, delivered in high spirits by a youthful Plant, who uses the upper part of his range and at times sounds strained, but he artfully works that to his own advantage. Jones's Hammond-organ chords mixed with Page's simple major progressions evoke the glory days of Traffic. Parts of the song take us back to the elementary rock'n'roll raunch of Free and Dave Edmunds, but also remind us of the slightly dated feel of the performance here among the later material scattered through the album. Still, the false endings are fun.

'The Wanton Song' provides more evidence that Plant is seeking a less punishing vocal style for his weathered voice: at the opening he uses a studio-distorted vocal to suggest extreme lust and lechery with intent. Page and Jones play a simple, spare but effective octave-bouncing riff while Bonham piledrives through the middle in typical fashion. But the real fun of this song comes in the bridge (0:59), where Page takes off on a completely untraditional series of chords and introduces a refreshing skew to the proceedings.

The instrumental playing on this track is thrillingly sharp and dynamic, suggesting a band at a real peak of inspiration and purpose, although why Page left his guitar out of tune in that bridge is a mystery. Strangely, the piece did not become a staple of the live set; it was quietly dropped after a few concert appearances. Perhaps Plant simply moved on from the blatant lusting depicted by the lyrics as he grew older and his life changed.

The next two pieces – 'Boogie With Stu' and 'Black Country Woman' – are enjoyable songs of no great consequence that would have made excellent cameos as single B-sides. Placed where they are on this double-album, neither contributes much. 'Boogie With Stu', a fourth-album outtake featuring Ian Stewart (or Stu) on piano, is a jam based on Richie Valens's 'Ooh! My Head' and is mercifully kept to under three minutes. Everybody on it realises that there is only so much mileage to be had from these things.

Years later, Page lamented ironically that he and Plant decided on this occasion to acknowledge their source. "Curiously enough, the one time we did try to do the right thing, it blew up in our faces. When we were up at Headley Grange recording *Physical Graffiti*, Ian Stewart came by and we started to jam. The jam turned into 'Boogie With Stu', which was obviously a variation on 'Ooh! My Head' by the late Ritchie Valens, which itself was actually a variation of Little Richard's 'Ooh! My Soul'. What we tried to do was give Ritchie's mother credit, because we heard she never received any royalties from any of her son's hits, and Robert did lean on that lyric a bit. So what happens? They tried to sue us for all of the song! We had to say bugger off!"[14]

'Black Country Woman', from the 1972 *Houses Of The Holy* sessions, starts with some wholly disposable pre-song chatter that also catches an aircraft flying overhead at Headley Grange. Then Zeppelin settle into a mandolin-and-acoustic-guitar shuffle worthy of 1930s blues stars The Mississippi Sheikhs. Plant delivers his plaint for a verse ("hey mama, what is wrong with you") before Bonham joins in with his bottomless bass-drum punctuating the beat. The instrumental accompaniment builds well, with Bonham contributing from his full kit

before the song is out. But Plant's economy with words here, his extreme stylisation of the delivery, and his unwillingness to develop the theme from its opening gambit make for a curiously static performance. Perhaps this explains why it stayed in the can when the *Houses* line-up was chosen. But at least it has a modicum of charm.

The concluding 'Sick Again' is swaggering Led Zeppelin heavy blues at its best, a slight kink in the riffing pleasingly disturbing expectations and keeping listeners alert. Bonham drums with brutal intensity, as if he's trying to drive everyone else out of the studio with the sheer weight of his sound. At times, especially in the release and at the song's end, Bonham sounds as if he's trying to show Ginger Baker how to play with real density rather than pussyfoot around. Page layers plucked and slide guitar tracks one over the other, providing a dense tapestry of blues wailing: a sort of Elmore James on acid.

Plant's lyrics, about shady sexual and romantic escapades on the road, are delivered with appropriate spleen and attitude. Plant had elaborated on this subject to *Rolling Stone* just prior to the album's release. He talked about his disenchantment when out on the road for too long and the increasingly predatory relationship between groupies and band members. "It's been a long time. Nowadays we're more into staying in our rooms and reading Nietzsche. There was good fun to be had, you know? It's just that in those days there were more people to have good fun with than there are now. The States were much more fun. L.A. was L.A. It's not L.A. now. L.A. infested with jaded 12-year-olds is not the L.A. that I really dug. ... If you listen to 'Sick Again' ... the words show I feel a bit sorry for them. 'Clutching pages from your teenage dream in the lobby of the Hotel Paradise / Through the circus of the L.A. queen, how fast you learn the downhill slide.' One minute she's 12 and the next minute she's 13 and over the top. Such a shame."[15]

With a slow fade, the album ends more or less where it started, digging deep into old blues and R&B territory, and reconstructing it as 1970s supersonic rock. It was something the band knew how to do in their sleep by then, but they still had the flair to make it work. At its conclusion, there is a sense that the band had worked something out of their system, clearing the decks in much the same way The Beatles did with the *White Album*. They were preparing for the future and a completely new set of songs written in the unfolding circumstances of 1975 and beyond. The album is a patchwork summation of all that had gone before and a suggestion of what the future might contain. That explains its breadth of scope as well as its unevenness and the lack of a unifying theme or angle. It also suggests the best way to approach *Physical*

Graffiti: not as a monolithic achievement to be digested whole, but as a smorgasbord of different treats, best enjoyed individually. It is the only Led Zeppelin album of which this is true.

Page felt it was an honest record, one that showed the band for what it was: a working unit making music collectively and enjoying the experience. "I look at it as a document of a band in a working environment. People might say it's sloppy, but I think this album is really honest. *Physical* is a more personal album, and I think it allowed the listener to enter our world."[16]

That was the album that stuck at Number 1 for six weeks and coincided with the second half of the band's US tour in the early spring of 1975. As they went back to work on the road the reviews began to pour in, most of them struggling to cope with the scale of the double album's ambition, especially given the one or two listenings that most music reviewers manage before committing their thoughts to paper.

In a leading review, *NME*'s Steve Clarke compared it with The Rolling Stones' *Exile On Main Street*, drawing the parallel further by suggesting that Zeppelin's *IV* was the counterpart to *Sticky Fingers*. "*Exile On Main Street* overflowed with peerless rock'n'roll, while just missing out on the polish that *Sticky Fingers* had. Likewise, with *Physical Graffiti* and *Led Zeppelin IV*; the former does not quite attain the perfection which the best of the earlier album does. Coming some two years after the fifth (best forgotten) album, *Houses Of The Holy*, *Physical Graffiti* is confirmation that the group has lost none of their inspiration and ability, even if it did take them a long time to deliver. ... Hard rock lives, and how."[17] The album sold very well indeed, and the forthcoming second leg of their US tour was a sell-out, so this was hardly a time for the band and its entourage to worry too much about what the critics had to say.

The second leg of the tenth American tour, running from late February to late March 1975, was mostly confined to the Southern states (especially Texas) and California, though there was the traditional visit to the extreme Northwest with two concerts each in Seattle and Vancouver. In Baton Rouge an overflow audience gave the band a tumultuous welcome. According to a local paper: "Led Zeppelin, reportedly the most popular rock band in the world, tried to destroy the LSU Assembly Center with sound Friday night."[18] Just another night at the office, then.

A week or so later, in Long Beach, California, the band came up against a similarly recalcitrant reviewer who found Zeppelin delivering "a numbing combination of intense, tenacious music and hopelessly limited imagination".[19] To his consternation, the crowd loved every minute of it. By this gig, the band were physically and mentally much stronger than earlier in the tour and able once again to finish their long concerts in style, the

In the same month as the release of album number six, **Physical Graffiti, Jimmy Page hoists his guitar aloft at the Nassau Coliseum in New York, February 13th 1975.**

set-list now running from 'Moby Dick' to old favourites 'Dazed And Confused', 'Stairway To Heaven', 'Whole Lotta Love', and 'Black Dog'.

In Seattle they added a couple of extras, 'Communication Breakdown' and 'Heartbreaker'. In San Diego, the night prior to Long Beach, the concert had been delayed by an hour and the capacity audience were restive, but within seconds of starting the band had an overwhelming two-way exchange going with the crowd that made for a standout event. The music was paced superbly by the light-show and complemented rather than dispersed by the appearance of dry ice. It may have taken a while for the band to find its feet on this tour, but by the time California sunlight was washing over them they were back to their best. After the concluding three-night triumphs at The Forum in L.A. on March 24th, 25th and 27th, they were convinced they had ensured their position at the top of rock's performance tree.

Yet the darker side of the band's touring existence persisted, and the shadows had grown longer. A year later, Page talked about the problems of "life in a bubble" while on such tours. He didn't think he got out of control. "Because if I did that, I wouldn't be able to play. It was more not being able to sleep, writing, fiddling about with tape recorders and TV sets, never settling: it was a feeling that somehow you'd touched the source of whatever creative drive you had and you didn't dare lose it. ... I

built myself up to such a pitch that I couldn't see myself ever coming down again.

"When you're actually on a tour and you look at it, you think you're never going to get through it. But then after a couple of days of staying up all night, your body gets used to this total thing, and your subconscious takes you on to this total thing, an assault upon the whole tour. You see a part of yourself which doesn't appear at any other time. ... It's got so much to do with the whole business of pacing, and waiting, too – the waiting before a concert, where there's nothing to do – but you can't quite relax because there's this thing coming up. ... Sitting down at a hotel at 3.00 in the afternoon waiting for 8.00 to come. ... There's only a certain number of things you can do in that situation."[20]

Tour manager Richard Cole remembered this tour as the one where heroin began to exert an active influence. As he recalled it: "Heroin circulated freely among our entourage. Although alcohol and cocaine were still much more prevalent, I frequently nourished my own smack habit, and at one time or another Jimmy, Robert and Bonzo tried some, too. ... No one was using any needles, and none of us seemed truly hooked in those days, although I'm not really sure about myself. ... On some level, I think we all knew the risks associated with heroin. But Led Zeppelin was like a teenager riding a motorcycle without a helmet. We thought we were infallible, that nothing or nobody could topple us from the throne."[21] Nothing apart from themselves, that is.

☐ Led Zeppelin in full flight at Madison Square Garden, New York City, February 3rd 1975.

UNFORSEEN CIRCUMSTANCES

- SWAN SONG SUCCESSES
- UK EARL'S COURT DATES, SOME FILMED
- PLANT CAR CRASH, AMERICAN TOUR CANCELLED
- 7TH ALBUM SESSIONS IN MUNICH
- 7TH ALBUM, PRESENCE, RELEASED

With the end of the tenth American tour in late March 1975, the band stalled any move back to Britain. Their phenomenal earning power, coupled with very high British income-tax rates for top earners, had made it imperative that they stay out of the country for a year. Similarly, they could not spend unlimited amounts of time in the USA as they would then be liable to US tax. A certain amount of juggling went on while management and accountants decided exactly where would be best for the band members to live. These dislocations alone made it difficult for Grant to co-ordinate band and business matters as well as he had in the past.

This was one of the reasons that the film project continued to languish, even though director Peter Clifton was still working hard on post-production. He found it difficult simply to get anyone to return phone calls, come to meetings or generally show a great deal of interest. He spent some time in Los Angeles early in 1975 while the band was still there, but found it virtually impossible to get them to concentrate on the film.

He did find Jones an exception – "very sweet, and [he] sparkled as a musician" – but otherwise he felt "they were like a bunch of footballers, crude and rude. In fact they took real pleasure in being rude to people. I remember them tying some girls up in their rooms at the Hyatt hotel in L.A. I walked into a bedroom only to find two of the guys asleep in bed together in their underpants. 'Excuse me guys, I'm trying to do some work here!' Then I walk into the next bedroom and there are all these groupies tied up. Dreadful girls. They weren't classy about who they hung out with".[1] Led Zeppelin never pretended they were, but it didn't aid progress when they were so distracted in so many directions at once.

Later the same month Page did manage to meet up with Clifton, in New York City. Clifton spoke at the time to *NME*, saying that Page had "recently finished dubbing the music at New York's Electric Lady studios, and only some quadraphonic dubbing remains to be done." However, he added, "No plans have yet been made about distributing the completed product."[2]

Knowing that the tax situation would keep the band away from Britain for the foreseeable future, Grant still wanted to promote *Physical Graffiti* there. He decided to use the number of days they were allowed into the UK without affecting their tax status to prepare and deliver three attention-grabbing nights at London's Earl's Court Arena in May.

The announcement of these dates came in mid March. The press statement from Swan Song's London office read: "Earl's Court was chosen for two reasons. Firstly it enables the largest number of people to see Zeppelin in an enclosed venue: a total of 50,000 will attend during the three days. And secondly, it is the most central of all London venues, particularly for those travelling from the provinces."[3]

The demand for tickets was enormous: 100,000 applications were received for the 11,000 tickets reserved for mail orders. The show's promoter Mel Bush agreed with Grant that two further shows should be added. This brought the collective audience for the five nights to a potential 85,000. It led to a huge acceleration in newsprint coverage in both the music and national press as it became clear this would be one of the great rock events of the year: Zeppelin would not be touring the country, had not played in Britain for nearly two-and-a-half years, and there seemed to be every likelihood that a similar wait would confront fans before they appeared at home again. Scarcity and demand could hardly have been better aligned: only the return of The Beatles could have trumped it. Led Zeppelin had the field to themselves.

During the spring and early summer of 1975 it seemed that Zeppelin and Grant had another runaway success on their hands with their Swan Song record company. In April, Bad Company had released their second album for the label in the US, *Straight Shooter*, which had gone Top 10, while the single 'Good Lovin' Gone Bad' reached the Top 40. The follow-up, 'Feel Like Makin' Love', hit Number 10 Stateside. Swan Song's other signings, Maggie Bell and The Pretty Things, had made the US album charts with their first releases, adding up to a 100 percent success rate at this early stage.

But this very success, combined with Grant's central role in the label's affairs, the current instability caused by the tax situation, and Grant's commitments to management business – he was attempting to look after Maggie Bell's career as well as Zeppelin's and Bad Company's – meant that the label was overstretched. There were not enough people with decision-making authority to do the work that needed to be done to keep everything expanding. Even at this early stage, opportunities were being missed, the right new talent was not being signed, and those acts they did have were often being overlooked by what was still a minimal staff.

Meanwhile, the band had Earl's Court to play. Their set was similar to that of the latter concerts on the US tour, apart from the return of the acoustic set, but much of it had not been heard live by a UK audience. The band had not played a British date since January 1973, before *Houses Of The Holy* had been issued.

The basic set-list at Earl's Court was 'Rock And Roll', 'Sick Again', 'Over The Hills And Far Away', 'In My Time of Dying', 'The Song Remains The Same', 'The Rain Song', 'Kashmir', 'No Quarter', 'Tangerine', 'Going To California', 'That's The Way', 'Bron-Yr-Aur Stomp', 'Trampled Under Foot', 'Moby Dick', 'Dazed And Confused', and 'Stairway To Heaven'. Encores were 'Whole Lotta Love' (including 'The Crunge') and 'Black Dog'. But each night had small variations and ad libs.

The band brought over the entire technical support from the US tour, including sound system, giant video screen and light-show. As in the States, this moved their image on dramatically from those early-1973 UK concerts – the last Zeppelin had played without a major light-show and the new state-of-the-art PA system. Each night had its little problems and highlights. On the first number of the first night, Page's guitar cord cut out, for example. Plant, pleased to be back in front of the home fans, was highly talkative between songs, a change from previous UK tours. At one point he referred sarcastically to the British Chancellor of the day, Denis Healey, and his onerous tax regimen that had forced the band into exile.

By common consent, the gem among the five nights was May 24th, the penultimate concert, when the band were simply red-hot and in an unstoppable groove. They even delivered a scintillating version of Joni Mitchell's 'Woodstock'. Some of the performances later appeared on the *DVD* set released in 2003; they were filmed more by "luck than anything" according to Plant in the accompanying booklet. According to him, they had just wanted some sort of record for themselves.

The footage shows just how far the band's stage presentation had moved on from their early 1970s sets. As at the Madison Square Garden concerts of 1973 they comfortably commanded the gigantic stage spaces rather than sticking together and working as a small tight-knit unit as they had tended to do on earlier occasions. They had all put distance between their early-1970s clothes-sense and their current ideas of themselves and were exploiting post-Glam ideas about stagecraft, although Plant kept his flowing locks and open-chested look. That was as much a trademark of the band as a burning zeppelin.

On the US tour Plant had been plagued by illness and the inevitable difficulties that accompany any below-par singer. But the Earl's Court footage proves conclusively that he had recovered his range and his power. Although there was now a coarsening in the upper range of his voice, as opposed to the chillingly solid banshee scream of earlier days, he was quickly learning to exploit it. Most of the old blues singers he so greatly admired – Blind Willie Johnson, Charlie Patton – had the ability to put in the grit and use it to their own expressive advantage. Plant's thorough schooling in blues tradition meant that he would hardly overlook that lesson.

Bonham by this stage had quite visibly gained a lot of weight, but the power he was generating behind the drums was as deep and overwhelming as ever and his precision was equally sharp. Jones, as Plant and Page had been saying for some time, was a more complete presence onstage now, moving effortlessly between a range of instruments, and not only playing them competently but creating something memorable in the process.

The 2003 *DVD* set captures most of the acoustic section of one of the concerts, showing Jones as a superb melodist on the mandolin in his accompaniment for 'Going To California' and 'That's The Way' (he's handy on footpedals, too). Both those numbers also demonstrate Page's sympathetic and notably unflashy guitar accompaniment. His folk and acoustic roots are fully in evidence, not so much in the style he adopts but in the discipline he imposes on himself in this role: it is hardly the work of an egomaniacal rock star.

The footage concludes with a fast but impressively smooth 'Stairway To Heaven'. It provides an opportunity to study Page's technique, split between the 12-string and six-string necks of his twin-neck Gibson guitar, and an insight into just how demanding is his role within this song and this band. The fact that the listener never feels the various transitions means that Page succeeds in sustaining a complete guitar role, even when he is soloing and there is no rhythm guitar to sustain him. This of course had been the case from the beginning, but it is laid bare in this performance.

With their UK commitments completed, the band scattered both to and from the country. Bonham went for a while to his West Midlands farm, where Chris Welch interviewed the drummer. He talked warmly of the Earl's Court nights. "I enjoyed those concerts: I thought they were the best shows that we've ever put on in England. … Everything went really well, and although we couldn't have the laser beams at full power, I thought the video screen was well worth doing. It cost a lot of bread, but you could see close-ups you'd never be able to see normally at a concert."[4]

The concerts had indeed been very expensive to mount, especially after bringing the entire rig over from the USA, and Zep's management claimed later that they'd made not a penny on the five nights. No matter: in their own minds, the entire band saw the Earl's Court concerts as a successful and temporary farewell to Britain. Plant said as much from the stage on the last evening, while Grant told Richard Cole: "The taxman is driving us out of England. These will be the last concerts here for a while."[5] Page, Plant and Jones were reported to have relocated to Montreux in Switzerland in early July. Bonham would exit the country soon afterwards.

In the weeks between the end of the US tour and the Earl's Court dates, Page, Grant and Plant had already agreed in principle the outline for a late-summer '75 American tour. This, they considered, would keep up the momentum and complete the year away from the UK that the tax rules demanded. After Earl's Court, Grant and Page advanced those plans in New York while Page worked on the film edits.

With everything decided, Plant and Page had planned a short Moroccan jaunt with their respective partners and family while the others spent their time separately with their own families. Page met up with Plant and his wife

Maureen in the latter part of June and they travelled in and around Morocco before going their separate ways. Page ended up back in London in early August for some more work on the Zep film, specifically the final edit on 'Dazed And Confused'. There was already a date fixed in mid August for the beginning of rehearsals for the upcoming American tour, set for a late August start. They were going to be kept busy in their tax exile.

Or so it seemed. It all changed on August 4th when the car that Maureen Plant was driving came off the road on the island of Rhodes in Greece. The car collided with a tree. All five of the Plant family were in the car, the three children in the back and Robert in the passenger's seat. The children sustained minor injuries but Plant had broken major bones in his arm and legs. Worst of all was Maureen. According to Richard Cole she broke her pelvis, fractured a leg, suffered cuts on her face and had a fractured skull. "She also had lost large amounts of blood, and because she had a rare blood type, doctors had to rely on her sister, Shirley, for immediate transfusions."[6]

Luckily, Page's girlfriend Charlotte Martin and Maureen Plant's sister had been following in another car, along with Page's daughter. Martin quickly contacted Cole back in London, who acted with great speed. None of the Zeppelin team was in London at the time, so he rounded up the best private medical care he could find and flew them all to Rhodes, where they immediately went to the hospital. Overcoming objections from the medical staff and manoeuvring around the local police, Cole got every one of the party back onto the plane and away to London in the briefest possible time. His actions quite possibly saved Maureen Plant's life and certainly aided in the party's long-term recovery. As it was, Maureen was in danger for a time and confined to hospital for weeks afterwards.

Robert, on the other hand, although badly injured and given no guarantee from his doctors that he would ever be 100 percent better, could not afford to continue receiving treatment in London. His tax-exile status demanded that he leave as soon as possible. Cole arranged for him to stay with a friend in Jersey. This British island near the coast of France enjoyed offshore tax status and is crowded with wealthy Brits living a convenient distance from the home country. Confined to a wheelchair, Plant suffered a painful regimen of physical therapy on his shattered legs for the next month and also tried to adjust to the enforced separation from his seriously-ill wife.

The day after the accident Grant cancelled the American tour. Everyone who had already purchased a ticket was entitled to a full refund. In early September, while his wife stayed behind in Britain to aid her own

By now, the strain of virtually constant touring and of keeping such a successful band on the rails was beginning to take its toll.

recovery and be with the children, Plant was moved to Malibu, on the California coast, where he met up with Page. They quickly decided that working on a project would be better for everyone, including Plant, than if they idly let time drift and depression set in too deeply. In that respect, Led Zeppelin's seventh album, *Presence*, would be the one fortuitous result of the Plant family's dreadful accident. It was no doubt with an unavoidable tinge of irony that Page flew back to London on September 24th to collect on behalf of the band not just one but seven different *Melody Maker* awards for the 1975 readers' poll, at a ceremony at the Carlton Hotel. In his acceptance speech he said: "I really wish we could all have been here to receive them, but I'm sure you'll understand."[7]

Back in Malibu, the band reconvened with the idea of rehearsing material for a new album, the only project they could realistically take on while their singer was so badly incapacitated. Plant confirmed in early 1976 that material was already under development prior to the Rhodes accident. "We already had some ammunition from our trip to Morocco – Jimmy and I had put together some epic sort of material – but every time we started listening and thinking about the ideas that we had already put together, we shied away."[8]

Using ideas sketched out in the previous weeks or evolved organically in rehearsals, all four musicians could see that a return to basics was essential under the circumstances. For Plant, this signalled a reinvigoration of his blues and rock roots; for Page it meant a new concentration on developing guitar strategies in collaboration with Jones and Bonham; and for the rhythm team it involved full-scale involvement in building everything from the ground up. Jones, in the meantime, decided to stick mainly to bass to maximise everyone's involvement in the process. During this period he had picked up an eight-string Alembic bass in a store and bought it. Delighted with the power and precision of the instrument and filled with renewed enthusiasm, he commissioned the California company to make him a four-string model as well, although this was not completed in time to be used at the *Presence* rehearsals or recording sessions.

"In L.A. we just rehearsed and rehearsed," Plant said a little later. "The whole band really wanted to play and had wanted to do that tour, so the same effort was put into the album. It was a unique situation where we rehearsed for three weeks – on and off, in true Led Zeppelin style, because we're not the greatest band for rehearsing. ... But this time it worked in the opposite way because the enthusiasm was contained in such a small space of time."[9]

But not everything was running smoothly. This was Led Zeppelin, after all. Page claimed later that Jones was never around when he needed him to play. Jones much later said it was the other way around. "Robert and I seemed to keep a different time sequence to Jimmy. We just couldn't find him. I wanted to put up this huge banner in the street saying 'Today's the first day of rehearsals'. Myself and my then roadie Brian Condliffe drove into SIR studios every night and waited and waited until finally we were all in attendance, by which time it was two in the morning."[10]

Bonham, away from home and resentful of his enforced exile from the UK and his family, repeatedly took himself off to the watering holes of Los Angeles and, getting as drunk as he could manage in as short a time as possible, found himself in situations that were, quite simply, degrading. He even managed to punch in the face a woman he vaguely knew who had been sitting alone eating a meal in a club and minding her own business. And still there was no one prepared to rein him in or help him get himself sorted out.

By the last quarter of October 1975, the band felt they had an album's worth of new material and were sufficiently on top of every new piece to begin recording. It had become impossible for them to record in LA due to more tax problems, this time a result of US laws. A new recording location had to be found. They discovered one in Munich.

Musicland was a top-flight recording studio located in the basement of the Arabella Hotel in the southern German capital. It had all the facilities the band needed to complete the job and the hotel could also accommodate the band and its entourage for the weeks of recording. Being self-contained was very important given Plant's continuing confinement in a wheelchair: he was able to exercise every day away from the chair with a walking stick, but otherwise was still largely chairbound.

They made the new record very quickly – the studio was booked for just two weeks and The Rolling Stones were due in the day after they finished. The speed with which the band worked shows in the consistency of sound and instrumentation they achieved on the album. There was also a unity of conception that had not been present on *Physical Graffiti* or even *Houses Of The Holy*. One aspect of this album stayed unique throughout the band's history: the real sense of pain, hurt, loneliness and occasional terror that haunts every song, and nowhere more so than on the adaptation of Blind Willie Johnson's 'Nobody's Fault But Mine'. As Plant said about the album a few weeks later: "It was really like a cry of survival. … There won't be another album like it, put it like that. It was a cry from the depths, the only thing that we could do."[11]

There was a dark undercurrent to that cry known only to those within the band's inner circle. As Richard Cole wrote later: "Bonzo, Jimmy and I used smack [heroin] during the daytime hours in Munich, and none of us seemed the worse for it. No one ever talked about the possible risks, and we probably didn't think about them, either. We felt trapped indoors by Munich's frigid air;

heroin, it seemed, made the time indoors pass more quickly."[12]

With the music completed, all but Page decamped to Jersey to unwind and take on board their troubled experiences. Page stayed on at Musicland, overdubbing, editing and mixing the tapes to the point of a finished master. Jones later confirmed that Page worked very hard indeed during the stay in Munich. Plant, reflecting on the album some years later, commented: "I think *Presence* has got some of the hottest moments Led Zeppelin ever had – agitated, uncomfortable, druggy, pained."[13] It was the fastest the whole outfit had produced an album since the very first one, back in 1968.

The original thought for the record's name was *Thanksgiving*. This had an obvious and entirely relevant resonance, but it didn't stick. The mastering sessions safely concluded, Page flew to Jersey where on December 10th, on a whim, Led Zeppelin gave their final concert of the year, to 350 amazed fans at a small venue, Beehan's Park West, in St Helier. Plant said later: "It was like a dancehall that was some place ten years gone by, in the best English tradition. Guys with dicky bows and evening jackets ready to bang your head if you stepped out of line, and chairs and tables lined up in escalation. Chicks wearing suspenders and stockings and a lot of rock'n'roll."[14]

This little gig in such an out of the way place suggested that 1976 would be a year of recovery and forward movement for the band. There were plenty of reasons to be cheerful as Plant and everyone in his family continued to make progress towards a full physical recovery. The band and manager Peter Grant could plan once more for a busy future.

Page took the first step in securing that future just prior to Christmas when he flew to New York to deliver the finished master of what was destined to become *Presence*. He also intended to make what he and director Peter Clifton hoped would be the final effort to complete the Led Zeppelin film. By this time relations between band and Clifton had reached a low point and Clifton was experiencing almost total breakdown in communication with anyone in the Zeppelin entourage. The trust that had existed in the first period after he took over from Joe Massot had evaporated, perhaps in part because of the extreme problems that had arisen elsewhere.

At such a time, the band had naturally retreated to doing what they knew and understood best: making music. Film, that alien and confusing medium, was one hassle that no one really needed. Plant aired his exasperation at the film-making process in an interview at the time. He said the band knew what they wanted from the filming because they knew their music and what it needed in visual support. But, he said, "Film people really puzzle me. The attitude and antics of the people involved with film, the way they follow their own odd trips, are really beyond my comprehension. ... The idea of the solitary man standing in front of the camera repeating himself time and time again to some irate lunatic sitting in a chair with Director written on the back – yeuch! No thanks."[15]

The selfsame lunatic with a chair was back in Los Angeles in February 1976 attempting to conclude a distribution deal for the film with Warner Bros. Something close to chaos reigned in many areas of Led Zeppelin's public and private existence, with manager Peter Grant additionally in the throes of a marital breakdown that would end with his wife leaving him. The meeting – designed to take the financial pressure off the band members, who had stumped up the capital for the film to be made by taking individual loans – was a key step towards getting the film out to its waiting public.

Clifton, alone in a room with the Warner top brass, filled in time for the moment of Grant's arrival, but it never came. Grant apparently had never left Britain. Richard Cole was sent at the last minute to deputise. Clifton remembered: "He turned up at the meeting coked out, armed with bottles of booze and with another of the band's roadies. The pair of them hadn't slept for days. And this is Warner Bros, not some party, right? They sit in a corner and start to mouth obscenities at the meeting. Richard is drinking and making all these inane comments, ... the Americans are saying, 'Oh my God, where's Peter Grant?' I had to stand up and say, 'Well, unfortunately Mr Grant is at a meeting.' After five or six hours of this, it became nonsensical, but we had to make the decisions without him. ... In fact, he had just stood up one of the most important meetings in his life for personal reasons. I was really upset, and having Richard Cole there – completely off his face – didn't help. I don't suppose he even remembers the meeting."[16]

Cole wasn't the only one with a monkey on his back. Just after this meeting, Cole was driving with Page to Los Angeles International Airport to return to London. They were snarled up in traffic when Page began a conversation, which Cole reported later. "'Chrissakes, Richard, don't get into this shit.' 'What do you mean?' I asked. 'Heroin. I think I'm hooked. It's terrible.' 'Have you tried to stop?' 'I've tried, but I can't. It's a real bastard.'" According to Cole, Bonham was also struggling with the first stages of a solid habit. Only Jones, Cole felt, "was nearly always able to avoid any traps that the rest of us got sucked into",[17] knowing when to turn away and keep walking from temptation.

In the absence of any coherent Led Zeppelin representation at the Warner meeting, the parties agreed to schedule the film – now titled *The Song Remains The Same* – for November 1976 release in the USA, with a premiere in New York City just prior to that, on October 20th. Ironically, this yawning vacuum at the centre of Zeppelin's business affairs was opening at the very time

that Plant was telling *Melody Maker*: "Peter is ultra-important, the fifth member of the group, and as much as we have a highly conscientious attitude about the material that we put out, so too has Peter with the responsibility on his shoulders." Plant went on to talk about the film and Richard Cole's role. "Richard deserves a feather in his hat, if we're going to wear them, because he's been such a great part of Zeppelin too. He's such a rock on the road, such a unique man. ... Ricardo knows what he's doing all the time, at least during the time he's supposed to: after that, who knows?"[18] Who indeed.

But at least Plant was responding to treatment and mending ahead of his doctors' prognosis. "They've called me a model patient," he said in February. "I was faced with a situation that dented every single thing I had going for me. My usual, er, sort of Leonine arrogance was instantly punctured by having to hobble around, so I'm having to take my time."[19] Meanwhile, Warner Bros had accepted *The Song Remains The Same* movie for US distribution on the condition that a string of expletives uttered by Grant backstage at Madison Square Garden be deleted. Clifton deleted the offending words from a print supplied to the authorities for certification, but left them in on every other print sent out later in the year. The film was definitely better for their inclusion.

In February, *NME* printed the results of its annual readers' poll. Plant and Led Zeppelin won in both the British and World sections, with Page topping the guitarist and producer categories of the General section. *Physical Graffiti* was album of the year, with Queen's *A Night At The Opera* second. The buzz of activity of 1975 had delivered the appropriate awards.

Presence was officially released on March 28th 1976, but the album's arrival in the stores was delayed because of production problems. Nonetheless it was the fastest Zeppelin album between recording and release since the very first. Page and Grant had used design team Hipgnosis, who had done the work for *Houses Of The Holy*, and they would also get the commission for the *Song Remains The Same* album jacket. Hipgnosis came up with the idea of 'the object' for *Presence*, which had appealed to Page's sense of humour as well as his taste for mystery.

The gatefold jacket presented a series of 1960s 'instructional images' as if they had been taken from handbooks, brochures or manuals, each with a black object placed in the pivotal part of the frame. The title of the record was embossed on the front cover. It was all very subtle, very kitsch, and a good joke, but it bore little or no relation to the music inside. The title itself was a fair reflection of the sheer weight and immediacy of recorded sound that the band and Page had been able to capture on tape in Munich, but it masked the urgent communication of their emotional states that overflowed from the music. *Presence* remains Zeppelin's most misunderstood and under-appreciated album.

The opening track – and the longest on the record – is 'Achilles' Last Stand'. The song was started in part in Morocco during the summer of 1975 and contains verbal reflections of the trip and the tax exile that prompted it. The title no doubt refers ironically to the fact that it was Plant's last holiday before the crash and the damage to his ankle and legs, occasioning the parallel with the invincible Achilles, brought low by an arrow in his heel, the only vulnerable spot in his body.

The Moroccan influence shows not only in the lyrics but in the way Page treats his guitar parts, especially the mysterious opening arpeggios. There is also the magical combination often to be found in Eastern music as the band commences a fast, complex rhythm over a beautifully voiced minor tonality. The combination of the two creates the special sense of reaching out and yearning that permeates the track and gives it the sense of a journey every bit as far-ranging as the one in 'Kashmir', though of a very different kind. All the motifs and figures on guitars and bass here are climbing, stressing the sense of need and impossible aspiration, almost supplication, as Page cleverly builds up successive layers of guitar accompaniment to bring the song's message to more than one climax.

Page is able to do this because of the tune's irregular construction. 'Achilles' starts with a conventional verse repeat and then a solo starting at 3:42 over the bridge section of the song with its yearning, ascending line and stop-time rhythms. Page's solo is astonishingly powerful, his long crying notes a reflection – not an imitation – of the beautiful melodies he had often admired in Eastern music. It is intense, compact and sustained, and one of his best on record. Soon after the album's release he said: "I guess the solo on 'Achilles' Last Stand' … is in the same tradition as the solo on 'Stairway To Heaven' on the fourth LP. It is on that level to me."[20] Fifteen years later he still closely identified with this solo. "I thought to myself: 'My god, that solo says a hell of a lot to me. What was going on there?'"[21]

With another verse the band falls into a different, tumbling riff pattern (around 5:55) that segues into the vocal tag "I know the rain". Another repeat of the stop-time section returns to the bridge and then a shortened verse full of Page's slide-guitar lines, propelling us into an extraordinary riff variation over the verse harmony (7:28) where Plant just makes guttural noises, as if spurring everyone on during this epic journey. From there the song builds to a second climax as more and more lines intersect with each other over the rhythmic cauldron. It all comes to an abrupt, crashing end at 9:42, only for Page's opening, mysterious guitar arpeggios to emerge once more and lead us away into the fading distance, like a mysterious desert guide or a chimera.

It is an extraordinary achievement for the whole band and one of which Page was intensely proud. Talking later to Steve Rosen about the proper application of harmonised guitar parts, he said. "'Achilles' Last Stand' is like the essential flow of it really, because there was no time to think the things out; I just had to more or less lay it down on the first track and harmonise on the second track. …

"I did all the guitar overdubs on that LP in one night. There were only two sequences. The rest of the band, not Robert, but the rest of them I don't think really could see it to begin with. They didn't know what the hell I was going to do with it. But I wanted to give each section its own identity, and I think it came off really good. … I thought I'd have to do it in the course of three different nights to get the individual sections. But I was so into it that my mind was working properly for a change. It sort of crystallised and everything was just pouring out."[22]

Jones confirmed many years later that there was some friction as 'Achilles' was mapped out. He was commenting on the time he began to take his new Alembic eight-string bass to Zeppelin sessions. "When Page starts soloing and goes up high there's a big gap, and you have the problem of filling it. We filled it with eight-string bass. … Page complained bitterly when the eight-string first appeared – he said: 'I'm not playing to that.' Then he realised how much sound it made and how it gave him a much better base to solo over. … Then he liked it. When Page came out with the first riff of 'Achilles' Last Stand' he said: 'What are we going to do with the rest of it?' I said: 'The 8–string bass.' … It fitted perfectly."[23]

The recording remained a personal favourite of Page's. In 1991 he discussed the selection of music for the first of the Zeppelin boxed sets. "The one where everyone said: 'My god, that was brilliant,' was 'Achilles' Last Stand'. That did sound brilliant, actually."[24]

'For Your Life' consists of simple musical building blocks but is cleverly arranged with stop-start riffs against a massive Bonham mid-tempo backbeat strut while Plant weaves in and out of the musical structure. It starts with blazing major chords that set up Plant's delayed entry. He treats this as a type of talking blues in the old tradition of telling a story in a semi-conversational way. The subject is "a cry for mercy in the city of the damned" – his experiences of alienation on the road.

The short bridge is a two-part affair that starts on a killer Zeppelin blues riff with a threatening edge to Page's guitar tone, leading to a 6/8 riff against Bonham's rock-steady 4/4 – a classic Zeppelin move. The verse after the bridge is completely empty, using the bridge riff and allowing the listener to take in the sheer nastiness of the sound, based on the famous so-called 'Hendrix chord' of 'Foxy Lady' and 'Purple Haze' fame but cranked up

John Paul Jones plays mandolin onstage to accompany 'Going To California' and 'That's The Way'.

tighter as Page continually steps it up by a tone after each verse.

Over this altered harmonic backdrop, Plant delivers some truly desperate vocals that reflect his distraught plight during the autumn months in Los Angeles. Page's solo is again top-drawer, full of unusual intervals, suspended rhythm and irregular phrases. He even uses a tremolo-effect wobble à la Hendrix at one point, but so elegantly that it becomes his own. Plant then returns for a final, almost bitter declamation and an end to the semi-conversation he has sustained for the entire track. It's a piece that uses elements common to many Zep tracks on previous albums, but it has a unique edge and tone.

Page thought he best captured his method of building layer after layer of guitars on 'Stairway To Heaven', 'Ten Years Gone', and 'Achilles' Last Stand', but 'For Your Life' is in the same category. He knew where his greatest talents lay. "My vocation is more in composition really than anything else. Building up harmonies. Using the guitar, orchestrating the guitar like an army – a guitar army. ... I'm talking about actual orchestration in the same way you'd orchestrate a classical piece of music. Instead of using brass and violins you treat the guitars with synthesisers or other devices ... so that they have enough frequency range and scope and everything to keep the listener as totally committed to it as the player is."[25]

The short clincher for the original side one of the vinyl release was 'Royal Orleans'. On it Plant rediscovers his humour and balance, depicting incidents from an earlier US tour with one of the band members in the New Orleans hotel of their choice, Royal Orleans. Again he tells a story of low-life fun and games, but as opposed to the conflict at the root of 'For Your Life', 'Royal Orleans' looks benignly on the world. The track, which has some overtones of the funk of 'The Crunge' and touches of gumbo quick-fire rhythm patterns, is one of the few rays of sunshine – albeit ironic – on an album dominated by other concerns.

Those concerns are laceratingly portrayed on the opening selection from the original side two, 'Nobody's Fault But Mine'. Plant, deep in the mire of misfortune, had again turned back to one of his earliest inspirations, spirituals singer Blind Willie Johnson (who had provided the raw material for 'In My Time Of Dying' on *Physical Graffiti*). Unfortunately, for all Plant's admiration of the great 1920s musician, Johnson's name is not to be found in either song's compositional credits. With money hardly an issue for any member of the band by 1975, one wonders why this happened. Page did offer an explanation of his role in 1998. "Robert came in one day and suggested we cover ['Nobody's Fault But Mine'], but the arrangement I came up with has nothing to do with the original. Robert may have wanted to go for the original lyrics, but everything else was a totally different kettle of fish."[26]

Regardless of its provenance, 'Nobody's Fault' is a blistering portrayal of a man looking for deliverance from his misdeeds and perceived sins. Plant sticks to Johnson's lyrics for the first couple of verses, but after the harmonica solo he improvises his own variant, singing about the "monkey on my back" with barely concealed desperation. It's clear from the later film of the Knebworth concert in 1979 that these lines cut deep with Plant; at that concert when he sings this song there is a remarkable rush of feeling evident across his face as he spits out the lines, a long way beyond any onstage posing for the crowd. This was one from the heart.

From a musical point of view, the track is again very simple in its component parts; a model of blues band playing, the rhythm trio working flawlessly together to inject incredible levels of feeling into the performance. The opening is like a supersonic 1970s interpretation of Johnson's beautiful slide guitar technique, the long, phased, sustained notes sighing and moving like trees in the wind or witnesses swaying in church. Plant's sighs add to that notion.

After that the band comes in like a ton of bricks – either that or a stroke of god's lightning – and Plant begins his confessional in front of the witnesses: "The devil he told me to go there / The devil he told me to go ... Nobody's fault but mine." As with other blues interpretations on earlier albums, Zep use the call-and-response method of dramatic construction, alternating between vocal and instrumental passages, but also using pauses and breaks to tighten the screw of tension to almost unbearable levels. This is released mid-song with a blistering miked-up harmonica solo from Plant that begins with a single sustained note, more like the shriek of a guitar or even a wounded animal. It's only when Plant moves from that note to the riffing that forms the rest of the solo that you realise it is in fact a harmonica. The ghost of James Cotton walks.

After another tortured vocal verse from Plant, Page adds his guitar commentary in a teasing, poised guitar solo. It hints at some sort of eventual salvation before the original band riff is reintroduced, this time cut short by a rising set of chords, punctuated by Bonham's crashing and Plant's stop-time pleading, and then a staccato finish.

As if to demonstrate the limited chance that the repentant will stick to his resolutions, the following song, 'Candy Store Rock', tells a story of unrestrained lusting, 1950s style, in an Elvis Presley/Gene Vincent pastiche. Like 'Royal Orleans' it is an enjoyable work-out for the band without being particularly distinguished, but at least it doesn't suffer from any pretension or ideas of grandeur. Zeppelin's members always insisted that the greatest thing about being in the band was the sheer fun they had playing together, whether onstage or in the studio. Tracks like this back up that idea.

'Hots On For Nowhere' is a shout of joy illuminating

the gloom of the larger efforts of *Presence*. This shuffle-swing song is strung together with bewitchingly constructed riffs and stops – one of which can be found in embryonic form in 'Walter's Walk' from 1972 – and has so much vitality that it feels almost as if this band were making their debut album, not the seventh. On the turnaround there is another of those clashing-metre riffs so beloved of the band when they worked on songs together, and which helps propel the whole unit back into the vocal. There is even a false ending, disguised by Page's double-tracked unaccompanied riffing settling on the tonic, before the band returns for another tag and a second, conclusive go at the riff tag.

'Tea For One' opens as if an extension of 'Hots On For Nowhere', with a heavy-metal riff that sounds like a Sherman tank grinding to a halt somewhere in a desert. That impression almost immediately gives way to a different type of desert as a slow 6/8 beat introduces one of Plant's most personal blues vocals. "How come 24 hours, baby, sometimes seem to slip into days … One minute seems like a lifetime, oh baby, when I feel this way." At over nine minutes, this is second only to 'Achilles' in length on the album. It contains a passionate, eloquent guitar solo from Page, who draws on his knowledge of the styles of earlier blues giants, especially B.B. King. But he introduces other elements – altered scales, jazz-like pauses – that those blues players never used. Page plays with maximum feeling and an equal level of refinement, and this poignant solo is one of his very best on record.

If there is a problem with this song, it comes with the recapitulation after the solo. Extra guitar lines heighten the atmosphere, but there is no response from Bonham, who remains unusually one-dimensional on this track. There is also an additional verse and chorus that extends the piece beyond a desirable length. While one can understand and sympathise with Plant's desire to sing all the lyrics he'd written, the performance sags under the extra weight, its original shape distorted and the unity of its message dissipated. It's a shame, for this otherwise moving blues ends the album, with the listener feeling in some unexplained way unfulfilled, as if an opportunity had been missed.

But there is no Led Zeppelin album with a perfect balance of all its constituent parts, even the fourth, and *Presence* does better than most in that respect. The album is not as diverse in inspiration and instrumentation as *III* or *Physical Graffiti*, but is on a par with any of them for sheer sustained inspiration and musicality. This is a band playing at its peak under extreme conditions. It's an extraordinary achievement for any band, let alone one with seven years of near-continual playing to its credit.

Page certainly felt positive about the album during the interviews that accompanied its release. He told Pete Doherty for *Sounds*: "There's a lot of urgency about it. There's a lot of attack to the music. … As far as laying [it] down, I suppose the word is orchestration, guitar harmonies and stuff. I've usually immersed myself in it, laid down things and there'd be room to amplify it with extra harmonies or whatever. With this one it came straight up. There's a hell of a lot of spontaneity about it. I think that's the element, really." As for this album's effect on the band's future, Page was adamant that the wells of inspiration were nowhere near dry. "We're only scratching the surface if you start relating it to classical work; it depends on how far you want to take it. There's such a wealth. There are no horizons as to what could be done. It just takes a lot of work, writing and recording."[27]

Plant, spotted by *Rolling Stone*'s Rich Wiseman at a January Pretty Things concert in Berkeley, California, agreed to give an interview in Los Angeles that February. Still in a leg brace, he was spending his time profitably by hanging out backstage with the likes of The Runaways and trading jokes with comedian Richard Pryor. He talked about the spirit the band had shown in adversity at the end of the last year. "My only alternative was to turn around and stand against the storm with my teeth gritted and fists clenched and make an album. All the energy that had been smouldering inside us getting ready for a lot of gigs came out in the writing and later in the studio. What we have is an album that is so Zeppelin. It sounds like the hammer of the gods." He talked about the unbending discipline the band had showed in making the record. "I'm really pleased with the whole thing because it took only 18 days to record and mix. We didn't go out one night. No riots."[28]

Over a year later, Page was still enthusing about the record. "*Presence* and my control over all the contributing factors to that LP, the fact that it was done in three weeks, and all the rest of it, is so good for me. It was just good for everything, really, even though it was a very anxious point, and the anxiety shows group-wise – you know: 'Is Robert going to walk again from his auto accident in Greece?'"[29]

Presence received very positive reviews throughout the UK music press and a largely positive reaction in America. For once *Rolling Stone* was kind to the band: in the same issue that saw a decidedly equivocal review for *Wings At The Speed Of Sound*, Steven Davis wrote that the new disc "confirms this quartet's status as heavy metal champions of the known universe. *Presence* takes up where last year's monumentally molten *Physical Graffiti* left off – few melodies, a preoccupation with hard rock rhythm, lengthy echoing moans gushing from Robert Plant, and a general lyrical slant toward the cosmos." After suggesting that 'Achilles' Last Stand' could be interpreted as The Yardbirds 12 years on, Davis concluded: "Actually there is some fine rock on *Presence*. 'Nobody's Fault But Mine' is strong, while 'Candy Store Rock' perfectly evokes the L.A. milieu in which Zep composed this album – it sounds like an unholy hybrid in which Buddy Holly is grafted on to the quivering stem of David Bowie. ... *Presence* is another monster in what by now is a continuing tradition of battles won by this band of survivors."[30]

The record enjoyed unprecedented pre-orders and went to Number 1 on both sides of the Atlantic that April. But with no tours planned and the failure of the one single from the album, 'Candy Store Rock' coupled with 'Royal Orleans', sales were not sustained. In Britain it avoided a clash with March's big-selling Status Quo album *Blues For You* and on its release in April bumped the TV soundtrack album of *Rock Follies* from the top spot, although *Follies* reversed the favour the following week. Then *Abba's Greatest Hits* came along and became the year's biggest seller, and *Presence* fell away.

The British market had become increasingly polarised in the previous couple of years between out-and-out pop, especially in the singles market, and heavy or progressive rock. The Glam days were well and truly over; even Roxy Music by 1975 were going for less of a tinsel-town image onstage and on their album jackets, while the inspiration of the blues had continued to evaporate. The impact of disco and Euro-rock in the form of Abba and Giorgio Moroder's Donna Summer epics had fundamentally changed the music scene.

Led Zeppelin, a band clearly in it for the long term, now had to present themselves as rock immortals – like The Rolling Stones, The Who, and Pink Floyd – whose music was in a sense above the petty issues of style and fashion, and whose every musical statement needed close attention. This would leave them exposed to the sustained attack they and other stadium rock headliners suffered in Britain from the music-press fashionistas, who by the end of 1976 would be hailing a younger generation of back-to-basics rockers as the new messiahs.

In America things weren't quite so volatile. Peter Frampton's *Frampton Comes Alive*, released around the same time, was to stay in or near the top spot for a large part of the year. *Wings At The Speed Of Sound* immediately preceded *Presence* at Number 1 and then fluctuated between positions in the Top 3. *Presence* made it to Number 1 on May 1st but stayed for just two weeks before the Stones' *Black And Blue* took over. Important albums that didn't exactly storm the charts but were released around the same time included Brian Eno's *Another Green World* and Laura Nyro's *Smile*.

Considering the emphasis that Led Zeppelin placed on playing live, it was a particular irony that they were removed from their natural constituency in 1976. At the end of that year the first British punk bands were beginning to proclaim their relevance to an emerging youth culture that took its live entertainment pretty seriously. Zeppelin had always stressed the importance of communicating with their audiences, whether in clubs or stadiums. Talking to a journalist soon after *Presence*'s release about the money to be made in rock, Page stressed the central importance of musical acceptance.

"Most of the people I know aren't even thinking about [money], they're thinking about how things are shaping up with their playing, how things are shaping up artistically. ... I relate much more to the actual communication with those people at the gig, which to me is more like the vibe of what it's all about than driving back through streets at six o'clock in the morning. If the audience is vibing you up and you're vibing them, you can get this gigantic feedback which can become quite magical. I relate far more to that, the communication between us and the people coming to see us."

Page's thinking was particularly acute, feeding into the wider view he held of his chosen profession. Describing rock'n'roll as "environmental music" and Chuck Berry's best songs as "anthems", he said: "I know there shouldn't be boundaries really, but as far as the statements go you've still got to own up that most of the people that are playing are self-taught people, even though there have been some that have come from a classical training. And then again if you want to relate it to music on a complete scale, relating it to the really serious composers in terms of the ideas and the textures they're laying down, then you're really going to start getting into deep water if somebody's saying that it's got that far, because I don't think it has."[31]

Led Zeppelin had now completed their 12-month stint as tax exiles. Plant, for one, couldn't wait to get back home. Talking to *Rolling Stone* back in February, he'd exclaimed: "In four days I should be treading in the Isle of the Blessed. For the first three months, I doubt I shall get out of bed. I owe my old lady quite a bit of backlog, you know."[32]

Given this overall mood in the camp, the band members had a relatively relaxed summer and autumn of 1976. Plant continued to repair his body, but the period was not without its controversies or tragedies. Plant's continual sniping at the British government's tax regime in the past year had irritated a number of people in the music business. The subject of income was red hot at a time when Britain itself was lurching from one currency crisis to another. Plant was not the only high-earner who had left the country for a year for tax reasons and talked about it. Ronnie Wood of The Rolling Stones had done the same thing.

Jethro Tull's Ian Anderson was so incensed by what he perceived as Plant and Wood's inability to grasp the truth

During a carefully managed gap in their tax-exile status, Led Zeppelin played five nights at Earl's Court in London in May 1975.

Overleaf: At Earl's Court, May 1975. "If the audience is vibing you up and you're vibing them," said Jimmy Page, "you can get this gigantic feedback which can become quite magical."

of the situation that he was quoted at length in *NME* on the subject. "Ron Wood suggests he pays 98 percent tax, but he couldn't pay 98 percent tax if he tried. Living in Britain, Ron Wood could pay no more than about 53 percent. And someone should tell Robert Plant that he's wrong. It's really sad that people go around spouting this out in public, because those ridiculous figures just don't exist. You pay 98 percent on non-earned income, but ours is earned income. … I would say that, overall, one can pay between 70 percent and 75 percent of all your income, whether it's earned abroad or in Britain."[33]

Plant had no direct answer to this because Anderson was in command of the facts, but he managed a catty quip when talking to *Melody Maker* at a Bad Company gig at L.A.'s Forum in May (a concert where he and Page made a couple of cameo appearances in the encores). Anderson had said in *NME* that he himself earned net "as much as a bricklayer who works really hard, and that's a lot of money". Plant's retort to *Melody Maker*'s reporter was: "So he only earns as much as a bricklayer, does he? Well, he writes songs like a bricklayer too, as far as I'm concerned."[34] Nobody stopped to ask a bricklayer how he felt about all this.

On a much more serious note, the British press carried the story that on May 14th ex-Yardbirds singer Keith Relf had been found dead in his London flat, a victim of accidental electrocution. He had been practicing guitar, working on songs for his latest band project, when a badly earthed guitar cord accidentally touched a live connection. Relf died from a heart attack. Distressingly, he was found by his eight-year-old son Danny, also in the flat at the time, who had the remarkable presence of mind to ring Relf's sister, Jane. But a rush to hospital in an ambulance was in vain. The gap between Relf's fortunes after the 1968 Yardbirds split and those of the band that Jimmy Page re-fashioned as Led Zeppelin was vast enough to be unbridgeable, both financially and in the popular eye. But Relf's death at the age of 33 was noted with sadness by music fans the world over.

At Earl's Court, May 1975. John Bonham: "I enjoyed those concerts. I thought they were the best shows that we've ever put on in England."

NOBODY'S FAULT BUT MINE

- SONG REMAINS THE SAME FILM RELEASED

- 8TH (SOUNDTRACK) ALBUM RELEASED

- 11TH AMERICAN TOUR

- PLANT'S SON DIES, REST OF TOUR CANCELLED

During the down-time after the release of *Presence* and the completion of interview commitments, Led Zeppelin's manager Peter Grant made some further business changes. He removed Danny Goldberg from the US arm of the band's Swan Song record company and virtually closed the UK operation, moving himself and the label to Montreux, Switzerland.

The band members too were attempting to restore some order to their private affairs, none more so than Jimmy Page. He said later: "It was a case of sorting out a year's problems in, say, a month, and not finding the whole process as simple as that. I mean, suddenly I had time to look around and I became aware of certain people who'd been taking incredible advantage of me in the year I'd been away."[1] Page reunited with Charlotte Martin, the mother of his daughter, but the domestic equation was never balanced for long during this period.

Zeppelin's public profile during the summer of 1976 was fitful, sustained mostly by the varying fortunes of *Presence* in reviews and charts worldwide. But behind the scenes, the band and Peter Grant were readying the long-delayed film *The Song Remains The Same* for an autumn premiere. Predictably enough, the project had not been progressing smoothly.

For a start, director Peter Clifton had been removed the project. For one reason and another, Grant had come to suspect that Clifton, who had been finishing the final mixes in Los Angeles, was living off the band and doing other work as well. Nothing was more likely to enrage him than the thought that someone was attempting to put one over on him financially. Clifton admitted that he had used a Led Zeppelin limo to pick up a print of another of his projects from a Los Angeles film lab, but said there was nothing else to it. At the time Grant chose not to believe him and organised a search of his rooms, suspicions that Clifton had 'stolen' the negative to the Zeppelin film he was still finalising.

"This was the film I had been working on for two-and-a-half years," Clifton said later. "As if I would have stolen it from the Technicolor lab. Could anything be crazier? It was nonsensical. The thing was, it was still my film at that stage because I had complete control of the negative, and they didn't know where the negative was stored. But it was at Technicolor – of course. It was complete paranoia."[2]

Clifton finished the film, added the appropriate credits and delivered it to Grant. Grant did two things in response. First, he organised a search of Clifton's London home for any Zeppelin outtakes while Clifton and his family were away. Second, he changed the film's end titles to reflect his own perspective on who deserved credit on a Led Zeppelin film. Although other details changed, Clifton's name stayed in the film but was eventually left off the posters and the advertising.

Clifton was furious on both counts, but especially about the confiscation of film remnants from his London home. He claimed later he'd created "a present for all the boys after we finished the film. It was all the best of the home-movie footage, which I was going to give to them. I had already given Peter Grant his copy. I had my son present it to his son Warren. So I tried to do the right thing. … We'd gone through all those fights to complete the film and now they'd sent these heavies around to my house. But nothing surprised me at this stage and my conscience was clear. I hadn't done anything wrong. As if I would sell pirated footage of my own film! It was true that they were paranoid about bootlegging, but in my business, if I screwed one pop star I would be out of business."[3]

Grant had his own perspective on all this. When it came to the credits, what he remembered was not the blow-up with Clifton but the tussles with Warner Bros in order to get the titles he wanted, created by the designer of his choice.

Somehow, eventually, sufficient progress was made for all parties to arrange premieres on both sides of the Atlantic. To complete the package, Page and his sound team also finished compiling the soundtrack album to accompany the film. Film and album releases were designed to coincide in the US in October and in the UK in November. This was the fastest follow-up LP in Led Zeppelin's history, released just seven months after *Presence*, although of course the concert-recorded music on the 'new' album was by then three years old.

In a separate development late that May, Bad Company, Swan Song's most lucrative signing after Zeppelin themselves, continued to go from strength to strength (incidentally putting more pressure on manager Grant), while the label's other band, The Pretty Things, broke up after three albums full of good music that had somehow failed to ignite buyers' passions and had consequently sold poorly.

In September 1976, *Melody Maker* published its annual readers' poll, revealing the extent to which live gigs had an influence on a group's placings. Top band in the UK and International sections was Yes, with Jon Anderson winning top British singer, while Robert Plant won the International section. Led Zeppelin came second to Yes in both band sections, while Jimmy Page came second to Steve Howe in the guitarist poll. Bonham likewise was second to ELP's Carl Palmer in the drummers' stakes.

That same month, Page and Bonham had some fun together in a Montreux studio. Using some fine solo drumming from Bonham as a basis, Page added synthesiser and studio effects to complete a diverting cameo, the first time a Led Zeppelin track had been dominated by drums since 1969's 'Moby Dick'. It was earmarked for the album due to follow *Presence*, but intervening events ensured that it was not issued during Bonham's lifetime. Instead it would turn up on 1982's *Coda*. Page gave it the title 'Bonzo's Montreux'.

Page returned to London in late September to find an interview published with film-maker Kenneth Anger that disgorged the story of Anger's film project *Lucifer Rising* into public view. Anger had hit bestseller lists that year with his revelations about old and dead film stars in his book *Hollywood Babylon* and was enjoying his new celebrity status, using it in a series of interviews that summer and into the following year to sink the knife into people he felt had let him down. A favourite subject was the long gestation of *Lucifer Rising*, his film that had been 'in the works' since 1967 and for which he'd asked Page to supply music. Anger was scathing in his comments about Page.

Page, a very private man who did not react well to criticisms of his music, let alone his character and lifestyle, made sure his point of view was represented. Interviewed for *NME* about *The Song Remains The Same* that November, he said to Nick Kent: "I must start by saying that I've lost a hell of a lot of respect for [Anger]. … I just wanted the bloke to finish the bloody film. Its whole history is so absurd anyway. I just assumed it was unfinished because he was such a perfectionist and he's always ended up going over his budgets. All I can say is, Anger's time was all that was needed to finish that film. …. I am totally bemused and really disgusted."[4] Page was right when he said to another journalist that Anger only had words with which to attack him, but Anger alluded in more than one interview that he thought Page was addicted to heroin. Although understandably hurt by the betrayal, Page probably felt it unwise to issue a flat denial.

The Song Remains The Same received its world premiere in New York City on October 20th 1976. The film had been mixed in quadraphonic sound, an early form of surround sound, and had only been booked into theatres with the requisite sound equipment, much to the band's frustration. They had no idea that there was no industry-wide acoustic standard for theatrical sound reproduction.

Peter Clifton was prevailed upon to supervise the sound mix at the premieres in New York and London, but not those in Los Angeles and San Francisco. "The band understood the need for good sound," he said, "but they didn't know how to balance the tracks. I had to mark the projectionist's controls to show where the volume settings were with a Chinagraph pencil. They needed me at the premiere because I was the only one who really understood the magnetic soundtrack system. Jimmy turned up in New York and told the projectionist to turn the sound up to full volume. If that had happened, there would have been terrible phasing on the surround sound and distortion."[5]

Everyone, fans and band alike, seemed happy with the New York premiere. The band were mobbed in their limousine on the way to the Manhattan movie house; *Rolling Stone*'s news column recorded that "a gaggle of kids leaped on the hood and roof, screamed, and generally acted very '64-ish".[6] Page in particular was gratified, after so much work in projection rooms getting the detail right with the technicians, to hear ordinary fans respond to the images and sounds with cheers, applause and laughter.

Reviewers, however, were not so kind. *Rolling Stone*, in the same issue as that news feature, slated the movie, Dave Marsh writing: "*The Song Remains The Same* isn't the landmark in Rock cinema Led Zeppelin would like it to be. In fact, it's barely a movie at all, just some concert footage interspersed with trick photography (in a fantasy sequence devoted to each member). This technique is supposed to unify the best qualities of *A Hard Day's Night* and *Gimme Shelter*, but it doesn't work; there is none of The Beatles' wit, and the horror is phoney. … It is hard to think of another major rock act making a film so guileless and revealing. Far from a monument to Zep's stardom, *The Song Remains The Same* is a tribute to their rapaciousness and inconsideration. While Led Zeppelin's music remains worthy of respect (even if their best songs are behind them), their sense of themselves merits only contempt."[7] Unfortunately for the band's sense of self-worth, it wasn't going to get much better than that elsewhere.

Meanwhile at the Los Angeles and San Francisco showings, with Clifton absent, "the sound was absolutely abysmal," tour manager Richard Cole wrote later. "Jimmy was so embarrassed he almost cowered under his seat. 'Why are you putting me through this?' he seethed".[8] There were many such problems to overcome in cinema theatres around the world where the film was shown. It received generally non-committal reviews in much of the music press, had a limited run in theatres, then vanished from sight. Years before the universal transference of films to video or DVD, it had nowhere else to go.

The soundtrack album, a double-vinyl effort with a clever Hipgnosis jacket, went to Number 1 in Britain in November 1976, making two chart-toppers in one year for the band in a year where they did not play a note in front of an audience. In America it rose only as far as Number 2, probably because the year's biggest selling album, Stevie Wonder's *Songs In The Key Of Life*, had been released almost simultaneously.

The album has become an unloved and neglected collection of live Led Zeppelin material, recorded in summer 1973 when they were exhausted at the end of a particularly long tour and puzzlingly devoid of any of the acoustic numbers played that year. It was even left out of the ten-disc Led Zeppelin boxed set of 1993 on the grounds that the CD collection was studio recordings only. The film, meanwhile, was eventually issued on video and then DVD and continues to sell steadily.

But as Page himself has said, it was a soundtrack

album and therefore had to reflect what the cinema audiences were experiencing. It cuts between different Madison Square Garden performances, with various elements patched from one version of a song to another. He didn't regard it as a true representation of the band's live work, having long been in favour of putting together a chronological album of Led Zeppelin concert performances that would have shown the band at each stage of their development.

Perhaps contemporary reviewers missed the distinction Page was trying to make, which is a valid one. Yet there is no way of disguising the fact that Plant's voice was not in best shape on that tour, and that this single fact had ramifications for the entire band's performance as they tried to compensate. At the same time, it would be wrong to write off the entire release as an abject failure. Even with all the caveats, there is some powerful music on the album, and it remains a portrait in sound of a band working very hard indeed to put over its musical message.

As far as the film itself goes, it is perhaps wrong to expect too much of any film about a rock group, especially one commissioned by the band and its management. There has to be a touch of the vanity project, just as there is with more or less every rock video that accompanies most new releases today. It may be that it is better to look for things other than a well-made and insightful glimpse into the workings of a rock band and its support team. What is presented to the public here is an insight into the mentality of the band, just as *Hard Day's Night, Help!* and *Let It Be* were into The Beatles. Any objective view of the film must conclude that it is awkward, overblown and sometimes downright foolish. The intercutting between live footage and band members' fantasies is perfunctory rather than inspired, but then it's difficult to see how the film-makers could have improved this without a complete restructuring and further shooting.

It was perplexing for Zeppelin fans who knew little of the band's interior workings that the film starts with several minutes shot in and around manager Grant's country mansion, portraying him and Richard Cole as 1920s gangsters. Why does a Led Zeppelin film open with a long and dull sequence starring a bunch of people who are unknown to the general public and who only prove they can't act? Why are they pretending to be gangsters? Who are these people and why are they given pride of place in a Led Zeppelin movie?

Such simple questions find no satisfactory answers. The sad truth is that by this time the Led Zeppelin camp had been inward-looking for so long that it had no idea of how it was perceived by the outside world. When it comes to indulging rock stars there is habitually some degree of latitude, as the cult of personality demands: there is a curiosity value attached to celebrities looning around doing anything at all. Or even nothing. But managers and tour managers?

In fact, if the vignettes prove anything at all, it is that none of the band can act adequately in the parts they've allocated for themselves. They all look wooden and camera-conscious, with Plant perhaps the most self-conscious of the four. Perhaps this is because he has gone for a storyline that demands a degree of skill in moving around, showing emotion and generally telling a story to the audience. As with all four of the band's cameos, his is without dialogue and accompanied by music from Madison Square Garden performances. Plant's mini-epic has him single-handedly storming a ruined castle defended by one or two keystone-cop knights in order to rescue a blonde maiden. She looks like she's just stepped out of a Los Angeles nightclub and has the brains to prove it. She might as well have stayed at home.

Page climbs a mount to discover a cloaked man who goes from old age to youth and back (all images of Jimmy Page), then waves things around like a mutant samurai. His sequence has the advantage of brevity and mysticism to protect it from accusations of bombast. Bonham's parade of hot cars, cattle and his family is harmless and takes our minds off 'Moby Dick', while Jones's film of masked men terrorising an 18th-century road and village is nonsensical however you look at it, even as an allegory for Led Zeppelin itself. Who cares? His 'unmasking' at home with his children is so telegraphed as to be a yawn. At least he looks happy to be there.

The best parts of the film are all at Madison Square Garden where there is a real sense of occasion and a febrile atmosphere, from Grant berating security staff backstage to the manoeuvres of gatecrashers as they are chased about. For the onstage sequences, there is an uneasy mix of Garden footage and the Shepperton reshoots, with all the players in the reshoots looking self-conscious and Page in particular hamming it up – something that he doesn't do live because he's normally so focused on making the music happen.

'Dazed And Confused', even interspersed with fantasy footage, is much too long, although there is one fascinating passage where Plant sings a snatch of 'San Francisco (Be Sure To Wear Flowers In Your Hair)'. This is something he did regularly on this tour; the interest comes from what Page, Jones and Bonham are playing behind him. Page plays the minor key, Moorish-tinged secondary guitar pattern from 'Achilles' Last Stand'. As he does so, Jones and Bonham look at each other as if to say, 'Well, what do we do now?' They count themselves in and then play along with him. This was two-and-a-half years before the song would be written in Malibu in late 1975. It is a perfect example of the methods that Page and the band used to compose and evolve their songs.

Jimmy Page in London. "I like change and I like contrast. I don't like being stuck in one situation, day to day. Domesticity and all that isn't really for me."

Although a very flawed film, *The Song Remains The Same* at least confirms that Zeppelin, even at the end of that punishing 1973 tour, was a staggeringly impressive live act. One exposure to the title piece, where the whole band is operating at 100 percent and in full flight, will convince even the most confirmed sceptic.

Unfortunately, in an episode that said as much about the current problems of the band as the film said about its 1973 aspirations, at its New York launch party a drunken Richard Cole picked a fight with *Melody Maker* journalist Chris Charlesworth, a long-time supporter of the band. Cole was thrown out of the party and then taken to task by a very irate Peter Grant. Plant twice apologised to Charlesworth in an effort to make it up to him; Charlesworth graciously accepted the apology and wrote a favourable review of the film. Here was another act of generosity from a bygone media age.

With the frustrations and delays of the film finally behind them and with Plant's physical injuries successfully mending through a programme of training and exercise, it was time to look for the best way to pull the band back into its more habitual rhythms of life. As usual, Grant was keen for them to tour, and this time, after the long lay-off, there were no dissenting voices. Planned properly, it seemed, even a long tour could be the right project for everyone.

It would be essential to work some pieces from *Presence* into the live set: this had happened every time a new album had been released in the past and there was no reason to change that pattern now. Songs like 'Achilles' Last Stand' and 'Nobody's Fault But Mine' would work superbly in concert, but 'Achilles' certainly needed rehearsing in order to arrange a workable live version. During November and December 1976 rehearsals were called and the band got back into the groove, playing sets together again while Plant rebuilt his stamina and confidence. Rehearsing at Emerson Lake & Palmer's studio in Fulham, west London, they had a number of old friends drop in. Steve Marriott was a vocalist whom Plant admired deeply, citing him as the "master of contemporary white blues", and he came to more than one of these sessions. Plant said later: "The two of us singing Muddy Waters songs was almost as hair-raising as our first gig."[9]

The band also had the opportunity to check out some of the younger bands coming through at the time. Plant saw The Sex Pistols at The Roxy in central London, Johnny Rotten mocking him from the stage for his pains. They saw The Damned at the same club. That same December The Damned had released their debut 45, 'New Rose', the first British punk single. Plant and Page in particular were impressed by the band's energy and edge when the four went to see them, also at The Roxy. Again, the admiration was not reciprocated.

Over the next year, Zeppelin would become a prime target of British punks such as the Sex Pistols, The Clash, and The Stranglers, all of whom saw them as easy meat, a living example of the perversion of the hippie dream through rock'n'roll excess and too much money. They were undoubtedly purveyors of rock'n'roll decadence who had more money than they knew what to do with. But as Plant said in February 1977: "If I and the rest of the band didn't honestly feel that there was something to achieve, we'd stay at home. You have to understand, it now goes far beyond how much one can gross on the gate. The bread doesn't come into it any more. Never mind the prissy things – that's something *Presence* taught us. No matter what some people may think, we still care enough to go plonking off around the world again."[10] They remained good musicians committed to their careers who, when they came together as Led Zeppelin, were still capable of commanding the top of the heap.

The 1977 US tour was planned for 51 dates, seven months and 30 cities. It was a sell-out before it even began, the organisers confidently expecting over 1,250,000 fans to attend. The band were expected to gross $10 million. It was originally scheduled to kick off at the end of February 1977, but Plant developed a sore throat, necessitating a re-scheduling. It must have seemed that his various infirmities would prevent the band from ever getting back onstage again. This had an unsettling effect on the entire band, but especially Page, who said: "When all the equipment came over [to America], we had done our rehearsals, and we were really on top, really in tip-top form. Then Robert caught laryngitis and we had to postpone a lot of dates and reshuffle them, and I didn't touch a guitar for five weeks. I got a bit panicky about that – after two years off the road that's a lot to think about."[11]

The tour, developing from the shape of the 1975 jaunt, was now split into three legs: the first would devour April 1977; the second would start in mid May and run until late June; the third was scheduled to run from mid July until mid August. This meant five months on the road with two extended breaks. When it came to getting the machinery up and running – someone with a bizarre sense of humour had put the opening concert in Dallas, Texas, on April 1st, All Fools' Day – the spirit was willing but the flesh weak. There were the usual catalogue of problems and negotiations to go through, but Grant, for one, was no longer inclined to deal with these matters as efficiently as before. Faced with his own escalating drug use and his impending divorce case, he had withdrawn from his role as the good-humoured cement that kept all the component parts of the band and the tours. Instead he relied on people such as tour manager Richard Cole and his attorney Steve Weiss to iron out difficulties as they arose.

Cole, although in poor shape himself as his heroin habit mushroomed, was aware that even before the tour got properly underway its dimensions were somehow wrong. "The Zeppelin entourage," he claimed, "had grown to ridiculous numbers, which was one of our problems during that spring and summer tour. Each band-member travelled with his own personal assistant: Dennis Sheehan, a roadie for Maggie Bell, joined us as Robert's assistant; Dave Northover, a pharmaciest and a rugby player, helped John Paul; Rex King, who had one of the meanest left hooks in England, came on board to keep an eye on Bonzo; and Rick Hobbs, Jimmy's chauffeur and butler in London, worked with him. I even had an assistant, Mitchell Fox, who came out of our New York office, and Peter had help from Johnny Bindon. ... Cliques were formed, and a very tight organisation became fragmented."12

Some of this was due to the increasing number of death threats and other random hints of violence against the band that had been an everyday part of touring with Led Zeppelin since 1973. But there was no doubt that the inward-looking paranoia within the band's entourage had grown too big to handle, with corresponding mistakes being made about systems and personnel.

The fact that Cole hired John Bindon, a London thug who had served time for murder, and that Peter Grant sanctioned such a move, spoke for itself. John Paul Jones saw these growing personal fiefdoms from another perspective, although he agreed that matters had deteriorated. But Cole was part of the problem, he said. "Things were getting a little crazy with Richard Cole and the likes of John Bindon. He was actually a nice bloke in the daytime, but at night just went crazy. I just avoided it all because I disliked all that violence stuff. I knew Robert never liked it and Jimmy was not around much on that tour. In fact Robert and I used to go out walking a lot to try and get a day-time existence."13 This could be seen as avoiding responsibility, but was there a realistic chance of Plant and Jones rehabilitating the Zeppelin operation while out on the road? It would have pulled the band apart, which was the last thing anyone wanted at that time. It should have been dealt with prior to the start of the tour but the opportunity had been missed. Now, the problem was not about to simply go away of its own accord.

Another more oblique symbol of the shift from hubris to downfall came when the touring party had to forgo the pleasures of the *Starship* aircraft they'd used for the previous two US tours. One of its engines had fallen off. Instead, they had to settle for a Boeing 707 owned by Caesar's Palace and modestly called *Caesar's Chariot*. Somehow the associations of that name seemed to fit Zeppelin's place in the scheme of things now.

The first leg of the band's 11th American tour, in April 1977, concentrated on the South and the rust belt. The set-list changed from gig to gig, but it normally included 'The Song Remains The Same', 'The Rover', 'Nobody's Fault But Mine', 'In My Time Of Dying', 'The

Star Spangled Banner'/'Achilles' Last Stand', 'Over The Hills And Far Away', 'White Summer'/'Black Mountain Side', 'Kashmir', 'Ten Years Gone', 'Battle Of Evermore', 'Going To California', 'Bron-Y-Aur Stomp', 'Black Country Woman', 'No Quarter', 'Sick Again', and 'Whole Lotta Love'. With such a repertoire, it was normal for the concerts to last three hours – just as they had back in 1973. There was often a pause around the half-way point to give the band and audiences time to regroup and refresh themselves. As before, there was a gigantic light-show, while the stage set became progressively more elaborate, as did Page's stage-wear.

At the opening Dallas concert, with Page self-confessedly panicky about his lack of practice, Plant was petrified about getting through the evening in one piece. He told *Melody Maker*: "For the first one or two gigs I was really measuring every move I made, to find if I'd gone too far or whatever. ... Ten minutes before I walked up those steps in Dallas I was cold with fright. Supposing I couldn't move around the stage properly? Because my right foot is permanently enlarged now. Well, it was killing for the first two gigs. I had to be virtually carried back on one foot. But once I'd got used to the concussive knocks of stage work it was OK, and now I've paced myself so I can work without anyone, hopefully, knowing I now have this thing to live with."14

The band had reinstated the acoustic set that had been a feature of previous tours, and for the first time they introduced 'The Battle Of Evermore', with Sandy Denny's vocal lines sung by John Paul Jones. Jones was using a triple-necked guitar designed for him by guitar-maker Andy Manson, incorporating mandolin, six-string and 12-string necks. He also used his Alembic eight-string bass on numbers like 'Achilles' Last Stand', an idea that had come from the original *Presence* recording sessions.

The opening dates on the tour were not only problematic for Plant. On the second Chicago date, Page collapsed onstage with severe stomach cramps. The concert had to be abandoned and the following night cancelled. It was officially announced as food poisoning, but Page's health had been fragile for some time, making him susceptible to a range of potential ailments.

Just their luck that *Rolling Stone* sent someone along to review the band this early on the tour when they had yet to get into their stride. In a throwback to the bad old days when the magazine interpreted anything Zep did in a negative light, writer John Millward was not kind. After comparing the band to a dragon, he described "bone-thin" Page as "at the heart of the beast" and Bonham and Jones as "the clumsiest rhythm section in rock". Plant was "a curly-locked, aristocratic peasant".

Having dismissed the other three members and set Page up for the unkindest cut, Millward didn't hesitate to deliver it. "Page's most inspiring trick on record is

restraint; his most famous solo, the blistering flurry that erupts in the middle of 'Whole Lotta Love', is 15 seconds long. In concert, with the three instrumentalists playing at sound levels just below the threshold of pain, such restraint is thrown out the window." After dismissing even Page's acoustic playing – it contained "particularly sloppy lapses" – Millward added: "Jimmy Page has kept the Zeppelin flying with bona fide metal classics – 'Kashmir' and 'Achilles' Last Stand' in particular – and it's these tunes that enliven the latter part of their set. These songs rampage like the dragon, sending thunderbolts of electricity out to a crowd that'll always be hungry for more. ... If Zep's show illustrates that mechanical foreplay can satisfy the mass audience, Page's grimacing climax makes the whole spectacle worthwhile." Considering that Page collapsed during this concert, one wonders if the reviewer had stuck it out to the end, especially when he writes of Page "partying onstage" during his solos.

The band soldiered on, slowly moving towards top gear. According to Plant, a fair number of the audience who had never seen the band live before and who had come attracted purely by their reputation were perplexed by the acoustic set the band continued to play. "They didn't know what the hell was going on. Kept looking at us, presumably thinking: 'Are they really that old?' ... Suddenly it burst through after six gigs, so that by the time we got to places like St Louis it had taken on another level of control, rather than merely trotting out the old favourites."15

Plant was obliquely referring to the major shifts in American rock that had taken place since the last Zeppelin tour. A softer option had emerged in the hands of Boz Scaggs, Peter Frampton, Bruce Springsteen, and the reborn Fleetwood Mac, who now featured Lindsey Buckingham and Stevie Nicks. While their 'Rhiannon' single of April 1976 had pointed the way, Fleetwood Mac's new album, *Rumours*, had been launched by their first Number 1 single, 'Dreams', in the very month of the first leg of this current Zeppelin tour.

Fleetwood Mac had been around as long as Led Zeppelin, if not longer, but an almost constant turnover of personnel at least kept the front line young and fresh in the eyes of late-arriving generations of teenagers. Zeppelin, with exactly the same personnel they'd started out with nine years earlier, were visibly of another generation by 1977, and either revered or scorned for that – depending on each fan's point of view. In America this was not so much a problem: you just had to go out there and prove to the kids that you could still deliver the goods as you always had done. After all, it's all showbiz, as Mr Lennon said.

In Britain, however, the generational divide had

become entangled in the fashion and politics of the day, where the emerging punk movement was taking all the favourite middle-class intelligentsia ideas of alienation, boredom and deep political cynicism and applying it to working-class lives. They were also mixing these notions with such timeless teenage weapons as ageism, a delight in obscenity and extreme fashions, all in an effort to upset the status quo. Of course, many of the most extreme ideas were given birth to and articulated by middle-class kids slumming it with their working-class mates in bands, writing for magazines or hanging out down the pub – but no one was going to own up to that at the time.

Contrary to the propaganda of the day that many continue to believe, the cutting edge of British rock barely touched Zeppelin at the time, in large part because the band were not playing in the country in 1977 and in fact hadn't played there since 1975, two years before punk made its mark in Britain. It is also true that punk was happening mostly far away from the private lives of Led Zeppelin. Speaking of another context, Swan Song director Alan Callan said: "In previous generations, people who accumulated wealth bought land. What came with the land was a community. When you are a rock star or a businessman you buy isolation, you don't buy community. There used to be a whole feudal system that bought stability. When you are a rock star ... you own a great manor but nobody is allowed to knock on the front door."16 That also applied to being out on tour, especially in the paranoid state of the Led Zeppelin entourage out on the 1977 US tour.

The band's concert in Cincinnati on April 20th – their second successive night there – confirmed that the band was as big a draw as ever, if not bigger, anywhere they cared to play in America. Over 1,000 fans tried to force their way into the already full Riverfront Stadium without tickets. Police made 100 arrests outside.

At this and the following concerts in Atlanta, Louisville and Cleveland, John Paul Jones played a bigger part in 'No Quarter' and the song's length began to increase correspondingly. This was not a typical Zeppelin crowd-pleaser, but a piece that invited fans to listen carefully and become absorbed in the atmosphere, as well as Jones's keyboard improvisations. The following night, the band broke its own attendance record at the Silverdome in Pontiac, Michigan, drawing a crowd of over 76,000 and clearing more than $790,000 gross at the gate. Even then, Jones later recalled that the atmosphere was not a happy one, with the crowd too far away in the dark and cold of the evening for the band to really be able to feel their response.

With that achievement under their collective belt, the band took a break of just over two weeks, with Jones, Bonham and Plant heading back to Britain for a spot of recuperation and time with their families. Page, however, was feeling restless. Spurred by a television programme

Robert Plant at the start of 1977. A personal catastrophe in July would turn it into the worst year of his life.

he'd been watching, he decided to act on a desire he'd had for some time to see Egypt. Cairo was one of Aleister Crowley's old haunts, and for that reason alone Page had long wanted to check it out. Now he had the time and the impulse. The guitarist was in a fragile physical condition throughout this period. The band even had a physician along for the tour to keep a watch on him and the recovering Plant in particular. Happily, he came through the Egypt visit unscathed and newly enthused.

As the second leg of this 11th US tour started in mid May 1977, Page continued to fret about his own performance. He said in June: "I'm still only warming up; I still can't co-ordinate a lot of the things I need to be doing."[17] Nonetheless, the band began the concerts in Birmingham and Baton Rouge at a higher level of energy than on the opening dates. They were more confident in their set and their physical ability to keep it together for the tour's length.

They were already looking into the future. In a long interview with Ray Coleman at the end of May, Plant jokingly referred to a general consensus within the band that they would like to have a go at sessions for a new album "in the autumn". Plant talked about the balance they were striking onstage for the fans. "It's got to be tight but loose. That's probably the title of the next album."[18]

They were certainly tight but loose in Houston and Fort Worth, Texas, where they crossed paths briefly with their record label stablemates, Bad Company. In Houston they brought Bad Company guitarist and old mate Mick Ralphs on to join them during an encore, playing Jerry Lee Lewis's old chestnut 'It'll Be Me'. In Fort Worth they contented themselves with joining forces to wreak havoc and devastation on the local hotel they shared.

Four consecutive nights in Landover, Maryland, close to Washington DC, continued to rack up new attendance records. The fans remained appreciative, with Plant in such good spirits by the final night that he burst into a few lines of the old Elvis Presley hit 'Surrender', a song the band knew well. But with the passing of May into June, matters rapidly began to unravel – although the band and management were not entirely aware of it at the time.

In Tampa Bay, Florida, Zeppelin were contracted to deliver two concerts on consecutive days. Since the earliest Zeppelin tours, planning had been meticulous so that when poor weather caused an outdoor concert to be cancelled, there were always 'rain dates' set aside so that fans could use their original tickets to come and see the band under better and safer conditions. Somehow, Zeppelin had signed a contract with Concerts West for the Tampa gig without noticing that there was no rain date and that the band were contracted to play whatever the weather. It was the type of slip that could happen to any hard-pressed organisation, but it was exactly the kind of detail that Grant would never have allowed to slip by when he was on top of everything in earlier years.

His own distractions and black mood had however left Grant vulnerable, and while he could blame others for the initial slip, he could not avoid escaping overall responsibility. He had committed Led Zeppelin to play whether or not it rained, something he had always avoided. Grant had harrowing personal experience of the hazards of mixing water and electricity: he had been the manager of Stone The Crows when their guitarist Les Harvey was electrocuted onstage by just such a mix.

Years later, Grant described the Tampa debacle as "a big mistake. Possibly one of our biggest, and all because we never realised there should be a rain date. It had been dreadfully wet for days in the area with rain like you've never seen."[19] Grant had compounded the mistake by not sending Richard Cole ahead to check the situation on the ground. "If Richard had gone he would have seen they'd set up a canvas roof instead of a metal one, which we always demanded. So when we get to the site there was something like 10,000 gallons of water resting over the drums. So now I have to make a decision about them going on."[20]

Mindful of his contractual obligations and the repercussions should he pull the band out, let alone the reaction of 70,000 expectant fans, and with a break in the weather, Grant reluctantly sent Led Zeppelin on. They lasted three numbers before the heavens opened once more and he waved them off. The crowd, intensely frustrated by this turn of events, reacted violently, as did the local police, who waded in with batons. Unsurprisingly, 60 fans and a number of police ended up in hospital. In the end, the concerts on that day and the following day were cancelled due to the appalling conditions. Grant, expecting to be nailed to the floor by all connected to the disaster, acted promptly to retrieve the situation and the band's reputation for giving value for money by taking out "a double page ad in the *Tampa Times*, or whatever it was, stating that in no way were we to blame and that Concerts West were taking responsibility. ... So no matter what the council said, we were in the clear for all to see."[21]

Glad to escape relatively unscathed, the band flew on to New York City, where no fewer than six straight nights at Madison Square Garden awaited them. The mini-break between a North Carolina gig and Tampa, plus the abandonment of both days at the Florida venue, meant that the band had scrambled a whole week off, giving Plant in particular a chance to rest and recover his voice and constitution.

Zeppelin's 11th US tour was their toughest yet: split into three sections, it ran from April through to August 1977.

Overleaf: "I think people tend to forget the impact of John Bonham," wrote one reviewer. "He was almost knocking people over in the first five rows with his ferocity."

On the first night in New York, Led Zeppelin were in top gear, with the crowd on such an adrenalin rush at first that everyone was carried along on their roars of approval. The set lost some of its urgency with a long 'No Quarter', where the audience was somewhat adrift in Jones's keyboard improvisations. Such things were not usually seen in rock concerts in 1977 unless you were a Yes or ELP fan.

But the acoustic set brought the fans and the band very close together. Plant constantly extended intimacies to the audience with throwaway lines and little gestures acknowledging their presence and enthusiasm. The end of their set included 'Achilles' Last Stand' and a short 'Whole Lotta Love', as well as a 'Star Spangled Banner' that guaranteed the band's acceptance by the New York audience and solid reviews from the critics. Not that they had to worry about filling the Garden for the next five nights: the place was already sold out before they'd played a note on that first evening.

In San Diego on June 19th they returned to another old favourite, 'Heartbreaker', and during the acoustic set broke into 'Mystery Train', made famous by Elvis Presley 20 years earlier. Led Zeppelin then flew to Los Angeles for six nights at The Forum, promoted by Bill Graham who hired his own 200-strong security staff for the event to ward off any crowd trouble or potential nutters. As in New York, some 120,000 people saw the band over the six evenings.

Everything about these concerts was massive – perhaps overly so – as the band aimed for an absolute high at one of their favourite venues. Plant in particular was in excellent spirits onstage after such a long struggle to regain his fitness. Page, however, did not look in good shape. All those around him feared that he would suffer some sort of physical collapse before the tour was out. He had little body weight and was often visibly under the influence of unspecified drugs, although he somehow managed to keep a dividing line between offstage and onstage life. He maintained his musical standards, although sometimes he was not playing with any great inspiration.

Two years earlier Page had talked to Cameron Crowe about his constant battle with the most debilitating effects of being on tour. Crowe had asked what were the possible advantages of lone travel to remote places. "Are you kidding?" said Page. "God, you know what you can gain when you sit down with the Moroccans. As a person and as a musician. That's how you grow. Not by living like this [on tour], ordering up room service in hotels. It's got to be the opposite end of the scale. The balance has got to swing exactly the opposite. To the point where maybe I'll have an instrument and nothing else. …

"I like change and I like contrast. I don't like being stuck in one situation, day to day. Domesticity and all that isn't really for me. Sitting in this hotel for a week is no picnic. That's when the road fever starts and that's when the breakages start."[22]

While they were in Los Angeles for the Forum dates at the end of June 1977, Page gave a long series of interviews to *Trouser Press* journalist Dave Schulps. The writer found the guitarist spectrally thin and often lacking in stamina, but on occasion able to rouse himself and talk enthusiastically about both Zeppelin and other bands around at the time. The last session lasted through most of one night, with Schulps glimpsing the glimmer of dawn from the hotel suite window as they concluded.

"During the course of the interview," Schulps commented, "Page made reference to his original demos and 'instrumental versions' of certain Zeppelin songs. At one point he went and pulled out a box of cassettes which he revealed as those tapes. After the interview ended, Page began illustrating certain points by playing for me a bunch of those tapes, including his original demo of 'Kashmir', featuring just himself and Bonzo. … Still wide awake and peppier than I'd seen him the entire time, [Page] put on his favourite current record."[23] This was The Damned's debut album, *Damned Damned Damned*. According to Schulps, Page then danced around the room as 'New Rose' blasted out from his stereo. Soon afterwards, the journalist crept off to bed, leaving Page to party on.

On the band's third night at The Forum, Who drummer Keith Moon pulled the type of stunt that Bonham had been playing on other bands for years. During Bonham's 'Moby Dick' solo, Moon wandered onstage and joined in on some tympani, to the delight of the boisterous crowd. Egged on by his success, Moon addressed the audience. To head him off, Plant went over and started playing some drums, then Page started up 'Whole Lotta Love' and the band took over once more. However, come the encore, 'Rock And Roll', Moon once again requisitioned the tympani and at the song's end announced he'd be back later in the year "with my own backing group". There were no grudges: Moon went along to the after-concert party with the rest of the band.

For the rest of the season at The Forum the band kept the stage to themselves and delivered more orthodox entertainment, even returning to 'It'll Be Me' for an encore. With those dates completed, the second leg of the tour was brought to a successful end and the band took off once more to Britain for a two-week break with friends and families.

Jimmy Page sometimes used a Gibson double-neck guitar onstage so that he could switch quickly between six-string and 12-string sounds. He is pictured here at the Pontiac Silverdome in Michigan, April 30th 1977.

Overleaf: John Paul Jones uses his Alembic bass onstage during Led Zeppelin's gruelling eleventh American tour.

For the third and final leg of their 11th US tour, Zeppelin flew straight from London to Seattle and settled into their favourite hotel there, the Edgewater Inn, as usual taking over an entire floor. The concert on July 17th, like the subsequent show three days later in Tempe, Arizona, was below par. In Tempe, Bonham was feeling unwell, while Page was hit by a firecracker, killing the atmosphere as well as his equilibrium.

By this time the mood within the Zeppelin camp was not a happy one: most of those involved were openly counting the days until the tour was due to finish in August. Part of the reason was the band's fragile health, especially Page's, while Plant's constitution was taking a pounding and he was often resorted to painkillers to quell the pains in his leg.

There was still a cloud over Grant, whose mood had been bleak and edgy all through the tour. His natural distress at the state of his personal life and the normal tensions of the tour were exacerbated by his own increased drug intake. The resulting ill humour from a normally upbeat man was hard to take on a long tour like this one. A relatively new member of the road crew felt it had a destabilising effect on the backup staff in particular. They were all scared of Grant's temper and so often carried out his demands all too literally. Jeff Ocheltree, one of Bonham's drum technicians at the time, said: "[Grant] was always bad-vibing people and he was just not a very nice person to be involved with, because you never had faith in the consistency of his behaviour. He had too much power and he viewed himself as a tough guy who was taking care of business."[24]

After the Tempe concert, the Zeppelin troupe disgorged itself into San Francisco for two consecutive nights at the Oakland Coliseum. As in Los Angeles earlier, legendary promoter Bill Graham, an early supporter of the band and of The Yardbirds before that, had organised both nights. The July 23rd concert lasted for no less than eight hours, with supporting groups Rick Derringer and Judas Priest warming up the crowd. Led Zeppelin delivered a long set greatly appreciated by their fans but which received less than glowing reviews in the local press. Critics found them a little self-indulgent. Nothing new there, then. But that was nothing to what was happening backstage while the band played on.

There was an incident relating to the removal by Peter Grant's son Warren of a wooden 'Led Zeppelin' door-sign from the band's portable dressing room. Witnesses from the Zeppelin party and promoter Bill Graham would recall different versions of the events, but the pivotal action concerned a severe beating for Graham security guard Jim Matzorkis involving John Bonham, Peter Grant, Richard Cole and Zep strong-arm man John Bindon.

After the assault the guard needed hospitalisation while two further casualties on Graham's team had bruises to tend. Apart from frayed tempers and damaged egos, the Zeppelin team were none the worse for wear. When the concert concluded, the Zeppelin party left for their hotels, passing up Graham's earlier invitation to attend an after-concert party. They figured they wouldn't be too welcome.

They were right. Bill Graham managed to contain his anger sufficiently to allow the band to complete their second (very subdued) concert the following night, July 24th. Apparently Page sat on a chair for much of the concert in reaction to the bad feeling backstage, presumably on the principle of 'don't get mad, get even'. But the atmosphere was gruelling. The band made their way to and from the Coliseum under heavy armed escort and no one from either side spoke to each other.

The next day, police arrived at the band's hotel and arrested Bonham, Grant, Bindon, and Cole on assault and battery charges, instigated by Graham. The promoter later recalled: "I watched those guys walk through with their hands cuffed behind their backs. That was worth everything. I saw them with their heads bowed down and their tails between their legs. As far as I was concerned every one of those guys in the band was accountable for that shit, because they allowed it to go on. And we weren't the only ones it happened to. We were just the last ones."[25]

They were taken to the precinct jail where attorney Steve Weiss had them released on bail a few hours later. Within hours the Led Zeppelin party had left San Francisco under a cloud; some of them headed for New Orleans, the location of the next concert, while others took a brief break in California. They didn't know it at the time, but those two unhappy nights in Oakland would be the band's last live dates in America.

A day later, three Graham employees brought a $2 million civil suit against the four men. Instantly, the assault was all over the US papers and made headlines back in Britain. This was sensational even in the decadent and debauched world of stadium rock, and no press hound was going to shy away from the story. It did untold damage to the band's image in America, for it was impossible to disassociate the band members from the violence when their own drummer had been cited in the legal action.

On July 26th the full entourage arrived in New Orleans and began to ready themselves for the concert in the city on the 30th; the third leg of the tour was just over a week old. While the band members were still sorting their things out in the hotel foyer, Plant received a call from his wife in England. He took it in his room. Some minutes later he came to Cole's room and told him that his five-year-old son Karac was near death. He had a

Robert Plant enjoying Madison Square Garden, June 10th 1977. "The bread doesn't come into it any more," he said.

respiratory infection that had not responded to emergency treatment. Two agonising hours later, Maureen Plant phoned again to tell him that his son had died. At that moment the tour was at an end.

Cole somehow organised flights for Plant, Bonham and himself on the next available plane to London, while Grant stayed behind to deal with the inevitable fall-out from having to close down the tour. Of all the things that can happen to a loving parent, the premature death of a child is perhaps the hardest to bear, and it would be a long time before Plant and his immediate family even began to come to terms with the loss of Karac Plant. The singer's own father was tracked down by *The Daily Express* for comment soon after he had collected Robert from the airport. "All this success and fame, what is it worth?" he said. "It doesn't mean very much when you compare it to the love of a family. Karac was the apple of my son's eye. He was a strong child, mischievous, bright and full of life. He had never been ill before. His death seems so unreal and so unnecessary."[26]

Many years later, Plant took a similar view. "After losing my son, I found that the excesses that surrounded Led Zeppelin were such that nobody knew where the actual axis of all this stuff was. Everybody was insular, developing their own world. The band had gone through two or three really big – huge – changes: changes that actually wrecked it before it was born again. The whole beauty and lightness of 1970 had turned into a sort of neurosis."[27] Of the three hammer blows on that tour – rained-off Tampa, the fights in Oakland, now this – Plant's loss of his son was by far the heaviest. Its consequences would last at least as long as the band.

Richard Cole, who had come back with Plant, commented on the pain he saw Plant suffering on the journey. "This 1977 tour had been so full of turmoil and hostility. The band members had drifted as far apart as they ever had on a tour. There was constant tension. There were arguments and anger. Nevertheless, when a real crisis like this one struck, it deeply affected all of us. All the disagreements and dissension that had seemed so

important over the past few weeks had suddenly become very insignificant."[28]

The death of his son caused Plant to question everything, not least his continuing involvement in Led Zeppelin. At such an exposed time, it is all too easy to make a false move, either through ignorance or stress. For a variety of reasons, Grant, Page and Jones did not make it back to Britain for Karac Plant's funeral later in the week. Cole and Bonham attended alongside a shattered Plant family. Cole claimed later that the absences cut Plant to the quick. According to Cole, Plant, back at his farm after the funeral, told him and Bonham: "Maybe they don't have as much respect for me as I do for them. Maybe they're not the friends I thought they were."[29] Plant had to wrestle with such thoughts, along with his family's bereavement, over the coming months.

The US tour was finally abandoned officially in mid August 1977. Plant and his family withdrew into mourning. Bonham had an accident in his Jensen car in early September, breaking two ribs. Then nothing. Nothing but rumours, because there was nothing to report.

Meanwhile, in an especially awful autumn for rock'n'roll around the world, Elvis Presley and Marc Bolan died: Elvis through a lethal combination of prescription and non-prescription drugs at Graceland, his home in Memphis; Bolan in a car accident when the Mini his girlfriend Gloria Jones was driving left the road and hit a tree on Barnes Common, less than a mile from Olympic studios, in west London. An especially touching tribute to Bolan came from The Damned, the punk band whom Bolan had hired as a support on his last British tour and encouraged along the way.

A troubled concert at the Oakland Coliseum, California, in July 1977.

Overleaf: Jimmy Page's guitars backstage, July 1977: two Martin acoustics, three Gibson Les Pauls, a Danelectro, a Fender Telecaster, and a Gibson double-neck.

OUT THROUGH THE IN DOOR

- CLEARWELL RECONVENING

- SESSIONS IN STOCKHOLM FOR 9TH ALBUM

- KNEBWORTH FESTIVAL LIVE COMEBACK

- 9TH ALBUM, IN THROUGH THE OUT DOOR, RELEASED

- 5TH EUROPEAN TOUR

- BONHAM DIES

- LED ZEPPELIN DISBAND

By November 1977 Jimmy Page was becoming exasperated at the number of times he had to deny that Led Zeppelin were breaking up. During an interview for *Melody Maker* Chris Welch asked the inevitable question. Page replied: "Definitely not! I've got to say to you right now there are areas that are bloody touchy. You see, I've never known a family to have such bad luck as Robert's, and it's really awful."[1]

Page, along with the rest of Led Zeppelin, was by then aware that Plant needed as much space and time as possible if he and his family were to overcome the tragedy of his son's death. At the same time, this meant that the incessantly active Page had nothing much on which to concentrate his energies. He had recently completed 15 years' work in putting a studio into his home. He talked to Welch about finally starting a project he'd long fancied, compiling a chronological live album from all the concert tapes the band had amassed over the years.

He also talked about the next studio album for the band. "I'm preparing material for the new LP, which I'll pace along with the live stuff. But I'd like the new album out first. I think I've spoken to you before about a long piece I'd written which was to have gone on *Presence*. I had it all planned out and arranged, but it was too dangerous to rely on because of the time factor. I knew how much time would be needed for the overdubs, and it wasn't the sort of thing John Paul Jones and I could do together. … It's basically an instrumental. The original idea was to have four sections for the vocals, coming back to the same theme each time. But there would be four separate melody lines dealing with the four seasons."[2]

This was the same idea that he'd described when planning sessions for *Physical Graffiti*, and perhaps even relates to long solo pieces he'd mapped out years before that. But he'd hit a huge wall. On the way back from America he'd lost a briefcase of cassettes that was brought through customs by someone else. The demos he'd made of the long piece were in that case and all were lost. The absence of a long track on the next Zeppelin album suggests that he never reconstructed it or that he lost interest due to a number of factors – including, according to Richard Cole's suspicions, an increasing involvement with heroin.

But that didn't mean that Page was not his usual inquisitive self about what was going on around him. He was already experimenting with a guitar synthesiser that would appear on the next Zeppelin album. He also revealed a detailed knowledge of the flourishing British punk/new-wave scene, claiming that The Damned were "a knockout".

He said: "They were the best initiation one could have had. So powerful and tight. Exactly what rock'n'roll is all about: sheer adrenaline music. I think that new wave is the most important thing that's happened since Hendrix."[3] Page went on to praise XTC as well, and The Sex Pistols, saying that "a couple of [Pistols] tracks are really great" although he didn't enjoy the band's negativity.

Ironically, given their stricken position, Led Zeppelin came top of many of the end-of-year readers' polls on both sides of the Atlantic. The 1977 tour and the attendant publicity had pushed them right back into the spotlight. It would seem that nothing could break the bond between the band and its long-term fans, but the new year of 1978 brought perhaps the quietest period in Led Zeppelin's ten-year career. There was little to do but wait for Plant and his family to adjust to their bereavement.

Away from the music, in February the federal case brought against Grant, Cole, Bonham and Bindon by Bill Graham's disgruntled employees was heard in the defendants' absence. They entered a plea of nolo contendere, meaning that a defendant does not admit guilt but accepts conviction, and can deny the charges in any separate case. The result was suspended prison sentences ranging from 12 months to two years each, plus nominal fines of under $1,000. Crucially, from Grant and his team's point of view, the plea left them able to defend themselves in any subsequent civil suit. Graham, intent on putting them all behind bars, was incensed, but there was nothing more he could do about that. The civil suit would drag on for another year or more before being settled. Meanwhile, Grant's health had suffered from the batterings of the previous two years. With a worsening diabetic condition and continual drug and alcohol abuse, he had a heart scare and ceased all business for a time in order to recuperate.

Plant was coming to terms with a new set of priorities. "Losing one's child is the bitterest pill to take," he said years later. "I tried to pick myself up and, as I did so slowly, I realised my family was more important than the luxurious life I'd been living in Led Zeppelin."[4] Plant said that since the day of his son's death he had rejected drugs altogether, although he still enjoyed a drink.

There was no collective band activity and little communication with Plant during the winter and early spring months of 1978, although Plant's oldest friend in the band, John Bonham, did maintain regular contact. Decades later, Plant revealed that he "really didn't want to go back" to the band.[5] He also claimed that Bonham was "the only guy that actually hugged me, that helped me at all".[6] Peter Grant said later that he regularly checked with the singer to see if he wanted to return. Grant felt it was "more a case of convincing him. After what he had gone through in losing his son during that last tour, I don't know how the man managed to hold everything together. But he did, and he came through with flying colours".[7]

By the end of April, Bonham and Grant felt that Plant was perhaps ready to meet the other two band members face to face. Grant called a meeting between them all with the idea of having them play together at Clearwell Castle, in the Forest of Dean near the English/Welsh border. Grant said: "That was after a long uphill battle to get him to work again. Robert kept saying he'd do it and then back down. But Bonzo was a tower of strength. We had a meeting at the Royal Garden Hotel [in London] and they started talking about Bad Company and Maggie [Bell] and all that, with their Swan Song hats on, and I said: 'What the fuck are you talking about? You should worry about your own careers.' So I suggested Clearwell, because Bad Company had been [there]. So Robert says he'd just like to do some jamming, so that's what they did."[8]

Although some observers have claimed that this reunion was a decisive and triumphant reaffirmation of the band's ability to come together and create great music again, Jones later begged to differ. "Getting back together at Clearwell was a bit odd. I didn't really feel comfortable. I remember asking: 'Why are we doing this?' We were not in good shape mentally or health-wise … but it wasn't easy to do much about. Perhaps nobody was strong enough to stop it – including our manager, who wasn't that well himself anyway. In the end it was like, 'Let's get through this and get back onstage.' … Around that time I did get closer to Robert. It's not that we didn't have a laugh at Clearwell, it just wasn't going anywhere." [9] Plant felt similarly, saying: "I felt quite remote from the whole thing. … I wasn't comfortable with the group at all. We'd gone right through the hoop and, because my hoop was on fire, I didn't know if it was worth it any more."[10]

This rather aimless gathering ended with options open for Plant. Sensibly, he paced himself, jamming from time to time through the summer with old friends and colleagues from the pre-Zeppelin days, testing his desire to go back to playing and singing professionally again. But months would pass before the time was right for new music.

The band lived separate lives through the summer of 1978 and on into September, when they briefly reconvened socially for Richard Cole's second marriage ceremony, at which Page was best man. Tragically, one of the band's hell-raising pals, Keith Moon, had died just the week before after launching himself into a clean-up, ceasing his binge-drinking and taking a substitute drug instead. An overdose of that drug had killed him.

Meanwhile, in an effort to keep busy and stay in touch with the larger music world, Bonham and Jones accepted Paul McCartney's invitation to appear in a Rockestra session at Abbey Road studio in October along with stars such as Denny Laine, David Gilmour, Hank Marvin, Pete Townshend, Gary Brooker, Kenney Jones, and Ronnie Lane. Two pieces were recorded, neither of them McCartney's finest moment, even if they were great fun for all participants: 'Rockestra Theme' sounds like a gigantic instrumental singalong while 'So Glad To See You Here' is simply one of McCartney's Wings-style rockers with lots of people playing on it.

In November 1978 Plant felt sufficiently recovered from the loss of his son to be able to concentrate properly on music again. He was ready to resume serious rehearsals with the band with a view to making a new record. In the intervening period of the band's inactivity there had been considerable change on the British rock scene, with the first wave of punk bands mostly running into the sands of internal discord and disputes with record companies and managers. Both The Sex Pistols and The Damned had broken with record labels and with themselves, while The Clash and The Stranglers carried on as a second wave of three-chord bruisers arrived, spearheaded by Sham 69.

But the revolution was running down. Few of these bands managed to achieve a real and sustained popular breakthrough, although Ian Dury and Elvis Costello – neither of them mainstream punks anyway – were two honourable exceptions. To the horror of the new generation of writers on *NME* and *Melody Maker* who had wholeheartedly embraced the new wave and punk bands, the UK charts were now dominated by disco hits and film soundtracks. During the whole of 1978, only The Boomtown Rats of the new groups managed a Number 1 single, with 'Rat Trap'. Other occupants in the top spot included singles from *Grease* sung by Olivia Newton-John and John Travolta (16 weeks combined), Boney M (nine weeks), Abba, and The Bee Gees.

In the British album charts, while Abba and Boney M managed a combined 11 weeks at the top, the soundtrack to *Saturday Night Fever* racked up 18 straight weeks at Number 1 from May to September, while the *Grease* soundtrack took a 13-week block-booking at the top from October through to the new year of 1979. There may be lies, damned lies and statistics, but it's difficult to argue at this distance that in 1978 the surviving punk and new-wave acts of the day were exciting more than the faithful and the already converted. Thus the real popular challenge to Led Zeppelin's ascendancy in Britain was disco and its pop culture offshoots.

When it came time to move on from rehearsals in London to a recording studio, in November the band accepted an invitation to make the new LP at Abba's studio in Stockholm. Abba had moved on from in-joke winners of the Eurovision Song Contest for Sweden in 1974 with their dipsy ditty 'Waterloo' to become a popular-music phenomenon, at one point challenging Volvo as the single largest Swedish company in terms of turnover. Abba, signed to Atlantic in America in 1974, had four top ten hits in the USA from then until 1980 but never managed the blanket domination of the US charts that they achieved in virtually every other pop-loving nation on earth in the 1970s.

From an early stage, musicians recognised the high

Overleaf: **Robert Plant battled with grief after his son's death in 1977, and it was only two years later that he began performing concerts again.**

quality of Abba's songwriting and the technical perfection of their productions, as well as the professionalism of the group's singing and playing. Abba may have been kitsch, but they were very high quality kitsch indeed. A man as technically astute as Page would have been well aware of the high production values evident in all Abba recordings made at their Polar studio in Stockholm, so it was only natural he and the rest of the band would have been receptive to the invitation. But there was another, less quoted, reason for the move. Led Zeppelin needed to record the album outside the UK for tax reasons. The Abba invitation happened to coincide. As Grant recalled: "Abba came to us and offered it. It was actually a slog to do it. We used to get the noon flight out on Monday and then return the Friday for the weekend. It was cold and dark all the time."[11]

At that time of the year in Sweden, darkness envelops all but a few fleeting hours in the middle of the day. There was already snow on the ground. So what Grant said was literally true. It was a more extreme version of the conditions when the band had made *Presence* in Munich in the cold of November 1975, three years earlier.

The band stayed at Polar for three weeks, travelling home each weekend as Grant said to see their families and, in the case of Page, maybe to listen to the tapes. Yet on this particular set of sessions Page was not the driving musical force that he had been on every Zeppelin album before. He had not been able to find the basic musical seeds that had always blossomed when he brought them into Led Zeppelin rehearsals in the past. There had been little or no creative dialogue with his regular songwriting partner Plant in the past months and scant creative impetus to give him a clear focus.

Page was, like Richard Cole, still struggling with drug problems that were certainly damaging his health and diminishing his vitality. Much of the time in Stockholm Page was late in arriving at the studio – as was Bonham, for similar reasons. The creative decisions had to be taken by others. Plant and Jones, distressed by the turn of events, at one point buttonholed Cole. "Jimmy, Bonzo, and I were becoming increasingly caught up in the quagmire of drugs," Cole said later, "enough to really anger Robert and John Paul. 'You're one of the people in charge of this operation,' Robert once told me, 'and it makes us nervous to see what's going on. Can't you see what's happening?'"[12] But Cole was struggling to accept the reality of his own situation and was in no position to help or guide Page and Bonham. And as Jones would remind later interviewers, back in the 1970s it was rare for rock musicians to have any recourse to help or counselling.

"For much of the time at those Polar sessions only Robert and I were turning up," said Jones. "There were two distinct camps by then, and we were in the relatively clean one. We'd turn up first, Bonzo would turn up later, and Page might turn up a couple of days later. The thing is, when that situation occurs you either sit around waiting or get down to some playing. So that's what we did in the studio … we made it happen."[13]

Jones and Plant 'made it happen' by putting down keyboards and guide vocals on tape tracks and then adding in the contributions of the others as they showed up. These were trying conditions for all concerned, but Jones enjoyed the added responsibility of creating pieces and, paradoxically, the freedom it gave him. He told one interviewer: "When I was playing keyboards I sort of had control of everything, tonally. If I wanted to change key, it would change key – sometimes inadvertently. … 'Carouselambra' and 'In The Evening' were all keyboards and drums to start with. The guitar was added on, as it were."[14] Grant concurred, saying later that "they were difficult conditions, but Jonesy was great on that. He put in so much effort".[15]

Cole noticed a few niggles. "Jimmy would take the master tapes to his home studio and do all the overdubs over the weekend before he'd fly back Monday morning. … Jimmy always resented the fact that when the writing credits came out, John Paul Jones was on every credit, because he had been working all the time.

"I think Jimmy kind of thought Jonesy was trying to take over as producer, which he wasn't. He was just making use of the time until the other two turned up. The truth of the matter was we never turned up until the middle of the night until we had scored. The other two got there when they were supposed to and just messed around doing stuff."[16]

This was a fundamentally different way of making music together, and it showed. Led Zeppelin had always worked on song ideas collectively, even when the songs in question were relatively fully formed by their writers in advance. Now, Jones and Plant were putting the structures together and recording them even before Bonham and Page had participated. It was taking the band in a different direction and into uncharted waters, asking them to adapt to a new system of creating their music.

"I think all four members had reached a maturity, so the music didn't send the same signals of abandon," Plant said years later. "My joy of life had been cudgelled and bashed so hard, I became a time-and-motion man for my own destiny. I was saying: 'If I go tomorrow, is this where I want to find myself, in a sex club in Stockholm being silly with Benny and Bjorn from Abba, while Agnetha and Frida are driving around trying to find out to which den of iniquity Led Zep has taken their husbands and how big was this guy's dong lying on the circular mattress?' There were some whimsical times. But it was very difficult for me, and I think the others felt it too."[17]

In the long term this change of procedure could have given the band a new life – or might have led to its dissolution through internal power struggles. That was something Led Zeppelin had rarely experienced in the past, when Page was universally acknowledged as its guiding and defining creative spirit. Jones said later: "It was a transitional period. It was a chance to see what else we could do. The next album would have been even more interesting had we followed that direction."[18]

The Polar sessions were completed and the band members returned to Britain just in time for Christmas 1978. In the new year, Robert and Maureen Plant had a baby boy, to their intense delight, and understandably in the months to come were intent on giving the new arrival top priority. At the same time, Page mixed the Stockholm tapes at home in Plumpton Place and put the songs into a running order. In a move that decidedly affected the particular character of the resulting album, he put to one side three tracks that showed the band's more traditional guitar-led rock and blues side. These were 'Ozone Baby', 'Darlene' and 'Wearing And Tearing'. The latter was a Plant favourite for a late spring 1979 single, but that idea came to nothing, in part because Page's idea was to put the three tracks out as a special souvenir EP or single to coincide with future live dates.

When the EP idea also came to nothing, the three tracks were left to gather dust, with the suggestion that they would eventually be given places on a later LP. Shifting tracks forward like this had been standard practice for the band since *Led Zeppelin III*, so there seemed little reason to doubt that this would happen once more. Page said later that plans for the next-but-one Zeppelin LP were by then well in hand and he would once more have guided the band back to its more traditional stylistic bases. "Bonzo and I had already started discussing plans for a hard-driving rock album after that. We both felt that *In Through The Out Door* was a little soft. I wasn't really very keen on 'All Of My Love'. I was a little worried about the chorus. I could just imagine people doing 'the wave' and all of that. And I thought: 'That's not us. That's not us.' In its place it was fine, but I wouldn't have wanted to pursue that direction in the future."[19]

With a full album in the bag and the band spread to their different corners of England, the next challenge was to decide upon the direction for the live work to promote the LP's eventual release, at that time pencilled-in for late spring 1979. There was a considerable difference of opinion. Jones favoured another American tour. Plant was not keen on touring and did not want to play America at all for fear of being too far and too long away from his family. Bonham hated long tours anyway. Page was keen just to get back out in front of an audience. Grant had his own reasons for not wanting an early return to America, where the ramifications of the Oakland incident with Bill Graham's staff were still unresolved. The American music industry at the time was broadly in sympathy with Bill Graham, who loudly proclaimed his position as the innocent party – a position it was hard to contest,

although Page in one interview that year tried to suggest that Graham was as big a bully as Grant.

A tour of Britain or Europe that summer seemed equally inappropriate: nobody was in a position to plan so far ahead, and a tour of the usual British venues was not the headline-making return that Grant was looking for. Eventually they decided to announce their return by a spectacular headlining appearance at a summer festival. Grant felt this would at one stroke put the band back at the top of everyone's agenda and also prove to the band members themselves that they still had something to give as a collective unit.

The Knebworth festival in August 1979 was the obvious choice. After Grant had convinced all four men that this was the right move, he quickly reached a deal with promoter Freddie Bannister. As usual, Grant extracted his own set of terms in order for his band to appear, including an asking price of £1 million. After initial wobbles, Bannister agreed and, in an attempt to meet the anticipated demand and also to give himself a chance to recoup the outlay, set two August dates, the 4th and the 11th.

Within two days of the announcement of the festival line-up around 260,000 tickets had been sold, the majority of them for the first weekend. In time-honoured Zeppelin fashion, *In Through The Out Door* was scheduled to be out in time for Knebworth, but eventually arrived in British stores on August 20th, nine days after the second concert. The new title had beaten Plant's idea of *Tight But Loose*, its original resonance now lost in the changed circumstances. The album had its new name because, Page quipped, that was the hardest way in. Or the hardest route back. There was certainly a return journey ahead of them now.

The band went into intensive rehearsals early in July 1979 in studios close to the village of Bray near Maidenhead, on the Thames to the west of London. The first task was to choose a suitable set. While it would come to closely resemble that used for most of the 1977 American tour, two tunes from the as-yet-unreleased *In Through The Out Door* were rehearsed, 'Hot Dog' and 'In The Evening'. The song chosen as the A-side of the July 12th US single, 'Fool In The Rain' ('Hot Dog' was the B-side), was not rehearsed and not played at Knebworth. The single reached Number 21, making it the best-performing Led Zeppelin single in the US since 'D'yer Mak'er', which had gone just one place better six years earlier, in November 1973.

The band had not played live for two years, so they arranged two warm-up gigs at the Falkoner Centret in Copenhagen, Denmark to clear the cobwebs out of their system and to break in the two new songs onstage. They played the Falconer on July 23rd and 24th 1979 – exactly two years after the Oakland fiasco that had signalled the end of their previous US tour. They played the same set both evenings, apart from the addition of 'Ten Years Gone' on the 24th. Page continued to substitute a solo guitar piece for 'Dazed And Confused', but rather than play 'Star Spangled Banner' to a European audience he delivered an unaccompanied bowed improvisation that served as the introduction to the downbeat, moody new piece 'In The Evening'.

For the Knebworth concerts, out to the north of London in Hertfordshire, Zeppelin had their own sound system and light-show flown over from the States to maintain their accustomed high-quality stage presence. Page and the other musicians visited the site in advance. "We've done a lot of rehearsing and checked things out," he told NME. "We've actually been down there and worked things out relative to the actual site. But then again it's like a natural amphitheatre, so I should imagine it's actually quite a good gig to be at."20

Promoter Bannister tried to keep the Festival line-up over the two weekends as close to identical as possible, and apart from one necessary substitution he managed to pull it off. The acts that appeared at both concerts were Led Zeppelin, Todd Rundgren's Utopia, Southside Johnny & The Asbury Dukes, The New Commander Cody Band, and Chas & Dave. In addition, Fairport Convention appeared on August 4th and The New Barbarians on the 11th. The New Barbarians were a one-off jamming band featuring Ronnie Wood, Keith Richards, Stanley Clarke, Bobby Keyes, Ian McLagan, and Joseph Modeliste.

Apart from Zeppelin, this wasn't the strongest line-up for a 1979 Festival. Page said in an interview straight after Knebworth that at one point he'd been hoping that the line-up would include Dire Straits, Joni Mitchell, and Little Feat, a combination with Led Zeppelin that would have been irresistible. As it was, there not even any of the new wave of 2-tone ska bands from the Midlands who were enjoying a runaway success in the British charts that summer: The Specials, The Beat, and Selecter.

Zeppelin's set on August 4th consisted of 'The Song Remains The Same', 'Celebration Day', 'Black Dog', 'Nobody's Fault But Mine', 'Over The Hills And Far Away', 'Misty Mountain Hop', 'Since I've Been Loving You', 'No Quarter', 'Ten Years Gone', 'Hot Dog', 'The Rain Song', 'Sick Again', 'White Summer'/'Black Mountain Side', 'Kashmir', 'Trampled Under Foot', 'Achilles' Last Stand', 'In The Evening' (preceded by Page's solo), 'Stairway To Heaven', then 'Rock And Roll', 'Whole Lotta Love', and 'Heartbreaker'. There were slight variants on the 11th when 'Ten Years Gone' was dropped, presumably because of technical problems when Jones swapped to his triple-necked guitar. Among the encores, 'Heartbreaker' was dropped in favour of 'Communication Breakdown'.

Plant told an interviewer just before the first show that, this time, the band were not expecting to indulge in the extended soloing and jams that had made their 1977 US tour dates regularly run over three hours. He particularly singled out 'No Quarter' in this respect, although as Jones was near enough to overhear him say this, it was probably a private wind-up between the two of them. Either that, or a case of pre-gig nerves, to which Plant had always been prone. But both nights went off without any major hitches.

The singer himself did not particularly enjoy the experience. Plant said recently: "I was watching it on the DVD and thinking: 'Christ, that was crap. That was a shit gig.' I know how good we had been, and we were so nervous. And yet within it all, my old pal Bonzo was right down in the pocket. And I'd thought he was speeding up on the night – I must have been so nervous myself that every single blemish and twist that was just a little away from what I expected was making me a little bit hyper."21

Plant's nervousness and the experiences of the past few years had fundamentally changed his reactions to his bandmates onstage. Where once he had embraced change and variation on every night they played, now he cringed with surprise and something near hurt. Yet as he said himself: "For all that had gone wrong, if you listen to 'Achilles' Last Stand' from Knebworth, it's absolutely spectacular."22

The set was uneven, with poor cohesion, and Page clearly found it difficult to find consistency as he played with his band onstage for the first time in two years. Yet the highlights were truly exciting, and the selection that appeared on the 2003 DVD set showed that the band had lost none of its power to move and excite.

All four musicians looked different, and not merely older. Jones was dressed in an all-white suit in direct contrast to his early hippie-look jeans and shirt. Bonham had dressed for the work at hand. Plant was dressed in cords and a nicely styled shirt while Page looked almost debonair in tailored trousers and shirt. With such a long lay-off and with only a handful of rehearsals and warm-ups plus some jams with local musician friends in the Midlands, Plant's voice was in particularly good repair. The sound system was excellent and the fans reacted with complete adulation.

Everyone at Knebworth knew this was a major event on the contemporary rock scene and were determined to savour it, even though they knew that the band had yet to return to the quality of their mid-1970s best. Grant said later that "it was a bit rusty". He pointed out, though, that a laser beam effect on Page's bow during his solo piece

Led Zeppelin's appearance at the Knebworth festival in England in August 1979 was their headline-making return to live concerts.

Overleaf: Jimmy Page working hard onstage at Knebworth, August 11th 1979.

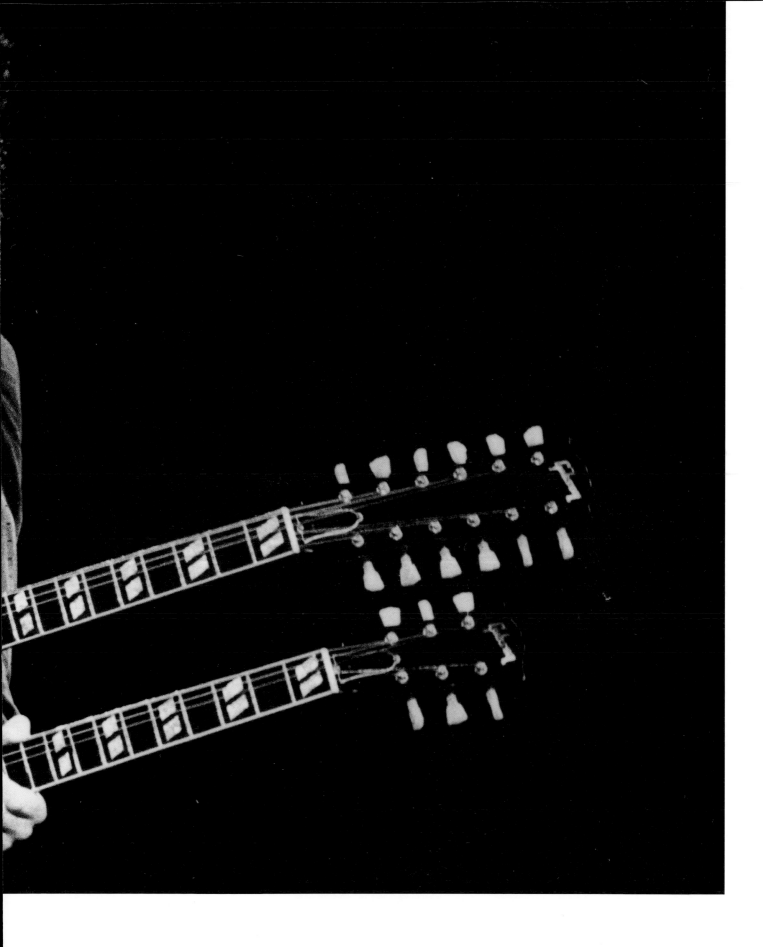

had been rehearsed "for hours". Grant felt "that really was a fantastic moment, watching that at the side of the stage."[23] Richard Cole recalled the entire crowd singing along in harmony with Plant on 'Stairway To Heaven' as an unforgettable experience.

The second weekend saw the band play to a smaller crowd. The audience had grown listless during a long day that had stalled badly just prior to Zeppelin's appearance when Ronnie Wood's all-star jam band had failed to ignite and then outstayed its welcome. All in a day's festival, but not something to best prepare the fans for the final act of the night.

The first concert had drawn a crowd officially counted at 140,000 (Grant had claimed 200,000; the police had said 100,000). The second failed to break into six figures, with Bannister claiming an attendance as low as 40,000 while others put it closer to 80,000. Apparently both the promoter and Grant had overestimated the band's pulling power over two successive weekends, and while the results were disappointing for all involved, Grant suspected Bannister was attempting to invoke an agreement for re-negotiation of Zeppelin's fees if the second night had delivered sub-par receipts.

After a stand-off, Grant and Bannister agreed that Led Zeppelin's manager would collect all gate receipts for the second concert. Bannister later released a statement – published as a full-page ad in a black border in *NME* – claiming: "There have been misconceptions reported in the press concerning Led Zeppelin and Knebworth, which as the concert promoter I would like to clarify. ... Led Zeppelin voluntarily reduced their guarantee by a substantial amount and were willing to accept an alternative arrangement in order to help ensure the best possible concert for the patrons and payment to all concerned, in the event there was insufficient funds to pay everyone. Peter Grant, manager of Led Zeppelin, was particularly concerned that all acts appearing at the concert be paid. Unfortunately, because of a large increase in production and staffing costs and increased VAT amongst other reasons, this substantial reduction by Zeppelin, while very helpful and very much appreciated, was unfortunately not sufficient."[24] Bannister was left with other major bills but not enough money to pay them. His company went into liquidation, making this fifth Knebworth his last.

With Knebworth behind them, the band returned to their private lives and waited to see the reaction to *In Through The Out Door* on its release the following week. As with 1976's *Presence*, it prompted more worldwide praise from reviewers than any of the albums released in their pomp. However, even though the record went to

John Bonham enjoying the band's return to concerts at the Knebworth festival, August 1979. Led Zeppelin had not played live for two years.

Number 1 throughout the world and stayed on the bestseller lists for weeks, it was their weakest studio effort by some distance.

The jacket itself speaks of a confusion of identity and a lack of direction. There were unconscious echoes of Ian Dury & The Blockheads' second LP for Stiff, *Do It Yourself*, released in mid 1979 with a variety of wallpaper designs as the background to a simple sleeve title and track listing. *Out Door*'s inner sleeve was a black-and-white photo of a New Orleans barroom scene. Only it wasn't, because no fewer than six photos were used and put together in assorted combinations that weren't revealed until the purchaser had taken the record home and taken off the brown paper bag that was the record's outside sleeve. Brown paper bag? This was putting into effect Grant's long-standing joke that Led Zeppelin would sell bucket-loads of records even if they were packaged in a brown paper bag. The only concession to retailers' sanity was a small stamp with the name of the band and the album title in one corner. This was exactly what the public bought, and in sufficient quantities to make it a much stronger seller than *Presence*.

In Britain Zep's new album went to Number 1 on September 9th and stayed there for two weeks. It had replaced *The Best Disco Album In The World*, which had been at the top for six weeks over the summer, and in turn was succeeded by Gary Numan's *The Pleasure Principle*, then *Oceans Of Fantasy* by Boney M, and finally Blondie's *Eat To The Beat* and The Police's *Regatta De Blanc*.

In America, the new Zeppelin album performed much more strongly. It arrived at Number 1 in September and stayed there for seven weeks, replacing The Knack's *Meet The Knack* (five weeks at Number 1) and finally replaced itself by The Eagles' *The Long Run*, that year's bestseller and a Number 1 for nine weeks.

In Through The Out Door was a curious collection, reflecting the disunity and confusion in which it was written and recorded. The opening song, 'In The Evening', is the only piece with an overwhelming Page influence in its conception. It starts with a haunting evocation of Eastern sunsets and music, with delicate decorations arising from Page's heavily produced guitar sounds. Then the band enters and a typically forthright guitar riff is marching in step with Bonham's emphatic drum beat. Plant's voice is given a heavy double-tracked effect that emphasises the drama but makes it difficult to disentangle the words, apart from the insistent chorus: "I need your love."

Page used another new technical device on 'Evening'. "There's a Gizmotron on it as well," he said later, referring to a hand-held 'infinite sustain' gadget. "Remember that mechanical device? It's like a hurdy-gurdy type of thing, an electronic wheel. You'd hold it near the bridge and depress whatever strings you wanted. It kind of rolled the strings. Lol Creme of 10cc invented

293

it. I think it never took off and was a financial disaster. I used it on 'Carouselambra' as well."[25]

The bridge of 'Evening' has a beautiful sequence of minor chords underlined by keyboards and etched by guitar multi-tracks. The drama and richness of this piece explain why the band decided to play it at Knebworth. It fits in the tradition of heavy ballads that extends from the first album right through to *Physical Graffiti*. In a nod to a friend and the not too distant past, Page quotes in the out chorus (6:02) an old Eric Clapton riff from 'Outside Woman Blues' on Cream's *Disraeli Gears*.

The follow-up, 'South Bound Saurez', gives Jones an opportunity to show off his Little Richard and Jerry Lee Lewis rock'n'roll piano technique. A slight song, it is nonetheless full of high spirits and hardly intended to be a Zeppelin magnum opus. This is the first indication that the production of the record will largely favour keyboards: Page's guitar is strictly used as back-up. His solo is perfunctory though quite tidy. Plant is completely committed in his vocals and he obviously enjoys playing the role of jiving lover in what amounts to a supercharged pub-band atmosphere.

'Fool In The Rain' again finds Plant in fresher voice than for some years, with little sign of fraying at the edges. Plant's lyrics talk of redemption through "the love that I've found" and the mood is positive. It starts with a slightly Caribbean-feel triple-metre riff over a slow-to-medium Bonham four-square beat, again with keyboards predominant, and then moves into a cod-calypso fast section that lets Bonham let fly with some entertaining Afro-Cuban patterns across various drum-heads.

A return to the original riff is used as accompaniment for a Page guitar solo. He employs electronics to create a parallel line an octave below what he is playing, probably generated by his guitar synthesiser. This type of effect had been in circulation since the mid 1960s and for a time was fashionable among saxophonists and trumpeters who felt that the doubled-up line helped them compete sonically with guitars. Jimi Hendrix used an Octavia unit for this purpose on 'Purple Haze' but chose to put the parallel octave line above what he was playing rather than below. Page's choice here makes his sound muddy, stilted and artificial; combined with one of his least connected-up and most meandering solos, it makes for an awkward melange of not particularly pleasant sounds and hardly one of Page's finest moments on record.

Plant re-enters to deliver his last verse and chorus with clarity and poise. The overall composition is sturdy and the song could have been developed into a very powerful Led Zeppelin statement. But there is little attention to detail, scant integration of all the varying parts and counter-lines, and no careful grading of instrumental colour, all ever-present Zeppelin constituents on other records.

Perhaps communication problems in the studio interfered with the proper realisation of the material at hand.

'Hot Dog' is a lark, a sort of hybrid between a tribute to early Elvis rockabilly and a tongue-in-cheek send-up of hayseed country music. But again it is musically unbalanced, with undue prominence for the excellently executed but mundane rhythm parts of Bonham and Jones. This was not because Jones and Bonham were on some kind of ego trip, but a result of Page's below-par playing. His gentle send-up of the staccato cotton-picking country style falls flat on its face because he can't maintain an even stroke and fumbles the execution of the long and difficult runs. Played live in front of an audience who would have enjoyed the joke, it wouldn't have mattered a great deal. Put on record for all time, it verges on embarrassing and can perhaps be counted as Led Zeppelin's second outright failure to master a particular feel and its execution, after 'D'yer Mak'er'.

'Carouselambra', which opened side two of the original vinyl LP, is much more ambitious. It is divided in sections like some of Zeppelin's best work from the past and contains some moving moments in its more than ten minutes duration. The greatest drawback is its reliance on Jones's keyboard work. He instigated the song and so is justified in taking a major role in its execution, but his jabbing chords in the major-key mid-tempo opening section are too high in the mix and their puny Farfisa-organ sound is singularly inappropriate for the grandeur of the tune's conception. Again, Page's guitar work in this section is slightly recessed in the mix – Page did the mix himself so this was not Jones's decision. Plant's vocals are recessed too, so much so that it is very difficult to decipher the words. This is a pity, as they are some of his best lyrics on the record. Plant later lamented this mixing decision. "I thought parts of 'Carouselambra' were good, especially the darker dirges that Pagey developed. And I rue it so much now, because the lyrics on 'Carouselambra' were actually about that environment and that situation. The whole story of Led Zeppelin in its latter years is in that song – and I can't hear the words!"[26]

Matters improve for the song when the introduction to the second section approaches and Page's gift for giant and glittering sounds is briefly revived. One suddenly catches a glimpse of what this composition could have been like had Page been functioning at the top of his capabilities throughout the sessions. With the arrival of the second section, Page relentlessly milks a slow and moody meditation by Plant across two guitar chords with the help of his guitar synthesiser, bringing every timbral effect he can devise. These are the "darker dirges" Plant mentioned. The full force of the piece suddenly hits the

And still the awards keep coming: Jones, Plant and Bonham suitably grateful at an industry ceremony in London, September 1979.

listener. Even then, Page's playing, although masked by the effects, is clumsy and at times rhythmically inaccurate.

The arrival of the third section brings Jones's keyboards back into prominence. He chooses another inappropriate sound from the selection at hand, this one not dissimilar to a worried hen pecking nervously at seeds. It sits uneasily with the grandeur of the pounding rhythms generated by Bonham and the huge sounds that Page is thrashing out of his guitar. With this the track fades. It is a missed opportunity on what could have been a major late-period Zeppelin odyssey. Anyone care for a remix?

'All Of My Love' is a pretty mid-tempo love ballad that again gives Jones's regrettably cheesy keyboard sounds prominence over Page's rather desultory guitar backing. Plant sings with great conviction and warmth, his voice once again in fine shape, and this time he gets a properly prominent place in the mix. But the worst is yet to come. The solo spot is handed over to Jones, who delivers something more akin to a Genesis or ELO record, in mock 18th-century classical-keyboard style, again using a tone that was fashionable in the late 1970s but now adds a triteness to the notes played.

'I'm Gonna Crawl' opens with Jones's keyboard intro that takes as its inspiration easy-listening organist Reginald Dixon rather than Yes, Roxy Music, or David Bowie. Its glutinous tones run as an undercurrent throughout the classic 6/8 ballad that Plant delivers. The singer is in terrific form, giving everything he's got to put across his point of view – he's gonna give the song's subject "every little bit of my love" and he means it.

Page takes his best, most poised solo of the entire record, touching on the eloquent phrasing that distinguished his work for years in the 1970s but which deserted him for much of these sessions. But you can't get away from the absence of Page's normally beautifully judged and variegated guitar that should be underpinning Plant's vocals. Instead we have Jones's wooden, unvarying keyboards. Towards the closing climax, Bonham works in some wonderfully expressive and controlled drum patterns to increase the intensity, but they are not as clearly articulated in the mix as they would have been on previous albums. It's another missed opportunity for a song that had great potential and another prime candidate for a remix.

In Through The Out Door is a tired album by a band searching for a way back and not quite finding the route. The unity of purpose and sheer impact of every other Zeppelin album is missing. It is understood that all four players are brilliant musicians. What is absent here is the overall vision of Page, who had created the characteristic Zeppelin angle on their own material for every other studio album. This is nobody's fault but Page's. Seemingly at a personal low point at the time, he simply was not functioning at his accustomed levels of creativity.

In later years he has rarely talked about that time,

though on one occasion he said: "*In Through The Out Door* was done in a little over three weeks. So I couldn't have been in that bad a shape. I'd never have been able to play, and I wouldn't have been able to keep my head together to do this, that and the other. What I remember about the Stockholm sessions is that the album took a different movement from, say, the earlier albums where we were consciously [trying not] to do choruses."[27] Considering the technical imperfections that litter his playing on the record, perhaps he was not as alert as he supposed.

With or without choruses, what is strange about the nature of *In Through The Out Door* is that the three tracks left off would have provided the missing qualities. Leavened among the brighter moments of *Out Door* and with that record's lesser tracks removed or remixed, they would have made for a much more dynamic and powerful album than the one released in summer 1979.

'Ozone Baby' starts off with the sort of patented Led Zeppelin guitar-bass-drums riff that one can imagine as an accompaniment to kicking in doors. It continues in the same vein, Plant singing brightly about his "own true love" while the band struts happily along, the big sound carrying all before it. This track could have held its own on any of Zep's previous albums and shows that, given the right context and the motivation, they could still function in top gear. It's a simple construction like the rockers on *Houses Of The Holy* and *Physical Graffiti* but tightly arranged and not allowed to meander, a delight from start to perfectly measured finish.

'Darlene' is the type of pastiche that the band were able to do easily and well, as opposed to their muddled attempts at reggae or rockabilly. This is an updated rock'n'roll eight-to-the-bar boogie that has Plant panting and pleading with Darlene in convincing style as Page, Jones and Bonham play along with panache, punch and a terrific control of dynamics. Jones's piano playing is characterful and well integrated into the overall sound of the band. Perhaps the three years between the mixing of *Out Door* and 1982's *Coda*, where these three tracks finally appeared, allowed Page to re-think his approach to these sessions at the mixing board. The walking bass section of the song – which ends in a long fade – swings like crazy and is the sound of a band ripping up the joint in grand style. So there was fun to be had in Stockholm after all.

'Wearing And Tearing', one of the relatively few Zeppelin tunes that sustains a seriously fast tempo throughout, is an exhilarating rock workout that would

The European jaunt of June and July 1980 would turn out to be the band's last tour. Page is pictured here onstage in Belgium on June 20th.

Overleaf: Led Zeppelin's final tour, with the band playing at the Ahoy Hallen in Rotterdam, Holland, on June 21st 1980. Just ten gigs later their live career would be over.

have made a sensational live choice. It's a simple piece with just four chords, possibly a result of Page and Plant's interest in new wave bands: the speed and the splashy sound, let alone Plant's screams and shouts in the last chorus, are like nothing so much as that to be found on The Damned's first album. Released as the last track on 1982's *Coda*, it came across as a melancholy what-could-have-been. Released on *In Through The Out Door* in 1979 it would have raised more than the odd eyebrow.

Between the August 1979 release of *In Through The Out Door* and the band gathering for the summer 1980 tour there was little Zeppelin business. Record sales in the USA had been spectacular, but there was no will to follow this up with any touring before Christmas. Few were in the right physical or mental shape to do such a thing, from the band members through to the back-up staff. In the coming months, Grant would have to re-think any arrangements for Zeppelin tours during 1980.

At the end of December, just before the new year dawned and with a fresh decade to look forward to, three members of Led Zeppelin were involved in a series of Concerts For Kampuchea in London. Robert Plant sat in with Dave Edmunds' Rockpile, a tight and hard-working rock'n'roll group featuring Nick Lowe, managed by Jake Riviera and then signed to Swan Song. Later on in the same show, Paul McCartney reassembled his Rockestra studio supergroup, featuring both John Paul Jones and John Bonham reprising their roles from the previous October. Jimmy Page, away on holiday in Barbados after a particularly distressing incident at his country house where a 19-year-old boy had died of an overdose, was not around to join in on the fun.

In April 1980, with Grant's plans for a summer tour of Europe advancing steadily, Led Zeppelin convened at The Rainbow in Finsbury Park, north London to begin rehearsals and the necessary selection of a live set. After a stuttering start there and later at the New Victoria Theatre in central London during late May and early June, they worked continuously to bring the set up to scratch at Shepperton studio, to the west of London.

Page and Grant had already discussed the nature of the proposed tour. Grant recalled: "We said: 'Let's forget the 320 lamps set-up and go back to 120 lamps, a back-to-basics sort of thing.'"[28] In that spirit, Page took the others right back to the very beginnings of the band by getting them to rehearse 'The Train Kept A-Rollin'', one of his perennial favourites from the Yardbirds days and the very first number that Zeppelin had ever rehearsed, back in Gerrard Street in summer 1968. It was to be the opening number for much of the upcoming European tour, emphasising the band's determination to scale back and reclaim its own blues-rock roots. Even 'Moby Dick' was dropped from the repertoire.

Meanwhile there were still some mountains to climb in order to harmonise the operation and have everyone facing the right way at the same time. Grant's ultimate aim since Knebworth was to get the band back to the USA and re-establish their concert-band supremacy and rock credentials to a new generations of fans who had never seen them. With that in mind he had been talking to the band members continually, but he met with sustained resistance from Plant.

Understandably, Plant had no desire to be away from his family for long periods. If anything should go wrong again, he would be in a darker hole than ever before. Grant said that Plant insisted he wouldn't go back to America, recalling the singer's recent on-stage speech at Knebworth. "'We're never going to Texas any more … but we will go to Manchester.' … As he's saying it he's eyeing me out at the side of the stage," Grant recalled. "So we did the European tour, but before it we had this big meet down at my house that went on all night. But all the others said it was down to me to get Robert to agree to go back to the States. I mean, we just had to go if we were to carry on, really."[29]

Another long-running problem had to be resolved before the tour started. Grant had to leave Richard Cole behind. "I'd paid for the doctor's visits and all that, and it just wasn't getting better," Grant said. "He had a massive problem, so I thought the only way to shake him up was to blow him out. So I told him I wouldn't want him in Europe, and he says: 'You can't do it without me.' But I said: 'Well, we've got to.'"[30]

Predictably, Cole, who had been with the band since its first tour, was angry and deeply hurt. Unable to confront his own addiction at the time, he lingered around London during the early summer, continuing to feed his by now spiralling habit. By mid June the band had left him behind and departed for Europe, with Phil Carlo now taking the tour manager's role. Meanwhile, on the first day of June, Page completed the purchase of a mansion on the River Thames at Windsor. He bought it from actor Michael Caine and looked forward to moving there in August from Plumpton Place.

The short European tour began in Germany, starting on June 17th in Dortmund to a crowd of 16,000 – smaller than on previous tours but certainly enthusiastic. True to their aims, the band stuck to a shortened set throughout the tour, adopting a pared-down approach. With few variations – mostly spontaneous workouts on old rock favourites – they played 'The Train Kept A-Rollin'', 'Nobody's Fault But Mine', 'Black Dog', 'In The Evening', 'The Rain Song', 'Hot Dog', 'All My Love', 'Trampled Under Foot', 'Since I've Been Loving You', 'Achilles' Last Stand', 'White Summer'/'Black Mountain Side', 'Kashmir', 'Stairway To Heaven', 'Rock And Roll', 'Whole Lotta Love', and 'Heartbreaker', the last two normally as encores. Once again the bookings concentrated on Germany as well as a smattering of gigs in Belgium, Holland, Austria and Switzerland. None in

France, however: according to the band, Paris, which would have seemed a reasonable place to play, didn't have a suitable venue at the time.

The tour generated little interest outside of the countries and cities where the band played. There has rarely been a time when the adventures of British bands in Europe were considered particularly newsworthy by the British music press, and although this was more or less a comeback tour by the band, in the eyes of London music journalists that comeback had been accomplished at Knebworth the previous August. They would wait for the band either to play the UK again or make a splash in America. It was only a matter of time before they would head across the Atlantic once more. Still, *Melody Maker* did eventually send Steve Gett out to catch the penultimate gig, in Munich on July 5th. As for the American press, Europe was another planet in terms of covering rock gigs. Or Japan. No US magazine sent journalists to cover the tour.

Reports from fans of the first few concerts enthused about the new material. They found it notable that the band had decided to drop the acoustic set for this stripped-down tour as well as some of the longer pieces, including 'No Quarter' – but also noticed that Page in particular was looking frail and unwell at times. Page's playing wavered between inspired and sloppy, depending largely on his physical condition.

Bonham was still apt to take on board copious quantities of drink and indulged in drugs, but was generally rock-solid, while the other two band members were fighting fit. Their stage attire echoed the sober, more adult image they'd projected at Knebworth ten months earlier. The band members were now in their thirties, not the first flush of outrageous youth.

Zeppelin endured two difficult concerts on June 26th and 27th. In Vienna, Austria some lunatic in the audience decided it would be hilarious to light a firework and throw it at Page. It exploded in front of his face, and the guitarist was lucky not to lose an eye in the brainless attack. The concert had to be stopped until he was ready to continue. After three numbers in Nuremberg, Germany the following night, Bonham literally fell off his drum stool onto the stage, passing out in the process. The concert was abandoned as he was taken away in an ambulance. It later transpired that, as Grant put it, "He'd had 27 bananas that night so it's not surprising he was ill!"[31]

Observers generally acknowledged that the tour hit a peak in Zurich, Switzerland, on June 29th, where the local Hell's Angels had been hired as security for the night. Thankfully for all concerned, the concert passed off without incident either onstage or off. The set lasted two hours, with Page once more on his mettle and, in a distinct change of pace, indulging in plenty of (for him rare) inter-song chat to the audience. Outstanding was the opener 'The Train Kept A-Rollin", which received a

massive cheer as it burst from the stage speakers, along with a bludgeoning 'Black Dog' and a thrilling encore of 'Heartbreaker' where Page took his outstanding solo of the night.

In Frankfurt, Germany, the fans were treated to Phil Carson of Atlantic Records coming onstage for an impromptu encore, playing bass while Jones played piano on the old 1960s favourite 'Money (That's What I Want)'. Keeping up the routine, the Munich gig five days later featured an encore with Bad Company's drummer Simon Kirke. In a pre-arranged move, at the conclusion of 'Stairway To Heaven' a second set of drums were brought out and set up. After a considerable pause while this took place, Kirke came out and joined Bonham for a twin-drums version of 'Whole Lotta Love'.

The Munich concert had around 10,000 people jammed into the Olympiahalle and thousands outside in the unusually cold summer air. Kirke explained later how this rendition of 'Whole Lotta Love' came about. Bonham, he remembered, "had phoned all the music dealers in Munich and said: 'I want a drum kit sent down, right away.' ... It's quite a complex arrangement to 'Whole Lotta Love' so Bonzo says to me, banging on his knees, 'Right, we do this, got that? Right, then Pagey takes over, bomp bomp. Got that? Great.' It was all done on the knees in the hotel room before we went onstage".[32]

The following day, July 7th 1980, in the still-divided city of Berlin, Led Zeppelin gave what turned out to be their last concert. It was originally to have been the first of two nights in the old German capital, but the second had been cancelled before the tour began. Thus the band played its final concert on the 12th anniversary of The Yardbirds' final gig – back in England, at Luton, in 1968. Led Zeppelin's last number in Berlin was an encore of 'Whole Lotta Love' that provoked the notoriously combustible Berlin crowd to explode in appreciation. It was a fitting and encouraging end to the three-week tour and one, Grant hoped, that would be a perfect facilitator for a return to the USA.

Grant's wish seemed on the point of coming true the following day. He said later: "I have an outstanding memory of coming off the Europe tour and landing in the Falcon jet in England and walking across the tarmac and Robert coming up to me and saying: "OK, I'll do it [play America], but only for four weeks.' ... We couldn't cover everywhere in four weeks, because Robert's schedule was always two days on and then one day off. But I reckoned that once Robert got over there and got into the swing he'd be OK."[33]

On that basis, as soon as the band were back in the country Grant started setting up an autumn US tour that he quickly dubbed 'Led Zeppelin The 1980s, Part One'. While the band members took a brief break to re-charge and see to their domestic lives the tour quickly took shape. It would start on October 17th in Montreal and

run through to four nights in Chicago starting on November 10th.

On September 24th the band gathered at Page's new manor house in Windsor to chat about their month off and then attend their first rehearsal for the upcoming US tour at Bray, just a few miles away. Bonham and Plant had driven there together. Plant recalled: "Bonzo was in one of those periods when he thought he was no good. ... He was saying: 'I don't want to do this. You play the drums and I'll sing.' We got to the studio and that's what happened. I played the drums and he sang a bit."[34]

After the rehearsal was finished they all returned to Page's house and had a mini celebration party. Bonham, who had been drinking all day, drank himself into a stupor by midnight and was laid on a bed in a guest studio by his roadie, Rex King. It would not have been the first time he'd been left to sleep it off. Only he didn't.

According to the coroner, Bonham had downed the equivalent of 40 measures of vodka in the 24 hours before he died during the night after inhaling his own vomit.

It may well be that Bonham had done similar things to himself in previous years and on previous occasions, but he was no longer 20 years old. On the recent European tour he had not been in the best of health, as his collapse in Nuremberg had shown. His body was no longer able to withstand such sustained bouts. Jones found him in bed the next day when he went up to wake him. "I think he had been drinking because there were some problems in his personal life," Jones said later, "but he died because of an accident. He was lying down the wrong way, which could have happened to anybody who drank a lot."[35]

Still stunned from what he had discovered, Jones had to go downstairs and tell Plant and Page, who were sitting and chatting amiably downstairs. From the moment Bonham's death was confirmed, all involved knew it was the end of Led Zeppelin. Robert Plant, who thought that the band at the time of Bonham's death "desperately needed to come together and create a new directive"[36], knew there was no point in continuing.

"We were very competitively close, and it broke me into little bits, really. My affinity to him was probably closer because we were both from the same neck of the woods. ... Really, I didn't have a great deal of incentive to carry on at all after he'd gone."[37]

Jimmy Page made no official comment, secluding himself away to deal with his own grief. He later told Richard Cole: "It would be an insult to find a replacement for John Bonham in order to keep Led Zeppelin aloft."[38]

John Paul Jones, reflecting on the situation many years afterwards, said: "At first the main emotion for me

was anger. It seemed such a waste. There was also a feeling of mortality – after all, it could have happened to any one of us. It was a difficult period."[39]

Grant recalled the beginning of that 'difficult period'. "After the funeral we all went to Jersey. But we all had that trouble with the [London] *Evening Standard* saying dreadful things. ... They came back from Jersey: I booked a suite for afternoon tea at the Savoy. And they all looked at me and asked what I thought. I said it just couldn't go on because it was the four of them, and they were all relieved because they had decided the same. ...

"You have to realise that for Led Zeppelin to make that music it needed the four of them to do it. And now that was gone."[40]

In December 1980 an official announcement was released confirming the end of Led Zeppelin's life as a band. "We wish it to be known that the loss of our dear friend and the deep respect we have for his family together with the sense of undivided harmony felt by ourselves and our manager have led us to decide we could not continue as we were."

To this day Led Zeppelin have been true to their announcement of December 1980. There have been three one-off performances. The first was in Philadelphia for Live Aid in 1985 (with Tony Thompson of Chic and Phil Collins both on drums, and Phil Martinez on bass while John Paul Jones was on keyboards). Next came the Atlantic Records 40th Anniversary bash in 1988 (with Jason Bonham on drums), and then their induction into the Rock & Roll Hall Of Fame in 1995 (again with Jason Bonham on drums). Page had been inducted into the Hall Of Fame three years earlier with The Yardbirds. But that is it.

Coda, released in 1982 to honour contractual commitments to Atlantic and also to cover tax demands on previous monies earned, cleared away close to all the leftover tracks from the various studio sessions of the 1960s and '70s. In recent years there have been the fine double-disc *DVD* set of goodies from various years and the *How The West Was Won* three-disc set of live concerts from 1972, but nothing newly recorded. There is no reason that there should be. Jimmy Page, interviewed in 2003 and asked if there is anything more to come from the vaults, commented that there are "some very interesting versions of songs. Alternate mixes, and alternative versions of songs, too. Maybe it'll take another 20 years for those things to come out ... . Of course there's quite a movement – and I'm helping to promote it – to [Dolby] 5.1, but that's another area with the studio albums. But ... in time we'll see what unfolds".[41]

Led Zeppelin's legacy is complete and strikingly consistent. It has stood the test of time and shows every sign of continuing to do so, as the three surviving members continue to pursue active but separate careers in music. It is the story of a band, not four individuals, and it ends here.

> After John Bonham's death in September 1980, manager Peter Grant called a meeting. "I said it just couldn't go on because it was the four of them, and they were all relieved because they had decided the same."

APPENDICES

ENDNOTES

Surnames alone in the endnotes are authors' names and refer to books listed in full in the Bibliography at the end of the book.

The quote on the jacket is from *Uncut*, May 2005. The quote on page 6/7 is from *New Musical Express*, April 6th 1974.

CHAPTER 1
Goodnight, Josephine

[1] Booklet notes *Yardbirds …Where The Action Is!* (New Millennium 1997) by Trevor Jones
[2] Booklet notes *Yardbirds …Where The Action Is!* (New Millennium 1997) by Trevor Jones
[3] Author's interview June 2004
[4] Carson p.66
[5] 'Zeppelin!' *Guitar Player* July 1977 p.36 by Steve Rosen
[6] Carson p.52
[7] *Zig Zag* December 1970
[8] 'Music In The Making' *Music Maker* November 1966 p.36 by John Kerr
[9] Author's interview June 2004
[10] *Zig Zag* December 1970
[11] *Zig Zag* December 1970
[12] Glenn Cornick, Russo p.78
[13] Booklet notes *Yardbirds …Where The Action Is!* (New Millennium 1997) by Trevor Jones
[14] Author's interview May 2005
[15] Author's interview May 2005
[16] Author's interview June 2004
[17] Booklet notes *Yardbirds …Where The Action Is!* (New Millennium 1997) by Trevor Jones
[18] *Melody Maker* June 22nd 1974
[19] Author's interview May 2005
[20] *Melody Maker* January 21st 1967 p.15 by Bob Dawbarn
[21] *Melody Maker* January 21st 1967 p.15 by Bob Dawbarn
[22] *Melody Maker* January 21st 1967 p.15 by Bob Dawbarn
[23] *Melody Maker* January 21st 1967 p.15 by Bob Dawbarn
[24] Welch Grant p.52
[25] *The Guitar Magazine* April 1998 by Michael Leonard
[26] Author's interview June 2004
[27] Author's interview June 2004
[28] Author's interview June 2004
[29] *The Guitar Magazine* April 1998 by Michael Leonard
[30] 'Sound Sense' *Music Maker* September 1967 p.45
[31] 'Sound Sense' *Music Maker* May 1967 p.45
[32] 'Sound Sense' *Music Maker* December 1966 p.53
[33] *Melody Maker* September 9th 1967
[34] *Guitar World* January 1998 by Brad Tolinski and Greg DiBenedetto
[35] *Zig Zag* December 1970
[36] Author's interview June 2004

CHAPTER 2
An Iron Butterfly By Any Other Name

[1] Russo p.123
[2] *Zigzag* December 1970 p.168
[3] Lewis Celebration II p.89
[4] Booklet notes *Yardbirds …Where The Action Is!* (New Millennium 1997) by Trevor Jones
[5] *Melody Maker* June 29th 1968
[6] *Oz* No.20 March 1969 by Felix Dennis
[7] *New York Times* June 15th 1968 by Robert Shelton
[8] Russo p.125
[9] Author's interview June 2004
[10] Author's interview June 2004
[11] *Go* July 1968
[12] *Uncut* May 2005 by Nigel Williamson
[13] *Melody Maker* September 12th 1970 by Chris Welch
[14] *Melody Maker* September 12th 1970 by Chris Welch
[15] *Uncut* May 2005 by Nigel Williamson
[16] Russo p.126
[17] *Zigzag* December 1970
[18] Author's interview June 2004
[19] Welch Bonham p.71
[20] *Zigzag* December 1970 p.168
[21] Welch Bonham p.74
[22] Welch Bonham p.74
[23] *Uncut* May 2005 by Nigel Williamson
[24] Welch Bonham p.75
[25] Welch Bonham p.75
[26] Lewis Celebration II p.116
[27] Welch Bonham p.75
[28] *Guitar Player* July 1977 by Steve Rosen
[29] Welch Bonham p.77
[30] *The Guitar Magazine* January 1998 by Brad Tolinski
[31] Welch Bonham p.76
[32] *Guitar World* January 1998 by Brad Tolinski and Greg DiBenedetto
[33] Welch Bonham p.77
[34] Welch Grant p.63
[35] *Guitar World* January 1991 by Joe Bosso
[36] Welch Grant p.63
[37] *Melody Maker* October 12th 1968 by Chris Welch
[38] Russo p.132
[39] *Zigzag* December 1970 p.169
[40] *Melody Maker*

CHAPTER 3
Happy Christmas, Mr Nixon

[1] Lewis Celebration II p.90

2 *Melody Maker* November 9th 1968
3 *The Guitar Magazine* January 1998 by Brad Tolinski
4 *Melody Maker* December 21st 1968
5 Yorkc p.83
6 *Sunday Denver Post* December 29th 1968
7 Welch Bonham p.83
8 Cole p.52
9 Yorke p.82
10 Yorke p.82
11 *New Musical Express* February 24th 1973 by Nick Kent
12 'Fillmore East' *Proximity V10* No.35 July 1993 by Hugh Jones www.buckeye-web.com/prox
13 Liner notes *Joan Baez In Concert* (Vanguard 1962) by Maynard Solomon
14 *Guitar World* January 1998 by Brad Tolinski and Greg DiBenedetto
15 Liner notes Jeff Beck *Truth* (EMI 1968)
16 *Guitar World* January 1991 by Joe Bosso
17 *Guitar World* January 1991 by Joe Bosso
18 *Uncut* May 2005 by Nigel Williamson
19 *Mojo* December 1994 by Colin Harper
20 *Guitar Player* July 1977
21 *Mojo* June 2003
22 *Guitar World* January 1998 by Brad Tolinski and Greg DiBenedetto
23 Guitar Player July 1977

CHAPTER 4
Tea Parties in Boston, Festivals in Bath

1 *The Guitar Magazine* January 1998 by Brad Tolinski
2 *Record Mirror* April 12th 1969
3 Cole p.81
4 *Dagens Nyheter* March 15th 1969
5 *Expressen* March 15th 1969
6 *Svenska Dagbladet* March 15th 1969
7 *Rolling Stone* March 1969
8 *Oz* No.19 March 1969
9 Author's interview May 2005
10 *Melody Maker* March 22nd 1969 by Chris Welch
11 *Oz* No.20 April 1969 by Felix Dennis
12 *Record Mirror* April 12th 1969
13 Yorke p.85
14 Davis p.79-80
15 Sander p.111
16 *New Musical Express* 10 May 1969 by Ann Moses
17 *Honolulu Advertiser* May 19th 1969
18 Sander p.114
19 Cole p.66
20 Cole p.66
21 Cole p.67
22 Sander p.118
23 Sander p.119
24 *Cash Box* June 14th 1969

25 *Billboard* June 14th 1969
26 Sander p.122
27 *Record Mirror* May 31st 1969
28 UK tour programme 1969
29 *Melody Maker* June 21st 1969
30 *The Guitar Magazine* January 1998 by Brad Tolinski
31 Carson
32 'Bath Blues & Progressive Music Fest 1969' by Mike de Voi http://tinpan.fortunecity.com/ebony/546/Zep-69-bath.html
33 *New Musical Express* July 5th 1969 by Nick Logan
34 *Disc & Music Echo* July 12th 1969
35 New Musical Express July 5th 1969 by Nick Logan

CHAPTER 5
Whole Lotta Newports

1 Goldblatt p.172
2 Goldblatt p.172
3 Goldblatt p.172
4 Balliett p.311-12
5 *Billboard* July 19th 1969
6 *Down Beat* August 21st 1969 p.26 by Ira Gitler
7 Balliett p.313
8 Welch Grant p.79
9 *Down Beat* August 21st 1969 p.26 by Ira Gitler
10 Welch Grant p.80
11 Steve Rosen book on Beck (Japan 1978)
12 Carson p.94
13 Cole p.83-85
14 Cole p.84
15 *Houston Chronicle* August 3rd 1969
16 Welch Bonham p.95
17 Balliett p.312
18 *Melody Maker* September 13th 1969
19 *Melody Maker* September 27th 1969 by Richard Williams
20 *Melody Maker* September 13th 1969
21 Cole p.98
22 *Record Mirror* September 20th 1969
23 *Down Beat* October 2nd 1969 p.26 by James D. Dilts
24 *Melody Maker* September 13th 1969
25 *Melody Maker* October 25th 1969 by Chris Welch
26 *Guitar World* January 1998 by Brad Tolinski and Greg DiBenedetto
27 *Melody Maker* October 25th 1969
28 Hewitt
29 *Guitar World* January 1998 by Brad Tolinski and Greg DiBenedetto
30 *Sounds* May 26th 1971 by Steve Peacock
31 Yorke p.97
32 Welch Bonham p.91
33 *Melody Maker* September 27th 1969
34 *Melody Maker* October 25th 1969 by Chris Welch

35 *New Musical Express* November 1st 1969
36 *Down Beat* April 2nd 1970 p.22 by Alan Heinemann

CHAPTER 6
Countess Bites Zeppelin: Nobody Hurt

1 *Melody Maker* December 20th 1969 by Chris Welch
2 Lewis Celebration II p.92
3 Lewis Celebration II p.92
4 Lewis Celebration II p.92
5 Yorke p.103
6 *Disc & Music Echo* December 20th 1969
7 *Disc & Music Echo* January 10th 1970
8 *Disc & Music Echo* January 10th 1970
9 *Disc & Music Echo* January 17th 1970
10 *Disc & Music Echo* January 24th 1970
11 *Record Mirror* January 31st 1970
12 *Melody Maker* February 21st 1970 by Chris Welch
13 Lewis Celebration II p.92
14 *Mojo* June 2003
15 *Led Zeppelin Interview Disc* (Atlantic promo 2003) by Dave Schulps
16 Welch Bonham p.98
17 Welch Bonham p.98
18 Welch Bonham p.97
19 Booklet notes *DVD* (Atlantic 2003)
20 Yorke p.110
21 *Melody Maker* February 21st 1970 by Chris Welch
22 *New Musical Express* April 11th 1970 by Ritchie Yorke
23 *Melody Maker* February 21st 1970 by Chris Welch
24 *Melody Maker* January 17th 1970 by Raymond Telford
25 *Led Zeppelin Interview Disc* (Atlantic promo 2003) by Dave Schulps
26 'News Extra' *Melody Maker* February 7th 1970
27 *Melody Maker* February 14th 1970 by Chris Welch
28 *Melody Maker* February 21st 1970 by Chris Welch
29 *Melody Maker* February 21st 1970 by Chris Welch
30 *Melody Maker* February 14th 1970 by Chris Welch
31 *Göteborgs-Posten* February 26th 1970
32 Cole p.111
33 *Melody Maker*

CHAPTER 7
Got Them Welsh Marin County Blues, Mama

1 *Melody Maker* February 28th 1970
2 *Melody Maker* February 28th 1970
3 Cole p.117
4 New Musical Express May 2nd 1970
5 Cole p.116
6 *Melody Maker* March 28th 1970
7 *Montreal Star* April 14th 1970
8 *Memphis Press* April 17th 1970

9 *New Musical Express* April 18th 1970 by Ritchie Yorke
10 *Disc & Music Echo* April 18th 1970
11 *Billboard* April 25th 1970
12 'Ask-In' *New Musical Express* April 11th 1970 by Richie Yorke
13 Davis p.119
14 *Mojo* June 2003 by Barney Hoskyns
15 *Mojo* April 2000 by Phil Sutcliffe
16 *Disc & Music Echo* June 6th 1970
17 *New Musical Express* June 27th 1970 by Roy Carr
18 *Disc & Music Echo* June 13th 1970
19 *Led Zeppelin Interview Disc* (Atlantic promo 2003) by Dave Schulps
20 Cole p. 128
21 *Mojo* April 2000
22 *New Musical Express* June 27th 1970 by Roy Carr
23 *Mojo* April 2000
24 *Guitar World* January 1991 by Alan diPerna
25 *Mojo* April 2000
26 *New Musical Express* July 4th 1970
27 *Record Mirror* June 27th 1970
28 'My Reminiscences' by Rip G http://www.geocities.com/SunsetStrip/Hotel/8117/Bath01.html
29 Cole p.132
30 'My Reminiscences' by Rip G http://www.geocities.com/SunsetStrip/Hotel/8117/Bath01.html

CHAPTER 8
Coming Through Slaughter

1 *Melody Maker* August 8th 1970
2 *Mojo* April 2000 p.61
3 *Rock* October 11th 1970 by Allan Rinde
4 Welch Grant p.73
5 *Honolulu Advertiser* September 7th 1970
6 Cole p.137-8
7 *Melody Maker* September 12th 1970 by Chris Welch
8 *Rolling Stone* November 26th 1970 by Lester Bangs
9 *Zigzag* 33 Vol.3 No.9
10 *Strange Days* October 23rd 1970 by Chris Hodenfeld
11 *Rock* October 11th 1970 by Allan Rinde
12 *Strange Days* October 23rd 1970 by Chris Hodenfeld
13 *Guitar World* January 1998 by Brad Tolinski and Greg DiBenedetto
14 *Record Mirror* October 24th 1970
15 *Guitar World* January 1991 by Joe Bosso
16 *Guitar Player* July 1977 by Steve Rosen
17 *Melody Maker* October 17th 1970
18 Russo p.114
19 *Melody Maker* October 17th 1970
20 *Melody Maker* October 17th 1970
21 *Disc & Music Echo* December 12th 1970

[22] John Paul Jones, Welch book p.96
[23] *Melody Maker* February 20th 1971
[24] *Melody Maker* February 13th 1971
[25] *Record Mirror* February 27th 1971 by Keith Altham
[26] *Melody Maker*

CHAPTER 9
Album? What Album?

[1] *Disc & Music Echo* November 13th 1971 by Caroline Boucher
[2] *Il Milanese* July 6th 1971 translation Godwin
[3] Cole p.156
[4] *Sounds* September 4th 1971
[5] Yorke p.143
[6] Booklet notes *Woody Herman At Carnegie Hall 1946* (Verve 1999) by Kenny Berger
[7] *Melody Maker* November 13th 1971 by Chris Welch
[8] *Honolulu Star-Bulletin* September 17th 1971
[9] Cole p.165
[10] *Zigzag* 33 Vol.3 No.9
[11] Author's interview May 2005
[12] Fyfe p.96
[13] Welch Bonham p.96
[14] *Guitar World* January 1991 by Joe Bosso
[15] Welch Bonham p.96
[16] Cole p.141
[17] *Guitar World* January 1991 by Alan diPerna
[18] Fyfe p.80
[19] *Guitar World* January 1991 by Joe Bosso

CHAPTER 10
Performing Pigs and Memories of Laughter

[1] Radio Perth February 16th 1972
[2] Cole p.175
[3] Author's interview May 2005
[4] *Go-Set* March 4th 1972 by Ian Meldrum
[5] *Times Of India* Pune edition July 7th 2001 by Nanu Bhende
[6] Author's interview May 2005
[7] *Disc* November 25th 1972 by Andrew Tyler
[8] Davis p.157
[9] *New Musical Express* April 4th 1972 by Roy Carr
[10] *Disc* April 22nd 1972
[11] Yorke p.158
[12] Lewis Celebration II p.119
[13] *Zigzag* 33 Vol.3 No.9
[14] Cole p.116
[15] Cole p.182
[16] *Melody Maker* July 1st 1972 by Roy Hollingsworth
[17] *Melody Maker* July 1st 1972 by Roy Hollingsworth
[18] *New Musical Express* August 12th 1972 by Roy Carr

[19] *New Musical Express* August 12th 1972 by Roy Carr
[20] *Sounds* December 9th 1972 by Steve Peacock

CHAPTER 11
Where's That Confounded Bridge?

[1] Cole p.191
[2] *Melody Maker* November 4th 1972 by Chris Charlesworth
[3] *Melody Maker* November 4th 1972 by Chris Charlesworth
[4] *Disc* November 25th 1972 by Andrew Tyler
[5] *New Musical Express* November 25th 1972 by Keith Altham
[6] *Disc* December 9th 1972
[7] *Sounds* December 9th 1972 by Steve Peacock
[8] *Melody Maker* December 23rd 1972
[9] *New Musical Express* February 24th 1973
[10] *Bravo* March 12th 1973
[11] Lewis Celebration II p.95
[12] Yorke p.165
[13] *Bravo* March 12th 1973
[14] Davis p.188
[15] Cole p.199
[16] Davis pp.188-89
[17] Davis p.187
[18] *Sounds* April 21st 1973 by Rob Mackie
[19] *Guitar World* January 1998 by Brad Tolinski and Greg DiBenedetto
[20] *Guitar World* January 1991 by Alan diPerna
[21] *Melody Maker* August 4th 1973 by Loraine Alterman
[22] *Zigzag* 33 Vol.3 No.9
[23] Welch Bonham p.97
[24] *Guitar World* January 1991 by Alan diPerna

CHAPTER 12
View From The Top

[1] *New Musical Express* April 21st 1973 by James Johnson
[2] *Sounds* April 21st 1973 by Rob Mackie
[3] *Circus* October 1973 by Howard Bloom
[4] Cole p.204
[5] *Disc* June 2nd 1973 by Lisa Robinson
[6] *Zigzag* 33 Vol.3 No.9
[7] *New Musical Express* June 23rd 1973 by Charles Shaar Murray
[8] Fyfe p.166
[9] Yorke p.180
[10] Yorke p.181
[11] *New Musical Express* June 16th 1973
[12] Cole p.218
[13] *Guitar World* January 1998 by Brad Tolinski and Greg DiBenedetto

14 *New Musical Express* August 11th 1973 by Ritchie Yorke
15 *New Musical Express* September 1st 1973 by Nick Kent
16 Welch Grant p.141
17 Lewis Celebration II p.119
18 Lewis Celebration II p.120
19 *New Musical Express* April 6th 1974 by Ritchie Yorke
20 *Circus* October 1973

CHAPTER 13
Taxing Concerns

1 *New Musical Express* April 6th 1974 by Ritchie Yorke
2 *Rolling Stone* March 18th 1975
3 *Led Zeppelin Interview Disc* (Atlantic promo 2003) by Dave Schulps
4 *New Musical Express* April 6th 1974
5 Welch Grant p.119
6 Lewis Celebration II p.120
7 'Random Notes' *Rolling Stone* January 13th 1977
8 Welch Grant p.126
9 Welch Grant p.126
10 Welch Grant p.127
11 *Melody Maker* June 22nd 1974
12 *Uncut* May 2005 by Nigel Williamson
13 Welch Grant p.150
14 Welch Grant p.134
15 Lewis Celebration II p.95
16 *New Musical Express* September 14th 1974
17 *Bottom Line* January 1977 by Robb Baker
18 *Bottom Line* January 1977 by Robb Baker
19 *Bottom Line* January 1977 by Robb Baker
20 *New Musical Express* February 1st 1975 by Lisa Robinson
21 *Circus* February 28th 1975
22 *New Musical Express* December 7th 1974
23 Lewis Celebration II p.96
24 *New Musical Express* November 2nd 1974
25 Welch Grant p.128
26 Lewis Celebration II p.119
27 Lewis Celebration II p.118
28 *Old Grey Whistle Test* broadcast BBC TV January 20th 1975
29 *New Musical Express*

CHAPTER 14
Whole Lotta Graffiti

1 *New Musical Express* November 2nd 1974 by Nick Kent
2 *Rolling Stone* March 18th 1975
3 *Rolling Stone* March 18th 1975
4 Welch Grant p.163
5 Davis p235

6 'Stairway To Excess' *Vanity Fair* November 2003 by Lisa Robinson
7 *Rolling Stone* March 18th 1975 by Cameron Crowe
8 *Uncut* May 2005 by Nigel Williamson
9 *Guitar World* January 1991 by Joe Bosso
10 *Rolling Stone* March 18th 1975 by Cameron Crowe
11 *Guitar Player* July 1977 by Steve Rosen
12 *Led Zeppelin Interview Disc* (Atlantic promo 2003) by Dave Schulps
13 Lewis Celebration II p93
14 Rooksby p.128
15 *Guitar World* January 1998 by Brad Tolinski and Greg DiBenedetto
16 *Rolling Stone* March 18th 1975
17 *Guitar World* January 1998 by Brad Tolinski and Greg DiBenedetto
18 *New Musical Express* March 1st 1975 by Steve Clarke
19 *Baton Rouge Sunday Advocate* March 2nd 1975
20 *Los Angeles Times* March 13th 1975 by Robert Hilburn
21 *Street Life* May 1st 1976 by Steve Peacock

CHAPTER 15
Unforseen Circumstances

1 Welch Grant p.130
2 *New Musical Express* June 21st 1975
3 *New Musical Express* March 15th 1975
4 *Melody Maker* June 21st 1975 by Chris Welch
5 Welch Grant
6 Cole p.265
7 *Melody Maker* September 27th 1975
8 *Circus* January 10th 1976
9 *Melody Maker* February 14th 1976 by Chris Charlesworth
10 Lewis Celebration II p.120
11 *Circus* January 10th 1976
12 Cole p.274
13 *Uncut* May 2005 by Nigel Williamson
14 *Circus* January 10th 1976
15 *Circus* January 10th 1976
16 Welch Grant p.135
17 Cole p.277-278
18 *Melody Maker* February 14th 1976 by Chris Charlesworth
19 *Melody Maker* February 14th 1976 by Chris Charlesworth
20 *Guitar Player* July 1977 by Steve Rosen
21 *Guitar World* January 1991 by Joe Bosso
22 *Guitar Player* July 1977 by Steve Rosen
23 Rooksby p.128
24 *Guitar World* January 1991 by Joe Bosso
25 *Guitar Player* July 1977 by Steve Rosen
26 *The Guitar Magazine* January 1998 by Brad Tolinski
27 *Sounds* March 20th 1976 by Pete Doherty

28 *Rolling Stone* March 25th 1976 by Rich Wiseman
29 *Guitar Player* July 1977 by Steve Rosen
30 *Rolling Stone* May 20th 1976 by Steven Davis
31 'Jimmy Page & The Beat of the Street' *Street Life* May 1st 1976 by Steve Peacock
32 *Rolling Stone* March 25th 1976
33 *New Musical Express*

CHAPTER 16
Nobody's Fault But Mine

1 Yorke p.209
2 Welch Grant p.131
3 Welch Grant p.131
4 *New Musical Express* November 20th 1976 by Nick Kent
5 Welch Grant p.136
6 *Rolling Stone* December 2nd 1976
7 *Rolling Stone* December 2nd 1976
8 Cole p.282
9 *Melody Maker* June 25th 1977 by Ray Coleman
10 *New Musical Express* February 26th 1977
11 *Guitar Player* July 1977 by Steve Rosen
12 Cole p.284
13 Jones Celebration II p.120
14 *Melody Maker* June 25th 1977 by Ray Coleman
15 RS 3 June 1977
16 *Melody Maker* June 25th 1977 by Ray Coleman
17 Welch Grant p.182
18 *Guitar Player* July 1977 by Steve Rosen
19 *Melody Maker* June 25th 1977 by Ray Coleman
20 Lewis Celebration II
21 Lewis Celebration II
22 Lewis Celebration II
23 *Rolling Stone* March 18th 1975
24 *Trouser Press* September 1977 by Dave Schulps
25 Grant Welch p.191
26 Graham
27 *Daily Express* July 28th 1977
28 *Mojo* June 2003 by Barney Hoskyns

CHAPTER 17
Out Through The In Door

1 *Melody Maker* November 5th 1977
2 *Melody Maker* November 5th 1977
3 *Melody Maker* November 5th 1977
4 *Uncut* May 2005 by Nigel Williamson
5 *Uncut* May 2005 by Nigel Williamson
6 *Mojo* June 2003 by Barney Hoskyns
7 Yorke p.239
8 Lewis Celebration II p.98
9 Lewis Celebration II p.120

10 *Uncut* May 2005 by Nigel Williamson
11 Cole p.6
12 Lewis Celebration II p.98
13 *Guitar World* January 1991 by Alan diPerna
14 Lewis Celebration II p.120
15 Lewis Celebration II p.98
16 Welch Grant p.212
17 *Uncut* May 2005 by Nigel Williamson
18 Lewis Celebration II p.120
19 *Guitar World* January 1998 by Brad Tolinski and Greg DiBenedetto
20 *New Musical Express* August 4th 1979 by Chris Salewicz
21 *Mojo* June 2003
22 *Mojo* June 2003
23 Lewis Celebration II p.98
24 *New Musical Express* October 6th 1979
25 *Guitar World* January 1991 by Joe Bosso
26 *Mojo* June 2003
27 *Mojo* June 2003
28 Lewis Celebration II p.98
29 Lewis Celebration II p.98
30 Lewis Celebration II p.98
31 Lewis Celebration II p.99
32 Welch Bonham p.119
33 Lewis Celebration II p.99
34 *Uncut* May 2005 by Nigel Williamson
35 Welch Bonham p.121
36 *Uncut* May 2005 by Nigel Williamson
37 Yorke p.256
38 Cole p.10
39 Lewis Celebration II p.121
40 Lewis Celebration II p.99
41 *Led Zeppelin Interview Disc*

LED ZEPPELIN ON DISC

ORIGINAL RELEASES

Albums

Led Zeppelin
Atlantic SD 8216 (US), 588 171 (UK)
Released January 12th 1969 (US), March 28th 1969 (UK)

SIDE 1
Good Times Bad Times
Babe I'm Gonna Leave You
You Shook Me
Dazed And Confused

SIDE 2
Your Time Is Gonna Come
Black Mountain Side
Communication Breakdown
I Can't Quit You Baby
How Many More Times

Led Zeppelin II
Atlantic SD 8236 (US), 588 198 (UK)
Released October 22nd 1969 (US), October 31st 1969 (UK)

SIDE 1
Whole Lotta Love
What Is And What Should Never Be
The Lemon Song
Thank You

SIDE 2
Heartbreaker
Living Loving Maid (She's Just A Woman)
Ramble On
Moby Dick

Led Zeppelin III
Atlantic SD 7201 (US), 2401 002 (UK)
Released October 5th 1970 (US), October 23rd 1970 (UK)

SIDE 1
Immigrant Song
Friends
Celebration Day
Since I've Been Loving You
Out On The Tiles

SIDE 2
Gallows Pole
Tangerine
That's The Way
Bron-Y-Aur Stomp
Hats Off To (Roy) Harper

Untitled fourth album
Atlantic SD 7208 (US), 2401 012 (UK)
Released November 8th 1971 (US), November 12th 1971 (UK)

SIDE 1
Black Dog
Rock And Roll
The Battle Of Evermore
Stairway To Heaven

SIDE 2
Misty Mountain Hop
Four Sticks
Going to California
When The Levee Breaks

Houses Of The Holy
Atlantic SD 7255 (US), K 50014 (UK)
Released March 18th 1973 (US), March 26th 1973 (UK)

SIDE 1
The Song Remains The Same
The Rain Song
Over The Hills And Far Away
The Crunge

SIDE 2
Dancing Days
D'Yer Mak'er
No Quarter
The Ocean

Physical Graffiti double-album
Swan Song SS-2-200 (US), SSK 89400 (UK)
Released February 24th 1975 (US & UK)

SIDE 1
Custard Pie
The Rover
In My Time Of Dying

SIDE 2
Houses Of The Holy
Trampled Under Foot

Kashmir

SIDE 3
In The Light
Bron-Yr-Aur
Down By The Seaside
Ten Years Gone

SIDE 4
Night Flight
The Wanton Song
Boogie With Stu
Black Country Woman
Sick Again

....

Presence
Swan Song SS-8416 (US), SSK 59402 (UK)
Released March 31st 1976 (US), April 5th 1976 (UK)

SIDE 1
Achilles' Last Stand
For Your Life
Royal Orleans

SIDE 2
Nobody's Fault But Mine
Candy Store Rock
Hots On For Nowhere
Tea For One

....

The Song Remains The Same soundtrack
double-album
Swan Song SS-2-201 (US), SSK 89402 (UK)
Released October 22nd 1976 (US & UK)

Recordings from Madison Square Garden, July 1973

SIDE 1
Rock And Roll
Celebration Day
The Song Remains The Same
Rain Song

SIDE 2
Dazed And Confused

SIDE 3
No Quarter
Stairway To Heaven

SIDE 4
Moby Dick
Whole Lotta Love

In Through The Out Door
Swan Song SS-16002 (US), SSK 59410 (UK)
Released August 15th 1979 (US), August 20th 1979 (UK)

SIDE 1
In The Evening
South Bound Saurez
Fool In The Rain
Hot Dog

SIDE 2
Carouselambra
All My Love
I'm Gonna Crawl

....

Coda
Swan Song 90051-1 (US), A 0051 (UK)
Released November 19th 1982 (US), November 22nd 1982 (UK)

SIDE 1
We're Gonna Groove
Poor Tom
I Can't Quit You Baby
Walter's Walk

SIDE 2
Ozone Baby
Darlene
Bonzo's Montreux
Wearing And Tearing

....

BBC Sessions two CDs
Atlantic 7567-83061-2
Released November 17th 1997 (UK), November 18th 1997 (US)

CD 1
(NB Not quite in this order on the CD)

Recorded March 3rd 1969
You Shook Me
I Can't Quit You Baby
Dazed And Confused

Recorded June 16th 1969
Communication Breakdown
The Girl I Love (She Got Long Black Wavy Hair)
Somethin' Else

Recorded June 24th 1969
What Is And What Should Never Be

Communication Breakdown
Travelling Riverside Blues
Whole Lotta Love

Recorded June 27th 1969
Communication Breakdown
I Can't Quit You Baby
You Shook Me
How Many More Times

CD 2
All recorded April 1st 1971
Immigrant Song
Heartbreaker
Since I've Been Loving You
Black Dog
Dazed And Confused
Stairway To Heaven
Going To California
That's The Way
Whole Lotta Love
Thank You

How The West Was Won three CDs
Atlantic 7567-83587-2
Released May 27th 2003 (US & UK)
Recordings from Long Beach Arena, June 27th 1972,
except those marked * which are from The Forum, Los
Angeles, June 25th 1972.

CD 1
LA Drone
Immigrant Song
Heartbreaker
Black Dog*
Over The Hills And Far Away*
Since I've Been Loving You
Stairway To Heaven
Going To California
That's The Way*
Bron-Y-Aur Stomp

CD 2
Dazed And Confused*
What Is And What Should Never Be
Dancing Days
Moby Dick*

CD 3
Whole Lotta Love*
Rock And Roll
The Ocean*
Bring It On Home*

Singles

All US releases only

Good Times Bad Times / Communication Breakdown
Atlantic 45-2613
Released March 10th 1969

Whole Lotta Love / Living Loving Maid (She's Just A Woman)
Atlantic 45-2690
Released November 7th 1969

Immigrant Song / Hey Hey What Can I Do
Atlantic 45-2777
Released November 5th 1970

Black Dog / Misty Mountain Hop
Atlantic 45-2849
Released December 2nd 1971

Rock And Roll / Four Sticks
Atlantic 45-2865
Released February 21st 1972

Over The Hills And Far Away / Dancing Days
Atlantic 45-2970
Released May 24th 1973

D'Yer Mak'er / The Crunge
Atlantic 45-2986
Released September 17th 1973

Trampled Under Foot / Black Country Woman
Atlantic SS 70102
Released April 2nd 1975

Candy Store Rock / Royal Orleans
Atlantic SS 70110
Released June 18th 1976

Fool In The Rain / Hot Dog
Atlantic SS 71003
Released December 7th 1979

Complilations

Only those that include previously unreleased or hard-to-find items are listed.

Led Zeppelin 'boxed set 1' four CDs

Atlantic 7567-8214-4
Released October 29th 1990 (US & UK)

Led Zeppelin 'boxed set 2' two CDs
Atlantic 7567-82477-2
Released March 19th 1993 (US & UK)

The Complete Studio Recordings ten CDs
Atlantic 7 82526-2
Released September 24th 1993 (UK), September 28th 1993 (US)

FILM

The Song Remains The Same
Warner DVD 7321900 113892
Released December 21st 1999 (US), June 5th 2000 (UK)

Performance footage Madison Square Garden July 1973 includes
Rock And Roll
Black Dog
Since I've Been Loving You
No Quarter
The Song Remains The Same
The Rain Song
Dazed And Confused
Stairway To Heaven
Moby Dick
Heartbreaker
Whole Lotta Love

DVD two DVDs
Warner 0349 70198-2
Released May 26th 2003 (UK), May 27th 2003 (US)

DISC 1
Royal Albert Hall January 9th 1970
We're Gonna Groove
I Can't Quit You Baby
Dazed And Confused
White Summer/Black Mountain Side
What Is And What Should Never Be
How Many More Times
Moby Dick
Whole Lotta Love
Communication Breakdown
C'mon Everybody
Somethin' Else
Bring It On Home

promo film 1969
Communication Breakdown

Danish TV March 14th 1969
Communication Breakdown
Dazed And Confused
Babe I'm Gonna Leave You
How Many More Times

Supershow March 25th 1969
Dazed And Confused

Tous En Scene June 19th 1969
Communication Breakdown
Dazed And Confused

DISC 2
Footage: Sydney Showground February 27th 1972 / Sound: Long Beach Arena June 27th 1972
Immigrant Song

Madison Square Garden July 1973
Black Dog
Misty Mountain Hop
Since I've Been Loving You
The Ocean

Earl's Court May 1975
Going To California
That's The Way
Bron-Y-Aur Stomp
In My Time Of Dying
Trampled Under Foot
Stairway To Heaven

Knebworth August 4th 1979
Rock And Roll
Nobody's Fault But Mine
Sick Again
Achilles' Last Stand
In The Evening
Kashmir
Whole Lotta Love

Sydney Showground February 27th 1972
Rock And Roll

LED ZEPPELIN ONSTAGE

First European tour (billed as The Yardbirds)
September 7th to September 24th 1968

UK dates
October to December 1968

First American tour
December 26th 1968 to February 15th 1969

UK dates
March 1969

Second European tour
March 14th to 17th 1969

UK dates
March and April 1969

Second American tour
April 18th to May 31st 1969

First UK tour
June 13th to 29th 1969

Third American tour
July 5th to August 31st 1969

Paris and London dates
October 1969

Fourth American tour
October 17th to November 8th 1969

Second UK tour
January 7th to 24th 1970

Third European tour
February 23rd to March 12th 1970

Fifth American tour
March 21st to April 18th 1970

Iceland & UK dates
June 1970

German dates
July 1970

Sixth American tour
August 15th to September 19th 1970

Third UK (& Ireland) tour
March 5th to 24th 1971

UK/European dates
May, July & August 1971

Seventh American tour
August 19th to September 17th 1971

First Japanese tour
September 23rd to 29th 1971

Fourth UK tour
November 11th to December 15th 1971

Australasian tour
February 16th to 29th 1972

European dates
May 1972

Eighth American tour
June 6th to 28th 1972

Second Japanese tour
October 2nd to 10th 1972

Montreux dates
October 1972

Fifth UK tour
1st leg November 30th to December 23rd 1972
2nd leg January 2nd to 30th 1973

Fourth European tour
March 2nd to April 2nd 1973

Ninth American tour
1st leg May 4th to June 3rd 1973
2nd leg July 6th to 29th 1973

European dates
January 1975

Tenth American tour
1st leg January 18th to February 16th 1975
2nd leg February 27th to March 27th 1975

Earl's Court dates
May 17th-18th, 23rd-25th 1975

Eleventh American tour
1st leg April 1st to 30th 1977
2nd leg May 18th to June 27th 1977
3rd leg July 17th to 24th 1977

Danish dates
July 1979

Knebworth Festival
August 4th & 11th 1979

Fifth European tour
June 17th to July 7th 1980

INDEX

AUTHOR'S ACKNOWLEDGMENTS

No book is written in a vacuum. I am grateful to all those people who have helped me along the way since this project was started.

As with my book on Jimi Hendrix, my biggest single debt is to my editor, Tony Bacon, whose continued belief in me however tangled the editorial situation may become is something I greatly appreciate and never take for granted. Even more, I am grateful for the fact that he is a true lover of music. I count my blessings.

Another music-lover is Nigel Osborne of Backbeat UK in London, a man who believes in quality as well as quantity. Long may he prosper. All in the Backbeat UK office in London have also been more than merely dutiful in their assistance, especially John Ryall.

On a professional level I have cause to be grateful to Greg Russo, whose enthusiastic pursuit of the facts I admire unequivocally in this compromised world. I also thank Ellen Sander for pointing the way towards her original published essay on Led Zeppelin's summer 1969 tour, a much-maligned, much-plundered and greatly misrepresented piece of writing I happen to admire. My sincere thanks are also due to Jim McCarty, whose courtesy and honesty when interviewed was refreshing and extremely helpful. Jeff Beck also proved approachable, insightful and articulate when we talked. Jon Newey was similarly exact and discerning in his recollections and Reynold D'Silva energetic, resourceful and generous with his time. I am glad Dave Lewis of *Tight But Loose* had the opportunity to check over the manuscript and give it a proper bout of authentication. I am also glad that so many journalists working when Led Zeppelin were in operation were so diligent in interviewing, documenting and reviewing the band. Without them it would be virtually impossible to write a book such as this. Equally, without the astonishing resources of the British Library it would be difficult to conceive of accomplishing the research needed for such a venture.

On a personal level there are people who contributed substantially to this book being written through their insights, suggestions and energy. Martin Armiger was unhesitating in his encouragement from the outset, as was Maureen O'Shaughnessy. Gary Norwell, Andrew Findlay, Sandra Russell, Jenny Bloomfield, Mike Wollenberg, Andrew Feitelson and Mike Segal were likewise enthusiastic from the moment the project was mooted. Max Easterman and Rosie Goldsmith have helped me through moments of doubt and Michael Horowitz has been unfailingly supportive during our talks about this book and my other writings. Lo Cole and Adam Horowitz also showed uncommon kindness and interest. Annette Peacock has been a long-term friend and morale booster whose advice and encouragement is deeply appreciated, while Diana Krall gave me support at a moment in time when I didn't realise myself how much I needed it.

Within my own family I am blessed. My two sons are real fans of the music and have never failed to encourage me to do my best with this project while my wife Alison has been unshakeable in her conviction that whatever I eventually produce will have been worth the effort. I also continue to share the endless exploration of music with my brother, who got me started on this particular journey, however inadvertently, and who still sends me CDs of weird music I've never heard before. I even like some of them.

PUBLISHER'S THANKS

Johnny Black; Dave Burrluck (*Guitarist*); Rick Conrad (Warner Strategic Marketing UK); Robert Elliott; Dave Gregory; Christopher Hjort; Achilles Last Stand website www.led-zeppelin.org; Dave Lewis tightbutloose.co.uk; Glen Marks; Tom Morris; John Morrish; Julian Ridgway; James Sowden.

BIBLIOGRAPHY

Books

Whitney Balliett *Collected Works: A Journal of Jazz 1954-2000* (Granta 2001)
Annette Carson *Jeff Beck: Crazy Fingers* (Backbeat 2001)
Alan Clayson *The Yardbirds* (Backbeat 2002)
Richard Cole *Stairway To Heaven: Led Zeppelin Uncensored* (Pocket Books 2002)
Stephen Davis *Hammer Of The Gods: Led Zeppelin Unauthorised* (Pan 1995)
Andy Fyfe *When The Levee Breaks: The Making of Led Zeppelin IV* (Unanimous 2003)
Ken Garner *In Session Tonight: The Complete Radio 1 Recordings* (BBC 1993)
Robert Godwin *Led Zeppelin: The Press Reports* (Collector's Guide 2001)
Burt Goldblatt *Newport Jazz Festival: The Illustrated history* (Dial Press 1977)
Bill Graham *My Life Inside Rock And Out* (Doubleday 1992)
Paolo Hewitt *Small Faces: The Young Mods' Forgotten Story* (Acid Jazz 1995)
Dave Lewis *A Celebration* (Omnibus 2003)
Dave Lewis *Celebration II – The Tight But Loose Files* (Omnibus 2003)
Tim Rice et al *Guinness British Hit Albums* (GRRR 1986)
Rikky Rooksby *Riffs: How To Create And Play Great Guitar Riffs* (Backbeat 2002)
Greg Russo *Yardbirds – The Ultimate Rave-Up* (Crossfire 2001)
Ellen Sander *Trips: Rock Life In The Sixties* (Scribner 1973)
Chris Welch *Peter Grant: The Man Who Led Zeppelin* (Omnibus 2002)
Chris Welch & Geoff Nichols *John Bonham: A Thunder Of Drums* (Backbeat 2001)
Joel Whitburn *The Billboard Book Of Top 40 Albums* (Billboard 1995)
Ritchie Yorke *Led Zeppelin: From Early Days To Page & Plant* (Virgin 2003)

Magazines

Bottom Line, Bravo, Circus, Crawdaddy, Creem, Disc (& Music Echo), Down Beat, Go, Go-Set, The Guitar Magazine, Guitar Player, Guitar World, Guitarist, Melody Maker, Mojo, Music Maker, New Musical Express, Oz, Proximity, Record Mirror, Rock, Rolling Stone, Sounds, Strange Days, Street Life, Tight But Loose, Trouser Press, Vanity Fair, Zigzag.

PICTURE CREDITS

For Beauty's nothing
but beginning of Terror we're still just able to bear,
and why we adore it so is because it serenely
disdains to destroy us. Every angel is terrible.

Rainer Maria Rilke, the First Elegy from The Duino Elegies, translation by J.B. Leishman and Stephen Spender, Hogarth Press 1939 and 1963